# Federalism in Asia

# Federalism in Asia

*Edited by*

Baogang He

*Deakin University, Australia*

Brian Galligan

*University of Melbourne, Australia*

Takashi Inoguchi

*Chuo University, Japan*

**Edward Elgar**

Cheltenham, UK • Northampton, MA, USA

Published by
Edward Elgar Publishing Limited
The Lypiatts
15 Lansdown Road
Cheltenham
Glos GL50 2JA
UK

Edward Elgar Publishing, Inc.
William Pratt House
9 Dewey Court
Northampton
Massachusetts 01060
USA

Paperback edition 2009

A catalogue record for this book
is available from the British Library

**Library of Congress Cataloging in Publication Data**
    Federalism in Asia / edited by Baogang He, Brian Galligan,
    Takashi Inoguchi.
        p.   cm.
    Includes bibliographical references and index.
    1. Federal government—Asia.   2. Democratization—Asia.
    I. He, Baogang, 1957–.   II. Galligan, Brian, 1945–.   III. Inoguchi,
    Takashi.
    JQ36.F43   2007
    320.45′049—dc22

                                                        2007001394


ISBN 978 1 84720 140 9 (cased)
ISBN 978 1 84844 798 1 (paperback)


Printed and bound by MPG Books Group, UK

# Contents

# Contributors

**Katharine Adeney** joined the Politics Department at the University of Shieffield in September 2004 from Balliol College at the University of Oxford where she had been a Junior Research Fellow in Politics since 2001. She received her BA from the University of Hull and her MSc and PhD from the London School of Economics. Her principal research interests include the countries of South Asia, especially India and Pakistan; ethnic conflict regulation and federal design; national identities; democratization in South Asia. Her recent publications include K. Adeney and L. Sáez (eds), *Coalition Politics and Hindu Nationalism* (2005), and K. Adeney, *Federalism and Ethnic Conflict Regulation in India and Pakistan* (2007).

**David Brown** is Associate Professor in Politics and International Studies at Murdoch University, Western Australia. He previously held positions at the National University of Singapore, Birmingham University, UK and Ahmadu Bello University, Nigeria. In 2003 he received a Fulbright New Century Scholar award to pursue research on ethnic conflict. He has numerous publications on the politics of ethnicity and nationalism, and has focused particularly on the region of Southeast Asia. Recent publications include *Contemporary Nationalism* (2000) and 'Ethnic conflict and civic nationalism', in James Parsonage, Patricia Thornton and Patrick Inman (eds), *Identity Matters* (2007).

**William Case** is Professor in the Department of Asian and International Studies, City University of Hong Kong. His research interests include democratization, elite theory, comparative political economy in East Asia, Indonesian politics and Malaysian politics. His recent publications include 'How's my driving? Abdullah's first year as Malaysian PM', *Pacific Review*, **18**(2) (2005); 'Political mistrust in Southeast Asia', *Comparative Sociology*, **5**(1–2) (2005); 'New uncertainties for an old pseudo-democracy: the case of Malaysia', *Comparative Politics*, **37**(1) (2005).

**Peter T.Y. Cheung** is Associate Professor and the Head of the Department of Politics and Public Administration at the University of Hong Kong. He holds a PhD in political science from the University of Washington, Seattle. His current research focuses on cross-boundary cooperation between Hong

Kong and Guandong province, the relations between Beijing and the Hong Kong Special Administrative Region and the politics of policy making in Hong Kong. He is also a former part-time member and research and planning director of the Central Policy Unit of the HKSAR government. His recent publications include 'Cross-boundary cooperation in South China: perspectives, mechanisms and challenges', in Anthony Yeh et al. (eds), *Developing a Competitive Pearl River Delta in South China under One Country Two Systems* (2006); 'Guangdong under reform: social and political changes and challenges in the 1990s', in John Fitzgerald (ed.) *Remaking China's Provinces* (2002); 'External relations of China's provinces', in David M. Lampton (ed.), *The Making of Chinese Foreign and Security Policy in the Era of Reform: 1978–2000* (with James Tang) (2001). His edited books include *Provincial Strategies of Economic Reform in Post-Mao China* (with Jae Ho Chung and Zhimin Lin) (1998).

**Brian Galligan** is the leading international expert on Australian federalism. He has been a Professor of Political Science at the University of Melbourne since 1995, and previously was a Professor in the Research School of Social Science at the Australian National University. He is a graduate in Economics and Commerce from the University of Queensland, and has a Masters and PhD in Political Science from the University of Toronto. Research interests are focused on Australian politics and political economy. Areas of particular interest include constitutional design, politics of the High Court, citizenship and rights protection, Australian political history and political economy. His recent books include *Australian Citizenship* (with Winsome Roberts) (2004); *Australians and Globalisation: the Experience of Two Centuries* (with Winsome Roberts and Gabriella Trifiletti) (2001); *Citizens Without Rights; Aborigines and Australian Citizenship* (with John Chesterman) (1997). His edited books include *Defining Australian Citizenship: Selected Documents* (with John Chesterman) (1999).

**Baogang He** is Chair of International Studies at Deakin University in Australia, the author of *The Democratization of China* (1996); *The Democratic Implication of Civil Society in China* (1997); *Nationalism, National Identity and Democratization in China* (with Yingjie Guo) (2000); *Balancing Democracy and Authority: An Empirical Study of Village Election in Zhejiang* (with Lang Youxing) (2002); *Multiculturalism in Asia* (co-editor with Will Kymlicka) (2005); and *The Search for Deliberative Democracy* (co-editor with Ethan Leib) (2006). He has co-authored and co-translated several books in Chinese (including John Rawls's *A Theory of Justice*), and has published 34 book chapters and more than 36 international refereed journal articles in English. His current research interests include deliberative democracy, Asian federalism, rural democracy and cosmopolitan international relations.

**Takashi Inoguchi** is professor emeritus at the University of Tokyo and Professor of Political Science at Chuo University in Tokyo, Japan. He obtained his PhD in Political Science from Massachusetts Institute of Technology (MIT) and his BA and MA from the University of Tokyo. His research interests are Political Theory, Comparative Politics and International Relations. He has published some 70 books in English and Japanese in the area of world affairs and international relations. Some of his more recent publications include *Reinventing the Alliance and the Uses of Institutions* (co-edited with G. John Ikenberry, 2003 and 2007 respectively), *Political Cultures in Asia and Europe* and *Citizens and the State* (both co-authored with Jean Blondel, 2006 and forthcoming respectively), *Values and Lifestyles in Urban Asia* (principal editor, 2005), *Human Beliefs and Values in Striding Asia* (principal editor, 2006), *Governance and Democracy in Asia* (co-edited with Matthew Carlson, 2006), *Japanese Politics* (2005). Since 2003 he conducts the AsiaBarometer Survey every year focusing on daily lives of ordinary people in Asia. He is also founding editor of two journals, *Japanese Journal of Political Science* (Cambridge University Press) and *International Relations of the Asia-Pacific* (Oxford University Press) and President of the Asian Consortium for Political Research. He has also contributed to encyclopedias such as *The International Encyclopedia of Social and Behavioral Sciences* (26 vols, Elsevier, 2000), *The Oxford Handbook of Political Behavior* (Oxford University Press, forthcoming), and *The International Encyclopedia of Political Science* (Sage Publications, forthcoming).

**Will Kymlicka** is the author of five books published by Oxford University Press: *Liberalism, Community, and Culture* (1989); *Contemporary Political Philosophy* (1990; 2nd edn 2002); *Multicultural Citizenship* (1995), which was awarded the Macpherson Prize by the Canadian Political Science Assocation, and the Bunche Award by the American Political Science Association, and *Finding Our Way: Rethinking Ethnocultural Relations in Canada* (1998); and *Politics in the Vernacular* (2001). He is also the editor of *Justice in Political Philosophy* (1992); *The Rights of Minority Cultures* (1995) and co-editor of *Ethnicity and Group Rights* (1997); *Citizenship in Diverse Societies* (2000); *Can Liberal Pluralism be Exported?* (2001); *Language Rights and Political Theory* (2003); and *Multiculturalism in Asia* (2005, co-editor with Baogang He). He is currently a Professor of Philosophy at Queen's University.

**Gurpreet Mahajan** is Professor at the Centre for Political Studies at Jawaharlal Nehru University, Delhi. She is the author of *The Multicultural Path: Issues of Diversity and Discrimination* (2001), *Identities and Rights: Aspects of Liberal Democracy in India* (1998) and editor of *The Public and the Private: Issues of Democratic Citizenship in a Comparative Perspective* (2003).

**R.J. May** was formerly a senior fellow in the Department of Political and Social Change, Research School of Pacific and Asian Studies at The Australian National University. He retired from the Department of Political and Social Change, of which he was a foundation member, in December 2004 and took up the position of Emeritus Professorial Fellow in the State, Society and Governance Project. He was formerly a senior economist with the Reserve Bank of Australia and later foundation director of IASER in Papua New Guinea (now the National Research Institute). In 1976 he was awarded the Independence Medal for his services to banking and research in Papua New Guinea. His research interests include comparative politics, particularly ethnicity and ethnic conflict, decentralization, parties and elections, and civil–military relations. His country focus is Papua New Guinea and the Philippines (especially Muslim Mindanao). His key publications include *State and Society in Papua New Guinea: The First Twenty-Five Years*, (2001); 'Muslim Mindanao: four years after the peace agreement', in *Southeast Asian Affairs 2001* (2001); and is co-editor, with V. Selochan, of *The Military and Democracy in Asia and the Pacific* (1998).

**Anthony Reid** is Director of the Asia Research Institute, National University of Singapore, and was previously Professor of Southeast Asian History at ANU and UCLA. His recent interests include the shaping of identities in modern Indonesia and Malaysia, and the way these have interacted historically with nationalism. His major books include *The Contest for North Sumatra: Atjeh, the Netherlands and Britain, 1858–1898* (1969); *The Indonesian National Revolution, 1945–1950* (1974); *The Blood of the People: Revolution and the End of Traditional Rule in Northern Sumatra* (1979); *Southeast Asia in the Age of Commerce, 1450–1680*, vol. I: *The Lands below the Winds* (1988); *Southeast Asia in the Age of Commerce, 1450–1680*, vol. II: *Expansion and Crisis* (1993); *Charting the Shape of Early Modern Southeast Asia* (1999) (North American and European rights with University of Washington Press, Seattle).

**Alan Smith** completed his PhD in 1991 at Monash University on the situation of West Papuan refugees in Papua New Guinea. Since 1993 he has been based in Thailand, initially as a Research Fellow of the Asia Institute, Monash University, working with Burmese opposition groups mainly with regard to the situation of ethnic minority groups. In 2001, he joined the staff of the Friedrich Naumann Foundation Regional Project based in Bangkok and he continues to be involved in political education, training and documentation work with Burmese community and political groups.

**Yongnian Zheng** is Professor and Head of Research at the China Policy Institute, University of Nottingham, UK. He is also a co-editor of *China: An International Journal*. He obtained his BA and MA in Law from Beijing University (1985, 1988) and PhD in Political Science from Princeton University (1995). He is the author of ten books, including *Discovering Chinese Nationalism in China* (1999); *Globalization and State Transformation in China* (2004); *Will China Become Democratic?* (2004); and his forthcoming book, *De Facto Federalism in China: Reforms and Dynamics of Central–Local Relations*. He has also co-edited 11 books on China's politics and society. Besides his research work, Professor Zheng has also been an academic activist. He served as a consultant to the United Nation Development Programme on China's rural development and democracy. In addition, he has been a columnist for the *Hong Kong Economic Journal* for many years, writing numerous commentaries on China's reform.

# Acknowledgments

This book developed out of the international workshop on federalism and democratization in Asia, held at Deakin University in February 2006, organized by Baogang He and Takashi Inoguchi. We invited a dozen scholars from different disciplines and countries to look at federalism in Asia. All chapters are structured around the central theme, with certain variations. In the wake of the workshop, we commissioned an additional two chapters.

We would like to thank the Japan Foundation for its grant, Edward Elgar for his encouragement, Professors Joan Beaumont and Geoffrey Stokes for their support, Alexandra O'Connell, Fethi Mansouri, Robert Macmahon, Kazumi Jushi, Goko Kimiko, Urara Murai and Eilidh Campbell St John for their various assistance.

B.H.
B.G.
T.I.

# Preface

Our aim in this volume is to explore the range of theoretical perspectives that shape debates over federalism in general, and territorial, multinational, hybrid and asymmetric federalism in particular in the region. We want to identify the areas of convergence and disagreement between these different perspectives, to evaluate their strengths and weaknesses, and to assess their long-term prospects. The authors have developed an understanding of how federal or quasi-federal institutions manage ethnic conflicts and accommodate difference, how democratization facilitates the development of federalism and how federalism facilitates or inhibits democratization in Asia.

This book has examined how federalism has fared in Asia, and why it has not been accepted as a very popular basis for Asian democratization and multinational representation. The huge exception, of course, is India and, to a lesser extent, Malaysia and Pakistan, so any explanation of Asian aversion to federalism must take account of these notable exceptions. China's de facto federalism must also be taken into account. Just as importantly, Indonesia's eschewing of federalism needs explanation, as do the ways in which various non-federal countries have achieved decentralization and accommodated multinationalism by other institutional means. Authors in this volume examine individual Asian countries to distil their particular constitutional and political features in order to explain whether and in what ways they are federal or not. Tony Reid highlights Indonesia's aversion to federalism by contrasting it with Malaysia's incorporation of partial federalism in its governance structure. Takashi Inoguchi shows, in Japan's case, that strong traditions of decentralization have underpinned democratization within a formal unitary system.

One major theme of the book is the relationship between federalism and democratization in Asia, which Baogang He examines extensively in Chapter 1, and the various country studies address in specific ways. A second major theme is the character of federalism and how it functions, or might function, in Asia. This is a large topic that is tackled in various ways: by Baogang He, who provides a summary of the debate on competing models of federalism and highlights hybrid federalism taking place in Asia; by Will Kymlicka, who sets out a model of 'multinational federalism' in Chapter 2; and by David Brown, taking a different viewpoint in Chapter 3, that he calls 'regionalist federalism'.

Eight Asian countries are examined in individual country studies, in chapters 4 to 12: India, Pakistan, Malaysia, Indonesia, the Philippines, Myanmar, Japan and China, with a separate chapter on Hong Kong, which forms a highly autonomous region within China.

Three of these countries are federal and are included in the roll-call of federal countries world wide by Ron Watts and Daniel Elazar. These are India, Pakistan and Malaysia, all founded in the immediate postwar period after extensive British colonial rule. Of these India is the outstanding functioning federation and democracy, despite some centralist features that allow national intervention in state government. It is also exceptional because of its vast geographic and demographic dimensions, serving more than a billion people across a subcontinent. Pakistan and Malaysia have weaker forms of both federalism and democracy, and more turbulent political histories. Pakistan has been the least stable country, experiencing wars of separation and division as well as long periods of military government. As well as a dominant military, it has a centralist administration that manages a system of 'illiberal federalism'. Malaysia has a centrally managed variety of 'semi-democracy' and minimalist 'federalism' controlled by a dominant party that continues in power at the national level. Neither of these countries can be conceptualized as multinational federalism; indeed, quite the opposite, with federalism being designed and managed so as to scramble and blunt ethnic differences. While Indian federalism has been spectacularly successful in representing and, at the same time, moderating ethnic populations, that has occurred within the large constitutional purpose of territorial representation in multiple spheres of government.

Other Asian countries that we might expect to have embraced federalism for multinational or decentralist purposes of government are Indonesia and the Philippines. Neither, however, has done so. Indonesia has been averse to federalism because of its more revolutionary founding and commitment to a national democratic ethos. Concern for secession of ethnically distinct regions has also been a factor against federalism, although the recent concession for Aceh gives special autonomy status to this distinctive and troublesome province. The Philippines is less averse to federalism that is currently being advocated as an appropriate means of resolving its multinational problems. This is somewhat alien to its tradition of central government with a well established system of local government for decentralist administrative purposes.

Japan is the leading unitary state in Asia and stands out as the most highly developed constitutional democracy with an elaborately entrenched constitution. For its amendment, Japan's constitution requires a referendum in addition to two-thirds majorities in both houses of its legislature. It is the only unitary country that comes within Lijphart's (1999, pp. 220–21) select list of countries with constitutions that are hardest to amend, requiring 'super-majorities' greater than two-thirds approval of both houses of the national legislature. The other countries in this top constitutional bracket are all notable federal countries: Australia, Canada, Germany, Switzerland and the United States. Japan is perhaps very well known in the West for its strong unitary system of government, but less well known for its centuries-old tradition of decentralization or quasi-federalism that has underpinned its democratic development and curtailed centralism.

Myanmar, previously known as Burma, is the polar opposite: a highly centralized and oppressive military dictatorship that eschews both democracy and constitutional government, so not surprisingly also federalism. Myanmar has dealt with its minority nations with suppression and the repression and expulsion of its leaders, although there are welcome signs of preliminary consideration of some partial return to constitutional government.

China holds special interest for the study of federalism because its revolutionary founding and Communist party rule over a vast territory and more than a billion people is ever more at odds with increasingly effective market capitalism. This is producing large disparities across China and providing the seaboard provinces with the economic base for greater political independence, so much so that China's political economy might be characterized as 'de facto federalism'. In addition, China has incorporated Hong Kong through a special status arrangement of 'One Country: Two Systems' that gives Hong Kong a high degree of autonomy.

The final chapter, by Brian Galligan, puts the discussion of federalism back into a broader historical and comparative perspective, showing that it serves multiple purposes, only one of which is multinational governance. Constitutional federalism allows for decentralization and complexity of government, and works best in liberal democratic political cultures characterized by tolerance and commitment to limited government. To work at all, federalism requires some significant presence of factors that will support a complex system of divided and limited government. Such an account of constitutional federalism draws upon the traditional meaning of federalism in Western political thought and constitutional design. It articulates some of the main attributes or propensities that have been identified in, or claimed by, studies of federalism. From this we can derive a more comprehensive understanding of the complexities of federalism that help our investigating why federalism has not been so prominent in Asian countries and, where it has, why that has been the case.

Finally we conclude with some observations on federalism in Asia that might be summed up in several propositions: one, that federalism has been relatively weak or non-existent in Asian countries that lack prior decentralist traditions, or where liberal democracy and market capitalism are weak; two, that in the broader sense of politically entrenched decentralization, hybrid federalism or quasi-federalism has more prevalence in some Asian countries; and three, that the need and potential for greater federalism in many Asian countries makes our sortie into this area worthwhile. While federalism is relevant to Asia, the working pattern of Asian federalism does not necessarily follow a Western style. Hybrid federal institutional design can be seen as an Asian strategy of managing ethnic conflicts through federal arrangements.

## CHAPTER OUTLINES

### Chapter 1    Baogang He, 'Democratization and Federalization in Asia'

This chapter provides an overview of theoretical and empirical issues for this edited volume. Section 1 maps the status and various forms of Asian federalism, section 2 outlines key debates over the competing models of federalism in Asia, section 3 argues that hybrid federalism is the form most appropriate to deal with minority issues and the national identity question in Asia, sections 4–5 develop an understanding of the complex relationship between democratization and federalization in Asia, and section 6 addresses the question of whether and how federalism can reduce or contain ethnic conflicts.

### Chapter 2    Will Kymlicka, 'Multination Federalism'

This chapter discusses an emerging trend in the West towards a model of 'multination federalism', which grants federal or quasi-federal forms of territorial autonomy to historic substate national groups. It argues that this model is working well to manage ethnic diversity peacefully, democratically and with respect for human rights, notwithstanding some continuing areas of controversy. It explores some of the factors that inhibit its adoption in Asia.

### Chapter 3    David Brown, 'Regionalist Federalism'

The case for multinational federalism is sometimes made in Asia by claiming that the demands of ethnonational minorities for territorial autonomy are rational reactions to their oppression by a dominant ethnic core and should therefore be acceded to as conducive to protective democratization. This chapter seeks to problematize this argument. It argues that the granting of federal autonomy to ethnic minority homeland regions is more likely to inhibit the further democratization of Southeast Asian nation-states than to promote it; and that regionalist federalism might be more conducive than a multinational federalism to the democratization of Southeast Asia. The conclusion is that the goal of deliberative democracy can best be promoted by a regionalist federalism conducive to a deliberative democratic national integration, rather than by multinational federalism.

### Chapter 4   Gurpreet Mahajan, 'Federal Accommodation of Ethnocultural Identities in India'

The chapter explores two questions: (i) the relationship between federalism and democratization, and (ii) the ability of federalism to resolve issues of ethnic conflict. Reflecting on the Indian experience it argues that, in post-colonial societies, federal structures were closely linked with co-option and annexation of territory. For this reason democratization and federalism are not often linked together in the collective memory of these societies. Nevertheless, over the years, federalism is gradually being linked with democracy and is being seen as a way of deepening democracy.

In India, federalism has created and expanded a plural public sphere, curtailed the intervention of the centre in the regions, nurtured the autonomy of the latter, provided new, and previously marginalized, groups with access to political power, brought these political élites into the national mainstream and given them an opportunity to influence and determine public policy at the national level. Above all, the federal framework has acted as a kind of safety valve by accommodating and deflecting dissent that was mounting against the centre and, by extension, the Indian State. In other words, the federal structure has enabled the state to address and accommodate dissenting voices. It has, in the process, played a crucial role in holding the nation-state together in the post-independence period.

### Chapter 5   Katharine Adeney, 'Democracy and Federalism in Pakistan'

The use of multinational federalism as a mechanism of ethnonational conflict regulation is controversial. It has been rejected as a structure of government by many of the decolonized states, especially multinational ones. This chapter argues, albeit with sweeping generalizations, that the structure of federalism implemented in Pakistan demonstrates that the main reason states reject federalism – that territorially homogeneous groups allotted their own territory are likely to secede – does not hold in all cases, and can be mitigated by additional structures. In so doing, it addresses the debate concerning the use of homogeneous versus heterogeneous provinces within multinational federations. The chapter examines the historical formation of federalism and current development of federalism in Pakistan and highlights the illiberal features of Pakistani federalism.

### Chapter 6    William Case, 'Semi-democracy and Minimalist Federalism in Malaysia'

Federalism is usually credited with promoting democracy. In Malaysia, however, it has been practised in ways that reinforce 'hybrid' politics, an amalgam of authoritarian controls and democratic procedures through which the government has efficiently perpetuated its incumbency. Federalist arrangements in Malaysia, then, have grown similarly skewed, with the central government assuming disproportionate power. Nevertheless, they retain enough substance for state-level governments still to be able to raise revenues and devise policies with some autonomy. This chapter demonstrates that Malaysia's federalist arrangements possess greater substance than is usually acknowledged. It shows that, by organizing federalism along territorial, rather than multinational, lines, the government disorganizes the social minorities that sometimes chafe under its rule. And by adjusting even its territorial federalism to minimalist levels, the government prevents regionalist sentiments from cohering in secessionist movements.

### Chapter 7    Anthony Reid, 'Indonesia's Post-revolutionary Aversion to Federalism'

States which achieve their current form through revolution have some advantages over those which evolve in the incremental manner of multiple compromises. They have powerful symbols, a clear identity, a centralized system of government and education, and an ideology which favours equality between citizens. France has these advantages in comparison with the United Kingdom, but it also has some disadvantages, particularly from the viewpoint of regions or minorities which feel themselves profoundly different. This chapter will look at a Southeast Asian pairing, post-revolutionary Indonesia and evolutionary Malaysia, to examine the costs and benefits of post-revolutionary centralization as against Malaysia's asymmetric federalism. It explores the possibilities of a kind of 'asymmetric Federalism' as a solution for Aceh following the peace agreement of 2005.

### Chapter 8    Ron May, 'Federalism v. Autonomy in the Philippines'

The Philippines does not have a federal system but, especially since 1991, it does have a fairly high degree of decentralization, which includes an

Autonomous Region of Muslim Mindanao and constitutional provision for an autonomous region in the northern Cordilleras (which has been rejected in two referenda). In recent years, however, there have been repeated calls for a federal system, endorsed in the context of proposals for constitutional review ('charter change'), in President Macapagal-Arroyo's 2005 State of the Nation address to Congress.

This chapter will provide a brief overview of decentralization under the Local Government Code in the Philippines, review the experience of autonomy initiatives in Muslim Mindanao and the Cordilleras, and look at the recent history of the idea of federalism in the Philippines. It will argue that, despite their limited success, autonomy arrangements probably offer a more promising way of dealing with issues identified in the present debate than a symmetrical federal system.

### Chapter 9    Alan Smith, 'Ethnicity and Federal Prospect in Myanmar'

The most important 'development' in Myanmar's political situation is undoubtedly the military's managed transition from total military control to something else, a new constitutional system. There are many opponents of the military's national convention and road map to 'disciplined democracy' (some highly vocal), including the National League for Democracy (NLD) and its political allies excluded from the process, and much of the international community, on the basis of its undemocratic process. Exile opposition groups are also highly vocal opponents, insisting that the only legitimate outcome is a democratic and federal Burma. The argument for a federal Burma relates to the ethnic dissatisfaction with the structure of the Union of Burma since its formation and of course armed rebellion (now largely in ceasefire) against the 'Union' government. A group of ethnic ceasefire groups broadly in favour of autonomy in ethnic states accepted the State Peace and Development Council's (SPDC) invitation to join the renewed National Convention (NC) process in 2004.

### Chapter 10    Yongnian Zheng, 'China's de facto Federalism'

China does not have a federalist system of government. Nevertheless, from a behavioural perspective we can see China's de facto federal structure. This chapter outlines an overall de facto federal structure in China's central–local relations. It identifies three main institutions which are embedded in China's de facto federal structure, namely, coercion, bargaining and reciprocity. The chapter also examines the prospect of the institutionalization of de facto federalism in China.

**Chapter 11    Peter T.Y. Cheung, 'Toward Federalism in China? The experience of the Hong Kong Special Administrative Region**

Hong Kong enjoys a higher degree of autonomy than most local authorities in federalist systems, such as in the area of monetary policy and external economic relations, although the interpretation of its Basic Law is still in the hands of the central authorities. Some scholars have argued that a federalist formula is perhaps one of the most feasible platforms for China's unification with Taiwan. Nonetheless, few scholars have examined what the Hong Kong experience means for China and whether it has further strengthened the federalist tendencies in the Chinese political system. This chapter is an attempt to address these questions. It provides an analysis of Hong Kong's experience in implementing the policy of 'One Country, Two Systems' in both theory and practice since 1997. The analytical focus is to examine how Hong Kong fares in light of the experience of federalist systems. The recent developments in Hong Kong's intergovernmental relations with both Beijing and south China will also be addressed. The chapter concludes by exploring the prospects of a federalist future for China and Hong Kong's impact on the process.

**Chapter 12    Takashi Inoguchi, 'Federal Traditions and Quasi-Federalism in Japan'**

In the West, Japan has long been regarded as a very centralized unitary state. Thus it is often forgotten that it has an even longer quasi-federal state tradition giving a solid autonomy to some 300 odd domains in early modern centuries (16th to mid-19th centuries). This quasi-federal tradition has survived alive and well for the last century in the form of very autonomous bureaucratic agencies at the highest level of central government. Confronted by the challenge of the deepening tide of globalization and of an increasingly self-expressive citizenry, Japan has been probing ways of meeting these challenges through the still uncertain mix of the two traditions. The chapter attempts to elucidate how Japan has been trying to adapt to changing environments. The postal privatization law legislated in 2005 is used to illustrate the argument. The chapter argues that Japan has been moving in the direction of loosening the tradition of a centralized unitary state to gear up the competitiveness of Japan and to tailor to the needs of those otherwise marginalized.

**Chapter 13    Brian Galligan, 'Federalism and Asia'**

This chapter examines comparative federal theory and practice to see how it might incorporate the multinational and regionalist perspectives in ways that deepen our understanding of federalism, or the lack of it, in the different Asian countries studied. It ends with some concluding observations on federalism in Asia.

B.H.
B.G.
T.I.

# 1. Democratization and federalization in Asia

## Baogang He[1]

The year 2005 was a watershed year in the contemporary history of Asian federalism. The formation of hybrid federalism in Indonesia was marked by the granting of substantial autonomy to the Aceh people in the 2005 peace agreement. In the Philippines, President Gloria Macapagal-Arroyo's 2005 State of the Nation address to Congress accelerated the process of federalization. These two events point to fundamental changes in Asian governance with regard to minorities and ethnic conflicts.

Conflicts over ethnic homeland rule, the right to territorial autonomy and even nation-statehood have been played out in Asia, where there have been debates over whether federalism in general and multinational federalism in particular is the best practice to reduce or contain ethnic conflicts. The international community has also questioned whether the multinational federalism of Spain and Canada offers a successful model and whether underlying norms and principles, such as the right to territorial autonomy, the right to self-determination and the right not to be assimilated, are acceptable as universal norms. This volume will examine the debates on federalism, the various practices of Asian federalism, the different paths toward federalism, and the spurs and impediments to federalism in Asia.

This introductory chapter aims to provide an overview of theoretical and empirical issues for this edited volume. Section 1 maps the status and various forms of Asian federalism; section 2 outlines key debates over the competing models of federalism in Asia; section 3 argues that hybrid federalism is the form most appropriate to deal with minority issues and national identity questions in Asia; sections 4 and 5 develop an understanding of the complex relationship between democratization and federalization in Asia, and section 6 addresses the question of whether and how federalism can reduce or contain ethnic conflicts.

# THE MAPPING OF ASIAN FEDERALISM

## Historical Overview

In the 1940s and 1950s, many Asian countries attempted to build federal systems, but most failed very quickly. Federalism was conceived as a way of holding the territories that eventually became India and Pakistan, and also Malaysia and Singapore. This imposition of a federated union upon the former colonies by the British failed in the era of nation building, resulting in the partition between India and Pakistan and the secession of Singapore from Malaysia. Nevertheless, federalism has been introduced after these events in India, Pakistan and Malaysia. Indonesia became a federated republic of ten provinces in 1948. This was a short-lived federation, however, as a unitary structure was firmly established and it was only later that regional governments were endowed with a measure of autonomy (see Seidler, 1955; Feith and Castles, 1970, ch. 10; Feith, 1973; Nasution, 1992). China attempted federation but never really manifested it and quickly rejected the Soviet type of federalism in the 1950s. The failure of federalism in South America, the Caribbean, Rhodesia and Nyasaland from 1953 to 1965, and in the British West Indies from 1958 to 1962, should also be noted.

In the first few decades following decolonization, states attempted to build unitary and homogenizing nation-states. They distrusted and discouraged federalism and regarded it as an aberrant phenomenon. Now all the old arguments about the dangers of federalism have been trotted out, but federalism is now perceived as an advanced form of government, and even as the ideal future form of governance at regional and global level. Multinational federalism is regarded as a desirable new form of governance in the world while, ironically, concern for ethnicity, the normative foundation for the construction of internal or external boundaries, is seen as backward.

Despite failure, frustration and obstacles, in most Asian countries, there have been calls for federalism. Even Singapore's former Prime Minister Lee Kuan Yew raised the question concerning the possibility of whether Malaysia and Singapore will be reunited as a federal entity one day (*Liange Zhaobao*, 2002, p. 22). The voice for federalism is much stronger in the countries when they face a national identity question. The pursuit of federalism takes place in countries like the Philippines, China, Burma, Indonesia, India, Sri Lanka and Pakistan, to name a few, where there has been resistance amongst ethnic and religious minorities, secessionist movements and even civil wars.

Indonesia witnessed many advocates for federalism (Kahin, 1985; Ravich, 2000; Dillon, 2006; King, 2006). In China the Dalai Lama's proposal for autonomy looks like a federal solution: the government of the People's Republic of China would remain responsible for Tibet's foreign policy while Tibet would be governed by is own constitution or basic law, and the Tibetan government would comprise a popularly elected chief executive, a bicameral legislature and an independent legal system (Dreyer, 1989, p. 284; He and Sautman, 2005–6). In The Philippines, it is argued that a federal system would be the ultimate solution to the Muslim separatist rebellion. In November 2000, a pro-federalist resolution was signed by 22 members of the 24-seat Philippines Senate. The resolution proposed amending the 1987 Philippines Constitution in a way that would convert the country's present 15 administrative regions into ten federal states, with a federal capital district (Manila) similar to Canberra in Australia or Washington, DC in the USA.

There are currently several stages of federalism in Asia. India is a well-developed federalist state that is often compared with the United States and Australia. India, Pakistan and Malaysia were former British colonies and their early federalisms, plus the semi-federal arrangement in Hong Kong, were associated with the decolonization of the British Empire.[2] The Philippines and Indonesia can be considered 'incipient' or 'infant' federalist states, since they are moving toward federal-style governance, although Indonesia may not accept the term. Hopes for federalism have been frustrated in Sri Lanka and Burma (Myanmar), leading to their classification as 'failed federalisms'. Mainland China and Hong Kong have developed somewhat authoritarian but nevertheless quasi-federal institutions. Other nation-states that could consider federalism include Thailand, in order to address the aspirations of Patani separatists in the south, and North and South Korea. Even Japan has been decentralized in favour of a form of federal politics (see Chapter 12).

The development of Asian federalism seems to fit the international trend. Since the end of the Second World War, and in particular since the late 1970s, federalism has increasingly become a paradigmatic practice. There are now 21 federations with about two billion people constituting 40 per cent of the world's total population (Elazar, 1995, pp. 5–18),[3] or 23 according to Adeney (2007, p. 14). Even Britain, with its devolved parliaments in Scotland and Wales, seems to be going down de facto the federal path; and the status of Northern Ireland has been compared to that of a federacy although it will have enormous difficulties in developing a new constitution in defining federal relations. Federalism has contributed to the restoration of democracy in Argentina and Brazil, to the extension of democracy in Venezuela, and to the transition from a one-party to a multi-party polity in Mexico (Elazar, 1995, p. 16). Spain and South Africa,[4] when embarking on democratization, have undertaken a transformation from a unitary to a federal state, while Russia as well as Bosnia and Herzegovina continued their practice of federation in the wake of democratization.

**Written Constitution**

There are at least two research paradigms or approaches to federalism: the formal institutional approach focuses on a constitutional order and a set of specific institutional arrangements, and the behavioural approach studies the functions of any federal practice. According to the *Blackwell Encyclopedia of Political Institutions*, federalism is 'a form of territorial organization in which unity and regional diversity are accommodated with a single political system by distributing power among general and regional governments in a manner constitutionally safeguarding the existence and authority of each' (Bogdanor, 1987, p. 228). In this definition, the political structure is understood in part by the wording of the constitution. In order to analyse federalism in Asia, it is necessary to examine the constitutional definitions of power relations, bicameralism, constitutional courts and autonomous rights.

Such analysis reveals that there are many approaches to federalism in the written constitutions of Asia. While the 1948 Myanmar Constitution defines Myanmar as 'the Federated Shan States and the Wa States', India is specified as a Union of States in its 1950 Constitution, and Pakistan was specified as a Federation. In Sri Lanka, the four central components of the draft constitutional document introduced by the government in 1997 were as follows: 1. Sri Lanka would change from a unitary state to an 'indissoluble union of Regions'; 2. Regions would have power over local land use, taxes, security and, to a lesser extent, media; 3. All national political parties would have representation in the regions; 4. The executive presidency would be replaced by a parliamentary system wherein the Prime Minister would be chief executive.

The State of Indonesia was clearly defined by Article 1 of the 1945 Constitution as 'a unitary state'. By contrast, federalism was written into the 1957 Constitution in Malaysia so that it has a federal system of government under an elected constitutional monarchy. Each of the 13 states has its own constitution and a unicameral state assembly that shares legislative powers with the federal parliament. The federal government has authority over such matters as external affairs, defence, internal security, justice (except Islamic and native law), federal citizenship, finance, commerce, industry, communication and transportation. The states of east Malaysia, however, enjoy guarantees of autonomy with regard to immigration, civic service and education matters.

In the beginning both the Chinese National Party and Chinese Communist Party (CCP) had an article on federalism in their party constitution. The Constitution of the Chinese Soviet Republic declared, in November 1931:

> The Soviet government in China recognizes the right of self-determination of the national minorities in China, their right to complete separation from China, and to the formation of an independent state for each national minority. Thus the Mongols, Moslems, Tibetans, Koreans and others inhabiting the territory of China enjoy the complete right to self-determination, that is, they may either join the Union of Chinese Soviets or secede from it and form their own state as they may prefer. (Louis, 1979, pp. 114–15)

This article was later dropped. The Basic Law in Hong Kong can be seen as a mini constitution which defined the power relation between Beijing and Hong Kong, and it has pioneered a new form of a quasi-federal system with Chinese characteristics.

**Bicameralism**

In a federal system a second chamber can promote national unity in that members of the second house can bring and balance regional interests into federal politics, act as a check on executive federalism and force the government to listen to the voice of minority parties that may soften a central government's extreme position. In Asia, several countries have developed bicameral legislatures, but the function of the system varies and needs to be studied further.

India has two houses, namely the Council of States and the House of the People. In Pakistan the Federal Assembly is now bicameral (it was unicameral between 1956 and 1973), comprising an indirectly elected and weak Senate which cannot veto money bills, and a popularly elected National Assembly. The power of the Senate was shown in 1998 when Nawaz Sharif was unable to introduce Shariah as the law of Pakistan because the Senate would not approve the bill passed by the lower house. The Republic of the Philippines has a bicameral Congress consisting of 24 senators and 250 representatives. Senators are elected, for a term of six years. In recent years, senators have been a driving force for the establishment of federalism in the Philippines.

In Indonesia, the House of Representatives holds the authority to establish law, and is responsible for legislation, budgeting and oversight. By the 2001 Constitutional Amendment, the House of Representatives of the Regions may propose to the House of Representative bills related to regional autonomy, participate in the discussion of bills related to regional autonomy, and may oversee the implementation of laws concerning regional autonomy. The People's Consultative Assembly has the authority to amend and enact the Constitution, and may dismiss the President and/or vice-President during his/her term of office according to the Constitution.

In Myanmar's Constitution the Chamber of Deputies shall be composed of members who represent constituencies determined by law; while the Chamber of Nationalities consists of 125 seats to be allocated among the states and territories.

**Constitutional Court**

Federalism necessarily contains within it the principle that powers are divided between regional and central governments, with each government having jurisdiction over different areas of government. For this principle to operate effectively, however, the principle of the separation of executive and judicial power must also be invoked, because the functioning of a federal system depends on whether a constitutional (or supreme, or high) court is autonomous and capable of dealing with any conflict between the federal government and any state or province government. Many Asian courts are subject to executive power and are not autonomous. India is a notable exception. Article 50 of India's Constitution stresses the necessity of the separation of judicial from executive power. The Supreme Court has original jurisdiction in any dispute between the Government of India and one or more States, between the Government of India and any State or States on one side and one or more other States on the other, or between two or more States (Article 131). A testing case was the dismissal of the Janata Dal government of S.R. Bommai in Karnataka by the Congress-controlled federal government on 21 April 1989. The Supreme Court found that the central government had not ascertained the *bone fides* of the 19 alleged defectors' letters, and 'acted in undue haste' in April 1994. Nevertheless such a ruling was unable to restore the already dismissed Assembly to power (Tummala, 1996, p. 380).

In Pakistan, the Supreme Court has original jurisdiction in any dispute between the Federal Government and a Provincial Government according to Article 184 of the Pakistan Constitution. Article 24 of the 2001 Indonesian Constitutional Amendment specifies that judicial power shall be independent and shall possess the power to organize the judicature in order to enforce law and justice. Article 24C stipulates that the Constitutional Court can determine disputes over the authorities of state institutions whose powers are given by this Constitution.

The 2000 draft of Sri Lanka's Constitution has a comprehensive provision concerning the Supreme Court which has jurisdiction in the areas of bills, review of Acts, statutes of regional councils, the interpretation of the Constitution and fundamental and language rights.

Chapter VIII of Myanmar's Constitution stipulates that the High Court shall have exclusive original jurisdiction in all matters arising under any treaty made by the Union and in all disputes between the Union and a unit or between one unit and another.

The Court in Hong Kong enjoys the power of final adjudication in all cases except those involving interpretation of the Basic Law. The power to interpret the Basic Law is vested in the National People's Congress. The Hong Kong court attempted to interpret the Basic Law once but such an effort was dismissed by the Beijing government. There is an echo here of the famous Webster–Hayne debate in the USA when Senator Robert Y. Hayne of South Carolina argued for the State's right to judge Federal Government violations of the Constitution. Such a right was never recognized (Belz, 2000).

## Autonomy

Autonomy is not equivalent to federalism, but constitutionally defined and guaranteed autonomy can be seen as a component in a federal structure, or a feature of asymmetric federalism, or at least quasi-federal practice.

In Malaysia, the legislature of the States of Sabah and Sarawak may make laws for imposing taxes. Article 89 of the Constitution (with reference to Malay reservation land) shall not apply to the State of Sabah or Sarawak. And Article 8 (with reference to political equality) shall not invalidate or prohibit any provision of State in the State of Sabah or Sarawak for the reservation of land for natives of the States or for alienation to them, or for giving them preferential treatment.

Articles 29 and 30 of India's Constitution provides a list of protection of interests of minorities, including the right of minorities to establish and administer educational institutions. In Pakistan, minority religious laws are protected in Articles 20–22. Article 28 provides that 'Subject to Article 251 any section of citizens having a distinct language, script or culture shall have the right to preserve and promote the same and, subject to law, establish institutions for that purpose.' Article 251 talks of the national language; and section 3 specifies that, without prejudice to the status of the national language, a Provincial Assembly may by law prescribe measures for the teaching, promotion and use of a provincial language in addition to the national language. In Sri Lanka, the Reserved List and Regional List in the 2000 Draft Constitution provided two long lists that define the scope of the power between the national and regional government. In Pakistan, while the Federal Legislative List defines the exclusive authority of the centre, the Concurrent Legislative List delineates residual authority assigned to the provinces. A Council of Common

Interests was mandated comprising the chief ministers of the four provinces and four federal ministers in order to protect provincial rights. However no council meetings were held under Benazir Bhutto (Day Banks and Muller, 1997, p. 637).

Hong Kong enjoys a very high degree of autonomy in an Asian federal context and even in the world history of federation. In the field of foreign relations, for instance, Article 116 of the Hong Kong Basic Law defines the set of provisions affecting the external dimension to the broad autonomy of the Regions: (1) to be a separate customs territory; (2) to participate in relevant international organizations and international trade agreements; (3) to be a member of delegations of the People's Republic of China in negotiations at a diplomatic level; (4) to maintain and develop relations, and conclude and implement agreements with foreign states and regions and relevant international organizations; (5) to participate on their own in international organizations and conferences; (6) to maintain the application in the Region of international agreements that have already been implemented; and (7) to host consular and other official and semi-official missions, with the approval of the Central People's Government.

**Extra-constitutional Federal Arrangement**

The above formal institutional approach is limited, however, in that it offers little understanding about how these federal institutions work in reality. The constitutionally defined union of the states of India contains many more federal elements and practices than does the constitutionally defined federation of Pakistan. Beautifully written constitutional provisions of federalism are often ignored in practice, while some unwritten practices surprisingly reveal certain federal features. It is therefore necessary to adopt a behavioural approach to the extra-constitutional federal practices which are extremely important in determining the future of political developments even though they are not written into the constitutions. As Schulz, the advocate of the behavioural school, argues, local government sometimes amazingly holds much greater powers than were thought of or defined by a constitution (Schulz, 1979).

Quasi-federal practices were manifest in the history of China and Japan, where there has been pragmatic recognition of regional autonomy and the sharing of sovereign practices (see Chapters 10–12). Federal projects in China and Japan can be seen as a form of restorative federalism, that is, restoration of the ancient elements of federalism with modern institutions. Of course, quasi-federal practices are merely customary practice with very little modern constitutional definition of the distribution of power between two levels of governments.

China is constitutionally a unitary state with limited federal elements in two critical areas: quasi-fiscal federal practice and semi-federal institutions with regard to Hong Kong. Hong Kong's special status has weakened the traditional unitary model of China. Hong Kong has its own currency and independent financial and legal systems. The Hong Kong model is rooted in Chinese tradition but is also in keeping with modern international trends. While Hong Kong's special arrangement can be seen as a revived form of traditional autonomous practice in the Qing dynasty, it also contains modern constitutionally guaranteed rights (see Chapter 11).

Since the economic reforms China has developed a quasi-federal fiscal system in which political units with substantial autonomy in the area of investment regulation compete for capital by providing a secure institutional environment (see Chapter 10). Montinola, Qian and Weingast's macro-level study (Montinola et al., 1966) found that Weingast's minimum requirements for de facto fiscal federalism were present in China: a hierarchy of governments with a delineated scope of authority so that each is relatively autonomous; primary authority for the provinces over the economy within their jurisdictions; national regulation of the common market across jurisdictions; limited revenue sharing between governments so that all governments face hard budget constraints; and an 'institutionalized degree of durability' so that this division of power cannot be altered unilaterally (Weingast, 1997, pp. 44–5).

In political terms, this fiscal 'federalism' has fostered a relationship of reciprocity between central and provincial officials, characterized by bargaining and compromise. Although the CCP top leadership in Beijing has ultimate authority over the provinces, the top leaders (including the general secretary, politburo members and standing committee) are chosen by an élite selectorate, consisting of members of the CCP Central Committee, revolutionary elders and top military leaders. So the rational provincial official, seeking to be promoted in the CCP hierarchy, can be 'played to' by the central authorities, who can gain support from provincial representatives in the selectorate by providing them with political incentives through the *nomenklatura*. Similarly, provincial officials can play to the centre because their votes are an important source of legitimacy and power for the senior central leaders (see Chapter 10).

The competing formal constitutional versus behavioural approaches offer different strategies of federalization, or two contrasting paths to federalism. While some advocate the designing of federal constitutions and the referendum process in making a choice for federalism (He, 2002b, pp. 67–97), others emphasize the importance of functional and informal approaches, that is, the development of de facto federal institutions and practices first, with consequent revision of the existing constitution later on. According to this approach it is only in the later stages that the development of federalism involves a process of institutionalization, in particular, the drafting of a federal constitution. As Hicks points out, the best way to develop a federation is to 'start in a small way with a few States so that it can adapt the Constitution gradually as it acquires more members as was the case with the original thirteen colonies of the USA . . . and the position of the early Swiss cantons' (Hicks, 1978, p. 176). Otherwise it is possible to devise or copy a nice federal constitution, but it may be just on paper and never operate in reality, as with Myanmar's constitution.

It is essential to achieve a certain balance between unity and diversity (or autonomy) in any move toward federalism. Federalism presupposes two things: the maintenance of unity and the satisfaction of the desire of minorities. The federal solution fails if it does not satisfy the desire of minorities or if it does not maintain the unity of the state. To establish and maintain federalism, one has to achieve what Watts calls 'relative balance' or 'approximate equilibrium' between the desire for union and the desire for regional autonomy (Watts, 1966). The success of the Indian federation seems to achieve such a balance through taking accommodationist measures with regard to secessionist Punjab. If the centre suppresses local autonomy in order to avoid the break-up of the state, there is little hope for federalism because, in the eye of the centre, the price of federalism is too high. If the region demands an extreme form of secessionism, for example, the Tamil Tiger's call for the return to homeland, and the Moro National Liberation Front's (MNLF) fight for separation, there is no hope for federalism either. As Ron May pointed out, a long time ago:

> Instability is inherent in the structure of federal decision-making in a dynamic context. Although for a time a balance may be achieved between the forces of separatism and centralism, in most cases federal systems either succumb to separatist tendencies, in which case either they disintegrate or they are held together by the coercion of the weaker by the stronger units, or national integration proceeds, in which case the original federal form becomes increasingly irrelevant to the political actuality. (May, 1970, p. 86)

## COMPETING MODELS OF FEDERALISM IN ASIA

The most important debate is over what kind of federalism can successfully achieve autonomy, contain and reduce ethnic conflicts, and facilitate and promote democracy. In this volume, Will Kymlicka examines the emergence of multinational federalism in the West, explains well the trend towards various forms of multinational federalism, evaluates the model of multinational federalism and discusses the relevance of this model to Asia (see Chapter 2). David Brown, by contrast, strongly argues against multi-national federalism being applied in Asia and favours regional or territorial federalism instead (see Chapter 3).

Regional or territorial federalism can be characterized as the universal protection of individual rights, the neutrality of the state with regard to different ethnic groups, the absence of an internal boundary for ethnic groups, the division and diffusion of power within a single national community, and regions rather than ethnicity being the basic unit of federal polity. The federalism of the USA and Australia can be seen as the examples of region-based federalism. Malaysian federalism is territorial rather than multinational. In recent years, Russia has attempted to introduce regional federalism and India contains a strong element of regional federalism.

The federalisms of Canada, Spain and Belgium can be seen as examples of *multinational federalism*, where federal constitutions accommodate concentrated ethnic groups; an internal boundary is drawn to enable minorities to exercise minority rights and self-determination, and to achieve an ethnonational homeland. Kymlicka defines 'multinational federalism' as 'creating a federal or quasi-federal subunit in which the minority group forms a local majority, and so can exercise meaningful forms of self-government', and where 'the group's language is typically recognized as an official state language, at least within their federal subunit, and perhaps throughout the country as a whole' (Kymlicka and Baogang, 2005, pp. 23–24; Kymlicka, 2006). Multinational federalism allows for language to be a determinant for the drawing of internal political boundaries. Taking India as an example, the organization of the state boundaries was based on ethnic language in the 1950s. Linguistic-based internal boundaries make a significant number of people happier, and are not inconsistent with liberalism, nor do they pose a threat to national unity. Multinational federalism seems much fairer than other systems in accommodating the desires and concerns of minorities.

The idea of federalism in Asia poses a set of interrelated questions which begin with the issue of whether Asian states can or should follow the Western models of federalism. Subsidiary questions are whether the American model of territorial federalism provides a stable,[5] but largely irrelevant, system for Asia; and whether the Canadian model of multinational federalism is relevant to Asia but inherently unstable. For David Brown, multinational federalism is unstable and problematic. He argues that, by its very nature, it solicits trouble, promotes more contentious violence and is likely, eventually, to break down the nation-state. Multinational federalism, by giving minorities pockets of majority power, creates difficulties for the functioning of democracy, whereas regional federalism can coexist with and promote democracy. In Québec, multinational federalism has fortified the minority French language at the cost of English, the language of the national majority. In Belgium, there is little sense of national identity and the future of Belgium is uncertain. The question of whether multinational federalism has been mistaken, premature and problematic in Western countries remains a contested issue.

The debate over regional versus multinational federalism has been manifest in Sri Lanka, where there exist two different conceptions of federalism. While the government of Sri Lanka and a majority of Sinhalese are interested in a region-based federal model combining shared rule and self-rule with limited autonomy for the Tamil Tigers, the Tamil Tigers' vision of federalism is a multinational one, more confederal in nature with maximal autonomy (Edrisinha, 2005, p. 261). In 2001, the Tigers rejected far-ranging decentralization of power as inadequate, and demanded an interim administration that would control police, judiciary, revenue and land issues in 2002. At the same time, the right-wing group among Sri Lanka's Sinhalese–Buddhist majority opposed the government's decentralization plan.

The key question is whether the state recognizes the right to territorial autonomy by ethnonational groups. It can perhaps be seen as a general rule that nation-states which opt for federalism are interested in pursuing a style of regional federalism in which common citizenship constitutes a civic homeland across different ethnic groups, and two levels of governments share power, while the ethnonational groups demand a sort of self-rule that is founded upon one ethnicity exclusive of other ethnic groups within a multinational federal polity.

Given the challenge of ethnonationalities, it would be extremely difficult for the Philippines and Indonesia to establish only a region-based federalism while rejecting multinational federalism completely. Regional federalism cannot deal with the challenge of ethnic conflicts adequately because of its failure to meet the special demands of minority nationalities. It is inevitable that some Asian countries will adopt a certain form of multinational federalism with asymmetric characteristics in order to deal with ethnic conflicts. A particular form of multinational federalism is needed in China, for example, to meet the demands of the Tibetan people.

Nevertheless, the model of multinational federalism cannot apply to the case of Hong Kong because most of the people of Hong Kong are Chinese, and multinationalities do not exist here. Likewise, if China and Taiwan were reunified by federal institution, this would not be a case of multinational federalism because Taiwanese are largely regarded as Han Chinese (*huaren*). Multinational federalism has its limits in Japan and in the two Koreas too. If the two Koreas were unified to establish a federal polity, the form of federalism would be unlikely to be multinational.

The wholesale implementation of multinational federalism is unrealistic in terms of the lack of a powerful driving force, problematic in terms of the subsequent difficulties it will bring, and misleading in terms of a narrow conceptual approach to federalism in Asia. Normatively speaking, one ethnicity cannot constitute a basis for federalism; and the federal state must pursue a mix of civic and ethnic interests. The Indian success story reveals that its federalism has blended both regional and multinational elements of federalism.[6] The achievement of the Indian federal accommodation of ethnic groups is due to both the multinational and regional federal mechanism (see Chapter 4). The success was not primarily from multinational federalism alone, but from a mix of regimes. One essential question is how Asian countries will develop mixed regimes, that is, generate a dynamic blending of elements of traditional rule, regional, multinational and asymmetric elements of federalism, and confederalism in different proportions at different times. Such a mix resists any simplistic conceptual theorizing.

## HYBRID FEDERALISM IN ASIA

Debate over region-based versus multinational federalism may be conceptually too narrow in East Asia. Such questions ignore or underrate the other models of Asian federalism. Pakistan and Malaysia, for example, have developed *illiberal federalism* where federalism coexists with, and even supports, the authoritarian structure. Indonesia, the Philippines and China have built up *hybrid federalism* with the key characteristics of regional autonomy.

The Western models of federalism – regional (territorial) federalism and multinational federalism – have not been widely implemented in Asia. Instead, a hybrid form of federalism has evolved in East Asia. It does not introduce wholesale Western federalization; rather, it is a piecemeal process that is more appropriate for some Asian countries. Hybrid federalism has a greater potential for success in Asia than does multinational federalism.

Hybrid federalism refers to the special mixed institutional arrangement where the centre and the main body of a polity remain a unitary system, while only one or two peripheral regions or units have been decentralized or offered the status of regional autonomy. This institutional configuration combines a unitary system with federal elements. It differs from the conventional unitary system because the special regional autonomy does not fall into the traditional category of central and local relations. The autonomy of Hong Kong and Aceh, for example, is defined and guaranteed by the Hong Kong Basic Law and the Law No. 11, 2006, passed by the Indonesian parliament in 2006, respectively; and the centre cannot change the autonomy law unilaterally. This hybrid federalism is also dissimilar to multinational federalism because the former only introduces federal elements in peripheral regions or units, while the latter has federalized the main body of polity.

Constitutionally defined and guaranteed regional autonomy, designed to satisfy the desires and aspirations of one nationality or ethnic group, constitutes a building block of hybrid federalism. Following political theorist William Riker's (1964, p. 11) minimal definition of federalism as being where '(1) two levels of government rule the same land and people, (2) each level has at least one area of action in the autonomy of each government in its own sphere, and (3) there is some [constitutional] guarantee . . . of the autonomy of each government in its own sphere', regional autonomy presents a possible Asian way toward hybrid federalism in Indonesia, the Philippines and China.

In a search for a hybrid federal system, India, Indonesia and China have attempted to combine and reconfigure unitary and federal elements in different forms with their distinctive characteristics. India's federal system, for example, contains some unitary elements. The president appoints governors, and can exercise direct presidential rule, and the prime minister can call for new state elections. The union government has power to override state governments with regard to the question of development and poverty. India is a mix of unitary and federal systems: unitary in a time of crisis, federalism functions at other times. The devolution process provides a legal definition of the relationship between the centre and the state, and the Supreme Court can make a decision against the union government. Both union and state parliaments can pass laws. The federal laws, however, have precedence if they are in conflict, for example if they both make a law relating to a power on the concurrent list.

Hybrid federalism is different from conventional federalism which has its necessary components of bicameralism and the arbitration role of a supreme court, among others. In particular, it adopts only a minimal form of federalism and, as a result, a large component of the unitary political system remains intact so that it has the advantage of maintaining the unity of the nation-state while avoiding the uncertainty of multinational federalism. (For a discussion of both the strengths and the weaknesses of multinational federalism, see Chapter 2.) Additionally, in relation to the Philippines, Ron May argues that special autonomy is better than wholesale federalization to deal with the existing problem in Mindanao because it can solve the problem without changing the whole system of the Philippines.

Hybrid federalism differs from multinational federalism in the following ways. As in the case of Aceh and Hong Kong, it is not purely ethnicity-based, nor does it guarantee political equality. It lacks a clearly defined internal boundary based on one ethnic language. Finally, as in the case of Hong Kong, hybrid federalism has the capability of achieving stability and peace at the cost of inter-group equality and even democracy.

Take a few examples of hybrid federal practices in Asia. Hong Kong enjoys a higher degree of autonomy than most federal sub-units. For instance, Hong Kong has a separate customs territory and is able to participate in relevant international organizations and international trade agreements. In Indonesia, quasi-federal institutions have emerged under the banner of regional autonomy. In the case of Aceh, Nangroe Aceh Darussalam (NAD), the autonomy law, recognized the Aceh people's long-sought religious sovereignty. The Acehnese may practise their Islamic laws (Shari'a). Under the NAD the Acehnese are entitled to receive 70 per cent of the revenues from oil and gas. Under the peace agreement of 2005, they may hold elections for a self-governing body. In the Philippines, the 1987 Constitution provided autonomous regions in Muslim Mindanao with legislative powers over administrative organization; creation of sources of revenues; ancestral domain and natural resources; personal, family and property relations; regional urban and rural planning development; economic, social and tourism development; educational policies; and preservation and development of cultural heritage.

Hybrid federalism is oriented toward stability, and has asymmetric features to achieve this aim. Asymmetry refers to, in Watts' words, 'the relative political power and influence' of the constituent units (Watts, 1999, p. 123). 'Asymmetric federalism', a phrase originally coined by Charles Tarlton (1965), means that the equality principle must be limited and modified accordingly. The argument for same treatment is often not a viable proposition. For instance, an asymmetric federal system needs to be developed in order to meet the different aspirations of the regions in Indonesia and provinces in the Philippines. The important issue is to avoid a simplistic notion of political equality which has been seen as the foundational block of federalism in the past. Political equality as one principle of democracy must be defended, but may need to be modified or even sacrificed in the federal institutional design in Asia. The equal number of senators in the USA and Australia despite the different population sizes is a good example of political equality in practice. As Watts points out, 'This [equal representation of the state in the senate system] ensured that differing state viewpoints would not be simply overridden by a majority of the population dominated by the larger states' (Watts, 1999, p. 92). The second chamber in different Asian countries, however, often takes account of difference; that is, some nationalities have more seats than others in the second chamber. Asymmetric federalism has long been practised in Malaysia, where Malaysian federalism favoured the indigenous group at the sacrifice of political equality for the Chinese and Indian communities. Malaysian asymmetric federalism is associated with the domination of the Malay ethnic group over and against the Chinese and Indian; in William Case's words, 'it did less to safeguard minorities than to institutionalize their inequalities' (see Chapter 6).

In order to meet both the desire for self-government and the need for maintaining the unity of the state, Asian countries adopt an asymmetric form of federalism. Federal institutions have to be asymmetric to maintain diversity and difference. To preserve diversity and difference, federalism must adopt differential treatment and asymmetric policy so that the con-stituent units of a federation do not possess identical powers: some should have special rights because of their social and political history (Agranoff, 1999). Asymmetric federalism can be employed as a means of conflict reso-lution to deal with secessionism and ethnic division. The driving force for Asian federalism comes from within; that is, from the threat to existing nation-states posed by internal groups. The national identity question (the choice between a separate political identity and a united national identity) constitutes a background condition for federalism.

The presence of national identity issues means that the most common form of federalism in Asia is 'hold-together federalism' rather than 'bring-together federalism'. Federalism in Indonesia, the Philippines, Sri Lanka, Burma (Myanmar) and China (with regard to Tibet) is designed to 'hold together' national unity. Hold-together federalism implies the primacy of maintaining the unity of the nation. It must adopt asymmetric character-istics because, in order to hold the country together, the centre makes a special deal with one group or subunit, and this special deal carries with it the asymmetrical distribution of power and rights with regard to the rest of the country. Malaysian federalism gave Sarawak and Sabah special powers to control migration, and the Indonesian asymmetric federal arrangement offers Aceh a set of special rights too. By contrast, 'bring-together' federalism is symmetric, as in the senate system in the United States and Australia. The provision for an equal number of senators from each state was designed to attract each state to the federal polity so that none of them felt in an inferior position when they joined the federal union.

If a federal solution were found to unify China and Taiwan, the federal form is likely to be asymmetric: different from both the United States and Australia. According to Deng Xiaoping's notion of 'one nation two systems', Taiwan would enjoy a high degree of autonomy, consisting of administrative and legislative power, judicial power including final judg-ment, the power to keep its own army, and certain powers in foreign affairs, such as signing commercial and cultural agreements with foreign countries (Chen, 1996, p. 1056). Taiwan would also have the power to issue its own currency. But only the PRC would represent China in the international arena; Taiwan would recognize the sovereignty of China, and its military arm would not constitute a threat against China. Deng Xiaoping's notion of 'one nation two systems' can be interpreted as an asymmetric federalism in which the federal state of Taiwan would enjoy more autonomy than Hong Kong and Tibet, but still have an unequal power relation with Mainland China.

Bring-together federalism would apply to the reunification of China and Taiwan, as well as South and North Korea. It is much more difficult to achieve bring-together federalism than hold-together federalism. States that struggle with national identity problems should therefore consider using federalism to hold their nationalities together before they become so different that bring-together federalism is the only option.

The initiating of hybrid federalism in Asia carries with it two apparent contradictions. First, the states which are most centralized, for example, Indonesia and China, are allowing special regional autonomy in practice. The second contradiction is that, despite the existence of asymmetric elements of federalism being implemented, both Beijing and Jakarta avoid the use of the term 'federalism', and favour the language of autonomy. While some Chinese dissidents openly call for a federal system, the official line bans any debate on federalism and sticks to Deng Xiaoping's idea of 'one country two systems'. This raises the highly contestable question of whether regional autonomy can be seen as a form of or an element in federalism.

The Asian form of hybrid federalism has a number of deficiencies. It institutionalizes unequal relations but it does not necessarily provide maximal minority rights for certain groups. The Hong Kong model of autonomy is an excellent example. Beijing made it clear that the ultimate source of power radiates from the centre to the regions and not vice versa. This is secured by two institutional arrangements. First, the central government has the power to appoint the Chief Executive in an autonomous system in which the executive body dominates the legislative body. Second, the power to interpret the Basic Law and to amend it belongs respectively to the Standing Committee of the National People's Congress and the National People's Congress of the PRC.

The Hong Kong model of autonomy was tested in 1999. In late January 1999, the Court of Final Appeal ruled that mainland-born children with at least one parent who is a Hong Kong permanent resident have, without restriction, the right to live in the territory. Perhaps most powerfully, the five judges added that the court had the authority 'to examine whether any legislative acts of the National People's Congress or its Standing Committee are consistent with the Basic Law and to declare them to be invalid if found to be inconsistent' (Ching, 1999, p. 21). Though the ruling could open the floodgates to immigrants, it was hailed in the local Hong Kong legal community as a victory for the rule of law and the independence of the judiciary.

Beijing, however, saw the ruling as an infringement of its sovereignty over Hong Kong. Chinese officials and legal scholars say the ruling exceeds the jurisdiction of the court, challenges the authority of China's highest legislative body, the National People's Congress, and violates the Basic Law, which was enacted by the NPC. Although it had delegated authority to Hong Kong courts to interpret certain sections of the Basic Law, the NPC has the final say. The NPC is 'the highest organ of state power', according to the Chinese constitution. Not even the Supreme People's Court can overrule it, let alone a collection of Hong Kong judges. Under pressure, the court 'clarified' its ruling on 26 February 1999, acknowledging the NPC as the supreme legislative body, whose authority cannot be questioned (see Chapter 11).

The long-term prospects for hybrid federalism are uncertain. It is possible that other regions or units will follow the example of special regional autonomy and demand similar treatment; thus more and more federal elements might be grafted into the unitary system. It is equally possible that the centre might be able to absorb the federal unit and transform it into an integral part of the unitary system. Hong Kong will be a test case to see which one will prevail in the long term.

## HOW DOES DEMOCRATIZATION FACILITATE AND IMPROVE FEDERALISM?

In today's world, democratization and federalization are linked in various ways with different forms. The close and complex association between democratization and federalization in real life requires a dialectical and sophisticated understanding of federalization and democratization.

In the context of multinational states, democratization can be understood as a process of federalization in which all parties are to achieve dual domains on, or dual sovereignty over, the same land and same people, and to make dual identities (national and subnational) compatible and complementary. Two or more peoples are not mutually exclusive but inclusively cooperative. Democracy is beyond one narrow ethnic definition of people. People's rule must be understood as *peoples'* rule; that is, the coexistence of shared rule by all the peoples and self-rule by one group of people. Democracy means a set of rights for everyone, including minority nationalities. Civic and political liberties enjoyed by minority nationalities must be upheld. If democratization is narrowly designed for one people, such a process will lead to anti-federal measures. Only if democratization is widely designed for two or more peoples can it contain federal elements and institutions.

In addressing the question of how democratization facilitates federalism, the existing federal states need to be distinguished from non-federal states because each requires different approaches in regard to the federalism project. In the case of non-federal states like Sri Lanka, Burma, Indonesia, the Philippines and China, the question is whether democratization will facilitate the introduction of federalism. In the case of existing federal states such as India, Pakistan and Malaysia, the question is whether democratization will help to improve or reform the existing federalism.

Different levels of democratization have different impacts. A higher level of democracy has contributed to the function of federalism in India. This needs to be distinguished from semi-democracy in Southeast Asia (Singapore in the 1960s, Malaysia in the 1970s, Thailand in the 1980s, Burma in the 1990s, Cambodia now) where semi-competitive elections are used to gain electoral legitimacy and extend tenure for the top leaders. Semi-democracy, as William Case describes in Chapter 6, provides an opportunity for the opposition to compete for limited power, and even come to power at the state level in Malaysia. The competition for votes gives the voters of the Chinese community much higher social value than they had before, and it slowly changes the federal polity. This semi-democratic country is different from China and Burma, where large-scale democratization is absent and this non-democracy factor inhibits the development of federalism.

The fact that the Philippines and Indonesia have embarked on a road toward federalism clearly demonstrates the effect of democratization on the process of federalization. While revolution has the logic of strengthening the central authority and developing a unitary state, as Tony Reid argues in Chapter 7, democratization offers a different normative order and logic in favour of federalist development. The effects of democratization on federalization can be grasped in the following ways.

Pressure for federalism comes from the process of democratization in which the idea of human rights dominates political debates, giving rise to an extension of rights awareness to minorities. In the politics of national identity, nation-states tend to stress all peoples as one common people, and do not treat minority nationalities as a separate people, while minority groups see everything through the eyes of distinctive ethnicity. The process of democratization provides an opportunity for minority groups to challenge the state's discourse on national identity, and to fight for their separate identity. Empowered by human rights discourse and institutions in the process of democratization, minorities have enthusiastically demanded

their cultural identity and rights. They openly criticized the state's undemocratic measures for a homogeneous cultural domination that threatens cultural liberty and diversity. In particular, some minorities who have had
historical experience of self-rule have been advocating and demanding
a federal system in which the subunits are granted certain powers to
control their own affairs. Democratization empowers minority groups and
increases their bargaining power in the process of federalization (He,
2002a, pp. 245–73).

Public debate and open advocacy for federalism have been closely associated with, and encouraged by, the process of democratization. With
freedom of speech and freedom of association, NGOs can oppose the
official line of autonomy and advocate federalism in Indonesia and the
Philippines.[7] In Taiwan and South Korea, there are numerous proposals on
federalism or confederation (Hwang, 1994, p. 293). The impact of democratization on federalism can be illustrated by the lack of democratization
and its impact in China and Myanmar, where public debate over federalism is banned by the authoritarian states;[8] using Allan Smith's phrase, federalism is 'not on the radar' in Myanmar; and the debates on federalism for
China and Myanmar can only be heard overseas.

In India the domination of a single political party and a single leader in
the 1980s 'turned the federal system virtually into a unitary system'
(Dubhashi, 1991, pp. 376–84). By contrast, party competition in the process
of democratization contributes to policy options with regard to federalism.
For example, in Taiwan, Zhou Yanshan, a former legislative member of the
New Party, suggested the model of a Chinese Commonwealth as a solution
(Zhou, 1995, pp. 19–24). The Kuomintang (KMT) considered federal or
confederate arrangements as a way to achieve unification, the DPP opposed
it in the 2000 general election. In Sri Lanka, parties offered different policy
options in the 2005 election. Public debate and party competition will eventually lead to debate over federalism in the parliament, for example in the
Philippines, where the senators have been arguing for a federal solution to
the Mindanao problem. The 2004 general elections in Indonesia strengthened the central government that was able to make a deal with regard to self-
government in Aceh. In Malaysia, limited competitive elections have eroded
the domination of United Malays National Organisation (UMNO) and
increasingly the non-Malay middle class has played an important role; these
changes have challenged the unequal basis of Malaysian federalism, but
whether these changes will make federal institutions more genuine and
equal remains to be seen.

The current lack of substantive federalization in Asia can be seen through
the perspective of *timing*. The third wave of democratization in Asia has
existed for a very short period and a certain time span is a necessary factor

for political transition toward federalism. For example, Belgium's transition from a unitary to a federal system took 30 years, from 1963 to 1993 (the introduction of the linguistic border line in 1963; the establishment of an equal number of ministries, and double majority in 1970; the federalization of Belgium in 1980, and the constitutional reform in 1993). In the Philippines, after nearly 20 years of democratization, federalism was on the government's agenda in 2005. In the wake of ten years of democratization, the Indonesian government started to implement policy concerning regional autonomy and self-government.

The sequence of democratization with regard to the development of federalism is different in Europe and Asia (He, 2001, pp. 97–119). Democratization in Spain and South Africa was simultaneously linked with the transformation from unitary to federal polities. There is, however, a sequence in which democratization precedes the establishing of federalism in Asia. India's case demonstrates that federalism and democracy were separate from each other in the initial stage of nation building, but developed in tandem with each other in the later stage (see Chapter 4). Myanmar, by contrast, has faced pressure for both democratization and federalization (see Chapter 9).

The denial of election results and the reversal of the democratization process often thwart the process of federalization. In the 1970 Pakistani election, the Awami League of East Pakistan won 160 out of 162 seats in the eastern wing, while the Pakistan People's Republic (PPP) secured only 81 out of 138 seats. If the election results were respected, it would have made the Pakistani federal system functional. Zulfikar Ali Bhutto, however, denied the right of the Awami League to form a majority government and did not convene the National Assembly. In the end, the state of Bangladesh was born (see Chapter 5). In the 1990 election in Burma, the Shans, which were the active ethnic group in the process of federalization before 1962, won the second-largest number of seats. The military regime justified its holding onto power by claiming the need to preserve the union; an opportunity of forming and developing federalism was thus lost.

The misuse of referenda has worsened the ethnic conflict problem in Sri Lanka. In the July 1977 general election, the United National Party (UNP) secured less then 52 per cent of the vote but gained 85 per cent of the parliamentary seats, a quirk of the 'first-past-the-post' electoral system. The Tamil United Liberation Front (TULF) became the opposition party in the parliament, for it had swept the polls in the predominantly Tamil northern region. By early 1978, the UNP replaced the Westminster model with a Presidential system and, in October 1982, Jayewardene of the UNP was elected president with a 53 per cent majority. In December of that year, a referendum was held to approve the extension of the term of parliament for six years as from August 1983. The Tamil minority saw an advantage to be gained in parliamentary elections expected in the following year and thus voted overwhelmingly against the referendum. Nevertheless, the referendum was passed with a favourable majority of 54.7 per cent out of the 71 per cent registered voters. After the referendum, relations between the government and the Tamils of the north deteriorated and, in July 1983, riots broke out in Tamil-populated regions of northern Sri Lanka (Smith, 1986, pp. 808–9). In any event, the TULF realized that its demand for regional autonomy, via devolution and decentralization, would not be granted. The weapon of parliamentary protest was replaced by a resort to arms (de Silva, 1987, pp. 20–22).

Sri Lanka lost several golden opportunities for making constitutional changes and accommodating the Tamil Tigers. In August 2000, Sri Lanka's parliament did not approve proposed constitutional changes. President Chandrika Kumaratunga dissolved parliament on 18 August 2000 and called parliamentary elections for 10 October, seeking a mandate from voters to pass the new constitution (Editorial, 2000, p. 12). In 2003, Sri Lanka's United National Front government attempted to negotiate with the Tamil Tigers to make peace. A dispute between President Kumaratunga and Prime Minister Ranil Wickremesinghe arose; and the United People's Freedom Alliance led by President Kumaratunga won the 2004 election and stopped the peace process. In 2005, the anti-federalism party won the election.

Given that the majority of the population in Sri Lanka is Sinhalese, elections and referenda are less likely to favour the minority North region. Here a crucial question is whether the national leaders ought to take courage and bypass the popular vote and go against majority rule in order to establish federalism in Sri Lanka. Historically, it was a group of élites who made the 'undemocratic' decision on federalism in India and the USA without going through a referendum. In Indonesia, the Aceh question was not an important issue in the 2004 general election campaign. The elected leader, Susilo Bambang Yudhoyono, has more autonomy than his counterpart in Sri Lanka to make a decisive decision. The apparently short-cut path toward federalism through referendum might turn out to be a longer route than was generally assumed. The case of Sri Lanka demonstrates that the misuse of referenda and majority rule has worsened ethnic conflicts and perpetuated the question of secession.[9] The constraint on majority rule, and cautious use of referenda and general elections with regard to the national identity question, the materialization of autonomy, and the protection of language rights could help to resolve the national identity issues in Sri Lanka. In establishing federalism, majority rule, the enemy of federalism, must be constrained. One 'demos' cannot decide the national identity issue alone. It is necessary to institute demos-constraining measures in federalization to deal with the danger of ethnonationalism.

Moreover, the function of federalism requires that all parties are committed to democracy; in particular, the political forces in the constituent units of federalism must be subject to the democratization process so as to achieve federalism. If the democratic element is absent, military forces are likely to be used to suppress other rivals. For example, the struggle for power and domination within the Tamil Tigers and the MNLF led to internal conflicts and the disruption of the peace process in both Sri Lanka and Philippines. The Liberation Tigers of Tamil Eelam (LTTE) stayed away from the Tokyo conference on 9–10 June 2002 in order to avoid making concessions on democracy and human rights.

## HOW DOES FEDERALISM FACILITATE THE DEMOCRATIZATION PROCESS?

Historically, federalism and democracy were separated from each other. Democracy in the United Kingdom and France occurred without federalism, while democracy was combined with federalism in the USA, Canada and Australia. An authoritarian form of federalism existed in the former Soviet Union and Yugoslavia, and today's Malaysia and China–Hong Kong. Substantive democratization and fuller federalization, however, are inherently interrelated and both must be established on the principle of consent.

Conceptually, federalism can be defined in democratic terms.[10] Sir George Young in 1941 described federalism as a form of democracy in the sense that federating functions develop a central governmental authority and administration, distribute governmental authority and decentralize administration. He suggested that federalism can revitalize democracy when its force has become deficient (Young, 1941). Generally speaking, federalism contains the features of democracy in the following senses: (1) the relationships between two governments are defined by the rule of laws and a set of procedures; (2) the independence of the court for the functioning of a healthy federalism ought to be maintained; (3) civic liberties and rights of minority nationalities are protected against majority rule, a sort of collective freedom for minority nationalities is preserved and a set of constitutionally guaranteed scopes of action are enjoyed by minority nationalities; (4) the idea of federalism relies on the idea of polycentricism (Ostrom, 1994), the practice of the division of power between federal and state governments, the balance of power and local autonomy. Federalism must operate in the three divisions of powers among legislature, executive and judiciary. If democracy is about sharing political power, federalism is about sharing powers between the centre and local, or between two levels of governments, or between mainstream nationality and minority nationalities.

Federalization can be seen as an effective way of deepening democratization in the senses of granting local autonomy and protecting minority rights, establishing new rules of the game with regard to the independence of the high court, and the democratizing of central and local relations. The idea that federalism facilitates democracy is largely a normative claim in the sense that any federalism has to recognize local or regional autonomy and this presupposes self-government associated with the fundamental democratic principle of people's rule.

A fuller federalization can be understood as a substantive democratization in terms of full franchise and authenticity. Full franchise means not only the mainstream nationality is able to vote, but also minority nationalities have the same rights and opportunities. Authenticity refers to the degree to which interaction is free from domination, manipulation, deception and self-deception. In this context, substantive democracy is needed in the struggle against authoritarian federalism in Malaysia and China.

In a well-functioning federal system, diverse voices of peoples are expressed and protected through bicameralism. This federal system promotes national unity and institutionalizes the democratic principle of equal representation. By contrast, in today's Burma where federalism is denied, minorities are advised to move away from national politics. Such a non-federal practice cannot promote national unity, let alone promote democracy. In a well-functioning federalism, moreover, élites from both the centre and state governments work together to address common issues; and consequently they have developed a mechanism of strengthening national unity. Functional federalism will also stop the centre from bullying the subnational governments, which enhances overall good governance. By contrast, in an ill-functioning federalism, such a good working relationship is absent and leads to discontent, especially when the centre tends to behave in a dictatorial manner ordering the subnational governments to act without proper consultation.

Federalism has deepened democratization and promoted the democratic institutions of India. James Manor argues that democracy in India functions to a large extent *because of* its federalist arrangement (Manor, 1998, pp. 21–35). Gurpreet Mahajan highlights two ways in which federalism contributes to democracy: diversifying and pluralizing the national elites and accommodating the previously excluded people who have no national standing at regional level. Federalism 'has helped to minimize the domination of the majority that controls the centre and provided space for different kinds of groups and communities to share power . . . it has resulted in a *plurality of elites* emerging in the political arena'. Very strikingly, within the federal structure, increasingly national coalition government relies on regional parties who compete for votes. As a result, 'in Northern India, the proportion of "Other Backward Classes" elected representatives went up from 11 per cent in 1984 to 25 per cent in 1996. Simultaneously, the percentage of Upper Caste representatives fell from 45 per cent to 35 per cent' (see Chapter 4).

It is necessary to reinforce the early conceptual distinction among territorial, multinational, hybrid, asymmetric and illiberal federalisms in order to develop an understanding of the impact of the forms of federalism on the process of democratization.[11] While genuine federalism contributes to democratization, other hybrid, asymmetric, illiberal, minimalist and quasi forms of federalism do not necessarily promote democracy. Illiberal federalism in Pakistan did not bring about substantive local democracy. The power of feudal landowners was increased through the local council elections under the illiberal federal structure in the 1960s (see Chapter 5). Malaysian federalism has dual functions. While it provides a structural framework in which the opposition party, the Parti Islam Se-Malaysia (Islamic Party of Malaysia), was able to control the state-level government in Kelantan between 1955 and 1978 and again after 1991, and in Terengganu between 1959 and 1961, and 1996 and 2004, it has also inhibited democratic development in the sense that the Malaysian style of minimalist federalism shores up the authoritarian system and its authoritarian structure prevents federal institutions from developing into a more meaningful and substantive system (see Chapter 6).

Hybrid federalism does recognize local rule but provides limited and constrained autonomy and often undermines and violates the principle of self-government. Authoritarian quasi-federal arrangements inhibit democratic development in Hong Kong, and the prospect of a semi-federal arrangement in Hong Kong is not bright, as freedom there has been decreasing. The fight for democracy in Hong Kong with a call for genuine self-government, including a directly elected chief executive by Hong Kong people, can be interpreted as a call for a genuine federal arrangement. The fight for genuine federalism can play a role in establishing democracy in China. Genuine federalism offers not only a much better alternative to the current Chinese authoritarian control over secessionist regions, but also a means to achieve China's unification with Taiwan, and a step toward democracy. An authoritarian form of federalism is exceptional, contingent, temporary and full of deficiencies. The collapse of the Soviet Union and the break-up of Yugoslavia demonstrated that an authoritarian federalism is unsustainable. In the end authoritarian federalism has to undergo a substantive change, as Soviet federalism did.

## CAN FEDERALISM REDUCE OR CONTAIN VIOLENT ETHNIC CONFLICTS IN ASIA?

Federalism has provided a set of mechanisms for managing national identity conflicts. They include representation, decentralization, regional autonomy, the independence of judicial review, financial commissions and inter-state tribunals. Malaysian federalism has successfully accommodated the desires and needs of Sabah and Sarawak, allowing them to control internal migration, thus skilfully containing the secession movement there, and preventing violent struggles for self-determination. Hybrid federal practice has helped to quell violent nationalism in Aceh.

India's federalism demonstrates that the federal state is capable of withstanding disruptive localism and promoting national integration and inter-ethnic harmony through territorial devolution, the guarantee of personal security and freedom of individuals to engage in economic and cultural intercourse across the regional borders (Ranapala, 1999, pp. 113–16). In 1935, India allocated special electoral seats for some minorities; this has pacified them and kept them under control. A concrete successful case is that of the Mizos, who engaged in 30 years of violent struggle and insurgency for their independence from the Indian State. In 1985, however, the Mizos were granted full autonomy and recognized as the 23rd state of the Indian Union. Now 84 per cent of the people of the state see themselves as Mizos and Indians (see Chapter 4).

Three factors or mechanisms contribute to the success of India's federalism in containing ethnic conflicts. Firstly, the language claims of minority nationalities were not anti-India per se and did not pose a threat to the life of the nation-state. The recognition of special language needs granted a special right to minority people who, as a consequence, gradually become respectable and responsible. Democratic inclusiveness and participation made people become pro-India and embody civic virtues. Secondly, collective regional identity did not translate into ethnic identity. Overlapping identities changed previously unique ethnic identity into regional identity, thus strengthening the national identity. Thirdly, there is a safeguard enabling the central government to deal with internal suppression when one ethnic group dominates. Federal institutions provided countervailing measures to reduce the domination of one ethnic group; and the centre has been strong enough to protect civic rights in provinces and sub-provinces.

While federalism contains and reduces ethnic conflicts, ironically, the decision to move to federalism is often related to violence and associated with a combination of international intervention and tense internal conflict. In the most violent areas, such as Cyprus and Sudan, the UN recommends federalism as a solution. In the international politics of national identity conflicts, there seems to be a hidden practice of rewarding insurgents. If one follows democratic and peaceful procedures, then the UN and the international community are unlikely to see a federal solution as the first option; and if one takes up arms, the international community is likely to favour the federal option and even the option of partition. In Burma, the whole society has been armed. While the military government insists on brutally cracking down on any dissident or secessionist movement, minorities take up guns to protect themselves to match the military regime. In such a situation, it is necessary for the international community to intervene so as to transform a brutal order where everyone fights each other to a just order where the dominant group will accept minority rights and the federalism solution. To minimize the violence that accompanies a transition to federalism, the international community should intervene to convince the parties to accept the federal solution.

Indeed, it was international governments and nongovernmental organizations that organized peace talks for Indonesia, Sri Lanka, Burma (Myanmar) and other countries. It was the international pressure against terrorism that forced the Tamil Tigers to give up their independence claim. The United States, United Kingdom, Australia, Canada and India declared the Liberation Tigers of Tamil Eelam (LTTE) as a terrorist organization; and, in November 2001, LTTE's leader, Velupillai Prabhakaran, withdrew his movement's long-standing demand for an independent homeland in Sri Lanka (Shastri, 2002, p. 182). It was a decrease in international capital flow and tourism that led the Philippines to adopt a reconciliatory approach to the independence force in Mindanao. The war against terrorism has made security the top priority and decreased international support for independence movements. As a result, federalism as a means of maintaining national unity and satisfying the demands of minorities is increasingly appealing.

## CONCLUSION

Various models of federalism exist in Asia. India adopts a combination of territorial and multinational federalism, and Indonesia and China are developing hybrid federalism. Japan offers us another model of quasi-federal practice. No model is able to claim a superior position; no single model can be applied across Asia. The international community needs to resist any simplistic notion of federalism in Asia and remain open to alternative models. Asian countries will need to generate a dynamic blend of various elements, including traditional rule, authoritarianism, democracy, federalism and confederalism. Furthermore, different situations will require these elements in different proportions, and a mix of regional, multinational and asymmetric elements of federalism will be desirable.

While we examine federalism and its various forms as a solution to ethnic conflicts, it is necessary to open our minds to other possibilities. For example, in Burma (Myanmar) there is a possibility that the military power holders will make a deal with minority nationalities without democratization or federalization. Some solutions may be based on an historical agreement or pragmatic concession, which does not necessarily involve a federal constitution, but nonetheless puts federal structures into practice.

This chapter has examined the complex relations between democratization and federalization. Democratization helps to speed up the process of federalization, which, in turn, facilitates the development of democracy. Taking Asia as a whole, one needs to strike a complicated balance between democratization and federalization. In the case of China and Myanmar, the problem is the lack of democracy. The absence of substantive democracy inhibits the establishment of federalism. The lack of internal democratic mechanisms in the Tamil Tigers and the MNLF put a stop to peace talks and delayed the process of federalization. By contrast, too much popular or majority rule in Sri Lanka has buried golden opportunities to move towards federation through supporting a unitary policy and strengthening the uncompromising position towards the minority.

A study of the status and failure of federalism in Asia reminds us of the existence of enormous obstacles to the federal project in Asia. Caution is needed to guard against excessive optimism. Having said that, the prospect of federalism can be viewed in historical terms. South Africa, Mexico, Nigeria and a long list of other countries who were regarded as failed federal states have now achieved a certain degree of federalism. K.C. Wheare (1964) regarded India as 'quasi-federal', but India is now deemed to be the most successful federation in Asia. These historical facts raise a question of whether quasi-federal practice in Indonesia, Japan and China might also be transformed into a more substantive federalism one day. Given the continuing trend of democratization in Asia, further federalization can be expected in the Philippines and Indonesia. If China were democratized, the institutionalization of China's quasi-federal arrangement (see Chapter 10) would be on the agenda. How China will be democratized and federalized remains to be seen and the impact of China's federalization would reach far beyond China and even Asia.

Overall, regardless of its weaknesses, hybrid federalism is the model most likely to succeed in some Asian countries. If all parties in Sri Lanka learn a lesson from the past failure, Sri Lanka is likely to follow the Indonesian path in making a peace deal and establishing an asymmetric federalism, blended with some elements of territorial and multinational federalism.

A sophisticated knowledge of the complicated working process of hybrid federalism in Asia will help the international community to construct a federal order in which both the nation-states and ethnonational groups are satisfied.

Originally, federalism was not invented to deal with national identity questions or serve a multinational purpose (see Chapter 13). The challenge of constructing a federal polity in a multinational context is a difficult task for federalists. It is not clear whether federalism is capable of resolving such thorny issues as ethnic division entirely, but it can be used to reduce or contain them within a functioning political system. To deal with these challenging issues, Asian states have already innovatively grafted some elements of federalism into the existing unitary system so that they can deal with the national identity issue while avoiding wholesale federalization. They will continue to develop innovative institutions different from conventional ones, and figure out their conceptual and institutional tools creatively.

## NOTES

1. The author would like to thank Katharine Adeney for her valuable comments, Will Kymlicka for his inspiring chapter, and Eilidh John for her editorial help.
2. The contribution of British colonial policy to federalism is well discussed in Chapter 6 in this volume. William Riker (1964, p. 32), however, argues that poor understanding of federalism by the British colonial official was responsible for the initial failure of Indian, Pakistani and Nigerian federalism.
3. Also see the special issue, 'New Trends in Federalism', in *International Political Science Review*, **17**(4), Oct., 1996.
4. Spain and South Africa are classified as examples of federalism by Watts, but not as federal states according to Britannica World Data, Derbyshire's handbook, and Elazar's work. See Lane and Ersson (2005, p. 169).
5. For a discussion of the limits of the US model, see Stepan (1999, pp. 19–34).
6. Multinational federalism is not an accurate description of federalism in Canada, where both regional and multinational elements exist. In addition, the special rights and an internal boundary in Québec were the product of fighting and negotiation between the then two great powers, Great Britain and France.
7. I have discussed the role of international NGOs in settling the national identity question. See Baogang He (2004). For NGOs' advocacy for federalism in the Philippines, see Chapter 8 in this volume.
8. In fact, originally I organized a workshop on Chinese federalism in Beijing in 2004, but my co-organizer pulled out in the later stages. As an alternative, I reorganized the workshop on Asian federalism in Melbourne.
9. This applied to the Philippines too. In 1976, the Tripoli Agreement was reached between the MNLF and the Philippine delegation. Of the 21 provinces of the Southern Philippines, 13 were granted autonomy, with a legislative assembly, an executive council and Islamic law courts. Given the favourable distribution of the ethnic population (four million Muslims and six and a half million Christians in 13 provinces), President Marcos called a referendum to decide whether the inhabitants of the region could have extended powers, under MNLF rule, or autonomy under the firm control of Manila. When Marcos won the referendum, Misuari called for a last-minute boycott and the MNLF

denounced it. Subsequently, in 1986, Marcos declared martial law in an attempt to suppress the southern secessionist movement.

10.  Of course there is the literature on the undemocratic elements and practices of federalism. Felix Morley argues that, in the United States, 'in the powerful Upper House of Congress the vote of a Senator from Nevada still has exactly the same weight as the vote of a Senator from New York'. The Supreme Court is even more undemocratic than the Senate because 'nine appointed judges, intentionally safeguarded from any popular control, are vested with power to nullify legislation approved by the elected representatives of the people'. In the executive, the Presidential veto can nullify financial legislation duly approved by both Houses of Congresses, as happened under President Franklin D. Roosevelt. Moreover, 'the quasi-autocratic committee chairs in both Houses of Congress continue to be chosen by the undemocratic seniority rule' (Morley, 1981, pp. 19–21). In a similar vein, anti-federalists argued against Australian federation on the ground that 'federation threatens many visible dangers to Victorian liberty', and that 'Queensland, South Australia, Tasmania, and Western Australia comprise only a minority of the people of Australia, but they will return 24 senators out of 36, and New South Wales and Victoria will be at the mercy of those 24 senators' (Anderson, 1977, pp. 1–2). These views, however, are based on a notion of democracy which is in favour of majority rule against the political equality of the senate system.

11.  Jan-Erik Lane and Svante Ersson (Lane and Ersson, 2005) use a set of data to address the question of whether federalism matters for democratic longevity. Such a statistical approach fails to make a distinction between different types of federalism.

# REFERENCES

Adeney, K. (2007), *Federalism and Ethnic Conflict Regulation in India and Pakistan*, New York: Palgrave.

Agranoff, Robert (ed.) (1999), *Accommodating Diversity: Asymmetry in Federal States*, Baden-Baden: Nomos Verlagsgesellschaft.

Anderson, Hugh (ed.) (1977), *Radical Argument against Federation 1897–1900, Victoria*, Richmond: Drummond.

Belz, Herman (ed.) (2000), *The Webster–Hayne Debate on the Nature of the Union*, selected documents, Indianapolis: Liberty Fund.

Bogdanor, Vernon (ed.) (1987), *The Blackwell Encyclopedia of Political Institutions*, Oxford: Basic Blackwell Ltd.

Chen, Qimao (1996), 'The Taiwan Strait crisis: its crux and solutions', *Asian Survey*, **XXXVI**(11), 1055–66.

Ching, Frank (1999), 'Judgment Call', *Far Eastern Economic Review*, 18 February, 20–21.

Day Banks, A. and T. Muller (1997), *Political Handbook of the World 1997*, New York: CSA Publications.

de Silva, Mervyn (1987), 'Ethnic conflicts respect no national boundaries', *Far Eastern Economic Review*, 3–9 July, 20–22.

Dillon, Dana A. (2006), *Indonesia and Separatism: Finding a Federalist Solution*, at http://www.heritage.org/library/execmemo/em670.html.

Dreyer, June Teufel (1989), 'Unrest in Tibet', *Current History*, **88**(539), 281–4.

Dubhashi, P.R. (1991), 'Reflections on the Indian policy and some suggestions for its reconstitution', *Indian Journal of Political Science*, **52**(3), 376–84.

Editorial (2000), 'Fighting war with reason', *The Asian Wall Street Journal*, 22 August, p. 12.

Edrisinha, Rohan (2005), 'Multination federalism and minority rights in Sri Lanka', in Will Kymlicka and Baogang He (eds), *Multiculturalism in Asia*, Oxford: Oxford University Press.

Elazar, Daniel J. (1995), 'From statism to federalism: a paradigm shift', *The Journal of Federalism*, **25**(2), 5–18.

Feith, Herbert (1973), *Indonesian Politics, 1949–57: the Decline of Representative Government*, Ann Arbor, MI: University of Michigan Press, pp. 84–123.

Feith, Herbert and Lance Castles (1970), *Indonesian Political Thinking, 1945–65*, Ithaca, NY: Cornell University Press.

He, Baogang (2001), 'The national identity problem and democratization: Rustow's theory of sequence', *Government and Opposition* (London), **36**(1), 97–119.

He, Baogang (2002a), 'Democratization and the national identity question in East Asia', in Yue-man Yeung (ed.), *New Challenges for Development and Modernization: Hong Kong and the Asia-Pacific Region in the New Millennium*, Hong Kong: Chinese University of Hong Kong Press, pp. 245–73.

He, Baogang (2002b), 'Referenda as a solution to the national identity/boundary question: an empirical critique of the theoretical literature', *Alternatives: Global, Local, Political*, **27**(1), 67–97.

He, Baogang (2004), 'Transnational civil society and the national identity question in East Asia', *Global Governance: A Review of Multilateralism and International Organizations*, **10**(2), 227–46.

He, Baogang and Barry Sautman (2005–6), 'The politics of the Dalai Lama's new initiative for autonomy', *Pacific Affairs*, **78**(4), 601–29.

Hicks, Ursula K. (1978), *Federalism: Failure and Success: A Comparative Study*, London: Macmillan.

Hwang, Kwan (1994), 'Korean reunification in a comparative perspective', in Whan Kihl Young (ed.), *Korea and the World: Beyond the Cold War*, Boulder: Westview Press.

Kahin, A. (ed.) (1985), *Regional Dynamics of the Indonesian Revolution*, Hawaii: University of Hawaii Press.

King, Peter (2006), 'Autonomy, federalism or the unthinkable: Indonesian debates and Papua's Future' (http://www.econ.usyd.edu.au/govt/cipa/PKFederalism. doc).

Kymlicka, Will (2006), 'Emerging Western models of multination federalism: are they relevant to Africa?', in David Turton (ed.), *Ethnic Federalism: The Ethiopian Experience in Comparative Perspective*, Ohio: Ohio University Press, pp. 32–64.

Kymlicka, Will and Baogang, He (eds) (2005), *Multiculturalism in Asia*, Oxford: Oxford University Press.

Lane, Jan-Erik and Svante Ersson (2005), 'The riddle of federalism: does federalism impact on democracy?', *Democratization*, **12**(2), 163–82.

*Liange Zhaobao*, 29 January 2002, p. 22

Louis, V. (1979), *The Coming Decline of the Chinese Empire*, New York: Times Books, pp. 114–15.

Manor, James (1998), 'Making Indian federalism work', *Journal of Democracy*, **9**(3), 21–35.

May, R.J. (1970), 'Decision-making and stability in federal systems', *Canadian Journal of Political Sciences*, **III**(1), 73–87.

Montinola, Gabriella, Yingyi Qian and Barry R. Weingast (1996), 'Federalism, Chinese style: the political basis for economic success', *World Politics*, **48**(1), 50–81.

Morley, Felix (1981), *Freedom and Federation*, Indianapolis: Liberty Fund.

Nasution, Adnan Buyung (1992), *The Aspiration for Constitutional Government in Indonesia: A Sociological Study of the Indonesian Konstituante 1956–59*, The Hague: CIP-Geguens Koninklijke Bibliotheek.

Ostrom, Vincent (1994), *The Meaning of American Federalism: Constituting a Self-Governing Society*, San Francisco, California: ICS Press.

Ranapala, Suri (1999), 'Freedom as response to ethnic regionalism', in Ian Copland and John Rickard (eds), *Federalism: Comparative Perspectives from India and Australia*, New Delhi: Manohar Publisher, pp. 111–36.

Ravich, Samantha F. (2000), 'Eyeing Indonesia through the lens of Aceh', *The Washington Quarterly*, **23**(3), 7–20.

Riker, William H. (1964), *Federalism: Origin, Operation, Significance*, Boston: Little, Brown and Company.

Schulz, Ann (1979), *Local Politics and Nation-States*, Santa Barbara, California: Clio Books.

Seidler, Arthur A. (1955), *The Formation of Federal Indonesia*, 1945–49, The Hague: W. van Hoene.

Shastri, Amita (2002), 'Sri Lanka in 2001', *Asian Survey*, **43**(1), 177–82.

Smith, Thomas B. (1986), 'Referendum politics in Asia', *Asian Survey*, **XXVI**(7), 793–814.

Stepan, Alfred (1999), 'Federalism and democracy: beyond the US model', *Journal of Democracy*, **10**(4), 19–34.

Tarlton, Charles (1965), 'Symmetry and asymmetry as elements of federalism: a theoretical speculation', *Journal of Politics*, **27**(4), 861–74.

Tummala, Krishna K. (1996), 'The Indian Union and emergency power', *International Political Science Review*, **17**(4), 373–84.

Watts, R.L. (1966), *New Federations: Experiments in the Commonwealth*, Oxford: Clarendon Press.

Watts, R.L. (1999), *Comparing Federal Systems*, 2nd edn, Montreal and Kingston: McGill-Queen's University Press.

Weingast, B.R. (1997), 'The political commitment to markets and marketization', in D.L. Weimer (ed.), *The Political Economy of Property Rights*, Cambridge: Cambridge University Press, pp. 44–5.

Wheare, K.C. (1964), *Federal Government*, New York: Oxford University Press.

Young, George (1941), *Federalism and Freedom: or Plan the Peace to Win the War*, London: Oxford University Press.

Zhou, Yanshan (1995), 'New thinking on the "Chinese commonwealth"', *Modern China Studies*, **6**, 19–24.

# 2. Multi-nation federalism

## Will Kymlicka

Minority nationalism is a universal phenomenon. As Walker Connor notes, countries affected by it

> are to be found in Africa (for example, Ethiopia), Asia (Sri Lanka), Eastern Europe (Romania), Western Europe (France), North America (Guatemala), South America (Guyana) and Oceania (New Zealand). The list includes countries that are old (United Kingdom) as well as new (Bangladesh), large (Indonesia) as well as small (Fiji), rich (Canada) as well as poor (Pakistan), authoritarian (Sudan) as well as democratic (Belgium), Marxist–Leninist (China) as well as militantly anti-Marxist (Turkey). The list also includes countries which are Buddhist (Burma), Christian (Spain), Moslem (Iran), Hindu (India) and Judaic (Israel). (See Connor, 1999, pp. 163–4.)

In all of these countries, national minorities are battling with the state – peacefully or violently – over issues of political representation, language rights, self-government, control over resources, and internal migration.

While the challenge of minority nationalism arises in all parts of the globe, the state's response to it varies tremendously from region to region. In this chapter, I will discuss an emerging trend in the West towards a model of 'multi-nation federalism', which grants federal or quasi-federal forms of territorial autonomy to historic sub-state national groups. In many Western countries the adoption of multi-nation federalism is quite recent, and so it is too early to provide a definitive assessment of its successes and failures. But I will argue that this model is working well to manage ethnic diversity peacefully, democratically and with respect for human rights, notwithstanding some continuing areas of controversy.

Can we hope or expect that this model will be adopted in other parts of the world? At first glance, the prospects are not encouraging. Despite its apparent popularity and success in the West, the model of multination federalism remains firmly resisted in most states in Asia and Africa. In those few post-colonial countries where multination federalism has been adopted, it has often been the fragile result of civil war. What explains these differing reactions? To answer this question, we must first understand the factors that explain why multi-nation federalism has become so widespread in the West. After all, until quite recently, it was also strongly resisted in the West itself. Yet various changes, in both the international geopolitical context and in local inter-ethnic relations, have dramatically lowered the risks of adopting multi-nation federalism in the West. In many other parts of the world, by contrast, it remains a high-risk strategy, although it may be nonetheless a relevant option for accommodating sub-state national groups, and possibly the only viable option.

In the first three sections of this chapter I describe multi-nation federalism in the West, explain its emergence and evaluate its strengths and weaknesses. In the fourth section I explore some of the factors that inhibit its adoption in Asia.

## MULTI-NATION FEDERALISM IN THE WEST

Many Western democracies contain minority groups which describe themselves as 'nations', and which mobilize along nationalist lines to gain or maintain self-government. This includes both sub-state national groups – such as the Catalans and Basques (in Spain), the Flemish (in Belgium), the Scots and Welsh (in Britain), the Corsicans (in France), Puerto Ricans (in the USA) and Québécois (in Canada) – and indigenous peoples, like the Sami (in the Scandinavian countries), Inuit (in Canada and Denmark), the Maori (in New Zealand), the Aborigines (in Australia) and American Indians.

In the past, the desire of these groups for self-government was typically suppressed, often brutally, as a threat to the state. Claims to distinct nationhood by a minority group question the basis of the legitimacy of the state, by denying that its citizens form a single nation or people, asserting instead that there are at least two separate peoples in the state, each with its own claim to popular sovereignty, and hence to self-government. It also jeopardizes the state's claim to parts of the territory of the state, which are asserted instead to be the homeland of another nation. Minority nationalism, in short, is the most direct threat to the legitimating ideology of the modern nation-state, and to the state's claim to rule over all its citizens and territory.

As a result, national minorities have typically been the first target of state nation-building policies.[1] Various efforts were made to erode this sense of distinct nationhood, including restricting minority language rights, abolishing traditional forms of local or regional self-government, and encouraging members of the dominant group to settle in the minority group's traditional territory so that the minority becomes outnumbered even in its historic homeland.

There has been, however, a dramatic change in the way most Western countries deal with substate nationalisms. Today, all of the countries just mentioned accept the principle that their substate national groups will endure into the indefinite future, and that their sense of nationhood and nationalist aspirations must be accommodated in some way or other, typically through some form of territorial autonomy. In some countries, this shift to territorial autonomy has been achieved by adopting a federal system, since federalism allows the creation of regional political units, controlled by the national minority, with substantial (and constitutionally protected) powers of self-government. Countries that have adopted federalism to accommodate national minorities include Switzerland (for the French- and Italian-speaking minorities), Canada (for the Québécois), Belgium (for the Flemish) and Spain (for the Catalans, Basques and Galicians).

In other countries, or for other national groups, there may be geographic or demographic reasons why federalism in the strict sense will not work. In these cases, we see the emergence of various quasi-federal forms of territorial autonomy. For example, Britain has recently adopted a quasi-federal system of devolution to Scotland and Wales, which now have their own legislative assemblies. And while Puerto Rico is not part of the American federal system (it is not one of the 50 states), it has a special self-governing status within the United States as a 'Commonwealth'. Similarly, while Italy and Finland are not federations, they have adopted special forms of territorial autonomy for the German-speakers in South Tyrol, and for the Swedes in the Aland Islands. In all of these cases, territorial autonomy enables national minorities to establish and govern their own public institutions, often operating in their own language, including schools, universities, courts and regional parliaments.

The use of quasi-federal forms of autonomy is even clearer when we consider indigenous peoples: Indian tribes in the United States and Canada are recognized as having rights of self-government, and are acquiring (or re-acquiring) control over education, heath care, policing, child welfare, natural resources and so on. Similarly, the Scandinavian countries have created Sami Parliaments; the Inuit of Greenland have Home Rule; and the Maori in New Zealand have increased autonomy.

In all of these countries, the goal of eliminating minority national identities has been abandoned, and it is now accepted that these groups will continue to see themselves as separate and self-governing nations within the larger state into the indefinite future. As a result, an increasing number of Western democracies that contain national minorities accept that they are 'multi-nation' states, rather than 'nation-states'. They accept that they contain two or more nations within their borders, and recognize that each constituent nation has a valid claim to the language rights and self-government powers necessary to maintain itself as a distinct society and culture.

Following Philip Resnick (Resnick, 1994), I will call these 'multi-nation federations'. They are not all federations in the technical sense, but they all embody a model of the state in which national minorities are federated to the state through some form of territorial autonomy, and in which internal boundaries have been drawn, and powers distributed, in such a way as to ensure that each national group is able to maintain itself as a distinct and self-governing society and culture. It is important to distinguish these 'multi-nation' federations from other federal systems where internal sub-units are not designed to enable minority self-government, such as the continental United States, Germany, Australia and Brazil. In these countries, none of the subunits was designed to enable an ethnonational group to exercise self-government over its traditional territory.[2]

Unlike many forms of multiculturalism which are often disparaged as tokenist or folkloric, multi-nation federalism involves a serious redistribution of political power and economic resources. The precise range of rights and powers accorded national minorities varies from country to country, but, at least in the case of the larger national minorities, they typically include the following three elements: (a) territorial autonomy, (b) the minority's language is accorded the status of an official language in that territory, either as a co-equal official language with the majority language or indeed as the primary or sole official language; and (c) the self-governing region exercises control over a broad range of public institutions, reflected most obviously in control over education all the way from primary to post-secondary education, including universities in their own language.

These three features are found wherever there are large national minorities in the West, like the Québécois, Puerto Ricans, Catalans and Walloons, all of whom have populations of over 2.5 million. But it is equally true of smaller national minorities, like Swedes in Finland (285 000), German-speakers in South Tyrol (303 000) or Italian-speakers in Switzerland (500 000). All of these groups have territorial autonomy, official language status at the regional level and schools (including universities) in their own language. Indeed, this three-fold package has now been adopted or offered for virtually every territorially concentrated national minority that is over 250 000 strong in the West.[3] Under these conditions, it is not an exaggeration to view the state as a union of two or more equal partners. Where national minorities are much smaller, as is typically the case with indigenous peoples, there may not be the critical mass needed to sustain official language status or a full set of public institutions. Yet, even here, we typically see at least some commitment to principles of territorial autonomy and cultural recognition. Indeed, all Western democracies containing indigenous peoples have accepted, at least in principle, some idea of indigenous self-government.

In short, we see a virtually universal trend towards multi-nation federalism in the West. Needless to say, the category of 'multination federalism' encompasses a broad range of institutional arrangements, and the details vary enormously in these different countries, most obviously in terms of the status of the ethnonational group at the central level. Is its language, for example, recognized as official at the central as well as the regional level? How is it represented in the central legislature (does it have veto rights, for example?) or central constitutional court? Does it have guarantees concerning representation in the central bureaucracy? It is on issues such as these that 'federal' and 'quasi-federal' regimes typically differ. In truly federal states, the substate units controlled by national minorities typically have strong guarantees of representation at the central level, including even veto rights on some issues. In quasi-federal systems, by contrast, such as Puerto Rico, the autonomous territory may have little representation at the central level.

How substate national groups are represented at the central level can be of pivotal importance. Having adequate representation at the centre can help offset the centrifugal tendencies of territorial autonomy. If power is shared, not only on a territorial basis, but also within the central government itself, this can strengthen the attachment of minorities to the larger state. As noted earlier, however, the details of the relationship between sub-units and the central state vary considerably across these Western countries. What is common to all forms of multi-nation federalism is the idea of territorial autonomy and, at least in the case of sizeable national minorities, official language status and a high degree of institutional completeness.

## EXPLAINING THE TREND

What explains this Western trend towards various forms of multi-nation federalism? It is important to note that this trend is just one example of a much broader trend in the West towards the greater accommodation of ethnocultural diversity. The last 30 years have also witnessed an equally striking shift in the treatment of immigrant groups. Older policies designed to exclude or assimilate immigrants have been replaced, in most countries of immigration, with new policies of immigrant 'multiculturalism'.[4] Why, then, has the West become more tolerant of ethnic diversity in general?

Any trend of this magnitude has multiple sources, and it would be impossible to discuss all of them here. But we can divide our question into two parts. First, why have ethnic groups become more assertive of their rights claims? And second, why have states and dominant groups become more willing to accept these minority claims?

In answering the first question, a key factor, I believe, is the human rights revolution, and the resulting development of a 'rights consciousness'. Since 1948, we have an international order that is premised on the idea of the inherent equality of human beings, both as individuals and as peoples. The international order has decisively repudiated older ideas of a racial or ethnic hierarchy, according to which some peoples were superior to others, and thereby had the right to rule over them. It is important to remember how radical these ideas of human equality are. Assumptions about a hierarchy of peoples were widely accepted throughout the West until the Second World War, when Hitler's fanatical and murderous policies discredited them. Indeed, the whole system of European colonialism was premised on the assumption of a hierarchy of peoples, and was the explicit basis of both domestic policies and international law throughout the nineteenth century and the first half of the twentieth. Today, however, we live in a world where the idea of human equality is unquestioned, at least officially. What matters here is not the change in international law per se, which has had little impact on most people's lives. The real change has been in people's consciousness. Members of historically subordinated groups in the West today demand equality, and demand it as a *right*. They believe they are entitled to equality, and entitled to it *now*, not in some indefinite or millenarian future.

This sort of rights-consciousness has become such a pervasive feature of modernity that we have trouble imagining that it did not always exist. But if we examine the historical records, we find that minorities in the past typically justified their claims, not by appeal to human rights or equality, but by appealing to the generosity of rulers in according 'privileges', often in return for past loyalty and services. Today, by contrast, groups have a powerful sense of entitlement to equality as a basic human right, not as a favour or charity, and are angrily impatient with what they perceive as lingering manifestations of older hierarchies.

Of course, there is no consensus on what 'equality' means (and, conversely, no agreement on what sorts of actions or practices are evidence of 'hierarchy'). People who agree on the general principle of the equality of peoples may disagree about whether or when this requires federalism, official bilingualism or consociational power sharing. But there can be no doubt that Western democracies historically privileged a particular national group over other groups who were subject to assimilation or exclusion. This historic hierarchy was reflected in a wide range of policies and institutions, from the schools and state symbols to policies regarding language, immigration, media, citizenship, the division of powers and electoral systems. So long as minority leaders can identify (or conjure up) manifestations of these historic hierarchies, they will be able to draw upon the powerful rights consciousness of their members.

A second key factor is democracy. At the simplest level, the consolidation of democracy limits the ability of élites to crush ethnic minority political movements. In many countries around the world, élites ban political movements of minority groups, or pay thugs or paramilitaries to beat up or kill minority leaders, or bribe police and judges to lock them up. The fear of this sort of repression often keeps minority groups from voicing even the most moderate claims. Keeping quiet is the safest option for minorities in many countries. In consolidated democracies, however, where democracy is the only game in town, there is no option but to allow minority groups to mobilize politically and advance their claims in public. As a result, members of minority groups are increasingly unafraid to speak out. They may not win the political debate, but they are not afraid of being killed, jailed or fired for trying. It is this loss of fear, combined with rights consciousness, which explains the remarkably vocal nature of ethnic politics in modern Western democracies.

Moreover, democracy involves the availability of multiple access points to decision making. If a group is blocked at one level by an unsympathetic government, they can pursue their claims at another level. Even if an unsympathetic right-wing political party were to win power at the central level, and attempted to cut back the rights of minorities, these groups could shift their focus to the regional level, or to the municipal level. And even if all of these levels are blocked, they could pursue their claims through the courts, or even through international pressure. This is what democracy is about: multiple and shifting points of access to power.

Where these two conditions are in place (increasing rights consciousness and multiple points of access for safe political mobilization) it is likely, perhaps even inevitable, that minorities will be more assertive in their claims. But why have dominant groups and the state accepted these minority claims? After all, minorities remain (numerical) minorities. They lack the numbers or coercive power to impose their will on majorities. In the end, the trend towards multi-nation federalism could not have occurred if it did not have the support of at least a sizeable proportion of the dominant group. In the past, dominant élites have been unwilling to support these claims, and indeed were willing to use considerable coercion to stifle them. What has changed?

There are two key factors here. First, states will not voluntarily accord greater powers or resources to groups that are perceived as disloyal, and therefore a threat to the security of the state. In particular, states will not voluntarily accommodate groups that are seen as likely to collaborate with foreign enemies. In the past, this has sometimes been an issue in the West. For example, before the Second World War, Italy feared that the German-speaking minority in South Tyrol was more loyal to Austria or Germany than to Italy, and would therefore support any attempt by Germany or Austria to invade and annex South Tyrol. Similar fears were expressed about the German minority in Belgium or Denmark. These countries worried that Germany might invade in the name of 'liberating' their co-ethnic Germans, and that the German minority would collaborate with such an invasion. Today, however, this is essentially a non-issue throughout the Western world, at least with respect to national minorities.[5] It is difficult to think of a single Western case where a state fears that a national minority would collaborate with a neighbouring enemy and potential aggressor.[6] Part of the reason for this is that Western states do not have neighbouring enemies who might invade them. NATO has been spectacularly successful in removing the possibility of one Western country invading its neighbours. As a result, the question of whether minorities would be loyal in the event of aggression by a neighbouring state has been removed from the table.

Of course, Western states do have more long-distance potential enemies, such as Soviet Communism in the past, Islamic fundamentalism today, and perhaps China in some future scenario. But, in relation to these long-distance threats, there is no question that national minorities in the West are 'on the same side' as the state. For example, if Scotland gains increased powers, or even independence, no one in the rest of Britain worries that Scotland will start collaborating with Al Qaeda or China to overthrow the British state. Scottish nationalists may want to secede from Britain, but an independent Scotland would be an ally of Britain, not an enemy, and would cooperate with Britain in NATO and other Western defence and security arrangements. So too with relations between Quebec and Canada, or Puerto Rico and the United States, or Catalonia and Spain. In the event of some future 'clash of civilizations' between the West and Islam, or between the West and China, there is no doubt about whose side these national minorities will be on. In all of these cases, national minorities are assumed to be allies, not enemies, and accommodating them poses no risk to the basic geopolitical security of the state.

This may seem obvious, but it is important to remember that, in most parts of the world, minority groups are often seen as a 'fifth column', likely to be working for a neighbouring enemy. This is particularly a concern where the minority is related to a neighbouring state by ethnicity or re-ligion, or where a minority is found on both sides of an international boundary, so that the neighbouring state claims the right to intervene to protect 'its' minority. Under these conditions, we are likely to witness what political scientists call the 'securitization' of ethnic relations.[7] Relations between states and minorities are seen, not as a matter of normal democratic politics to be negotiated and debated, but as a matter of state security, in which the state has to limit the normal democratic process in order to protect itself. Under conditions of securitization, minority political parties may be banned, minority leaders may be subject to secret police surveillance, and free debate on certain issues, such as autonomy or secession, may be illegal. Even if minority demands can be voiced, the larger society and the state will flatly reject them. After all, how can groups that are disloyal have any legitimate claims against the state? The securitization of ethnic relations erodes both the democratic space to voice minority demands, and the likelihood that those demands will be accepted. In the West, however, minority nationalist political mobilization has been almost entirely 'desecuritized'. Minority nationalist politics is just that – normal, day-to-day politics. Relations between the state and national minorities have been taken out of the 'security' box, and put in the 'democratic politics' box.[8]

A second factor that explains the willingness of states to accept minority claims is the existence of a deep consensus across ethnonational lines on basic values of liberal democracy and human rights. As a result, it is taken for granted that any powers of self-government granted to national minorities will be exercised in accordance with shared standards of democracy and human rights. Everyone accepts that these substate autonomies will operate within the constraints of liberal–democratic constitutionalism, which firmly upholds individual rights. In virtually every case of multi-nation federalism in the West, substate governments are subject to the same constitutional constraints as the central government, and so have no legal capacity to restrict individual freedoms in the name of maintaining cultural authenticity, religious orthodoxy or racial purity.[9] In fact, these basic liberal freedoms and human rights are typically protected at multiple levels: regionally, nationally and internationally.

It is not only legally impossible for national minorities to establish illiberal regimes, but they have no wish to do so. On the contrary, all of the evidence suggests that members of national minorities are at least as strongly committed to liberal–democratic values as members of dominant groups, if not more so. Indeed, substate autonomies often adopt more progressive policies than those adopted at the central level. Policies on gender equality or gay rights, for example, are more progressive in Scotland than in the rest of Britain, more progressive in Quebec than in other parts of Canada and more progressive in Catalonia than in other parts of Spain. Moreover, support for cosmopolitan values is also typically higher in these substate regions than in other parts of the country, including support for foreign aid, or for strengthening the role of the European Court of Human Rights, or other international human rights instruments.[10]

This removes one of the central fears that dominant groups have about multination federalism. In many parts of the world, there is a widespread fear that, once national minorities acquire self-governing power, they will use it to persecute, dispossess, expel or kill anyone who does not belong to the minority group. In the West, however, this is a non-issue. There is no fear that self-governing minorities will use their powers to establish islands of tyranny or theocracy. More specifically, there is no fear that members of the dominant group who happen to live on the territory of the self-governing minority will be subject to persecution or expulsion. The human rights of English residents of Scotland are firmly protected, not only by Scottish con-stitutional law, but also by European law, and this would be true even if Scotland seceded from Britain. The human rights of English–Canadian residents of Quebec, or of Castillian residents of Catalonia, are fully pro-tected, no matter what political status Quebec or Catalonia ends up having.

Where there is a strong consensus across ethnic lines on liberal–democratic values, people feel confident that, however claims to self-government are settled, their own basic civil and political rights will be respected. No matter how the claims of ethnonational and indigenous groups are resolved – no matter what language rights, self-government rights, land rights or multiculturalism policies are adopted – people can rest assured that they will not be stripped of their citizenship, or subject to ethnic cleansing, or jailed without a fair trial, or denied their rights to free speech, association and worship. Put simply, the consensus on liberal–democratic values ensures that debates over accommodating diver-sity are not a matter of life and death. As a result, dominant groups will not fight to the death to resist minority claims. This is the other side of the human rights revolution mentioned earlier. On the one hand, the global diffusion of a human rights consciousness has inspired non-dominant groups to resist inherited ethnic and racial hierarchies; on the other hand, it has also given confidence to dominant groups that the resulting minority rights will operate within a framework that firmly protects the basic indi-vidual rights and security of all citizens.

I believe that these two factors, the desecuritization of state–minority relations, and the cross-ethnic consensus on liberal–democratic values – have dramatically changed the views of states and dominant groups about multination federalism in the West. Where there is no fear that minorities will collaborate with external enemies, and no fear that they will violate human rights or create illiberal regimes, the two most pressing objections to multi-nation federalism have been removed.

This does not mean that members of dominant groups in the West have become enthusiastic supporters of multi-nation federalism. As I discuss below, there remain important concerns about this model. It is now accepted, however, that demands for multi-nation federalism can no longer be dismissed as evidence of disloyalty, or as a threat to democracy. Multi-nation federalism is accepted as a legitimate topic for political debate, and a legitimate goal of minority political mobilization. And where minorities can present compelling arguments that adopting multi-nation federalism would in fact remedy historic injustices and reduce inherited hierarchies, and where minority nationalist parties receive a clear and consistent democratic mandate for their claims, it becomes difficult for dominant groups to avoid entering into negotiations. Faced with strong and determined minority nationalist mobilization, states are confronted with a choice of either entering into democratic negotiation with minorities or engaging in the undemocratic suppression of them. When fears about external security and/or internal tyranny can be invoked, the choice of suppression may seem reasonable, and indeed prudent. But when those fears are no longer credible, it is difficult to justify the choice of suppression over democratic negotiation. The result is a slow but steady trend towards the (grudging) acceptance of multi-nation federalism across the West.

## EVALUATING THE TREND

How should we evaluate this trend towards multiculturalism and minority rights in the West? Are multi-nation federations in the West working well? Should we view these models as a 'success' or a 'best practice', to be celebrated, and perhaps even to be encouraged in other regions, such as Asia? In some cases, it is simply too early to tell. The federalization of Spain and Belgium, for example, is comparatively recent, and devolution in the United Kingdom is only a few years old.

If we look across the broad range of cases, however, I think we can make some judgments about their strengths and weaknesses. Multi-nation federalism in the West has clearly been 'successful' along some dimensions and, equally clearly, a 'failure' along others. I would argue that it has been successful along at least the following five dimensions.

1. *Peace and individual security*: the multi-nation federations referred to above are managing to deal with their competing national identities and nationalist projects with an almost complete absence of violence or terrorism by either the state or the minority.[11]
2. *Democracy*: ethnic politics is now a matter of 'ballots not bullets', operating under normal democratic procedures, with no threat of military coups or authoritarian regimes which take power in the name of national security.

3. *Individual rights*: these reforms have been achieved within the framework of liberal constitutions, with firm respect for individual civil and
   political rights.
4. *Economic prosperity*: the move to multi-nation federalism has also been
   achieved without jeopardizing the economic well-being of citizens –
   indeed, the countries that have adopted multi-nation federalism are
   amongst the wealthiest in the world.
5. *Inter-group equality*: multi-nation federalism has promoted equality
   between majority and minority groups. By equality here I mean non-
   domination, such that one group is not systematically vulnerable to the
   domination of another group. Multi-nation federalism has helped
   create greater economic equality between majority and minority;
   greater equality of political influence, so that minorities are not continually outvoted on all issues; and greater equality in the social and
   cultural fields, as reflected for example in reduced levels of prejudice
   and discrimination between groups.

On all these criteria, multi-nation federalism in the West must surely be
judged a success. These multi-nation federations have not only managed the
conflicts arising from their competing national identities in a peaceful and
democratic way, but they have also secured a high degree of economic prosperity and individual freedom for their citizens. This is truly remarkable
when one considers the immense power of nationalism in the past hundred
years. Nationalism has torn apart colonial empires and Communist dictatorships, and redefined boundaries all over the world, yet democratic
multi-nation federations have succeeded in taming the force of nationalism.
Democratic federalism has domesticated and pacified nationalism, while
respecting individual rights and freedoms. It is difficult to imagine any
other political system that could make the same claim.

There are at least two important respects, however, in which multi-nation
federations have not lived up to expectations. First, the lived experience
of inter-group relations is rarely a model of constructive intercultural
exchange. Multination federalism emerges in response to the assertion of
substate national identities, but it also tends to reinforce and institutionalize those identities, and to reinforce the sense of boundaries (geographical
and cultural) between groups. Over time, this can tend to reduce, rather than
enhance, intercultural contact. At best, most citizens in the dominant group
are ignorant of, and indifferent to, the internal life of minority groups, and
vice versa. At worst, the relations between different groups are tinged with
feelings of resentment and annoyance. Despite the significant reforms of
state institutions in the direction of multi-nation federalism, substate
national groups still typically feel that the older ideology of the homogenous

nation-state has not been fully renounced, and that members of the dominant group have not fully accepted the principle of a multi-nation state
(or have not fully accepted all of its implications). By contrast, members of
the dominant group typically feel that members of the minority group are
ungrateful for the changes that have been made, unreasonable in their expectations and impossible to satisfy. As a result, inter-group relations are often
highly politicized, as members of both sides are (over)-sensitive to perceived
slights and misunderstandings. As a result, many people avoid inter-group
contact, or at least do not go out of their way to increase their contact with
members of the other group. When contact does take place, it tends to
reduce quickly to rather crude forms of bargaining and negotiation, rather
than any deeper level of cultural sharing or common deliberation.

The result is sometimes described as the phenomenon of 'parallel societies'. Consider, for example, the Flemish in Belgium or Québécois in
Canada. Multi-nation federalism has enabled these national groups to live
more completely within their own institutions, operating in their own language. In the past, these groups often faced extensive economic, political
and social pressure to participate in institutions run in the dominant language. For example, the courts, universities and legislatures were conducted
in the dominant language. Yet today, as a result of multi-nation federalism,
these groups have been able to build up an extensive array of public institutions in their own language, so that they can gain access to the full range
of educational, economic, legal and political opportunities without having
to participate in institutions that are primarily run by members of the dominant group. In effect, these sorts of multi-nation federations allow groups
to create 'parallel societies', coexisting alongside the dominant society,
without requiring much interaction between them.

In short, increased fairness at the level of state institutions has not been
matched by improvements at the level of the lived experience of inter-group
relations. The state has become more just, inclusive and accommodating,
but inter-group relations remain primarily relations of indifference and
sometimes resentment. This is the first failing of multi-nation federalism in
the West.

Second, and more importantly, multi-nation federations have not
removed secession from the political agenda. On the contrary, secessionist
ideas and secessionist mobilization are part of everyday life in many
Western multi-nation federations. Secessionist parties compete for political
office, and citizens may even be given the choice of voting for secession in
a referendum (as has happened in Puerto Rico and Quebec). To date, no
such referendum on secession has succeeded in the West, and no democratic multi-nation federation has fallen apart. This fact alone suggests that
the adoption of federalism has reduced the actual likelihood of secession,

since it is almost certain that one or more of these countries would have broken up long ago without federalism. Had Canada, Belgium and Spain not been able to federalize, they might not exist as countries today.

But even if federalism reduces the likelihood of secession, it does not remove secession from the political agenda. Secessionists are on TV, in newspapers, and compete freely for elected office. And secessionist political parties often get substantial support in elections: 40 per cent in Quebec; 30 per cent in Scotland; 15 per cent in Flanders, the Basque country or Catalonia; and 5 per cent in Puerto Rico. This means that secessionists are present in parliament and on government commissions, and they use these platforms to articulate their views. So, while multi-nation federalism may have reduced the actual likelihood of secession, it has not removed it from everyday political life, or taken it off the political agenda. It has not 'solved the problem of secession'.

Under these circumstances, it is potentially misleading to describe multi-nation federalism as a success, let alone as something to celebrate. Celebration is hardly the spirit with which most Western citizens view the institutions of multi-nation federalism. And yet, beneath the reservations and ambivalence, there is also the sense that this is the best, and perhaps the only, way for liberal democracies to deal with substate nationalisms. After all, what matters most to citizens is the security of their individual rights and liberties, economic prosperity and democratic freedom, and multi-nation federalism has proved itself capable of securing these basic goods. However much people are disappointed with the strained quality of inter-group relations, and however much they regret (and resent) the persistence of secessionist mobilization, they know that these problems are firmly contained within the bounds of liberal–democratic norms. Inter-group relations may be matters of indifference or resentment, but there is no danger of communal riots or ethnic cleansing. Secessionist politics may be present, but there is no danger of civil war, revolution or of a *coup d'état*.

Accommodating minority nationalism through multi-national federalism, therefore, poses no threat to people's basic rights and interests. By contrast, any attempt to suppress minority nationalism would require restricting liberal–democratic rights, and might even drive minority nationalists away from peaceful mobilization into violent conflict. It is sometimes said that multi-nation federalism reflects a 'communitarian' approach to the state, with which 'liberals' are uncomfortable. My view is the opposite. Multi-nation federalism scores very well on liberal criteria of individual rights and democratic freedoms, but involves abandoning the communitarian dream that the modern state can embody a unitary political community united by bonds of communal friendship. Multi-nation federalism accepts that multi-nation states will always be divided societies, but insists that this division can be managed in accordance with liberal–democratic norms.

Perhaps the best evidence for this overall acceptance of the legitimacy of multi-nation federalism is the fact that no country in the West has attempted to revoke its federalizing reforms. While several Western states that were once unitary and monolingual have shifted towards territorial autonomy and official language status for their national minorities, no Western state has moved in the opposite direction. And indeed there is no major political party in any of these countries that is attempting to reverse these reforms. While their initial adoption was controversial, and their continuing operation remains a source of dispute, these reforms have quickly become an accepted and taken-for-granted part of the political life of these countries. Indeed, there has even been debate within the Council of Europe about enshrining a norm of territorial autonomy for national minorities as one of the 'European standards' of minority rights that all European countries should respect.[12]

Multi-nation federalism in the West, then, has four distinctive features. First, it arose in response to a particular sort of problem, namely the problem of competing nationalisms within a single state. Second, it attempts to manage this problem through a threefold package of reforms, involving territorial autonomy for national minorities, official language status for the minority's language, at least on a regional level, and a high degree of institutional completeness. Third, the adoption of this model was made possible by several important changes in the local and geopolitical context in the West, particularly the desecuritization of ethnic relations and the emergence of a cross-ethnic consensus on liberal–democratic values And fourth, these facilitating conditions have helped to ensure that multi-nation federalism has been successful, not in the sense of removing conflict or creating harmony, but in the sense of ensuring that conflicts between national groups are contained within the bounds of peaceful, democratic politics.

## RELEVANCE FOR ASIA

With this background, we can now turn to Asia. Would multi-nation federalism be an appropriate model for those national minorities demanding greater autonomy in Asia, such as the Karens and Shans in Burma, the Baluchis in Afghanistan and Pakistan, the Tibetans and Uighurs in China, the Sikhs and Kashmiris in India, the Acehnese (and East Timorese, until recently) in Indonesia, the Bougainvilleans in Papua New Guinea, the Moros in the Philippines and the Tamils in Sri Lanka?

There are strong parallels between these minority nationalisms and those in Western democracies, such as the Québécois, Flemish, Scottish or Catalans. In both contexts, these groups are seeking some form of regional autonomy; in both contexts, this mobilization was often triggered, or intensified, in response to the threat posed by majority nation building (for example, imposing the Sinhalese language on Tamils in Sri Lanka and eliminating political autonomy in Tibet); in both contexts, this has generated demands for the adoption of federalism as a mechanism for accommodating minority nationalisms and, in both contexts, there is the threat of secession if this desire for autonomy is not met.

In the Western experience, federal or quasi-federal forms of territorial autonomy are increasingly seen as the only or best solution to these conflicts. Yet territorial autonomy is strongly resisted virtually everywhere outside the West, whether in Eastern Europe, the Middle East, Africa or Asia. As Nandy puts it, 'Any proposal to decentralize or to reconceptualize the state as a truly federal polity goes against the grain of most postcolonial states in the third world' (Nandy, 1992, p. 39). Most post-colonial states object to the very idea of empowering national minorities, and would rather suppress than accommodate minority nationalisms.

We can see this dynamic in many parts of Asia. Most Asian states have responded to minority nationalisms with suppression. Indeed, they have often used the same tools to suppress minority nationalism that Western countries historically adopted. These include settlement policies designed to swamp national minorities in their historic homeland with settlers from the dominant group (for example, government policies to promote ethnic Bengali settlement in the Chittagong Hill Tracts of Bangladesh; ethnic Javanese settlement of East Timor or the Aceh area of Indonesia; Christian settlement of the Moro areas of the Philippines; ethnic Han settlement of Tibet and Eastern Mongolia in China or Viet settlement of the Champa and Montagnard areas of Vietnam). Minorities have also been stripped of their traditional self-government, through either the centralization of power or the redrawing of boundaries. As in the West, this disempowering of minorities has often occurred even where promises had been made to respect the autonomy of minorities, as in Baluchistan in Pakistan, Arakan and Kachinland in Burma/Myanmar, the South Moluccas in Indonesia, East Turkestan in China, or Bougainville in Papua New Guinea. We also find cases of oppressive language policies, such as the attempt to impose the majority Sinhalese language on the Tamils in Sri Lanka, the Persian language on the Arabistans in Iran, the Dzongkha language on the Nepalese in Bhutan, the Burmese language on the Mons in Burma, or the Urdu language on the Sindhi in Pakistan.

India stands out as an interesting exception to this trend. It is one of the few countries outside the West to have voluntarily federalized to accommodate minority nationalist claims for autonomy. Moreover, I would argue that this experiment has been a success. Earlier fears that the linguistic reorganization of the states in India would lead to the breakdown of the country have not materialized, and most commentators now argue that is has on the contrary helped to reduce violence and increase stability. Indeed, some commentators describe it as a 'remarkable success' (Schwartzberg, 1985, p. 177; Lijphart, 1996, p. 263).

One might think that the success of the Indian model would have inspired other countries in Asia to adopt federal or quasi-federal forms of territorial autonomy in response to the aspirations of national minorities, and indeed one can find many academic commentators who argue that federal or quasi-federal forms of territorial autonomy are the only viable solution for other states in the region facing the challenge of minority nationalisms, including Afghanistan (Their, 1999); Burma (Smith, 2005); China (Yan, 1996; Davis, 1999); Sri Lanka (Edrisinha, 2005); Pakistan (Ahmed, 1997) and Indonesia (Anderson, 2004), to name a few. Moreover, a recent attempt to draft the principles for a regional charter of minority rights in South Asia endorsed 'devolution of power, autonomy and federalism' as one of their fundamental principles (ICES, 2003).

Yet India (along with the Federated States of Micronesia) remains the exception in the region. In most countries, the idea of federal autonomy for national minorities remains a taboo. Many countries have engaged in civil war rather than concede this sort of autonomy, and have only been prepared to contemplate multi-nation federalism when a military solution has become too costly or protracted.[13]

What explains this striking opposition to a model that has worked well in the West, and in India? There is a range of possible explanations. One focuses on differences in *values*. Some commentators, like Baogang He, argue that Western liberal models of multination federalism are at odds with the more 'communitarian' Confucian heritage of East Asia, which stresses ideas of harmony and fusion (He, 1998, 2004, 2005). Such contrasts between a 'liberal West' and a 'communitarian East' are intensely controversial since they tend to exaggerate both the extent of agreement within each region and the extent of disagreement across regions.

But even if such contrasts can be sustained as broad generalizations, it is unclear how they explain the issue at hand: namely, differing attitudes towards multi-nation federalism. It is not clear why Western liberals would be inherently inclined to support multi-nation federalism, while Asian communitarians would be opposed. One might make the opposite prediction.

Historically, most liberals in the West have endorsed the idea of equal and undifferentiated citizenship within a unitary nation-state, and have viewed ideas of multi-nation federalism as a regressive compromise with pre-modern ethnic allegiances. Conversely, one might expect that communitarians in Asia would be sympathetic to ideas of multi-nation federalism, since they provide shelter for already existing communities built around a sense of common history, language and culture. Why would communitarians want to give a centralized state, often itself the product of artificial colonial boundaries, the power to suppress these actually existing communities in the name of some new political identity built around the post-colonial state?[14]

The link between philosophical values like 'liberalism' or 'communitarianism' and support for political institutions like 'multi-nation federalism' is not direct or straightforward. It is mediated by many intervening assumptions and expectations. And it is differences in these intervening assumptions, I believe, not differences in foundational values, which explain differing attitudes towards multi-nation federalism in the West and Asia.

Consider the changing attitude amongst Western liberals towards multi-nation federalism. Why have many liberals in the West gone from being liberal nation-statists to liberal multi-nation-federalists? The answer, in part at least, lies in the trend, discussed earlier, towards a consensus on liberal–democratic norms across ethnonational lines. It is increasingly clear that accommodating minority nationalism can occur within the framework of liberal constitutionalism, including the firm protection of individual civil and political rights. In such a context, multi-nation federalism involves a redistribution of powers, but does not affect the extent to which those powers are exercised within a liberal–democratic constitutional framework.

In other regions of the world, by contrast, many liberals worry that substate autonomies will become petty tyrannies that flout the rule of law, deny human rights and oppress internal minorities. There are indeed reports of such problems in the new regional governments of Indonesia (Bell, 2001) and in the ethnolinguistic states of India (Weiner, 1998). As a result, many liberals in Asia believe that substate autonomies for national minorities should be delayed until firmer protections of individual rights and the rule of law are in place. In other words, whether liberals are attracted to multi-nation federalism depends in large part on empirical assumptions about the likely enforcement of individual rights.

Differing empirical assumptions are similarly crucial in determining the attitude of communitarians towards multi-nation federalism. In both the West and the East, communitarians have historically hoped that the political community could indeed be a unified 'community', untroubled by divisions along ethnic and linguistic lines. In the West, however, this dream has slowly been recognized as unrealistic in countries with strong minority nationalist movements. Attempts to preserve the ideology of 'one language, one nation, one state' through the assimilation or exclusion of national minorities have proved futile. National minorities are too numerous, and too politically conscious of their rights, to simply disappear.

In Asia, by contrast, many communitarians still cling to the hope that minority nationalism will fade away. They believe that substate nationalism is really a transient by-product of some other problem that will disappear over time through the processes of modernization or democratic transition. Some people assume that minority nationalism will fade as the economy improves, or as democracy is consolidated, or as communications and media become globalized. In this view, if Asian states have the strength to hold out against minority demagogues and ethnic entrepreneurs, the problem will gradually solve itself. This, of course, is precisely the expectation that Westerners have gradually relinquished, since minority nationalisms have in fact strengthened rather than weakened as Western states have become more democratic, prosperous and globalized.

The expectation that minority nationalism will fade helps to explain, not only the resistance to adopting the 'Indian model' of multi-nation federalism, but also the popularity of the 'Singapore model' of unitary nation building. For example, some of the commentators who oppose adopting federalism in Sri Lanka have suggested that Sri Lanka could instead follow Singapore's model. But, insofar as one thinks of the Singapore model as a success (and it has been a success in terms of peace and prosperity), this success is predicated on the fact that all of the three major groups are predominantly formed through immigration to Singapore. None of the groups claims Singapore to be its historic homeland, and none claims historic rights of self-government over it. In short, the typical problem of minority nationalism simply does not arise. Tamils in Singapore do not make the same kinds of claims as Tamils in Jaffna or Tamil Nadu. So too with the Malays and Chinese: they were all primarily brought to Singapore by the former imperial powers.

Put another way, it would be inaccurate to say that Singapore has found an alternative way of dealing successfully with the problem of a national minority that has mobilized along nationalist lines to defend its homeland against encroachment by a larger state into which it was involuntarily incorporated. Singapore never faced that particular problem. As a result, to suppose that Singapore provides other countries with a model for dealing with minority nationalism is, in effect, to suppose that the distinctive demands associated with minority nationalism will disappear. To hope that Tamils in the Jaffna peninsula of Sri Lanka would accept the same status as Tamils in Singapore is to suppose that the former would abandon all of the political aspirations and nationalist identities that have been built up around the ideas and myths of a historic Tamil homeland and of a historic Tamil kingdom. It is to suppose that Tamils in Sri Lanka would give up the ideas that have inspired their political mobilization for over 50 years. This is the sort of hope that has long been given up by most people in the West in relation to their minority nationalist groups.

In comparing East and West, then, we see a curious set of contrasts. In Asia, many intellectuals and politicians are deeply pessimistic about the prospect that substate national groups can exercise territorial autonomy in accordance with liberal–democratic norms, yet they are surprisingly optimistic about the possibility that substate nationalism will simply disappear. The former explains why liberals oppose multi-nation federalism, and the latter explains why communitarians still dream of creating unified political communities. In the West, by contrast, public opinion is optimistic about the capacity of substate national groups to govern within liberal–democratic constraints, but pessimistic about the likelihood that substate nationalism will disappear as a result of processes of modernization, democratization, development or globalization. I believe it is these differing forms of optimism and pessimism, rather than differences in values per se, which account for some of the differences between the West and East.

There are, however, other factors at work as well. One crucial factor concerns issues of security. As noted earlier, states will not accord greater powers or resources to groups that are perceived as disloyal, and therefore a threat to the security of the state. In particular, states will not accommodate groups that are seen as likely to collaborate with foreign enemies. Under these conditions, the 'securitization' of ethnic relations erodes both the democratic space to voice minority demands, and the likelihood that those demands will be accepted.[15]

As noted earlier, this dynamic no longer applies to national minorities in the West, thanks mainly to the protective regional security umbrella created by NATO. In large parts of Asia, however, state–minority relations remain highly 'securitized'. In several cases, security fears arise from the belief that the minority's main loyalty is to a (potentially hostile) neighbouring kin-state with whom it may collaborate: we see this in India regarding the Kashmiri minority (and the Muslim minority more generally); in Sri Lanka regarding the Tamil minority; in Afghanistan regarding the Uzbek minority; in Cambodia regarding the Vietnamese minority; in Pakistan and Bangladesh regarding the Hindu minority; in Bangladesh regarding the Biharis; in Thailand regarding the ethnic Malays; and in Vietnam regarding the Chinese minority. In several of these cases, there have even been policies to encourage or force the allegedly disloyal minority to 'return' to their 'home' country.

A related problem arises when a particular national group is found in two or more countries, divided by modern international boundaries, and who may have dreams of forming (or regaining) a common state. The classic case in the Middle East is the Kurds, divided between Iran, Iraq, Turkey and Syria, who have longed to create an independent Kurdistan. A comparable situation in Asia concerns the Baluchis, spread across Afghanistan, Iran and Pakistan, who have sometimes expressed the desire for an independent state. The Pashtuns (Pathans) who are divided by the Afghan/Pakistan border have also periodically expressed a desire to be unified in a single state.

In both of these contexts, the state fears that the minority will collaborate with its kin across the border, whether it be a neighbouring kin-state or just a neighbouring kin-group. But there are other ways in which minorities can be suspected of collaborating with hostile external powers who threaten the state. In some cases, these external powers are former imperial powers (as with the South Moluccans in Indonesia, who are seen as collaborators with the Dutch; or the Montagnards in Vietnam, who are seen as collaborators with the French and Americans). In other cases, minorities are seen as collaborating with international movements that threaten the state. In the past, this often involved the fear that minorities were part of an international Communist conspiracy set upon overthrowing capitalist countries. More recently, this has been replaced by the fear that minorities are part of an international movement of radical Islamists to overthrow secular states (as in Aceh and Mindanao). In yet other cases, the concern is that minorities are serving as agents of foreign capital, fomenting rebellion to gain preferential access to natural resources.

In all of these cases, minorities are seen (rightly or wrongly) as allies or collaborators with external powers that threaten the larger state. To an outside observer, these minority groups might appear to be weak and marginalized, with little power or resources to challenge the state, but, from the state's point of view, these minorities are the local agents for larger regional or international powers or networks that are very strong, and pose a credible threat to the state.

In short, there are at least three major obstacles to multi-nation federalism in Asia: (a) scepticism about the likelihood that substate autonomies will respect human rights and liberal–democratic values; (b) the belief that ethnic mobilization, including substate nationalism, will disappear over time as a result of modernization and development; and (c) the fear that minorities will collaborate with enemies of the state.[16] By contrast, in the West, most citizens are (a) optimistic about the liberal–democratic credentials of substate autonomies; (b) resigned to the long-term existence of ethnic politics and minority nationalist mobilization; and (c) confident that minorities will be allies, not enemies, in any larger regional or international security conflicts.

As a result, multi-nation federalism in Asia is typically resisted across the political spectrum, by liberals, communitarians and statists alike. Under these conditions, the prospects for multi-nation federalism in Asia seem limited, except as the outcome of violent struggle, or perhaps of international pressure.

## NOTES

1. This raises the question whether modern Western states are 'nation-building or nation-destroying', in Connor's famous phrase (Connor, 1972). In reality, they have been both: they have attempted to build a sense of common nationhood throughout the territory of the state by attacking any pre-existing sense of distinct nationhood held by minorities.
2. For more on the difference between multination federalism and other forms of federalism, see Kymlicka (2001, ch. 5).
3. The most obvious exception is Corsica, although France has recently passed a law granting autonomy to Corsica. Other possible exceptions include Northern Ireland, where Catholics are not territorially concentrated, and Cyprus, where a civil war broke out over the refusal by the dominant Greek community to share power with the Turkish minority. Even in these cases, however, we see movement in the direction of greater recognition of minority nationalism. Northern Ireland has recently adopted a peace agreement that explicitly accords Catholics a number of guarantees in terms of representation; and Cyprus has been debating a UN-brokered proposal to adopt a form of multination federalism, based partly on the Belgian model.
4. For a discussion of this trend, see Kymlicka (2001, ch. 8).
5. Since 9/11, there are security concerns in some Western states about their Muslim immigrants, but there is no comparable concern about their long-standing national minorities.
6. Cyprus is the closest example, where the Turkish minority is seen by the state as likely to collaborate with intervention by Turkey.
7. For the 'securitization' of ethnic relations, see Kymlicka and Opalski (2001, pp. 66–8, 366ff; Kymlicka, 2004a, Kymlicka, 2007).
8. This desecuritization even applies to the issue of secession. Even though secessionist political parties wish to break up the state, it is typically assumed that they must be treated under the same democratic rules as everyone else, with the same democratic rights to mobilize, advocate and run for office. This is true of secessionist politics throughout the West, be it in Scotland, Flanders, Quebec or Catalonia. One reason for this remarkable tolerance of secessionist mobilization is the assumption that, even if substate national groups do secede, they will become allies, not enemies.
9. A partial exception is Indian tribal governments in the US, which are exempted from some provisions of the US Bill of Rights, and this exemption has allowed some tribes to adopt policies that violate liberal norms. While many tribal governments defend this partial exemption from *domestic* constitutional norms, they typically do not object to the idea that their self-government decisions should be subject to *international* human rights norms and international monitoring. See, on this, Kymlicka (2001, ch. 4).
10. For some of the evidence, see Kymlicka (2001, chs 10–15).
11. The Basque Country is the main exception, although the ETA campaign of violence began in the 1960s and 1970s as a response to the highly centralized Fascist regime, and is unlikely to have emerged had Spain been a democratic multi-nation federation. Cyprus is another example, although here too violence arose in response to attempts by the state

to subvert the multi-nation federal arrangements adopted at independence. It was the abrogation, not the adoption, of multi-nation federalism that generated violence.

12. These attempts have so far been unsuccessful, for reasons I discuss in Kymlicka (2007, ch. 6).

13. As happened in the late 1980s in the Philippines, and as is happening at the moment with Sri Lanka, and may happen in Indonesia and Burma, all in response to inconclusive armed struggles.

14. I have elsewhere explored the puzzle that defenders of communitarianism in Asia support state policies that are profoundly anti-communitarian, making it impossible for individual members of minority groups to fulfil the communal obligations that these defenders say is at the heart of their value system. In most Asian countries, as elsewhere around the world, it is the centralizing state, not minority political claims, that is eroding inherited ideals of community (Kymlicka, 2004b).

15. For examples of laws banning various forms of minority nationalist claims, see Shastri (1997, pp. 151–3) (banning advocacy of secession in Sri Lanka) and Ganguly (1997, pp. 257, 264) (prohibiting discussion of 'sensitive issues' in Malaysia).

16. Another factor in some of these cases is the perception that minorities have historically been privileged by colonial powers at the expense of the dominant group. In such circumstances, perceptions of historic injustice are invoked by the dominant group to reject demands for minority rights.

# REFERENCES

Ahmed, Samina (1997), 'Centralization, authoritarianism and the mismanagement of ethnic relations in Pakistan', in Michael Brown and Sumit Ganguly (eds), *Government Policies and Ethnic Relations in Asia and the Pacific*, Cambridge: MIT Press, pp. 83–128.

Anderson, Benedict (2004), 'The future of Indonesia', in Michel Seymour (ed.), *The Fate of the Nation-State*, Montreal: McGill-Queen's University Press.

Bell, Gary (2001), 'Minority rights in Indonesia: will constitutional recognition lead to disintegration and discrimination?', *Singapore Journal of International and Comparative Law*, **5**, 784–806.

Connor, Walker (1972), 'Nation-building or nation-destroying?', *World Politics*, **24**, 319–55.

Connor, Walker (1999), 'National self-determination and tomorrow's political map', in Alan Cairns (ed.), *Citizenship, Diversity and Pluralism*, Montreal: McGill-Queen's University Press, pp. 163–76.

Davis, Michael (1999), 'The case for Chinese federalism', *Journal of Democracy*, **10**(2), 124–37.

Edrisinha, Rohan (2005), 'Multination federalism and minority rights in Sri Lanka', in Will Kymlicka and Baogang He (eds), *Multiculturalism in Asia*, Oxford: Oxford University Press, pp. 244–61.

Ganguly, Sumit (1997), 'Ethnic policies and political quiescence in Malaysia and Singapore', in Michael Brown and Sumit Ganguly (eds), *Government Policies and Ethnic Relations in Asia and the Pacific*, Cambridge: MIT Press, pp. 233–72.

He, Baogang (1998), 'Can Kymlicka's liberal theory of minority rights be applied in East Asia?', in Paul van der Velde and Alex McKay (eds), *New Developments in Asian Studies*, London: Kegan Paul International, pp. 20–44.

He, Baogang (2004), 'Confucianism versus liberalism over minority rights', *Chinese Journal of Philosophy*, **31**(1), 103–23.

He, Baogang (2005), 'Minority rights with Chinese characteristics', in Will Kymlicka and Baogang He (eds), *Multiculturalism in Asia*, Oxford: Oxford University Press, pp. 56–79.

International Centre for Ethnic Studies (2003), 'Statement of principles on minority and group rights in South Asia', Colombo: ICES.

Kymlicka, Will (2001), *Politics in the Vernacular: Nationalism, Multiculturalism, Citizenship*, Oxford: Oxford University Press.

Kymlicka, Will (2004a), 'Justice and security in the accommodation of minority nationalism: comparing East and West', in Alain Dieckhoff (ed.), *The Politics of Belonging: Nationalism, Liberalism and Pluralism*, New York: Lexington, pp. 127–54.

Kymlicka, Will (2004b), 'Universal minority rights? The prospects for consensus', in Morigiwa Yasutomo, Ishiyama Fumihiko and Sakurai Tetsu (eds), *Universal Minority Rights, A Transnational Approach*, Stuttgart: Franz Steiner Verlag, pp. 13–57.

Kymlicka, Will (2007), *Multicultural Odysseys: Navigating the New International Politics of Diversity*, Oxford: Oxford University Press.

Kymlicka, Will and Magda Opalski (2001), *Can Liberal Pluralism be Exported? Western Political Theory and Ethnic Relations in Eastern Europe*, Oxford: Oxford University Press.

Lijphart, Arend (1996), 'The puzzle of Indian democracy: a consociational interpretation', *American Political Science Review*, **90**(2), 258–68.

Nandy, Ashis (1992), 'Federalism, the ideology of the state and cultural pluralism', in Nirmal Mukarji and Arora Balveer (eds), *Federalism in India: Origins and Development*, Delhi: Vikas Publishing, pp. 27–40.

Resnick, Philip (1994), 'Toward a multination federalism', in Leslie Seidle (ed.), *Seeking a New Canadian Partnership: Asymmetrical and Confederal Options*, Montreal: Institute for Research on Public Policy.

Schwartzberg, Joseph (1985), 'Factors in the linguistic reorganization of Indian states', in Paul Wallace (ed.), *Region and Nation in India*, Delhi: American Institute of Indian Studies, pp. 155–82.

Shastri, Amita (1997), 'Government policy and the ethnic crisis in Sri Lanka', in Michael Brown and Sumit Ganguly (eds), *Government Policies and Ethnic Relations in Asia and the Pacific*, Cambridge: MIT Press, pp. 129–63.

Smith, Alan (2005), 'Burma/Myanmar: struggle for democracy and ethnic rights', in Will Kymlicka and Baogang He (eds), *Multiculturalism in Asia*, Oxford: Oxford University Press, pp. 262–87.

Thier, Alexander (1999), 'Afghanistan: minority rights and autonomy in a multiethnic failed state', *Stanford Journal of International Law*, **35**, 351–88.

Weiner, Myron (1998), *Sons of the Soil*, 2nd edn, Delhi: Oxford University Press.

Yan, Jaiqi (1996), 'China's national minorities and federalism', *Dissent*, Summer, pp. 139–44.

# 3. Regionalist federalism: a critique of ethno-national federalism

## David Brown

Democratization is relatively shallow in Southeast Asia, not just because of the absence of fair competitive elections in Burma, Brunei, Laos and Vietnam, but also because those Southeast Asian governments which are elected have continued to evince various authoritarian tendencies – populist, bureaucratic–authoritarian, or neopatrimonial – which inhibit political pluralism. The purpose of this chapter is to develop an argument which suggests that, in such circumstances, the granting of federal autonomy to ethnic minority homeland regions is more likely to inhibit the further democratization of Southeast Asian nation-states than to promote it.

The chapter takes as its point of departure the recent edited book, *Multiculturalism in Asia* (Kymlicka and He, 2005). That volume began by advocating the merits of liberal multiculturalism and suggesting that, despite some barriers, 'throughout South and East Asia, countries are now debating, and sometimes adopting, new policies to accommodate minorities' (ibid., p. 1). He and Kymlicka thus depicted a 'new politics of diversity in Asia' (ibid., p. 2). Most of the case-study chapters, however, expressed some scepticism as to whether there has yet been a discernible shift towards the enhanced accommodation of ethnic minority claims in Asia.[1] Several also expressed doubts as to whether Asian societies can be, or ought to be, held accountable before the bar of Western liberal multiculturalism. The doubts were expressed in nuanced ways, in the context of particular countries and ethnic minorities, but two themes recurred.

First, the liberal multiculturalist prescription of differential ethnic rights is sometimes seen to be incongruent with the contextual fluidity – the 'pattern of continuous and trivial local diversity' (Moerman, quoted in Pholsena, 2005, p. 103) – which characterizes identity construction in these societies.[2] The result of introducing ethnically differentiated citizenship rights can therefore be to exacerbate the already prevalent top-down reification of ethnic identities in Asia, by setting them in institutional cement, thus further promoting the misrecognition and ethnic stereotyping they were intended to combat, and marginalizing those made invisible by the 'flattened and homogenized' ethnic categories (Chua, 2005, p. 183). Further, the granting of territorial federal rights to ethnic minority communities might not be applicable to the many Asian ethnic communities which claim to have migrated to their residential homeland during or prior to the period of state formation. Even in the case of non-migrant communities, such as the Acehnese, the granting of multinational federal rights would imply accepting at face value their contested claims to sole-homeland status in the bounded autonomous territory, thus disempowering Gayo, Javanese and other ethnic minorities resident in the province (Bowen, 2005).

Doubt about the wisdom of advocating ethnicity as the basis for political rights, even for the purpose of favouring marginalized communities, is sometimes accompanied by a recognition that national (nation-state) identities might be more powerful and more 'authentic' as the basis for a sense of identity and belonging than is sometimes implied by advocates of liberal multiculturalism. This is suggested by Vatthana Pholsena in relation to Lao national identity,[3] and developed by Chua Beng Huat in relation to Singapore. He argues that the power of national identity derives, not just from the hegemonic nature of state ideology, but also from the 'vernacular communitarianism' reflecting the nested relationships of everyday interactions, between individual, family, ethnie and nation. These relationships function in practice to prioritize the 'needs of the nation-as-community' (Chua, 2005, p. 178), so that, in the Singaporean case, citizens acquiesce in the costs which this implies for each ethnic community, including the ethnic majority (p. 193).

These points provide the basis for the discussion which follows. It will be argued that a regionalist federalism might be more conducive than a multinational federalism to the democratization of Southeast Asia. Conceptually, the distinction between the two is clear, between the federal autonomy of a regional polity constituted as a civic homeland granting equal status to all its residents, and that of a region which constitutes itself as an ethnic homeland so as to give priority to its ethnonational core. On the ground, the distinction is more complex, since it depends on the kind of norms and structures which develop in the course of political practice, as well as on constitutional provisions. This does not make it any the less crucial to try to analyse the implications of the two forms of federalism, since awareness of the distinction can enhance the capacity to influence the direction, and thence the political impact, of democratization.

# DEMOCRATIZATION AND FEDERALISM

The case for multinational federalism in Southeast Asia derives primarily from the facts of the recent civil conflicts between minority ethnonational separatist movements and state forces, notably in Burma, Indonesia, the Philippines and Thailand. Since the minority ethnonational movements claim the right to some form of territorial political autonomy from the existing nation-state, and since violent conflict has arisen from the refusal of the state regimes to grant such territorial autonomy, it might seem merely common sense to suggest that the conflicts could be resolved if there were either a negotiated secession or an agreement to reconstitute the disputed territory as an autonomous federated region. The secession of East Timor from Indonesia, and the recent peace agreement on Aceh, seem to validate the argument. However, the recognition that a short-term peace might be obtained by acceding to the autonomy claims of separatist ethnic nationalist movements does not deal with the issue of whether federalism would offer a stable, just or democratic formula for accommodating ethnic diversity within Southeast Asia's nation-states.

It has indeed been suggested that the introduction of asymmetrical multinational federalism might be even more problematic in Asia than it has been in the West (Kymlicka, 2005). Firstly, the Asian states are in several cases more authoritarian or illiberal than their Western counterparts; and secondly, some of the minority ethnonational movements have a longer or more mass-based tradition of violent protest in pursuit of their goals.[4] As a result, there is the fear both that federalism might produce autonomous provinces governed by militant ethnonational elites imposing undemocratic 'islands of local tyranny' (ibid., p. 35) and also that the illiberalism, both of the state élites and of the ethnonational élites, might undermine the federal compromise once the gaze of international opinion is averted, so that federalism might pave the way for political disintegration and instability (Kymlicka, 1998), rather than for 'a world that offers justice to all its peoples, majorities and minorities' (He and Kymlicka, 2005, p. 21).

The case for or against multinational federalism depends, however, on more than whether it precedes or follows democratization. More fundamentally, the normative case for multinational federalism depends upon how democratization is conceptualized. Democracy refers to the political equality of citizens,[5] but its institutionalization may take diverse forms. In the functioning democracies of the modern world, several forms of institutionalization coexist in tension, but when we advocate democratization we usually do so in order to prioritize some particular institutionalization. In examining the normative merits of multinational federalism, we need to refer to two characterizations of democracy, as 'protective democracy' (Held, 1987), and as 'deliberative democracy' (Habermas, 1990).

## Protective Democracy

Protective democracy derives from the classical liberal concern for the protection of individual liberty rights against an oppressive state. Its central tenets were those of 'natural rights' and 'limited government'. When it became clear that a central government elected by the majority of the populace, and governing in the name of 'the people' might become even more oppressive of liberty than a monarchical tyranny, the need for democracy to be institutionalized as constitutional 'checks and balances', became clear, at least to Tom Paine. In the absence of such constitutional constraints, and also of the constraints provided by a pluralistic civil society, the governing élites might tend to use the machinery of 'democratic' elections to give political priority to their own interests and values, and to seek to impose these on the citizenry. If these interests and values were predominantly bourgeois, this might generate a proletarian reaction, with workers seeking to defend themselves from bourgeois domination. If they were patriarchal, a feminist movement might begin to demand the protections of gender-based affirmative action. If the state élites were imbued with the interests and values of a particular ethnic community, the ethnic minorities might begin to need, and to demand, appropriate protections. Such an ethnic bias on the part of the state élites might be particularly likely were they to be recruited from an ethnic majority which they could mobilize as their constituency for electoral purposes; or when the state élites belonged to an ethnic core community whose preferential access to education, or wealth, or military leadership, gave them priority access to state power. The state might then become the agency of an ethnic core community, seeking to promote its cultural values and material interests at the expense of the ethnic minorities. In such a situation, the national identity promoted by the state in its policies, symbolism and rhetoric would function as the vehicle for the promotion and prioritization of the interests and values of the dominant ethnic culture. The civic norms and structures of the nation-state, or its institutions offering multiculturalist accommodations, would thus be revealed, on examination, as facade elements within the nationalist ideology, functioning to camouflage and promote the prioritizing of ethnic core values, and the cooptation and marginalization of ethnic minorities.

On grounds of protective democracy therefore, the case for multinational federalism is clear: to provide those subordinated and marginalized ethnic minorities resident in their ancestral homelands with the constitutional and institutional means to protect themselves from the dominant ethnie, 'in response to the threat posed by majority nation-building' (Kymlicka, 2005, p. 37). The main danger is that even multinational federalism might still function to promote ethnic cooptation. But if such federalism did prove insufficient to protect an ethnic minority from a state acting as the agency of an oppressive ethnic core, there would be protective democracy grounds for advocating full secession based on ethnic self-determination.

**Deliberative Democracy**

The case for multinational federalism looks more problematic, however, if the primary goal of democratization were to be conceptualized as deliberative democracy. The classical liberal idea of a foundational 'social contract' implied a model of democracy as the formation of 'a people', a political community formed by the participation of all individual citizens in the exercise of authority (Dunn, 2005, pp. 63–4). Participation in such a deliberative community might begin merely as a defence of self-interests, but it engenders democracy only insofar as the defence of individual and minority interests begins to give way to a primary concern with sustaining the deliberative processes of collective accommodation (Habermas, 1990), thereby engendering outcomes fair to all (Gutmann and Thompson, 2004).

In Habermas's formulation, the attempt to create such a deliberative democracy, in situations where some ethnic minorities have hitherto been marginalized or alienated, will need to involve, not only the granting of equal individual citizenship rights to all residents of a territory regardless of ethnicity, but also various ethnically affirmative minority group rights. However, the criterion for the recognition of such rights must be their effectiveness in reducing the marginalization and alienation of ethnic minorities, so as to promote the goal of their progressive inclusion in the civic polity (Habermas, 2000, pp. 143–6). The accommodation of ethnic diversity thus promotes the goal of a political equality which is ethnically blind. Such a polity would not be a 'nation' in the sense of comprising an ethnically homogeneous community, but it would be a nation in the sense of comprising one discursive community, containing 'a plurality of different individual and collective experiences, histories, commitments, ideals, interests, and goals' (Young, 2004, p. 230), but sharing the civic cultural values of 'inclusion, equality and reasonableness' (p. 229).

Iris Marion Young suggests, however, that the concept of an ethnically blind civic polity is not just difficult of attainment, but is an incoherent conception, since 'the public sphere is . . . governed by norms which appear to be universal or culturally neutral, but which in fact reflect the cultural values of the dominant social categories' (Miller, 2000, p. 63). But the fact that a civic polity might not be culturally neutral in relation to all markers of difference, including for example class or gender, presumably does not invalidate the ideal of its attaining neutrality as to one such difference, for example ethnicity. The civic culture which promotes a pluralistic and liberal civic polity tolerant of ethnic difference should perhaps not be depicted as the opponent of the 'politics of difference', so long as the character of its public norms is the subject of deliberative democratic debate seeking the goal of inclusive cohesion, rather than the subject of contending power-based interest rivalries.

If democratization were to be conceptualized as progress towards the normative goal of constructing nation-states as civic deliberative democracies, the case for multinational federalism becomes problematical. It must rest on the hope that ethnonational regional assemblies will progressively overlap and intertwine with other sites of discursive debate within the nation-state, as sometimes occurs in states whose federalism is constructed on a regionalist rather than a multinational basis.

## The Southeast Asian Context

The dominant view in the literature on Asian nationalism and ethnic politics has long been that most Asian nation-states were constructed so as to favour one dominant cultural community at the expense of the diverse indigenous, migrant or ethnonational minorities. As Crawford Young put it 30 years ago, 'the nation-building process, through which the state seeks the sanction of nationality, frequently involved utilization of the symbol system associated with the historically dominant culture' (Young, 1976, p. 507). What followed from this was the concern of this ethnic core to promote its culture as the 'instrument of cultural dignity and progress' (p. 507) amongst the peripheral populations. This view of the Asian nation-state has generated a widespread tendency towards analysis which portrays ethnic minorities as legitimate defenders of their rights against such ethnocultural domination. As Bowen notes in relation to the Free Aceh Movement:

> international commentary on the struggle in Aceh sometimes portrays it as a liberation struggle by the 'Acehnese people', sometimes described as an 'indigenous people'. Drawing this conclusion would, however, take the movement's self-characterization at face value ... Aceh illustrates the ways in which international categories of 'minorities' and 'peoples' not only fail to capture local histories and meanings, but in fact weigh in on one side of a conflict. (Bowen, 2005, p. 160)

The argument that protective democratization is promoted by multinational federalism derives from the depiction of the Southeast Asian nation-states as the agency of a dominant ethnic core, and the depiction of the autonomy claims of ethnonational minorities as reasonable reactions to such ethnic domination. In order to develop the counter-argument, that multinational federalism inhibits deliberative democracy, we need therefore to challenge this tendency to portray the minority ethnonationalist movements as innocent victims, and to portray the dominant ethnies as racist oppressors.

## ETHNIC MINORITIES AND REACTIVITY

For liberal multiculturalists, the primary cultural communities within which individuals define their identity and pursue their development are the ethnic group, the ethnic nation, or the 'tribal' indigenous communities. If individuals embedded within such communities are to pursue their self-realization, the various ethnic communities must, it is argued, be granted institutional respect and recognition by the state, and accorded various forms of self-determination rights. But the word 'ethnicity' is often avoided by liberal multiculturalists in favour of terms such as 'cultural community' or 'minority'. This is partly because 'ethnicity' has acquired pejorative connotations.

As has frequently been noted, the word derives from the Greek term for non-Greeks – other people with distinctive cultural or biological characteristics, who were different 'peripheral, foreign barbarians' (Hutchinson and Smith, 1996, p. 4). It came into modern usage from the 1950s onwards to refer primarily to minority groups, and to focus attention on the emotional power of their reactive oppositions to national integration and modernization; thence the depictions of ethnicity as an irrational and regressive 'primordial' bond (Geertz, 1963).

The term was subsequently employed to refer to non-minority communities, whose bonds to 'blood and soil' seemed particularly powerful and politically salient, and who seemed to behave in many ways as if they *were* minorities, reacting against more powerful communities. The outcome of this has been the widespread assumption that ethnic nationalism (denoted sometimes as cultural or ethnocultural nationalism) is somehow intrinsically emotionally 'excessive and militant' (Kohn, 1962, p. 24), or 'illiberal and belligerent' (Miller, 1995, p. 8). Its aggressive character is explained as arising from a sense of inferiority in relation to a perceived threat from a powerful other. It is thus a reactive form of consciousness which emerges only in a 'collectivist–authoritarian' form (Greenfeld, 1992, p. 11).

There are good reasons to be critical of the easy elision, in much of this literature, of ethnicity with illiberalism and aggression (Brown, 2000, pp. 53–7). Nevertheless there might be a 'germ of truth' hiding there.

The insight becomes clearer when the potential shift of minority ethnic consciousness, from rational to non-rational reactivity, is outlined.

Ethnic consciousness forms, and develops into 'ethnonationalism', when the expansion and intensification of state interventionism threatens the autonomy and cohesion of minority communities (Connor, 1994).[6] The minority ethnic communities may of course be objectively mistaken in their perception of such threats, but their ethnonationalist reactions can nevertheless be seen as involving an instrumental rationality, an attempt to defend group values and self-interests against the perceived threat of state oppression, by using the available 'weapons of the weak' (including direct action) to seek the removal of such state oppression. Ethnonationalism emerges, then, as 'resentment at foreign rule' (ibid., p. 36) that can be seen to have a rational reactive basis. But resentment is a painful emotion, especially if an ethnic minority begin to feel that the power-scales are tipped against them. It has been suggested that, in such circumstances, some ethnonational activists may begin to develop a *ressentiment* consciousness, and transmit this to their followers. Nietzsche's idea of *ressentiment* can be employed to illuminate a process which involves the following changes:

a.   Awareness develops amongst the ethnic minority community that they are marginalized or relatively deprived in some respects, and powerless to rectify this. Initially this might generate a 'colonial mentality': the resignation of the marginalized, and the acceptance that the ethnic minority culture is inferior. The corollary of this is the development of feelings of admiration and envy directed towards the culture of the dominant groups (Mannoni, 1991).

b.   Some amongst the ethnic minority come to perceive that their social disruption and relative deprivation derive, not from complex social forces, but from the oppression of the minority community by a specified oppressor community which is allied with, or which controls, the state. Thus, for example, even if the economic deprivation of a minority community was derived primarily from the poverty of its economic resources, it is likely to be perceived by some ethnic minority élites as arising from 'internal colonialist' exploitation by a dominant core. This gives rise to feelings of hatred towards the dominant groups.

c.   The inability of the marginalized ethnic minority to act on this hatred and defeat the oppressor leads to a reformulation of the relationship. They experience a growing dissonance between traditional values and the egalitarian rhetoric of state nationalism, and also between both of these and the social realities of their disruption and marginalization. One solution for this anomic dissonance is *ressentiment* (Greenfeld, 1992, 2005). In the *ressentiment* process, shame of the 'defeated' ethnic minority culture is replaced by its depiction as a virtuous culture characterized by purity, asceticism and communitarian spirit. By contrast, the envy of the oppressor's culture gives way to its depiction as immoral: materialistic, decadent and corrupt. This *ressentiment* reformulation involves an element of illusion which enables those who are marginalized and deprived to feel good once more about themselves; 'one can feel happy and superior to the poor individuals who possess the now devalued and ridiculed values' of the dominant culture (Morelli, 1998, p. 5).

d. Once the oppressor has been depicted as immoral, and the ethnic minority as virtuous, ethnic nationalist action can be mobilized on moralistic grounds, employing the emotive language of the right to ethnic minority self-determination, and the injustice of exploitative colonialism. The complexities of politics thus become simplified, in the language of ethnic nationalism, into a formulaic 'good Us versus evil Other' ideology.

e. The self-depiction of the ethnic minority as the virtuous victims of the oppressors is characteristically articulated in the primordialist language of ethnicity. If the community can be seen as defined by a cultural distinctiveness arising from its common ancestry, it can claim the moral authenticity associated with organic naturalness. Moreover, if this self-depiction includes the claim to continued occupancy of an ancestral homeland, the ethnie can be portrayed as the nation, and thence as the legitimate holders of collective self-determination rights.

f. Dominant groups thus come to be evaluated, not by their personal behaviour, but by the imposition of a collectivist ethnic stereotype, as the immoral ethnic oppressor. The result is that minority ethnic nationalism develops as a powerful ideological formula offering a simple diagnosis for contemporary problems and a simple prescription for their resolution: 'Once we were cohesive and secure in our ethnic homeland. Things went wrong when this homeland was infected or invaded by the ethnic other. If the infection or invasion can be rectified by restoring the autonomy of our ethnic homeland, then we will once again be cohesive and secure.' Such a formulation becomes a self-validating cognitive and moral filter, since most contemporary grievances can be depicted as arising from the disruptive interventions of the dominant Other. It can therefore easily develop in a morally absolutist direction. Once the dominant Other has been stereotyped as immoral and untrustworthy, negotiations with this Other become increasingly problematic. Even the offer of 'genuine' federal autonomy is likely, therefore, to be rejected as a 'trick'.[7] Such a depiction of ethnic minority nationalism, not as the rationally and morally legitimate reaction to objective oppression, but rather as an illusory ideological response to anomic dissonance, would help to explain why political accommodation is so difficult in ethnic conflicts.

In the case of Patani separatism in Southern Thailand, for example, the recent upsurge in separatist violence occurred after the government had shifted from assimilationist oppression, towards policies which promoted the teaching of Malay and Islam in the schools of the southern provinces, and which enhanced Malay–Muslim recruitment into the administration, parliament and government. In the 1990s also, the Malay–Muslim provinces had gained political leverage from democratization, as successive central governments began to rely upon support from Malay–Muslim constituencies. Initially it looked as if this shift to ethnic accommodation had promoted a 'deradicalized' Malay–Muslim cultural consciousness which renounced separatist violence (Jory, 1999), but when violence erupted again in the early 1990s, it was promoted by 'an expanded pool of alienated youth who became prime targets for recruitment by [Islamic] extremists' (Croissant, 2005, pp. 30–31).[8] They were able to mobilize village communities where coexistence between Malays and Thais was breaking down, in the 1990s, because of the impact of state and market interventions on everyday life. Villagers resolved this crisis by increasingly identifying themselves by reference to an imported 'high Islamic culture . . . to reassert cultural identity and to overcome cultural marginalization'. This has transformed the south, 'from coexistence to hatred' (Horstmann, 2004, p. 92). High Islam has functioned as a political ideology to promote 'the mobilization of hatred [which] has inspired a political nostalgia of a lost state of Patani' (p. 89). Separatist violence is committed by a small minority, but it is probably facilitated by this political ideology of hatred, espoused also by non-violent Malay–Muslim ethnonationalists who demonize the state by ignoring its recent accommodations so as to sustain their portrayal of it as the assimilationist oppressor, pursuing 'the policy of Thaisation [which] goes back centuries' (quoted from BERSATU leader Wan Kadir, in Noor, 2005). The result of this negative stereotyping of the state is that, 'sadly, there is some quiet satisfaction the police are getting killed' (quoted in Horn, 2002).

If such *ressentiment* elements were significant in the consciousness of minority ethnonationalist activists, it would seem to imply that the appropriate test of an offer of federalism would be its potential impact in reducing the *ressentiment* basis of their ethnonationalist mobilization, rather than simply the extent to which it accorded with the minority's own self-determination claims.

# THE AUTHORITARIAN TENDENCIES OF SOUTHEAST ASIAN GOVERNMENTS

Southeast Asian states have displayed clear authoritarian features, and ethnic minorities have frequently been amongst the victims of this authoritarian tendency. This has sometimes been explained as arising from the state's role as the agency of a dominant ethnie, seeking to impose its values on, or to marginalize and exploit, the ethnic minorities.

Such an explanation of ethnic minority oppression is indicated in He and Kymlicka's depiction of an 'important difference' between Asia and the West. They argue that, in the West, ethnic minorities feel that they have been mistreated at the hands of the ethnic majorities. But in Asia, it is frequently the case that the ethnic majorities feel they have been mistreated at the hands of the minorities which collaborated with foreign colonial powers. In the post-colonial Asian states, therefore, the ethnic majorities now feel justified in asserting their ethnic dominance, in order to 'remedy this historic injustice' (He and Kymlicka, 2005, p. 8). This depiction of Asian ethnic cores as acting towards their ethnic minorities on a reactive basis is sometimes complemented by the widespread depiction of Asian state-nationalism as itself reactive, first against colonial domination and, more recently, against Western neocolonialism or the dominant influence of 'Western values'. Asian authoritarian regimes have thus sometimes been depicted as the agency of slighted ethnic majorities intent on reasserting their dominance, and therefore acting towards their minorities in ethnocentric and racist ways. Daniel Bell has argued that this tendency was sometimes constrained by authoritarian regimes, but is now promoted by the 'democratic' electoral mobilizations of ethnic majorities (Bell, 2004). From such a perspective, then, national integration is equated with ethnic oppression.

There is a related argument, that the authoritarian tendencies of Southeast Asian states might be explainable in terms of illiberal 'Asian values' which prioritize the collective good over individual and minority rights. Such values could be seen as facilitating the ethnic core's concern to pursue its ethnic self-interests, thus generating the state's oppression and exploitation of ethnic minorities. This seems unlikely. The communitarian bent of Asian values might just as easily imply the prioritizing of the family or the ethnie over the nation, as of the nation over the family or the ethnie. It seems more likely that the prioritizing of the national collectivity over individual and minority rights derives, not from Asian values, but rather from the authoritarian isolation of the state from society.

The simplest explanation for the authoritarian tendencies of Southeast Asian governments emerges from the depiction of its regimes as comprising ruling classes intent on prioritizing their own self-interests over those of the societies they govern. If such governments do represent the interests of another societal group, this is usually identified, in the 'political economy' literature, not as the ethnic majority, but as the emergent or dominant bourgeoisies. It may be that, as in Malaysia, governing élites seek to legitimate their policies by claiming that they favour the ethnic majority community, the *Bumiputra*; but this merely camouflages policies which favour the trans-ethnic bourgeoisies (Gomez, 2004). Once Southeast Asian states are depicted as the agencies of their dominant bourgeoisies rather than the agency of their ethnic cores, the reason for oppressive policies towards ethnic minorities becomes clear. The capitalist economic development of these nation-states depends in part on their capacities for transforming the economies of their pre-capitalist peripheries. The location of ethnic minorities, in particular the 'indigenous peoples', in such pre-capitalist peripheries thus explains the interventionism of the state, and the societal disruptions which stimulate ethnic minority mobilization. State policies towards ethnic minorities derive more from a concern with economic integration than with ethnic domination.

## THE ETHNIC CORE AND THE NATION-STATE

There is, however, a second reason for doubting the proposition that Southeast Asian governments function as the agencies of dominant ethnies imbued with 'collective–authoritarian', and thus defensive–aggressive, forms of consciousness. Anthony Smith has shown how modern nation-states derive their legitimacy and affective power by constructing national identity on the basis of ethnic symbolism. However, as Smith goes on to note, the development of ethnic majority consciousness does not usually precede the formation of the modern nation-state, but rather develops conterminously with it, so that the two intertwine (Smith, 1981, pp. 18–20). This implies that the consciousness of Asia's dominant ethnies should not be understood simply as an ethnic consciousness; but rather as a consciousness deeply imbued with values of state patriotism and state nationalism which transcend ethnicity. Three key elements in this consciousness of Southeast Asia's dominant ethnies may be indicated.

### The Internally-Generated Element in the Consciousness of the Dominant Ethnie

During the early and middle twentieth century, a new public space fed by the growth of print media emerged within the state territories created by colonial rule. Civil society associations began to use this space to promote indigenous cultural values and the claims of diverse interest groups. These associations began to articulate a new 'imagined community' which was pan-ethnic in the sense that it encapsulated diverse groups with cultural or dialect variations as one community denoted partly by ideas of race, language or religion, but also by appeals to the idea of an ethnic homeland focused on, and increasingly bounded by, the new territorial state. This sense of identification with the territory of the state gave a civic dimension to the consciousness of the dominant ethnie, which became interwoven with the new ethnic identity. Thus, for example, the Thais of Thailand began to identify themselves as distinct from the broader Tai-Lao linguistic group of which they were a part. Initially this emergent ethnic identity was counterposed to the civic idea of a nation-state. By the 1920s, 'commoner nationalists shifted the meaning of a nation from the people enclosed within the national territory and bound by loyalty to the sovereign, to a community defined by ethnic origins, a long and unique history, and a common language' (Baker and Phongpaichit, 2005, p. 113). By the 1930s, Thailand's national identity was being articulated by the liberal Pridi, so as to link this idea of the ethnic nation with the idea that a state constitution 'fuses us all together as one unity' (p. 124).

The collective consciousness of this dominant ethnie in the state territory was neither purely ethnic in character, nor simply a civic patriotic attachment to the emergent nation-state. It was an interplay between the two, a hyphenated ethnic–civic nationalist consciousness. Because of its origin in a pluralistic civil society sphere, it was imbued with an internally generated developmental optimism which manifested itself as an 'investment in national prestige' (Greenfeld, 2005, p. 327). This developmental optimism was then fed by the attainment of state sovereignty and modern statehood, by the increasing vibrancy of civil society and, for the NICs, by the transformation of the national economy. The dominant ethnie thus became conscious of themselves not just as an ethnic community, but as the ethnic core of the nation whose future depended on the integrity and development of the nation-state. The mix of ethnic and civic elements in this consciousness remains one of the main bases for the development of civil society in Southeast Asia, and thence for the democratic and pluralist pressures in modern politics.

The strength of this element in the consciousness of the ethnic core varies significantly from country to country, but it implies a view of national integration as an enterprise of 'civilizing the margins': promoting the national identity already attained by the ethnic core, amongst the ethnic minorities. Liberal multiculturalists would object to such national integration, even in the absence of state efforts at ethnic assimilation, oppression or exploitation, as being incompatible with the ideal of ethnic minority self-determination. If most members of the ethnic core are deeply imbued with nation-state identity, it is clear that they will seek the development of the nation-state by incorporating the ethnic margins into the culture of the nation with which they, the ethnic core, already identify. Even if this is done sensitively, seeking to accommodate ethnic minority traditions and languages while providing access to the national culture and national language, as in the 'relative bright spot' of the treatment of minority ethnic groups in the Philippines (Eder and McKenna, 2004, p. 56), it is likely to work to the detriment of the traditional way of life of the ethnic minorities, and to evoke, in some cases at least, their opposition.

## The Reactive State-Generated Element in Ethnic Core Identity

The state regimes of Southeast Asia have remained 'semi-authoritarian'. Government has remained in the hands of military leaders, elitist professionals or business groups, but the resultant regimes have increasingly needed to mobilize mass support for electoral purposes, and to legitimate their authoritarianism. Authoritarian leaders can most easily claim to be the sole legitimate spokesperson for the nation-state by constructing the nation as a unique ethnically defined collectivity whose sovereignty depends on the subordination of individual and minority 'vested interests' to the collective 'national interests' (Greenfeld, 1992). What follows from this is either the assimilation or the marginalization of ethnic minorities. In order to legitimate authoritarian rule the state élites have articulated and promoted a portrayal of the dominant ethnie as a collectivity intolerant of internal pluralism or external difference. This authoritarian–collectivist portrayal employs 'the masculine imagery of the strong-state' (Baker and Phongpaichit, 2005, p. 138). It depicts the ethnic core as insecure and defensive, reactively asserting itself against ethnic and or nation-state others. It comprises an attempt to 'create a new culture . . . by using the power of the state' (p. 126). The degree of success of this state-generated endeavour to influence the consciousness of the ethnic core has varied greatly from case to case. At its strongest, it generates the kind of 'authoritarian democracy' which Satha-Anand saw emerging under Thaksin in Thailand after the Tak Bai killings in 2004, when the government employed the media to promote a 'patriotic outrage' (Pathmanand, 2005, p. 12), so as to evoke public approval of the government's use of violence against Muslims (Satha-Anand, 2004). In the Malaysian case, the authoritarian–collectivist ideology was actively promoted by Malay state bureaucrats and aristocrats in order to defend their interests as aspiring state élites. They promoted a reactive Malay consciousness constructed as defensive and insecure, particularly in relation to Chinese culture. There were indeed internally generated elements in the emergent Malay/Malayan identity, articulated by a secular Malay-educated intelligentsia which 'looked to the creation of a Greater Malaysia or Greater Indonesia' (Steinberg, 1987, p. 337). But the reactive–collectivist construction of Malay identity, which depicted Malayan and then Malaysian nationality as a defence of the Malay community against the non-Malay minorities, became central to the state-building enterprise.

Even in the Thailand and Malaysian cases, it would be misleading to depict the authoritarian state as acting as the agency of an ethnic core characterized by a reactive and aggressive ethnic consciousness. Rather, the authoritarian state has tried to legitimate its authoritarianism by promulgating a collectivist and reactive depiction of ethnic core consciousness, precisely in order to contain and remould the more liberal, pluralistic and self-confident elements in the ethnic–civic consciousness of the dominant ethnie, which continually threaten to undermine the legitimacy of authoritarianism.

### The Ressentiment Element within the Ethnic Core

The uneven impact of development within the ethnic cores can generate a *ressentiment* mentality amongst at least some of their downwardly mobile sections. From such a *ressentiment* perspective the long-standing conflicts involving the ethnic separatist movements can be simplistically depicted as security threats to the nation. Just as in the West, it seems likely that this racist, 'redneck' right-wing populist element within the ethnic core has only limited appeal, and limited impact on state policies. In Southeast Asia, its clearest manifestation is in the rise of extremist Islam as a small minority within the Muslim majorities of Malaysia and Indonesia, from which the state élites have carefully distanced themselves.

The consciousness of the dominant ethnies thus has both civic and ethnic dimensions, and contains elements of an internally generated developmental optimism which tends to openness and tolerance, elements of a reactive state-generated ideology which takes a collective–authoritarian form, and elements arising from the *ressentiment* of those marginalized within the ethnie. Variations in the interplay between these elements of consciousness influence divergent patterns of national integration. But the recognition of these diverse elements in the consciousness of the ethnic core, and of the variations they generate in the politics of national integration, serves to undermine the claim that the character of the state, and in particular the authoritarian tendency of states in Southeast Asia, derives in any direct sense from the consciousness of the dominant ethnie.

# THE CIVIC DIMENSION OF DEMOCRATIZATION

The civic values associated with national identity (the ideals of legal equality, equality of political rights, equal access to education and to state welfare and so on) are already politically powerful normative claims in Southeast Asia, which clearly exert some effectiveness as pressures towards democratization, as in the catalyst role of student *reformasi* demands in securing the removal of Suharto in Indonesia (Aspinall, 1999). This might relate to the changing structure of globalized capitalism in Southeast Asia. It is frequently suggested that modern capitalist development demands and promotes a retreat from coercive authoritarianism, towards a politics which requires the 'manufacturing of consent'. Cooptation and accommodation would seem to be better for national economic development than are coercion and violence. This might coincide with the adoption of electoral bases for government, and thence the need to mobilize electoral support beyond the confines of the ethnic core. The implication is that the legitimatory language of domination (the need to sacrifice individual and minority interests for the good of the collective development) begins to give way to the legitimatory language of accommodation: the claims of fairness, equity and equality. Rather than such civic values being seen merely as fraudulent camouflage for ethnic oppression, they should perhaps be recognized as having the capacity to inhibit (albeit in some cases weakly) such oppression.

Democratization requires a shift of political focus away from the politics of ethnic majority versus ethnic minority, and towards the politics of collectivist civic nationalism versus liberal civic nationalism. There were some signs of this recently in the trans-ethnic support for *reformasi* in Indonesia and Malaysia. In Malaysia, the public alignments arising from clashes between Anwar and Mahathir crossed ethnic lines, and related to the tensions between their opposing liberal and collectivist visions of Malaysia's national identity. Both signalled the need to begin moving from a politics of pro-Malay affirmative action towards a 'new Malaysian' position of inter-ethnic integration (Lee, 2005). The trend is most visible in civil society politics. Judith Nagata notes that 'many Malaysians are now prepared more openly to think and act along less ethnically exclusive lines, and to participate in emergent civil society activities' (Nagata, 2004, p. 245). Meredith Weiss sees the same signs: '[the] *Orang Malaysia baru*, or "new Malaysians" seem to be spurring a new nationalist discourse and praxis. This nationalism is cosmopolitan' (Weiss, 2002, p. 197). The state still acts to constrain this trend, as it has in Thailand. The debates concerning the 1997 Thailand constitution focused on the issue of whether democratization should take a pluralist direction, implying 'an expansion of the concept of Thai identity to include a more pluralistic notion of what it means to be "Thai"' (Jory, 1999, p. 349), or a more collectivist direction, as it has taken under Thaksin.

Such contentions between pluralist and collectivist visions of a more civic national identity have direct and major implications for the policies adopted towards ethnic minorities. But the significance of the shift of focus in political language, from ethnic majority versus minority, to collectivist–authoritarian versus liberal pluralist national identities, is that it begins to change the vision of democratization, away from the goal of protective democracy, and towards the goal of deliberative democracy.

If progress towards liberal–civic national integration were to be recognized as central to democratization in Southeast Asia, it is clear that the first step, for several countries, is the offer of citizenship to all residents, regardless of their ethnicity (for example, to Thailand's Hill Tribes, to Hong Kong and Singapore's domestic workers, to Vietnamese in Cambodia). Progress towards a national deliberative democracy is also clearly inhibited by the lack of access of some ethnic minorities to the national language, and by the often limited extent of inter-ethnic interactions. In Malaysia, the reification of ethnic differences, the state's promotion of ethnically based social and political institutions, and the continued salience of ethnic divisions of labour, have all inhibited national integration. The danger is that multinational federalism might exacerbate rather than ameliorate such problems of national integration.

## FEDERALISM AND NATIONAL INTEGRATION

If democratization is understood as progress towards the ideal of liberal civic national integration, it becomes clear that all marginalized residents, including those marginalized on grounds of ethnicity, need whatever supplementary legal protections or material resources are required for them to gain full access to citizenship rights, while sustaining the values and practices associated with ethnicity, so as to enable 'nested nationalities'. As Will Kymlicka and Wayne Norman have noted, state accommodation of the claims of ethnic minorities is often conducive to, rather than incompatible with, the liberal civic goal of a deliberative democracy of equal citizens: 'generally speaking, the demand for both representation rights and multicultural rights is a demand for inclusion' (Kymlicka and Norman, 1995, p. 306). A key principle of deliberative democracy is that all citizens affected by a decision should take part in the decision-making discussions within and across numerous sites within the polity. David Miller argues that such a deliberative democracy can be fair to disadvantaged ethnic groups (Miller, 2000, p. 159). This, however, seems inconsistent with his advocacy

of protective multinational federalism even in cases of 'nested nationalities', where some citizens espouse dual identities, and where the overlapping ethnic and national cultures 'are sufficiently convergent so that
participants in each can readily understand the other' (p. 132). Miller recognizes that it is the historical interweaving of each ethnic community
within the common institutions of the nation-state which have fostered the
overarching national identity (p. 135). It seems reasonably likely, therefore,
that the formation of the multinational federalism which he advocates
would reduce that interweaving, reduce the tendency towards the dualiza-
tion of identities, and thus inhibit the potentialities for a trans-ethnic deliberative democracy within the nation-state.

In all nation-states, citizens disagree in their vision of national integration. Some prioritize assimilation into the ethnic core; others seek ethnically blind equal citizenship, and others seek the just accommodation of
ethnic group rights. Political stability and national integration are
enhanced so long as state élites employ the symbolism, rhetoric and policies of the nation-state to interweave these divergent ideals, so that the
diverse ethnocultural, civic and multiculturalist interpretations of equality,
justice and democracy can be employed ambiguously in the course of deliberative debate, rather than become definitionally counterposed to each
other in the form of contending self-interested rights claims (Brown, 2000).
Since there is clear danger of a clash between *ressentiment* assertions of
ethnic majority rights and *ressentiment* assertions of ethnic minority rights,
it is the norms and values of civic nationalism which play the crucial
buffering role.

This means that moves to accommodate demands for federal autonomy
are more likely to promote national integration and political stability if
they are framed in the language and symbolism of civic values: to end the
abuse of human rights, to promote the individual liberties of minorities, or
to enhance democracy, rather than as an inalienable right of ethnonational
self-determination. The alienation of ethnic minority activists is likely to be
eased, as Mahajan notes, if they are granted 'positive affirmation'
(Mahajan, 2005, p. 309) and 'recognition' (p. 310); but if their *ressentiment*
ethnonationalist ideologies are to be transcended rather than cemented,
such recognition must take the form of their inclusion in the liberal–democratic structures of the nation-state, rather than their protective ethnonational autonomy from that nation-state.

Multinational federalism seems directly antithetical to democratic
national integration because 'Self-government rights . . . are the most complete case of differentiated citizenship, since they divide the people into separate 'peoples', each with its own historic rights, territories, and powers of
self-government, and each, therefore, with its own political community'

(Kymlicka and Norman, 1995, p. 307). The reason for this, however, is the multinational basis for federalism, not federalism itself. If federal autonomy is granted to an ethnonational separatist movement, it makes it more likely that the *ressentiment* ideology of its activists will be legitimated and thereby promoted. It gives them a platform from which to demand that fuller secessionism which will protect the virtuous Us, from the demonized Other, thus eroding the sense of national political community required for deliberative democracy. It also legitimates their claim to embody the will of the ethnonation, and thus to suppress dissent within the federated region.

In established democracies, these dangers can be ameliorated by the counter-pressures derived from coopting ethnonationalist élites into the procedures and structures of intergovernmental debate. Nevertheless, federalizing concessions to ethnonational separatists in democratic states served in several cases to whet the ethnonationalist appetite for greater independence, as in Quebec, Flanders and the Basque Country. It is, however, in states where democracy has been shallow and weak that federalizing concessions have proved most destabilizing, since they have frequently been perceived by separatist ethnonationalists as a sign of the weakening of the central state, and of the legitimation of ethnic homeland rights over minorities. This was evident in the break-up of the USSR. Gorbachev's attempts to 'renew' the Soviet Union by promoting a decentralized federalism helped to precipitate declarations of independence by several of the republics (Beissinger, 1993, pp. 107–8). In Georgia, for example, the accession to governmental power in 1990 of the nationalist dissident, Gamsakurdia, facilitated his demand for independence, accompanied by a 'Georgia for the Georgians' campaign directed against ethnic minorities in the republic. In Azerbaijan, the Azeri nationalist Elchibey won the 1992 elections by espousing liberal–democratic beliefs, but proceeded to pursue anti-Russian policies and to launch an 'it is our land' campaign against the ethnic minorities in Azerbaijan. The problem was not simply that such individual leaders had authoritarian tendencies but, more fundamentally, that, once the claim to ethnonationalist homeland autonomy had been legitimated by the promise of multinational federalism, this became the most powerful source of legitimacy for any leader seeking to mobilize mass support. Thus, in Azerbaijan, even the anti-nationalist Aliyev was impelled to proclaim the ethnonationalist goal of independence as a means of attaining governmental power. *Ressentiment* is not just an ideological mindset of ethnonationalist activists; it is also translated by multinational federalism into a dominant basis for governmental legitimacy.

Regionalist federalism organized on a non-ethnic basis can, on the other hand, perform an integrative function, as is argued elsewhere in this volume in relation to the Australian case. Regionalist federalism might possibly promote such integration even when there is some de facto ethnic clustering within the federated regions. As Martin Dent argued in relation to Nigeria's shift from the large three ethnically-defined federal regions which existed prior to the civil war, to the 36 smaller non-ethnically defined federal units formed after the 1979 Constitution, 'a federal system that calls its constituent parts by ethnic names is asking for trouble' (Dent, 2000, p. 164). He then cites the disintegrative impact of ethnically-based federalism in the Yugoslavian case, and notes (perhaps over-optimistically):

> Nigeria avoided this danger by using the geographical area as surrogates for ethnic identities, although no one doubts that the inhabitants of five of the states in the former West are overwhelmingly Yoruba, those of five in the former East are overwhelmingly Ibo, and those of nine in the former North are overwhelmingly Hausa/Fulani . . . Ethnic identity is very often the language of the market place, but in federal matters it is not to be mentioned and, like sex in polite conversation, it is usually described by a synonym. (Dent, 2000, p. 164)

In the Malaysian case, federalism functions effectively, within the predominantly Malay states, to provide some democratic space, and some interregional equity, within an authoritarian polity.[9] However, it is least effective in the predominantly non-Malay states of Sabah and Sarawak, where a stronger form of federalism was introduced in 1963, precisely to protect the Kadazans in Sabah, and the Iban in Sarawak, from Malay domination. In effect, however, these terms of federation have fostered Kadazan and Iban ethnic consciousness and thus have 'engendered conflict between building loyalties at state level and at national level' (Cheah, 2002, p. 55).

Non-ethnic federalism is sometimes supplemented by other agencies to promote the access of marginalized communities to citizenship rights, and to ease the disruptive impacts of rapid social change, as with Malaysia's 'Department of Aboriginal Affairs' for the *Orang Asli* communities (Endicott and Dentan, 2004). Even where this is done, the tendency to ethnic stereotyping is most effectively inhibited by defending the interests of all marginalized citizens, as was done in India in relation to the issue of religious diversity. The redrawing of state boundaries to give self-government to linguistic communities in India has, however, marginalized some linguistic groups at the expense of others. This has succeeded in reducing some sites of ethnic conflict, but it has engendered others:

> The overlapping of cultural and political boundaries has at times yielded particularistic chauvinism. The expression of such sentiments has been sharpest

in regions where the regional linguistic élite did not occupy prestigious social, economic and political positions. Here linguistic identity movements, on securing statehood, have endorsed exclusionary policies and been hostile to other, especially powerful, linguistic groups within the region. (Mahajan, 2005, p. 302)

For Mahajan, 'the ethnic violence unleashed by such expression as "sons of the soil" . . . movements suggest that protection of the rights of all people in the region should perhaps be a condition for granting separate rights, like those of self-governance or separate statehood, for identified national minorities' (p. 302).

The implication, then, is that, if the institutions of federalism are to promote the development of the nation as a deliberative democracy, they must facilitate interactions between groups and individuals of diverse ethnicities, promote interactions between the state and federal levels of politics and of government, and potentially also facilitate the interplay between federated province, nation-state and the various 'state fragments' at the supra-state regional and global levels of politics. If deliberative democracy is the goal, then federalism is desirable only if it is institutionalized and symbolized in territorially inclusive, rather than ethnically exclusive, terms and if it functions to reduce the alienation of those in the marginalized provinces so as to promote their state–national integration, rather than their ethno-national self-determination.

The peace agreement on federal-type autonomy for Aceh, signed in August 2005, is important because it derived crucially from Gerakan Aceh Merdeka's (GAM) agreement to give up its demand for independence, in favour of an agreement that it be allowed to contest provincial elections. There are two interpretations of GAM's goals. The first is that it seeks a pluralistic democracy in an autonomous Aceh within Indonesia. The second is that it envisions provincial elections as resulting in a GAM victory and thence a referendum leading to full separation from Indonesia. As a recent ICG paper has noted, these divergent interpretations of GAM's aim (and of its level of support within Aceh), reflect the two different directions in which Aceh's federal-type autonomy might lead. One scenario is that it provides the model for provincial parties, representing diverse communities and interests within each province of Indonesia, to participate in both the provincial and the central parliaments, so that the two levels of a decentralized democracy can interweave, creating an Indonesia 'where local parties [are] absolutely essential to the institutionalization of democracy'. The other scenario is that it ushers in a move towards multinational federalism which engenders, not democracy, but 'the disintegration of Indonesia by encouraging ethnic and regional identities at the expense of a national one' (ICG, 2005, pp. 10–11).

# NOTES

1.  The use of the term 'ethnic' is always problematical, partly because it refers to a dimension of identity consciousness, but is often employed to denote cultural groups defined by language, race or religion. It is also problematical because it has the effect of treating the continuous gradations of nested identities as if they were bounded categories. Note that some multiculturalists prefer the synonyms, 'cultural community', 'minority' and 'majority', for reasons discussed in this chapter.
2.  See similar comments by Mika Toyota, in relation to the 'Hill Tribes' of Thailand, in the same volume (Toyota, 2005).
3.  Pholsena notes that nation-state sentiments may be constructed on the basis of powerful cultural affinities which fulfil people's needs for 'commitment and sharing' (Pholsena, 2005, p. 107). She recognizes that such a construction of Lao national identity on the basis of the recent state-sponsored revival of Buddhism, might favour 'the dominant Tai-Lao ethnolinguistic group' and therefore be 'troubling' for the non-Lao minorities (p. 97). But she also insists on the distinction between Lao dominance (the Lao *mandala*) and the universalistic and democratic elements in Buddhism which give it some potentiality as a culture of national integration.
4.  The net result is reflected in the violence of the confrontations. In 1994, Gurr and Harff estimated the deaths in Northern Ireland and the Basque conflicts as 200 and less than 100, respectively. The figures for Burma were 130 000; for Aceh, 10–20 000; and for the Moro conflict in the Philippines, 50 000 (Gurr and Harff, 1994, pp. 160–66).
5.  In John Dunn's arresting formulation, democracy is 'a demand to accept, abide by, and in the end even submit to, the choices of most of your fellow citizens. There is nothing enticing about this demand, and no guarantee ever that accepting it will avoid fearsome consequences and may not involve hideous complicities' (Dunn, 2005, p. 24).
6.  Walker Connor, who stresses the emotive power of ethnicity, and Michael Hechter, who offers a 'rational choice' view of ethnicity, may disagree about the relative primacy of cultural grievances and economic grievances in ethnonational mobilization, but they nevertheless agree on seeing ethnic nationalisms as constituting defensive assertions of self-determination which arise from awareness of a 'serious threat to the lifeways of the various ethnic groups' (Connor, 1994, pp. 36–7).
7.  In the case of Aceh, it seems clear that the current settlement, the outcome of intermittent negotiations since 1999, depended crucially on the GAM's deep distrust of the Indonesian government as an instrument of Javanese domination, being outweighed by trust in the international community, in particular the Finnish mediators and the EU and ASEAN monitors.
8.  Croissant notes that the southern provinces did benefit from Thailand's economic development, but that their relative deprivation increased, with average household income falling from 120.7 per cent of the average for the whole country in 1962, to 91.8 per cent in 2000 (Croissant, 2005, p. 29).
9.  Jomo and Wee examine the finance-related tensions of Malaysian federalism arising from increased central control over the states, and note that the use of this control to discriminate against Parti Islam SeMalaysia (PAS) state governments in Kelantan and Terengganu, as well as against the Sabah and Sarawak states, has some potential to 'undermine the legitimacy and unity of the Malaysian federation' (Jomo and Wee, 2003, p. 455). Nevertheless, they see federalism as having had some overall effectiveness in reducing regional disparities in Malaysia: 'With greater financial resources, there has been greater attention to federal government efforts in reducing inter-regional welfare disparities and ensuring more equitable development' (ibid., p. 446).

# REFERENCES

Aspinall, E. (1999), 'The Indonesian student uprising of 1998', in A. Budiman, B. Hatley and D. Kingsbury (eds), *Reformasi: crisis and change in Indonesia*, Clayton, Australia: Monash Asia Institute.

Baker, C. and P. Phongpaichit (2005), *A History of Thailand*, Cambridge: Cambridge University Press.

Beissinger, M.R. (1993), 'Demise of an empire-state: identity, legitimacy, and the deconstruction of Soviet politics', in C. Young (ed.), *The Rising Tide of Cultural Pluralism: The Nation-State at Bay?*, Madison: University of Wisconsin Press.

Bell, D.A. (2004), 'Is democracy the "least bad" system for minority groups?', in S. Henders (ed.), *Democratization and Identity: Regimes and Ethnicity in East and Southeast Asia*, Lanham: Lexington.

Bowen, J. (2005), 'Normative pluralism in Indonesia: regions, religions and ethnicity', in Kymlicka and He (2005).

Brown, D. (2000), *Contemporary Nationalism: civic, ethnocultural and multiculturalist politics*, London: Routledge.

Cheah, B.K. (2002), *Malaysia: the making of a nation*, Singapore: Institute of Southeast Asian Studies.

Chua, B.H. (2005), 'The cost of membership in ascribed community', in Kymlicka and He (2005).

Connor, W. (1994), *Ethnonationalism: the quest for understanding*, Princeton: Princeton University Press.

Croissant, A. (2005), 'Unrest in South Thailand: contours, causes and consequences since 2001', *Contemporary Southeast Asia*, **27**(1), 21–43.

Dent, M. (2000), 'Nigeria: federalism and ethnic rivalry', in M. O'Neill and D. Austin (eds), *Democracy and Cultural Diversity*, Oxford: Oxford University Press.

Dunn, J. (2005), *Setting the People Free: the story of democracy*, London: Atlantic Books.

Eder, J.F. and T.M. McKenna (2004), 'Minorities in the Philippines: ancestral lands and autonomy in theory and practice', in C.R. Duncan (ed.), *Civilizing the Margins: Southeast Asian government policies for the development of minorities*, Ithaca: Cornell University Press.

Endicott, K. and R.K. Dentan (2004), 'Into the mainstream or into the backwater? Malaysian assimilation of Orang Asli', in C.R. Duncan (ed.), *Civilizing the Margins: Southeast Asian government policies for the development of minorities*, Ithaca: Cornell University Press.

Geertz, C. (ed.) (1963), *Old Societies and New States: the quest for modernity in Asia and Africa*, New York: Free Press of Glencoe.

Gomez, E.T. (2004), 'Governance, affirmative action and enterprise development: ownership and control of corporate Malaysia', in E.T. Gomez (ed.), *The State of Malaysia: ethnicity, equity and reform*, London: RoutledgeCurzon.

Greenfeld, L. (1992), *Nationalism: five roads to modernity*, Cambridge, Mass.: Harvard University Press.

Greenfeld, L. (2005), 'Nationalism and the mind', *Nations and Nationalism*, **11**(3), 325–41.

Gurr, T.R. and B. Harff (1994), *Ethnic Conflict in World Politics*, Boulder, Col.: Westview.

Gutmann, A. and D. Thompson (2004), 'Deliberative democracy beyond process', *The Journal of Political Philosophy*, **10**(2), 153–74.

Habermas, J. (1990), *Moral Consciousness and Communicative Action*, Cambridge, Mass.: MIT Press.

Habermas, J. (2000), *The Inclusion of the Other: studies in political theory*, Cambridge, Mass.: MIT Press.

He, B. and W. Kymlicka (2005), 'Introduction', in Kymlicka and He (2005).

Held, D. (1987), *Models of Democracy*, Cambridge: Polity Press.

Horn, R. (2002), 'Gunning for cops', *Time Asia Magazine*, 5 August, **160**(4) (www.time.com/time/asia/magazine/printout), accessed 14/11/2005.

Horstmann, A. (2004), 'Ethnohistorical perspectives on Buddhist–Muslim relations and coexistence in Southern Thailand: from shared cosmos to the emergence of hatred?', *Sojourn*, **19**(11), 76–99.

Hutchinson, J. and A. Smith (eds) (1996), *Ethnicity*, Oxford: Oxford University Press.

ICG International Crisis Group (2005), 'Aceh: a new chance for peace', *Asia Briefing*, **40**.

Jomo, K.S. and C.H. Wee (2003), 'The political economy of Malaysian federalism: economic development, public policy and conflict containment', *Journal of International Development*, **15**, 441–56.

Jory, P. (1999), 'Political decentralisation and the resurgence of regional identities in Thailand', *Australian Journal of Social Issues*, **34**(4), 337–52.

Kohn, H. (1962), *The Age of Nationalism*, New York: Harper and Row.

Kymlicka, W. (1998), 'Is federalism a viable alternative to secession?' in P.B. Lehning (ed.), *Theories of Secession*, London and New York: Routledge.

Kymlicka, W. (2005), 'Liberal multiculturalism: western models, global trends, and Asian debates', in Kymlicka and He (2005).

Kymlicka, W. and B. He (eds) (2005), *Multiculturalism in Asia*, Oxford: Oxford University Press.

Kymlicka, W. and W. Norman (1995), 'Return of the citizen: a survey of recent work on citizenship theory', in R. Beiner (ed.), *Theorizing Citizenship*, Albany: State University of New York.

Lee, J.H. (2005), 'UMNO factionalism and the politics of Malaysian national identity', Murdoch University PhD thesis.

Mahajan, G. (2005), 'Indian exceptionalism or Indian model: negotiating cultural diversity and minority rights in a democratic nation-state', in Kymlicka and He (2005).

Mannoni, O. (1991), *Prospero and Caliban: the psychology of colonization*, Ann Arbor: University of Michigan Press.

Miller, D. (1995), *On Nationality*, Oxford: Clarendon Press.

Miller, D. (2000), *Citizenship and National Identity*, Cambridge: Polity Press.

Morelli, E.M. (1998), 'Ressentiment and rationality', paper for the Twentieth World Congress of Philosophy, Boston, Mass.; Paideia archive (www.bu.edu/wcp/Papers/Anth/AnthMore.htm), 21 January, 2005.

Nagata, J. (2004), 'Elusive democracy: appropriation of "rights" ideologies in Malaysian ethnic and religious political discourse', in S. Henders (ed.), *Democratization and Identity: regimes and ethnicity in East and Southeast Asia*, Lanham: Lexington.

Noor, F.A. (2005), 'Dr. Farish A. Noor interviews the head of the Patani BERSATU movement', *Brand New Malaysian* (www.brandmalaysia.com/movabletype/archives/2005/06), 9 November.

Pathmanand, U. (2005), 'Thaksin's policies go south', *Far Eastern Economic Review*, July/August, **168**(7), 8–13.

Pholsena, V. (2005), 'A liberal model of minority rights for an illiberal multiethnic state?', in Kymlicka and He (2005).

Satha-Anand, C. (2004), 'Fostering "authoritarian democracy" with violence: the effect of violent solutions to southern violence in Thailand', paper prepared for the Empire Conference, National University of Singapore, September.

Smith, A.D. (1981), *The Ethnic Revival*, Cambridge: Cambridge University Press.

Steinberg, D.J. (ed.) (1987), *In Search of Southeast Asia: a modern history*, Sydney: Allen and Unwin.

Toyota, M. (2005), 'Subjects of the nation without citizenship: the case of "Hill Tribes" in Thailand', in Kymlicka and He (2005).

Weiss, M.L. (2002), 'Contesting race and nation: Malay dominance and multiracial coalitions in Malaysia', in R. Starrs (ed.), *Nations under Siege: globalization and nationalism in Asia*, New York: Palgrave.

Young, C. (1976), *The Politics of Cultural Pluralism*, Madison and London: Wisconsin University Press.

Young, I.M. (2004), 'The deliberative model', in C. Farrelly (ed.), *Contemporary Political Theory: a reader*, London: Sage.

# 4. Federal accommodation of ethnocultural identities in India

## Gurpreet Mahajan

## ASPECTS OF THE INDIAN FEDERAL SYSTEM

Article 1 of the Indian Constitution states: 'India, that is Bharat, shall be a *Union of states*' (emphasis added). Although the Constitution has all the features of a federal system and refers to the territories of the states (regions) and the territories of the Union, distinguishes between two tiers of government and divides the powers of the central and state governments, it does not use the term 'federation'. This was intended to highlight one distinctive characteristic of the Indian federal structure. As the Chairman of the Constituent Assembly (the body that framed the Constitution of independent India), Dr Ambedkar, explained, the federal framework was not the result of an agreement by the states. Hence, no state had a right to secede from it. The federation was, in this sense, 'a union; it had all the features of a federal polity but it was indissoluble' (CAD, vol.VII, p. 43).

Against this backdrop it is easy to understand why the nature of the Indian federal system has been a prominent subject of public debate and discussion ever since the Constitution came into effect. While the fact of India being a federation is not in doubt or dispute, there are different representations of its federal character. Some analysts describe it as 'quasi-federal' (Wheare, 1963, p. 27), others see it as a 'quasi-federal union with several important features of a unitary government' (Munshi, 1967, p. 1) or a 'federation with strong centralizing tendency' (Jennings, 1953, p. 1). These different, though not incongruent, descriptions point to some essential differences between the Indian federal system and those of Canada or the USA, but, above all, they draw our attention to provisions of the Indian Constitution that give an edge, and at times an overriding authority, to the centre within the federation.

The centre is privileged in many different ways. Among other things, it has the authority to (i) reorganize the territorial boundaries of states and form new states by separating the territory from an existing state or by merging together existing states; (ii) issue administrative directives to the states to ensure compliance with the Union law(s) which apply in that state; (iii) appoint and dismiss a governor (the formal head of the executive in a state); (iv) declare a state of emergency if the President is satisfied that there is a threat to the security of the country, or to any of its territories, from external aggression or internal disturbances; (v) declare 'President's rule' (rule by the central government) if the governor reports that a constitutional crisis exists and the state cannot function in accordance with the provisions of the Constitution.

Of all these provisions it is the authority to declare an Emergency and President's rule that has been the most controversial and indeed the most powerful instrument of central intervention. It has been used frequently to counter movements for autonomy and secession, and to protect the interests of the ruling party at the centre (see, Nakade, 1969; A. Khan, 1997). In the recent past, however, the Supreme Court of India has asserted that the proclamation of an Emergency under Article 356(i) is not immune from judicial review and the court can strike down the proclamation if it is found to be 'mala fide or based on wholly irrelevant or extraneous grounds' (*S. R. Bommai* v. *Union of India*, 1994). The present debate on the use of constitutional provisions, and the manner in which centre–state relations have been redefined with the emergence of strong regional parties, is not, however, the subject of this chapter. There are a number of studies already available on these subjects (Jain, Keshyap and Srinivasan, 1972; Maheshwari, 1973; Dua and Singh, 2003) and they reveal that the presence of different parties at the national and regional level has significantly altered centre–state relations. It is now more difficult for the centre to dictate terms to regional governments when a different party is in power there.

Moving away from the overwhelming concern with the management of centre–state relations in India, this chapter focuses on the capacity of federalism to deepen democracy and protect diversity. Since its independence, India has been a federal democracy. Except for a brief interlude of 19 months when an Emergency was declared and democratic rights were suspended, India has been governed by democratically elected governments. Unlike many other post-colonial societies, both within this region and elsewhere, where military regimes and dictatorships seem to be the order of the day, India stands out as a remarkable story of the success of democracy. Here democracy has not only survived and prevailed, it has in fact been strengthened. While many Western democracies today are facing a decline in the participation of people in the electoral process, in India more and more people are participating. On average, the voter turnout for the General Elections to the central Parliament is about 60 per cent and the voter turnout for the state legislative assemblies is approximately 70 per cent. Participation at the local level, in the Pachayati Raj institutions, is even higher, with about 80 per cent voter turnout.

It is in the context of this deepening of democracy that this chapter explores the link between federalism, democracy and diversity. Federalism involves division of power and authority between the central and regional government so that power is not concentrated in the hands of one body or set of institutions.[1] To the liberal mind, this form of institutional arrangement is desirable as it distributes power and provides more avenues for participation and access to authority. By delineating separate spheres of legislation for the centre and the state (regional) government it complements the goal served by horizontal division of power through the doctrine of separation of powers.

In recent times federalism has been linked to democracy in yet another way. In addition to creating plural centres of power, it is said that regional governments can offer more opportunities for a territorially located community to influence decision making. Federalism can provide space for such communities to govern themselves and determine their own affairs in identified areas. This means that, in addition to providing avenues for greater participation in public and political life, the federal framework has the capacity to accommodate diverse cultural groups and communities. In situations where cultural communities are concentrated in one geographical space, federalism can offer them the right to self-governance within the existing structure of a sovereign nation-state. It can in this way deepen democracy and, what is equally important, minimize sources of ethnic conflict.

The process of homogenization involved in creating a shared national culture and the failure to accommodate different cultural communities on an equal footing are today the major sources of ethnic conflict in all societies. Ethnic conflicts in turn pose a serious danger to national and international peace and security. While the greater part of the twentieth century was haunted by conflicts between states, since the 1990s it is ethnic conflicts emerging within a nation-state that have gradually escalated into wars involving other states. Lingering discontent stemming from a sense of being unequal is therefore a threat not only to democracy but also to the survival of existing nation-states. Federalism is expected to serve the interest of democracy and the nation-state by offering an opportunity to communities to govern themselves and determine their future in accordance with their own way of life. Implicit here is also the belief that federalism can enhance and accommodate diversity, thereby minimizing, if not eliminating, an important source of conflict within society.

Has the federal framework in India fulfilled these expectations? Has it helped to accommodate diversity and deepen democracy? These are questions that this chapter seeks to address by taking as its reference point the experience of India. India is the largest and most populous democracy in the world. It is also a country with an enormous degree of religious and linguistic diversity. Many scholars have argued that federalism was a natural choice for a country inhabited by so many socio-cultural groups. For them, India could not be anything but a federation (see, for instance, R. Khan, 1992). The present organization of state territories tends to reinforce this picture as it makes cultural community the basis of the federation. What were the consequences of linking cultural identity with the political right to self-governance? Analysing the Indian experience in this regard will, it is hoped, throw some light on the purported link between federalism, democracy and diversity. In particular, it may help us to understand whether federalism is the natural and direct result of diversity, and whether it is a preferred option for a diverse democratic polity.

## PAST LEGACIES AND FUTURE ORIENTATION

When India gained independence in 1947 it was a foregone conclusion that it would be a parliamentary and federal democracy. While alternatives to each of these were debated in the Constituent Assembly, the vision of India that had emerged in the course of the freedom struggle prevailed. The British colonial rulers had introduced elements of a parliamentary and federal form of government in India. These measures had been necessitated by the growing support for the anti-colonial struggle and the corresponding demand for self-government in the country. The rationale for these institutional structures changed after independence, but aspects of the administrative framework that had developed under the colonial rule were retained. In other words, decolonization did not translate into rejection of everything that existed under colonial rule. Whether it was the legal structure with its plural civil codes and common criminal code, or the administrative services, several institutions that emerged during the period of colonial rule continued even after independence.

The Government of India Act of 1935 made provisions for a federal form of government. Although a federal structure did not eventually materialize it was strongly suggested by the Cripps Mission. Subsequent proposals for 'Dominion Status' for India also presumed a federal form of government. Hence, the idea of a federal framework had emerged long before independence. Indeed, the presence of region-based political communities had been acknowledged by the Indian National Congress, the organization that provided leadership to the national movement for independence. From 1918 onwards, many of the Congress Provincial

Committees were organized along linguistic lines. There was, in other words, recognition of and an emerging consensus on the desirability of having a federal structure.

For the British a federal design was not an aid to democracy. It was intended neither to increase avenues for popular participation nor to give territorially located communities the right to self-government. For them it was simply a necessary aid in the process of colonization that could be used effectively for annexing territories. A federal arrangement with its dual government formed the basis of a number of treaties with separate princely kingdoms. Being part of federal India, as part of the British Empire, offered these rulers the best chance of retaining their kingdom while accepting the domination of the colonizing power. To the British, who had vast trading interests in this region, a federal arrangement enabled them to protect and pursue their interests by entering into special treaties and arrangements with these kingdoms (see Seervai [1967] 1991, pp. 9–18).

Subsequently, when the movement for independence gained momentum, a federal constitution was formally proposed as a way of accommodating popular sentiment. While power remained essentially in the hands of the Governor General, elected representatives of the local population could now be given some share in the process of governance in the provinces. With elected representation, however, came the system of separate electorates. The institutionalization of a separate electorate for the Muslim population was from the beginning viewed with suspicion: members of the Indian National Congress felt that it was a way of dividing the society permanently.

No matter how we assess the Act of 1935, the point that remains is that federalism had a checkered past. Under the British rule, it was a handy instrument for furthering the colonial interests in different ways at different times. Hence, in the popular imagination, it was neither associated with democracy nor seen as a way of strengthening the polity. In the present context when a federal arrangement is often suggested for erstwhile colonies, it is perhaps necessary to remember that, in the experience of many of these colonies, federalism was not unambiguously linked to democracy. For many, the gains of federalism are dubious and often suspect.

Despite the mixed bag of legacies, India became a federal polity and its Constitution elaborated the structure of central and regional government, identified separate sources of finance, and areas of jurisdiction. Although it appears that a country of India's size and diversity requires a federal framework, pragmatic considerations rather than concerns of democracy were critical in this decision. There were more than 500 princely states at the time when India gained independence. Most of these joined the Indian Union and in this situation it was politically expedient to treat some of these states as new provinces or to merge them with adjoining territories. The federal arrangement provided space for their incorporation and offered a way of holding different territories, with diverse histories, together as a single unit.

The Indian federation began with three types of states, which were identified in the Constitution as Part A, Part B and Part C types of states. Part A states, nine in number,[2] were mostly regions that were previously provinces of British India placed under the jurisdiction of the Governor General. Part B states, eight in number, were formerly ruled by princes, many of whom had treaties with the British through which they recognized the sovereignty of the latter. Part C states included both provinces of British India and princely states.[3] Each category of states had a distinct form of government. Part A states were under the authority of a governor and an elected state legislature. Part B states were governed by a *rajpramukh*, who was often a former prince, along with an elected legislature. Part C states were placed under a chief commissioner who was appointed, like other heads of executive, by the President of India. There were in addition union territories, and the state of Jammu and Kashmir had a special status.

These units of the federation were formed primarily for reasons of administrative continuity and convenience, in addition to political necessity. Cultural identities received little or no recognition in the formation of states. The framers of the Constitution were acutely aware of the existing diversity; they also recognized the need to treat different communities as equals, but after the partition of the country they were extremely reluctant to make cultural identities the basis of political identity at any level. Cultural communities were accommodated through special cultural rights, but not political rights. In the political arena, citizens were by and large treated as citizens and their particularities more or less ignored.[4] The cultural realm, like the liberal private space, recognized and accommodated differences through a web of constitutional provisions and special considerations.

At the time of independence, concerns of national unity and integrity dominated and provided the core reasons for keeping the political arena free of cultural identities. This liberal logic, however, faced a serious challenge in the post-independence period. The late 1950s saw a spate of agitations by linguistic communities. In Andhra Pradesh, Potti Sriramulu went on a fast-unto-death demanding that the Telegu speakers be identified as a separate community and the territories of the state be redrawn accordingly. The riots that followed his death compelled the first Prime Minister, Pandit Jawaharlal Nehru, to constitute a Commission to look into the reorganization of state boundaries. Subsequently, other communities, notably the Marathi, Tamil and Punjabi communities, raised similar demands. Eventually, the State Reorganization Commission redrew the boundaries of states in phases. In the first phase, territories primarily of Part A states were reconstituted so that linguistic communities that were living in contiguous areas could form one unit of the federal polity. In the second phase, new states were constituted in the Northeast and, through this process, several tribal communities received territorial and political autonomy. In each process of reorganization, cultural and community identity became the ordering principle of the federation in the post-independence period.

Today, a large number of states are organized on the basis of a shared cultural identity, although there are exceptions and, in the last few years, concerns of unequal development have also been factored into the forma-tion of new states. But by and large, states are organized around a shared language or a shared community (tribal) identity; and federal units provide an opportunity for these cultural communities to enjoy some degree of political autonomy in their region.

In a country where the census recognizes the presence of more than a hundred spoken languages, it is virtually impossible to ensure that all lin-guistic groups have their separate territory and constitute a separate state or federal unit. There are several groups, such as Sindhi and Urdu speakers, who are scattered across different states and many others who are waiting to be recognized as distinct cultural and political communities. Almost every-where the recognized cultural group is the numerically dominant group, but there are sizeable numbers of other linguistic groups that constitute a minority. Even in states like Andhra Pradesh, where more than 80 per cent of the population speak Telegu, there are sizeable numbers of Urdu-speaking Muslims in the Hyderabad region, and Tamil and Kannada speak-ers in the south and south-west parts of the state. These communities, despite being concentrated in a specific region, remain minorities in the state, though some of them are a majority some distance away in another region.

Thus, while linguistic identity is the primary ordering principle and has meant recognition for many cultural communities, applying this norm has not been easy. When there are enormous numbers of competing identities, which group gets recognition is itself a matter of political adjudication and contestation. It is not, in other words, a clear and simple process of recog-nizing existing nationalities.When the difficulties of identifying territories that are to be included in a given state are added, there exists a volatile situ-ation that is always liable to political manipulation and mobilization. The issue of linguistic boundaries is far from settled even today. There are regions, for instance Belgaum in Karnataka, which are still under dispute. The Maharashtra government wants this area to be merged with them and there are local communities that also wish the same. The application of the cultural principle has yielded many challenges of this kind and there are no ready formulae that can be invoked for negotiation in these cases. Today, it is not the fear of fragmentation but the difficulties in accommodating the range of existing diversities that question the use of a cultural criterion in designing political institutions. As far as non-religious identities are concerned, most people would accept that multiple identities can coexist within a democratic polity.

## TAPPING THE POTENTIAL: FEDERALISM AS A RESOURCE

Two elements need to be emphasized: (i) the organizing principle of the federation has changed in post-independence India. Today, cultural identity is the basis of identifying separate units of the federation. While there are a few exceptions and many other cases where cultural communities are still seeking recognition, most of the existing states are formed on grounds of a shared linguistic or cultural identity; (ii) the existence of a federal structure provides space for accommodating diverse cultural identities. This is not a role that the founding fathers had envisaged for the federal framework, nevertheless it came to perform this role fairly successfully. Retrospectively, one can say that, at different moments of the country's history, it has created opportunities that have, when used, made the difference between fragmentation of the polity and its unity.

Most political analysts in the 1950s and 1960s predicted the 'collapse of the Indian state' (Harrison, 1960, p. 339). They believed that, with its enormous religious, linguistic and ethnic diversity, India could not survive long as a single political entity. It would inevitably fragment into many different units. After all, independence had come with the partition of the country and the creation of a separate state of Pakistan as the homeland for the Muslim minority. Dissenting forms of nationalism continued to mark their presence even after independence. In the north-east, Nagas and Mizos not only asserted their cultural distinctiveness, they claimed that they were never a part of India. They pressed their demand for independence and secession from India. In other parts of India there were movements for the reorganization of linguistic identity. The nation-state was thus under pressure, if not threat, in at least a few areas.

In this situation of growing discontent, the presence of a federal structure played a critical role in accommodating these communities and keeping the country united and one. It allowed the possibility of recognizing several cultural communities by redrawing the boundaries of the states.

The fact that India was a federal polity allowed the state to respond to the voices clamouring for recognition. The reorganization of the boundaries of the state enabled these 'sub-nationalisms' to take a positive form, wherein they could enrich the existing diversity instead of posing a threat to the territorial integrity of the country. Linguistic communities wanted recognition within the state, they were never opposed to a united India and, today, culturally distinct units of the Indian federation coexist with reasonable ease within a united and integrated India. While non-recognition may have pushed them in the direction of dissenting nationalism, their accommodation has strengthened and not diminished national unity and integrity.

The fact that cultural identities can coexist with national identity is amply evident from the continued existence of India as a united and democratic polity. In fact recent surveys revalidate this assessment. A recent poll seeking to measure citizens' trust in their political institutions and sense of pride in their nationality shows that 61 per cent of Indians said they were 'very proud' and 28 per cent 'quite proud' of being an Indian. What is even more striking is that states which had for long periods of time challenged the authority of the centre and battled for greater autonomy registered even higher degrees of pride in being a citizen of India. In Tamil Nadu, 68 per cent of the people said they were 'very proud' to be an Indian; Punjab, another region that was torn by militancy and demands for autonomy and at times even secession, registered an even higher positive response. Here, cumulatively, 92 per cent said they were 'proud' or 'very proud': this was three points higher than the all-India average (Linz et al. 2007, pp. 80–83).[5]

What is equally significant is that a majority of the people in these regions identified themselves as Indian along with another cultural identity. India was part of their political imagination and they saw themselves as having multiple and complementary identities. There are of course variations across regions and communities that cannot be ignored. In areas or communities such as the Nagas, that are still aspiring to be separate nation-states, the sense of identity with India is lower. But what is noteworthy is that identities that have been successfully accommodated through the federal arrangement, and recognized as distinct cultural groups, have been able to nurture a sense of pride in their national identity.

Federalism has in all these situations been a valuable resource. This is not to say that accommodation of cultural identities is easy or readily accepted even when these resources exist. Most states, and the dominant hegemonies within them, try to maintain a status quo. India is no exception. Here too the state and the centre have often resisted demands for recognition. Concessions leading to the recognition of a group as a separate, self-governing community have been made as a last resort when other options had failed or yielded inadequate results. This is particularly true of cases where cultural identities used anti-national rhetoric and employed violent means to assert their demands.

The most striking case of successful accommodation within the federal framework is that of the Mizo community. The claims of an independent and separate Mizoram had gained momentum after a severe famine in the late 1950s. By the mid-1960s the Mizo National Volunteers, the armed wing of the movement, had seized the capital of Aizawal. They had, in their attempt to secede, taken control of other key towns in the Mizo Hills. In this context of growing militancy and violent insurgency the creation of the union territory of Mizoram paved the way for negotiation with the Mizo National Front. By 1976, a secret agreement was reached between the Mizo National Front and the Government of India (see Bhaumik, 1996). Even this limited form of recognition resulted in a significant change in the attitude of the militant underground organization. It agreed to accept Mizoram as an integral part of India. In 1986, when Mizoram became the 23rd state of the Indian Union, and the leader of the Mizo National Front, Laldenga, became its chief minister, the once underground movement came above ground and became a part of the democratic process.

The Mizos had lived with 30 years of insurgency and resistance against the Indian State. The Indian state had during this period countered the expressed militancy with a show of force, yet, today, an astounding 84 per cent of the people of the state favour democratic governance and the majority see themselves as Mizos and Indians. Only 32 per cent identify themselves as Mizos only (Linz et al., p. 38). The two identities of membership of the Indian state and the Mizo cultural community have thus come together. A sense of their cultural identity, distinctiveness and pride can be gauged from the following statement that can be seen on some of their officially maintained websites.

> Mizoram is our homeland
> It is not given or gotten as a gift
> It is not acquired by privilege
> Or potential contracts
> It is not bought with gold or held by the force
> No, it is made with us the sweat of the brow
> It is the historic creation
> And the collective enterprise of a people
> Bodily, spiritual and moral
> Over a span of generations.[6]

One must reiterate the fact that the Indian state followed the path of recognition very cautiously, and often hesitatingly. Like most nation-states, it tried to counter the demands of the Mizo community and its militant wing with force and repression. It used coercion in different forms; besides using armed personnel, it resorted to such measures as relocation of community members and sealing of the international borders with Bangladesh. These measures did not yield the desired results as the leaders of the movement went underground and continued their resistance.

Meeting the challenges of a secessionist movement, however, entailed a willingness to learn from mistakes and the readiness to experiment with new solutions. This process of learning took considerable time during which the Indian state was not always accommodating. But, retrospectively, what is striking is that recognition of the Mizos as a separate and distinct nation within India played an important role in winning the loyalty of the community members and fighting the growing militancy among the members of the community. The creation of Mizoram as a separate state within the federal structure helped enormously in transforming dissent that was otherwise challenging the territorial integrity of the nation-state.

Whether it is the case of accommodating multiple identities, as in the case of linguistic movements for recognition, or the right of culturally distinct groups to govern themselves, particularly in the north-east, or the desire for greater autonomy from the centre, as in Punjab and Kashmir, the challenges to the Indian state have required in one form or another the strengthening of federal institutional structure (see Manor, 1996). It is only when the state has acknowledged this and acted to reinforce and deepen the federal framework that India has been successful in holding the diverse communities together as one. Federalism has, in this sense, certainly been as asset.

## THE CREATION OF A PLURAL PUBLIC SPHERE

Besides offering a framework within which dissent could be transformed into cooperation, federalism has deepened democracy in one specific respect in India. It has helped to curb, or at least minimize, the dominance of the majority that controls the centre and provided space for different groups and communities to share power. While federalism may not have bridged the gap between the political elite and the people, it has resulted in the emergence of diverse and plural elites in the political arena. In the first three decades, political power was concentrated in the hands of one political party (the Congress) and even though the party had several regional units, the regional leadership was steadily marginalized. The creation of ethno-regional states within the framework of federalism, however, assisted the formation of a political community within the region. Shared concerns and needs eventually triggered discontent with a party that was dominated by a national elite. Even more significantly, it culminated in the emergence of regional parties; that is, political groups that have a strong presence in a specific region rather than the entire country.

Initially regional parties challenged the hegemony of the national elite in the regional states. In some of the most populous states in North India, particularly Uttar Pradesh and Bihar, socially marginalized groups, designated as the 'Other Backward Classes' (OBCs), emerged as a strong political presence. In Northern India, the proportion of OBC elected representatives went up, from 11 per cent in 1984 to 25 per cent in 1996. Simultaneously, the percentage of Upper Caste representatives fell from 45 per cent to 35 per cent. No matter which party came to power, the Chief Ministers were mostly from the OBC communities (Jaffrelot, 2002, pp. 150–60). The emergence of these classes as an important political power was not the result of federalism, but the presence of the federal framework allowed for the consolidation of political interests within the regions. Groups that could not come to power directly at the centre got an opportunity to consolidate their numbers, forge region-based coalition of communities, and assert their political power at the regional level. In the absence of a federal system this might have been more difficult to accomplish.

Some scholars have represented this shift in political power as the 'silent revolution' (ibid.); others have referred to it as the 'second democratic upsurge' (Yadav, 2006) that challenged the hegemony of the dominant social classes. Whether the emergence of a political elite has empowered these groups is a matter of some dispute, but it is undeniable that it has resulted in the diversification of the political elite.

Today, regional parties are a formidable force in Indian politics, representing the voice of diverse social communities and classes. Their emergence has meant a significant reduction in the influence of the national parties. This is starkly evident from the fact that, since the 1990s, no national party has been able to secure a simple majority in the central parliament. Coalition governments that have been formed rely heavily on regional parties for support. In a situation where no political party has a clear majority, these regional parties, as coalition partners, have been able to the influence the agenda of the government. Federalism has thus facilitated power sharing between classes and given a share to the social and political elite from different regions in the decision-making process of the country.

In addition to yielding a coalition of communities, and minimizing the influence of the majority or the dominant classes, the federal structure has also nurtured a plural public sphere. In 2001, there were publications in 101 languages and dialects. Apart from English and the 18 languages recognized at that time by the Eighth Schedule of the Constitution, there were publications in 82 other languages and dialects. Indeed it is the non-English media that is registering greater rates of growth. The Indian Readership

Survey of 2005 indicates a decline in the readership of the leading English daily, *The Times of India*, but a steady increase in the readership of other language media. This is significant because *The Times of India* is the only English newspaper that ranks among the top 20 dailies in terms of their circulation. A closer look at this list reveals that the readership of Hindi papers outranks the English papers and, other than one English paper and three publications in Hindi, it is publications in regional languages that enjoy wider readership.

The growth in the regional language press and media is an indicator of the plurality emerging in the public sphere. If political analysts in the late 1970s pointed to the domination of an urban-based, English-speaking elite in social and political life, today the public sphere is much more heterogeneous. Issues reflecting the problems specific to a particular region as well as points of view that arise from that location are finding a place in the public domain, and are helping to constitute new communities of citizens. Once again, federalism is not the immediate cause of this democratization. A large number of related factors have played a crucial role here: the increase in literacy rates and the creation of regional states with a distinct linguistic identity have both contributed to the revolution we are witnessing. But there is no denying the fact that this reorganization of state boundaries as well as recognition of linguistic identities was possible only within the federal framework. Thus, while the federal arrangement was not chosen with all these consequences in mind, its presence, along with other policies of recognition, have enhanced participation and helped to keep the country united.

## CROSSING THE LINE: FROM PARTICIPATION TO MAJORITARIANISM

Over the years the federal structure has been strengthened and so has the process of democratization. The merit of a federal system is that it provides space for territorially located communities to present their demands effectively and to influence decision making. When the territorial community is also a cultural community that has existed over a period of time with a distinct identity, federalism offers a way of transforming the nation-state into, what Kymlicka calls, 'a multi-nation state'. Federalism, in such a context, deepens democracy by giving national communities the opportunity to govern themselves within the framework of the existing state. It allows minority nations to survive and preserve their culture while simultaneously protecting the unity of the state.

In India, identified linguistic communities have benefited from the federal arrangement. As is evident from the previous section, federalism has given these communities space to grow, flourish and place their agendas in the public domain. But, in a developing society where there is competition for limited resources, it has also intensified the struggle between communities. Although the dominant linguistic community constitutes the numerical majority in every state, there are sizeable numbers of other linguistic communities that continue to live in the region. The federal arrangement that has helped in the consolidation of the majority linguistic identity has simultaneously transformed some communities into minorities. In some cases where the minority was previously economically or politically powerful, it unleashed a form of exclusionary majoritarianism that systematically attacked minorities. Perhaps the worst manifestation of this was seen in Assam, where more than five thousand people died in ethnic violence between 1980 and 1986.

In other regions where the process of consolidation of the new majority did not take a violent form, the 'sons of soil' sentiment manifested itself in other ways. Public jobs and prestigious administrative positions were linked to official language and this obviously tilted the balance in favour of the majority. Thus, while diversity has certainly been enriched, protecting the rights of minorities has posed serious concern. Linguistic communities that felt marginalized within the nation-state and for this reason demanded some degree of territorial and political autonomy have not been sensitive to the concerns of minorities within. Indeed, once they became majorities within the region, they have behaved more like a nation-state rather than a multi-nation state.

When we have communities who have lived as separate entities with their own distinct institutions for a long period of time, their accommodation through federal arrangements poses relatively fewer problems. In India, however, language yielded distinct communities but these communities had not always lived as separate nations. Language, religion and region constituted a web of complex relationships that were neither completely discrete nor entirely overlapping. In these circumstances, the drawing of boundaries along the lines of language alone served a political purpose. It allowed these emerging communities either to consolidate or to challenge existing relations of power. Nation building by linguistic communities did not pose a threat to the sovereignty and unity of the state, but it affected the lives of other communities significantly. Sharing of power and rotation of elites is an important part of democracy, but the conversion of some groups into permanent minorities is a matter of concern, and it calls for some protective measures.

The governments at the centre have been aware of this responsibility. They have tried to mitigate the effects of this process of minority creation by mandating due consideration for the legitimate claims of these communities. State governments are required to publish official notifications in the language of the minority community in areas where these groups are concentrated.

Likewise, in schools where approximately a third of the children are from a minority linguistic community, education must also be provided in the mother tongue of the latter. In most cases these policy recommendations have remained unheeded; most states claim that they do not have the resources to provide education in different languages. As a result, minorities are almost always expected to assimilate. Even states like Manipur in the north-east that were previously more accommodating of their internal diversity are now witnessing this problem.

These difficulties not withstanding, the effects of region-based majoritarianism has been eased, to some extent, by the constitutional provisions for minorities, particularly Articles 29 and 30 of the Constitution. Article 29(1) gives citizens having a distinct language, script or culture the right to 'conserve the same'; and Article 30 provides for 'all minorities, whether based on religion or language . . . the right to establish and administer educational institutions of their choice'. The Supreme Court of India has interpreted these provisions to imply that minorities may set up educational institutions that are devoted to teaching their language as well as other subjects in that language. In the case of education where the context is the region, it has identified communities that are numerically smaller in the region as minorities. Thus the Arya Samaj sect of the Hindu community is identified as a minority in the state of Punjab and the Telegu-speaking community in Tamil Nadu is also identified as a minority, even though they constitute a majority in the state of Andhra Pradesh.

In other words, communities that are a majority in one part of India have been identified as a minority in another and, as and when they set up their educational institutions, they can use their own language as the medium of instruction. Further, in situations where these institutions receive financial support from the government, they must leave 50 per cent of the seats open to members of other communities. As a result, even though the language of the majority enjoys dominance and state-run educational institutions expect minorities to assimilate, it is minority educational institutions that provide different minority communities as well as members of the majority with effective choice. Their presence cushions the effects of majoritarianism prevalent in the region. It is therefore not surprising to see that the number of minority educational institutions has over the years steadily increased, in the field of both primary and higher education.

## THE TASKS AHEAD

Advocates of multiculturalism have for some time now emphasized the need to acknowledge and accommodate different nations living within a country. In lieu of building a nation-state around a single, homogenizing national culture, they have stressed the desirability of recognizing differences and nurturing a multi-nation state. This is without doubt an important task, but it needs to be further supplemented. Positive recognition of diversity at the national level needs to be supplemented by a similar acknowledgment of diversity at the regional level. We need to create multinational democracy at all levels, and this is not easy.

India is by most measures a multi-nation democracy and the federal system has enabled these different nations to govern themselves. Yet, even though this transition was made in the 1960s, we find that communities engaged in nation building at the regional level do not show the concern they have themselves received as minorities to existing minorities within the region. Besides, federalism offers a way of accepting diversity within the polity, but we need still to devise structures and policies by which diversity may be respected within each region.

Supplementary institutional arrangements are also required in another sphere. Federalism can only be a way of recognizing communities that are living together in one region. In situations where minorities have been living together on the same territory for a long period of time, the conventional federal institutional structure is by no means adequate. We need to look for other ways of accommodating minorities and maintaining a balance between the existing communities within the region. In India, where several minorities within a region are located in one part, it has at times created sub-regional federations. This is one way in which the claims of internal minorities have been accommodated without dividing the country into small and unviable units. In most cases, such arrangements have only had a limited degree of success. While they have helped to restrict ethnic conflict for short periods of time by giving power to the marginalized minority within the region, the government in the region has not always been supportive of such arrangements. More innovations are therefore needed within the federal framework for protecting the rights of internal minorities. In addition, we need to search for non-territorial modes of accommodating minorities and design institutions that do not simply visualize individuals as members of specific communities. There must be space for the participations of persons as individuals, as members of the region and as members of specific groups.

While these are areas that call for innovations, the federal form of organization has also presented new problems and challenges and these also need to be considered carefully. With a dual system of government, the federal arrangement is always more open to conflicts internally: conflicts between states, and conflicts between centre and one or more states. Taking cognizance of this the Constitution of India provides, under Article 263,

means for setting up Interstate Councils. A number of councils have been
set up in the post-independence period for enhancing coordination in planning and policy, and discussing matters of common interest. Such arrangements, however, have not been uniformly successful. In fact, on most crucial
issues there have been deadlocks and differences more often than cooperation, a case in point being the use of river water. Although special
tribunals have been set up by the central government to take up specific
conflicts between states involving the use of river water, many of them
remain a source of continuing tension between neighbouring states.

In part this problem arises from a deeper contradiction implicit within
the federal structure: it creates a sense of political community within the
region. The government of each federal unit, with an eye on competitive
politics, tends to pursue policies that work to the advantage of the people
in that region rather than the cumulative good of the larger whole. This
makes emerging areas of conflict between states fairly intractable, and often
subject to political manipulation by political parties. How then can we
create institutions that are forums of effective deliberation and cooperation? How do we ensure that political posturing, reflecting political party
positions, makes way for decisions that take note of the welfare of citizens
as a whole?

The dilemma is that federal political arrangements are more juridical in
nature. They require, and are more dependent upon, external intervention
and adjudication by a court of law. Thus, even as we welcome the increase
in participation that comes with federalism, as a form of government federalism is more combative by nature. A second, and deeper, problem relates
to the determination and pursuit of the common interest and well-being of
the citizens as a whole. In most federations, basic concerns of individuals,
such as law and order, education and health, are matters that are entrusted
to the regional state. As a consequence, we often confront gross inequalities
between regions. In some regions, productivity is high, literacy rates are up
and quality of life is better, while in others people are forced to migrate in
search of work and basic facilities. Such regional imbalances, leading to
inequality of opportunities, are a commonly observed phenomenon in
India. What are the responsibilities of the centre and other states to the
people living in a region which, for reasons of internal administration or
government, is lagging behind? What are the responsibilities of the centre
to the citizens of the state, irrespective of where they live, when their basic
rights are violated? These are areas of ambiguity and concern within federalism that need to be considered carefully.

Most often there is reluctance to authorize the intervention of
the federal government and there are good reasons for this. In India the
centre has a long history of intervening and at times even dismissing

the government in office on account of what is designated as a breakdown of the law and order machinery. Since the right to intervene can be, and often was, used for securing political advantage by the government in power at the centre, it is always suspect. At the same time, when the regional state is implicated in targeting particular communities and is unable to protect the lives of some of its members, should we not empower the centre to intervene to protect the rights of the vulnerable minorities? Should intervention by the federal government wait for a formal request for assistance to come from the state?

These are the dilemmas that present themselves in a federal form of government. They need, however, to be addressed within a framework that complements rather than supplants federalism. Federalism may not always be a tool of democratization and countries may not become federal as they democratize, nevertheless, federalism is a resource: it offers opportunities that can, when used, nurture democracy and the unity of the polity.

## NOTES

1. Jean Blondel described federalism as an institutional arrangement that 'aims at achieving optimum de-centralization' (1969, p. 289).
2. Part A states were Assam, West Bengal, Bihar, Bombay, Madhya Pradesh, Madras, Orissa, Punjab, Uttar Pradesh.
3. States that comprised Part C were Delhi, Kutch, Himachal Pradesh, Bilaspur, Coorg, Bhopal, Manipur, Ajmer, Tripura.
4. An exception was made only in the case of Scheduled Tribes living in identified hill regions, particularly of the North East. As they already enjoyed special protection, their desire for segregated or separate existence was recognized. But an attempt was made to include them in the political process by reserving seats for Scheduled Tribes in all legislative bodies, the idea being that the political arena must aspire to be universal. If some communities wilfully stayed away, an effort was to be made to include them so that the universalizing capacity of the political was not undermined.
5. These values are based on the State of Democracy in South Asia Study (2005) conducted by the Centre for the Study of Developing Societies, Delhi. Linz et al. show that these finding conform by and large with the findings of the World Values Survey.
6. See http://Mizoram.nic.in; site developed and maintained by National Informatics Centre, Mizoram State Unit based on the content provided by the State Government, Ministry of Communication and Information Technology.

## REFERENCES

Bhaumik, Subir (1996), *Insurgent Crossfire*, London, Delhi: Lancer Publications.
Blondel, Jean (1969), *Comparative Government*, London: Weidenfeld & Nicolson.
*Constituent Assembly Debates* (CAD) (1946–50), Official Reports, 12 vols, Delhi.
Dua, B.D and M.P. Singh (eds) (2003), *Indian Federalism in the New Millennium*, Delhi: Manohar.

Harrison, Selig S. (1960), *India: The Most Dangerous Decades*, London: Oxford University Press.

Iqbal, Narain and Arvind K. Sharma (1969), 'The emerging issues and ideas of Indian federalism – a post-fourth general election review', in S.C. Keshyap (ed.), *Union–State Relations in India*, New Delhi: Institute of Constitutional and Parliamentary Studies.

Jaffrelot, Christophe (2002), *India's Silent Revolution*, Delhi: Permanent Black.

Jain, S.N., S.C. Keshyap and M. Srinivasan (eds) (1972), *The Union and the State*, Delhi: National.

Jennings, Ivor (1953), *Some Characteristics of the Indian Constitution*, London: Oxford University Press.

Khan, Arshi (1997), 'The importance of Article 356 in centre–state relations in India; a critical review of its use and misuse', in Rasheeduddin Khan (ed.), *Rethinking Indian Federalism*, Simla: Indian Institute of Advanced Study.

Khan, Rasheeduddin (1992), *Federal India: A Design for Change*, New Delhi: Vikas Publishing House.

Linz, Juan J., Alfred Stepan and Yogendra Yadav (2007), ' "Nation state" or "state nation"? India in comparative perspective', in Shankar Bajpai (ed.), *Democracies and Diversity: India and the American Experience*, Delhi and Oxford: Oxford University Press.

Maheshwari, B.L. (ed.) (1973), *Centre–State Relations in the 70s*, Calcutta: Minerva Associates for the Administrative Staff College of India.

Manor, James (1996), 'Ethnicity and politics in India', *International Affairs*, **72**(1), 459–75.

Munshi, K.M. (1967), *The President under the Indian Constitution*, Bombay: Bhartiya Vidya Bhawan.

Nakade, Shiv Raj (1969), 'Article 356 of the Constitution', in S.C. Keshyap (ed.), *Union–State Relations in India*, New Delhi: Institute of Constitutional and Parliamentary Studies.

Seervai, H.M. ([1967] 1991), *Constitutional Law of India*, 4th edn, vol. I, Bombay and London: N.M. Tripathi Private Ltd & Sweet and Maxwell Ltd.

Wheare, K.C. (1963), *Federal Government*, London: Oxford University Press.

Yadav, Yogendra (2006), 'Understanding the second democratic upsurge: trends of Bahujan participation in electoral politics in the 1990s', in Zoya Hasan, R. Bhargava, B. Arora and F. Frankel (eds), *Transforming India: Social and Political Dynamics of Democracy*, Delhi: Oxford University Press.

# 5. Democracy and federalism in Pakistan

## Katharine Adeney

Federal forms of government are diverse. There is no 'ideal type' of federation. We should therefore not analyse federations according to whether they conform to a standard set of institutions, as classical institutional scholars of federalism did (see Wheare, 1963, p. 33). Federations differ according to their democratic status, whether they are multinational or territorial, whether they recognize diversity, and, if they recognize diversity, how they do so. There may also be alternative mechanisms that operate within a federal system that are vital to the accommodation of diversity but that we would not characterize as being part of the federal form.

An examination of the history, formation and operation of federalism in Pakistan requires an answer to these questions. Federalism has been a contested form of government, especially in divided societies. Scholars and statesmen have been concerned that conceding federal autonomy to territorially concentrated groups will be an encouragement to secession (Nordlinger, 1972, p. 32). Recent debates surrounding the appropriate constitutional form in Afghanistan and Iraq have seen a resurgence of these concerns. These fears were at the forefront of elites' minds in the decolonizing countries in Asia.

Pakistan was formed from the partition of India into the states of India and Pakistan by the British Raj in 1947. Pakistan was cast as the seceding state, dependent on India's 'generosity' for its financial and administrative resources. It was therefore in a precarious position and the conflict over Kashmir soon after partition increased the power of the army (Jalal, 1995, ch. 2). Pakistan shared a colonial inheritance with India, but, as authors such as Talbot have illustrated, the power structures of north-west India had operated in a more authoritarian fashion than did those in Bengal or the rest of India (Talbot, 2005, pp. 54–65). Although to talk of democratic development in the other parts of India is problematic, these authoritarian legacies have been important and were compounded by post-partition insecurity. This insecurity increased the power of undemocratic institutions which, because they were dominated by particular ethnic groups, led to difficulties in creating inclusive and, ultimately, democratic federal structures.

## FEDERAL FORMATION IN INDEPENDENT PAKISTAN

Federalism in South Asia had a long history. Devices of territorial autonomy were used as means of managing diversity and as methods of effective government in the time of the Mughals (1526–1857). The British also understood the importance of federal institutions of government as a mechanism of divide and rule, as well as a necessary administrative tool. The British Raj operated through de facto federal forms in India from at least 1919 and gradually extended the powers and responsibilities of the provinces that would become part of India and Pakistan. Constitutional proposals made by both the Congress Party (speaking ostensibly on behalf of all Indians but, in reality, mostly Hindus) and the Muslim League (speaking ostensibly on behalf of all Muslims, but in reality for Muslims in Hindu majority provinces) operated within this federal framework. Debates over community rights and power sharing at the centre were intimately connected into the debates over federalism. The Muslim League was aware that territorial autonomy provided little protection for minority rights in the state as a whole (Adeney, 2002, pp. 8–33).

After independence, Pakistan had to build its state institutions from scratch in addition to writing a new constitution. Unlike India, which inherited the institutions and political identity of the British Raj, Pakistan was cast as the seceding state and had two wings, separated by 1000 miles of (increasingly hostile) Indian territory. Pakistan was composed of the Muslim majority provinces of Sindh and the North West Frontier Province (NWFP), the Muslim majority areas of the Punjab and Bengal, as well as princely states such as Bahawalpur, Khairpur, Kalat and the Baluchi States Union, and other territories which were not recognized as provinces under British rule, and were notionally governed directly from the centre; the Federally Administered Tribal Areas (FATA). Almost all the princely states acceded to Pakistan after independence. Kalat was the exception – attempting to remain independent and ultimately coerced into joining Pakistan in early 1948. It should be noted that India pursued similar policies with the princely states of Hyderabad and Junagah. The situation of Kashmir, also a princely state, was more complicated. It was not completely surrounded by either India or Pakistan, but bordered both. It was a Muslim majority state, but its ruler, the Maharaja, was Hindu. He entertained notions of becoming independent. This was not acceptable to either India or Pakistan.

The name of Pakistan, coined by Cambridge student Ramat Ali in 1933, incorporates **P**unjab, **A**fgahni (NWFP), **K**ashmir, **I**rani (Baluchistan) and **S**indh ('tan' means land). Coincidentally, it also translates as 'land of the pure'. Significantly, the acronym does not include Bengal. In 1948, Pashtun tribesmen, who most observers accept were sponsored by the Pakistan government, invaded Kashmir. Panicked, the Maharaja requested Indian assistance, which was granted on the condition that Kashmir accede to India. This accession duly took place (with a condition that a plebiscite be held to determine the wishes of the people of Kashmir), leading to the first war between India and Pakistan in 1948. This war resulted in the division of Kashmir along the Line of Control, which has been redrawn by subsequent conflicts between the two countries. The plebiscite was never organized, India refusing to do so while part of Kashmir remained 'occupied' by Pakistan. Despite Article 370 of the Indian Constitution guaranteeing Kashmir special status, the parts of Kashmir held by India were integrated into India through constitutional and legal amendments in the 1950s (Bose, 1997, p. 33). Notwithstanding current peace moves, the status of Kashmir remains disputed.

The Pakistani-controlled part of Kashmir is divided into two territories, the Northern Areas and *Azad* ('free') Kashmir. Neither has been integrated into the governing structures of the Pakistani state. The Northern Areas, including Gilgit and Baltistan, are ruled directly from Islamabad, and do not possess any local representation of their own, a source of growing local grievance. *Azad* Kashmir in contrast, possesses its own constitution, parliament, Prime Minister and President. But it is subordinate to the Pakistan Government; '[d]espite the emergence of institutions and indeed the Legislative Assembly in Azad Kashmir [which did not come into being until 1970], the powers of Azad Kashmir functionaries are always subject to the likes and dislikes of the government in Islamabad' (Ellis and Khan, 1999, p. 276).

Politically it is independent from Pakistan; its elections are not scheduled at the same time as the other provinces, the most recent ones having occurred in July 2006. Nominally, therefore, *Azad* Kashmir is autonomous from Pakistan, but in practice, elections are not free and fair. This is firstly because candidates have to swear allegiance to Pakistan, an impossibility for movements such as the Jammu and Kashmir Liberation Front that seeks the independence of Kashmir (from both India and Pakistan). In total, 50 parties were barred from competing in the July 2006 elections as a result of this clause. Secondly, even within these parameters, election rigging by Islamabad is often alleged and, in the July 2006 elections, the allegations were even more widespread than usual (BBC, 2006).

These asymmetrical federal arrangements, which ostensibly provide autonomy for a contested region with disputed status, are therefore, in reality, a sham. The region does not possess a separate status from the rest of the federation because of its cultural attributes, only because to integrate it would be to legitimize the division of Kashmir between India and Pakistan. The Pakistani Constitution (Article 257) provides that '[w]hen the people of the State of Jammu and Kashmir decide to accede to Pakistan, the relationship between Pakistan and the State shall be determined in accordance with the wishes of the people of that State'. Other than to acknowledge that *Azad* Kashmir has been economically and politically underdeveloped (see Ballard, 1991, pp. 513–17; Ellis and Khan, 1999) the rest of this chapter will concentrate on the provinces that are integrated into the political and constitutional structure of Pakistan.

It is vitally important to understand the demographics of Pakistan to facilitate understanding of the debates over the structures of federalism. At independence, Bengalis comprised 54 per cent of the population. Punjabis comprised 28 per cent, Pashtuns 6 per cent, Sindhis 5 per cent, Urdu speakers 3 per cent and Baluchis 1 per cent. The majority of the population (54 per cent), Bengalis, were concentrated within one single province, the eastern wing of Pakistan. The western wing not only contained a minority of the population, but it was divided into several different provinces. The Bengali dominance thus posed a heightened 'threat' to the elites of the western wing, especially those elites who were not elected. As will be discussed in further detail below, these elites belonged to particular ethnic communities rather than others.

After partition, Pakistan worked under the British Government of India Act 1935 (re-titled the Indian Independence Act of 1947), which had established a federal constitution, even though the federal provisions of that Act had not come into being under the Raj because of the refusal of the princely states to participate. Pakistan did not finalize its own Constitution until 1956, *nine* years after independence. Progress on writing the constitution had started in earnest in 1949 with the publication of Liaquat Ali Khan's Objectives Resolution, setting out the parameters within which the state would operate. In 1951, the Basic Principles Committee Report set out a draft of a constitution based on the principles of equal representation in the upper house, but left the composition of the lower house unclear. This was unacceptable to the Bengalis, who comprised a majority of the population. Bengali demands that they have a majority in both houses of parliament were equally unacceptable to the provinces of the western wing.

Various proposals, all of which involved a federal structure, shuttled back and forward (see Samad, 1995a) before the (Prime Minister) Mohammad Ali Bogra Formula of 1953 was accepted. This formula 'solved' the problem of

Bengali over-representation by creating equality through a bicameral legislature: East Bengal had a majority of seats in the lower chamber, but the provinces of the western wing had a majority of seats in the upper chamber. When added together, the eastern and western wings had an equal number of seats. This was satisfactory to both wings because of the provision that

> [i]n the case of difference of opinion between the two Houses in respect of any measure, the following step will be taken: a Joint Session of the two Houses will be called; the measure may then be passed by a majority vote, provided the majority includes 30 per cent of the members present and voting from each zone. (Bogra, 1953, pp. 5–6)

This provision codified a form of what Arend Lijphart would come to define as a mutual veto (Lijphart, 1977). The Bogra Formula was translated into the constitution that was passed by the Constituent Assembly in 1954, but this constitution did not come into force. The protracted constitution formation process had provided the conditions for the army and bureaucracy to increase their influence, already strong because of the conflict over Kashmir. Both the army and the bureaucracy were dominated by Punjabis and Mohajirs. These communities were unwilling to permit a constitution to be adopted that would give Bengalis control of the state and undermine their own power. Therefore, the Constituent Assembly that had adopted the Bogra Formula as the basis for a constitution was immediately dismissed by Governor General Ghulam Mohammad. The constitution had also sought to curb the power of the Governor General. The Constituent Assembly was eventually reconvened after extensive judicial wrangling (see Samad, 1995a, p. 172), but a new political landscape had emerged. The Muslim League was reduced from 60 seats out of 80 to only 33; its representatives replaced by more recently elected non-Muslim League Bengalis. The Assembly now comprised representatives elected by the Provincial Assemblies, elected between 1951 and 1954, rather than ones elected in 1946. A new constitution was proposed, one that 'solved' the problem of Bengali demographic dominance. It created parity between the two wings by merging the provinces of the western wing. Renamed West Pakistan and East Pakistan, each wing had 150 seats in the National Assembly, a unicameral legislature.[1] This created a 'dangerous' bipolar federation; dangerous because federations with a smaller number of units are much more likely to fail. (See Adeney, 2007, p. 172.) At the same time, Bengali was recognized as a joint official language with Urdu,[2] thus assuaging some concerns about the new constitutional arrangement and loss of demographic dominance. Machinations involving the dismissal of Chief Ministers and false promises about the location of the capital of West Pakistan (the Chief Minister of NWFP was promised that the capital of the merged state would be located in Peshawar, in NWFP. In the event it was located in Lahore, in Punjab) ensured that the proposal passed the Provincial Assemblies of NWFP, Punjab and Sindh. The Constitution came into force in 1956. It was a centralized federation, and possessed similar emergency provisions to those of India.

> If . . . a grave emergency exists in which the security or economic life of Pakistan, or any part thereof, is threatened by war or external aggression, or by internal disturbance beyond the power of a Provincial Government to control, [the President] may issue a Proclamation of Emergency. (Pakistan, Government of, 1956, 191.1)

> During such an emergency '[p]arliament shall have power to make laws for a province [and give] . . . direction to a Province as to the manner in which the executive authority of the Province is to be exercised'. (Pakistan, Government of, 1956, 191.2)

But before national elections could be held under this constitution, indeed, some would argue, to *prevent* national elections being held, Iskander Mirza, President of Pakistan, and Ayub Khan, the Commander in Chief of the army, seized power in 1958. Talbot notes that, 'Ayub's coup of 1958 had indeed been prompted precisely by the desire to head off elections which would deliver a populist challenge to the dominant elites; domestic and foreign policy interests' (Talbot, 2005, p. 193). Mirza was soon deposed by Ayub Khan, who ruled until 1969, when street protests brought about by an economic crisis, and his loss of authority caused by the defeat of Pakistan in 1965 by India, forced him to resign. Yahya Khan took over, restored all the provinces in the western wing and called the first national elections in Pakistan's history, on the basis of one person one vote. These were held in 1970, in which the success of the Awami League started a process culminating in the secession of Bangladesh.

## MULTINATIONAL VERSUS TERRITORIAL FEDERALISM?

The model of federalism that Pakistan adopted in 1956 was not a multi-national one. A multinational federation 'creat[es] a federal or quasi-federal subunit in which the minority group forms a local majority, and so can exercise meaningful forms of self-government' (Kymlicka, 2005, pp. 23–4; see also McGarry and O'Leary, 2005, pp. 263–96). Pakistan cannot be classified as a multinational federation because, in contrast to India, the boundaries of the units of the federation were not revised to accommodate territorially concentrated linguistic communities. During the movement to secure Muslim autonomy in a united India, linguistic or regional identities were viewed by the Muslim League as detracting from Islamic unity. Although Jinnah had not opposed the linguistic reorganization of the Hindu areas in united India, in 1924 he had opposed any 'territorial redistribution that might . . . affect the Muslim majority of population in the Punjab, Bengal and N.W.F. Province' (Pirzada, 1969, p. 578).

After independence, the concerns of the Muslim League leadership in Pakistan remained the same. The threat from India and the perceived precarious existence of the newly created state contributed to an atmosphere of insecurity.

The new state also refused to recognize 'regional' languages. Instead, it adopted Urdu as the national language. The adoption of Urdu can be understood in two ways. Firstly, it was an attempt to unify the population around a 'neutral' language. Although it was spoken as a mother tongue by only 3.24 per cent of the population, Urdu was ostensibly a neutral language, similar to the adoption of Bahasa Indonesian rather than Javanese in Indonesia. Secondly, it had the distinction of being the language of the Islamic resistance to Hindu Raj in the United Provinces.[3] In addition to the national language policy, the 1956 Constitution did not permit provinces to adopt a provincial language (although Article 19 provided that '[a]ny section of citizens having a distinct language, script or culture shall have the right to preserve the same') (Pakistan, Government of 1956, p. 19). This language policy was in sharp contrast to the Indian multicultural one (Adeney, 2007, ch. 5). Nevertheless, Pakistan after 1956 cannot be classified as a territorial federation according to Kymlicka's definition: 'the protection of individual rights, the neutrality of the state with regard to different ethnic groups [and] the absence of an internal boundary for ethnic groups' (He, 2007, pp. 1–57). It is true that it did not seek to restructure the boundaries of its units to recognize the territorial concentration of diversity, rather pursuing the opposite option, merging all the units of its western wing into one. This created a province dominated by Punjabis, as shown in Table 5.1, but with substantial minorities, all of which were territorially concentrated. But it cannot be said that there was an absence of an internal boundary for all ethnic groups as the eastern wing was extremely homogeneous, as Table 5.1 demonstrates. The eastern wing was the eastern half of the province of Bengal that had been partitioned by the British when they left the subcontinent in 1947. It had been a linguistically homogeneous province before partition, but had been divided along lines of religion. Partition made this division permanent. Significantly, the reorganization of the western wing into one unit increased the political importance of this homogeneity, especially as 56 per cent of the population lived within East Pakistan.

*Table 5.1   The percentage of speakers of different languages within the wings of Pakistan after the creation of the One Unit Plan*

|  | Population | Bengali | Punjabi | Pashtu | Sindhi | Urdu | Baluchi | Other | Total |
|---|---|---|---|---|---|---|---|---|---|
| West Pakistan | 44% | 0.02 | 61.86 | 14.84 | 11.85 | 6.50 | 2.80 | 2.13 | 100% |
| East Pakistan | 56% | 98.16 | 0.02 | 0.00 | 0.01 | 0.64 | 0.00 | 1.17 | 100% |

*Source:* Pakistan, Government of (1951), Census of Pakistan.

*Table 5.2   The percentage of speakers of different languages within the provinces of Pakistan in 1998[4]*

|  | Population | Urdu | Punjabi | Sindhi | Pashtu | Baluchi | Saraiki | Others |
|---|---|---|---|---|---|---|---|---|
| N W F P | 13.4% | 0.78 | 0.97 | 0.04 | 73.9 | 0.01 | 3.86 | 20.43 |
| Punjab | 55.6% | 4.51 | 75.23 | 0.13 | 1.16 | 0.66 | 17.36 | 0.95 |
| Sindh | 23% | 21.05 | 6.99 | 59.73 | 4.19 | 2.11 | 1 | 4.93 |
| Baluchistan | 5% | 0.97 | 2.52 | 5.58 | 29.64 | 54.76 | 2.42 | 4.11 |
| All Pakistan |  | 7.57 | 44.15 | 14.1 | 15.42 | 3.57 | 10.53 | 4.66 |

*Note:* Population figures do not round to 100 per cent because they exclude FATA and the capital territory.

*Source:* Population Census Organization, Government of Pakistan.

In addition, the Pakistani state did not adopt 'neutrality . . . with regard to different ethnic groups'. Neither the national language law nor the creation of the One Unit Plan was ethnically neutral. The adoption of Urdu as the sole national language privileged the Mohajir community, of which it was the mother tongue. The term 'Mohajir' refers to refugees from India who migrated from India after partition to urban Sindh, notably the cities of Karachi (the capital of Pakistan until 1960) and Hyderabad.[5] Most of these people had migrated from India, from the United Provinces (now Uttar Pradesh) and Bihar. In general they were the elite (whom Hamza Alavi has called the Salariat (Alavi, 1990, pp. 19–72) who had pushed for the formation of the Muslim League to protect their interests against Hindu encroachment in a united India, the ultimate culmination of which was the formation of Pakistan.[6] After partition this elite sought to protect its position within Pakistan, but lacked the power base to do so. The adoption of Urdu as the language of government therefore privileged the job opportunities of this community above all others. Additionally, the adoption of Urdu as the sole 'national' language was extremely problematic for the majority of the population who spoke another language, specifically the Bengalis. Some 54 per cent of the population of Pakistan spoke Bengali as their mother tongue, but it was not until 1955, eight years after independence, that Bengali was accepted as a joint official language alongside Urdu.

The adoption of Urdu had a final ethnic dimension. As will be elaborated on below, the institutions of state in which power came to reside – the army and the bureaucracy – were dominated (and still are) by Pashtuns (primarily resident in NWFP), Punjabis and Mohajirs. Urdu had been the language of the lower levels of government in NWFP, 'British' Baluchistan and Punjab before independence. This contrasts with Sindh and Bengal, which operated in Sindhi and Bengali, respectively. Vast differences of status exist between languages: Urdu, Sindhi and Bengali were strong languages of literature and literacy, while Punjabi on the Pakistan side of the border was primarily a spoken language. (See Adeney, 2007, pp. 102–3.) Therefore, although some of the Punjabi elite claimed they were willing to sacrifice recognition of their language in the interests of national unity, in reality (Pakistani) Punjabi would not have been a practical choice as a written language of government.

Since 1971, Pakistan ostensibly looks more like a multinational federation. The secession of Bangladesh in 1971, achieved with Indian military assistance (although the cause of the secessionist movement was internal to Pakistan), radically altered the demographics and geography of Pakistan. Even before the secession of Bangladesh, Yahya Khan in 1970 abolished the One Unit Plan, but after the secession Pakistan became a territorially contiguous state with four provinces. However, although the three provinces (Punjab, Sindh and NWFP) were reconstituted (incorporating princely states within their pre-1955 borders) and Baluchistan became a province for the first time, two provinces in particular were not homogeneous. As Table 5.2 demonstrates, all provinces have significant linguistic minorities; Punjab is the most homogeneous, with 75 per cent of Punjabi speakers.[7] Even NWFP has a significant proportion of non-Pashtu speakers, namely Hindko speakers in the north and east of the province. Sindh and Baluchistan are most heterogeneous. In Sindh, this was caused by the migration of the Mohajirs into the urban areas of the province, discussed earlier. Mohajirs extended their identity as a distinct community and dominate the commercial capital of Pakistan, the city of Karachi, which is the capital of Sindh. But there are also a large number of Punjabi and Pashtu speakers who have migrated into the province, predominantly into Karachi. This has caused serious conflict.[8] The situation of Baluchistan is more complicated. At independence, what is now Baluchistan was split between 'British' Baluchistan with a sizeable Pashtu-speaking community (41 per cent) and the Baluchi States Union, which was predominantly Baluchi and Brahvi speaking. After the One Unit Plan was dissolved in 1970, the two areas became the province of Baluchistan. The demographic mix was further muddled after the 1979 invasion of Afghanistan led to the influx of predominantly Pashtu-speaking refugees, many of whom settled in refugee camps in Baluchistan. This mix has come about to the chagrin of both Baluchis and Pashtu speakers, and a movement exists to join the Pashtu-speaking areas to the NWFP, or, failing that, to create a separate province of the Pashtu-speakers of Baluchistan. The lack of homogeneity in these provinces has caused tensions between communities, but also between the centre and the province.

The Constitution of 1973, adopted after consultation between the political parties elected in the first national elections in 1970, retained a federal system, but amended the constitution to create a bicameral legislature. In the upper chamber, the four units of the federation were equally represented – a demos-constraining element in Stepan's language (Stepan, 1999, pp. 19–34). But the lower and more powerful chamber, the National Assembly, was elected on the basis of population, with one province, the Punjab, possessing the majority of seats. The 1973 constitution also marked a significant shift in language policy. Urdu became the sole national language, but provincial languages were now permitted. Significantly, Sindh was the only province that changed its provincial language from Urdu (to Sindhi).[9] The other provinces retained Urdu. On one level this was a sign of the 'successful' integrationist policy adopted by the centre at Partition: a link language had been created. But the reason for Urdu's retention as a provincial language in the other provinces must also be attributed to the (relatively) sizeable number of linguistic minorities in both NWFP and Baluchistan. Adoption of Baluchi in Baluchistan or Pashtu in NWFP would have caused conflict with their linguistic minorities (the majority of the 'others' in the table in NWFP are Hindko speakers). In addition, Punjab was used to operating in Urdu before independence and, as a primarily oral language (on the Pakistan side of the border), Punjabi was not a realistic candidate for a provincial language.

## ILLIBERAL FEDERALISM

In common with other chapters of this volume, this chapter considers the concept of illiberal federalism, a concept that has definite relevance to Pakistan. Illiberal federalism is defined in the introductory chapter as occurring where federalism coexists with, and even supports, the authoritarian structure. Federations can be both democratic and non-democratic. In 2006, there is only one non-democratic federation, the United Arab Emirates, but until the end of the cold war the USSR and Yugoslavia were both non-democratic federations. Pakistan today is nominally democratic, but the democratic mandate of the Presidential referendum of 2002 was suspect, and the 2002 National and Provincial Assembly elections were also flawed (although not to the same degree) (European Union, 2002).

The relationship between federalism and democracy cannot be understood without investigating different types of democracy. Democracy can be minimally understood as requiring elections (Huntington, 1991) or, maximally, requiring human social and economic equality (Sen, 1999, pp. 3–17). Democracy is understood below as a continuous rather than a dichotomous variable. At the heart of democracy is the value of equality – every vote counts for the same amount. This, however, says nothing about the *type* of democracy. Democracies can be either majoritarian or consociational (Lijphart, 1977). Democracy in its most basic form does not guarantee minority rights, and even liberal democracy with its respect for individual rights (Parekh, 1992, pp. 160–75) may not provide opportunities for minority groups to influence political action.

Is this a problem? On one level it is not: the people should rule, therefore the majority of a political community have the final say. But this becomes more of a problem when groups are divided into different communities, and the boundaries of these communities are hard. In such a situation, when people are self-defined or other-defined by their religious, linguistic, cultural, racial or regional affiliation, groups can be permanently excluded from power and influence in a democracy. Such a situation violates the equality assumption of democracy – if a person is excluded from power and influence because of their ascriptive affiliation.

Federalism can also be both majoritarian and consociational. There is nothing inherent within federalism that protects minority rights. Territorial federalism may deliberately not recognize identities and seek to protect individual rather than group rights, but integrationist nation building tends to benefit dominant communities, as does majoritarian democracy (McGarry and O'Leary, 1993, p. 18). This was the case in Pakistan. Even when multinational federalism exists, where the boundaries of the federal units are drawn to encompass particular groups, and cultural rights are given to these territorially defined cultural communities, such a community may lack access to real power at the centre. In such situations federal structures may be seen as a form of segregation (in a similar manner to the homelands of Apartheid South Africa). Even when the situation is not so extreme, a territorially bounded community may feel itself excluded from power, as were the Bengalis in Pakistan.

The process leading to the creation of 'indigenous' federal structures in Pakistan contributes to our understanding of illiberal federalism. The constitution-making process was so protracted precisely because of the implications of permitting one person one vote. This was a problematic concept for the Pakistani elite of the western wing because the majority of the population resided in the eastern wing. The western elite had no intention of subordinating themselves to Bengalis, who were viewed as racially and religiously inferior.[10] The federal form that was ultimately adopted, through the One Unit Plan, created parity between the two wings. This would not necessarily have been an illiberal federation, even if the motivation of the elites behind its creation was to perpetuate authoritarian structures. Consociational democracy seeks to safeguard minority rights through the institutional tempering of majoritarian democracy. Therefore, parity between the two wings could have coexisted with democracy, but national elections were never held.

Many explanations for the lack of national elections have been advanced. The prime reason was that the elite of Pakistan who dominated the non-democratic institutions of state did not trust politicians. The Muslim League had factionalized after independence, its organization atrophying, and the leaders of the newly created Republican Party, one of its offshoots, were never tested on the electoral stage. The Muslim League had also been decimated in the provincial elections in East Bengal in 1954. The 'old elite' of the United Provinces were therefore under challenge by parties such as the Awami League that were better organized. These organizations were perceived by the bureaucracy and the army to be a threat to the stability of Pakistan. The eventual acquisition of power and declaration of martial law by President Iskander Mirza and Commander in Chief, Ayub Khan, in 1958 must be understood in this context. This takeover facilitated the centralization of the state.

Ayub Khan soon dismissed Iskander Mirza and introduced a new centralized Constitution. Based around 'basic democracies' – locally elected councils – it was a system of indirect election, through several levels, culminating in the national and provincial assemblies. Pakistan remained a federation but definitely an illiberal one, as Ayub distrusted politicians. 'They have all been tried and found wanting. I am now certain that if the country is left to them we should expect nothing but ruin' (Khan, 1967, p. 61) and was convinced that democracy was unsuitable for Pakistan (Talbot, 2005, p. 153). Party-less indirect elections were held in 1962 for the National and Provincial Assemblies, but the basic democracies consolidated the power of feudal landowners, hardly the most democratic force in Pakistan.

After Ayub was removed from office in 1969, his successor, Yahya Khan, called elections on the basis of one person one vote, abolishing the parity between the two wings of Pakistan. This was a bold but dangerous move. In the 1970 elections the regionalist party, the Awami League of East Pakistan, performed extremely well. It managed to secure all but two seats (160 out of 162) in the eastern wing of the country, giving the party an overall majority in the National Assembly. This was politically explosive. No one had expected the Awami League to be in such a powerful position after these elections; they had expected the party system to factionalize in the eastern wing. The result created an impasse. Zulfikhar Ali Bhutto, the leader of the Pakistan People's Party (PPP) in the western wing (which had won 81 out of 138 seats in the western wing, doing much better than predicted) was unwilling to let the Awami League form a majority government, seeking a share in political power. The Awami League was unwilling to concede such a role, although it was willing to discuss issues with the parties of the western wing. The military supported Bhutto and the National Assembly was not convened (Talbot, 2005, p. 203). Ultimately negotiations failed, and on 25 March 1971 the Pakistan army was sent to East Pakistan to crack down on the agitation. 'Operation Searchlight' led to the deaths of at least 300 000 Bengalis, the creation of approximately ten million refugees and, ultimately, Indian intervention in the conflict to curb the 'demographic aggression' of the Pakistanis (as the ten million refugees had relocated themselves within India's border states) (Marwah, 1979, pp. 549–80).[11] The state of Bangladesh was thus born.

After the secession of Bangladesh, a new Constitution was written. As noted, the constitution of 1973 returned Pakistan to a parliamentary federal system. The constitution was negotiated between the parties elected in the western wing in the 1970 elections, the vast majority of whom supported it. The opportunity to create a democratic and truly federal constitution was never stronger. The army had been severely weakened, initially by its defeat by India in the 1965 war, and then by the successful secession of Bangladesh, aided by India. The army was therefore in no position to oppose the charismatic and popular Zulfikhar Ali Bhutto, but the emergency provisions remained in the constitution.[12] The PPP and Bhutto may have had their base in Sindh, but Bhutto was just as much a centralizer as previous Pakistani rulers. Bhutto was also a charismatic politician, in the style of Mujibur Rahman in Bangladesh and Indira Gandhi of India.[13] Of course, centralization is compatible with a democratic system of government, but all three operated in ways that undermined democracy in their respective countries.

In Pakistan after 1973, Punjab province possessed (and still possesses) the majority of seats in the National Assembly, although not in the upper house.

No ruler of Pakistan could articulate regionalist issues, or support the claims of others demanding changes, without alienating the Punjab, the heartland of Pakistan. Pakistan's emergency provisions were shortly turned against the National Awami Party (NAP) provincial government in Baluchistan as demands for autonomy escalated in the province. Bhutto claimed that the provincial government was encouraging secessionism, and that the violence between tribes in Baluchistan that had emerged after the secession of Bangladesh was a prelude to a wider secessionist war. Most observers conclude that it was 'not a war aimed to create a separatist Baluchi state, it was merely an attempt to hold the centre to a commitment on federalism' (Hewitt, 1996, p. 60). Bhutto saw the NAP as an electoral threat as the PPP had failed to win any seats in Baluchistan, and only one in NWFP (Amin, 1988, p. 122); 80 000 armed troops were sent into Baluchistan, leading to the deaths of 9000 people. The conflict crystallized perceptions of Punjabi domination and only served to further alienate Baluchis. In addition, it placed the army centre stage and renewed its purpose and legitimacy.

These events provide further demonstration that democracy does not always make federalism work in an accommodationist fashion, and that democracy may exacerbate conflict between communities. Democratic federalism does not necessarily lead to the inclusion of minority communities even if it is not 'reinforcing authoritarian structures'. The dichotomy between democratic and non-democratic federalism, while important, is only part of a wider story about how the structures of a particular federation are operated.

Bhutto was arrested and executed by General Zia-ul Haq after the 1977 elections, during which Bhutto was alleged to have connived to have a political opponent murdered. The opposition Pakistan National Alliance (PNA) declared that the election had been rigged and major street demonstrations erupted. Although most observers conclude that the PPP would have won the elections in any event, irregularities had occurred. After his assumption of power, General Zia declared martial law and dismissed the National and Provincial Assemblies, which were not reconstituted until the party-less elections of 1985. Zia's rule has become infamous for its promotion of Islam in the army and society, but must also be noted for its promotion of the interests of the Punjab and Pashtuns (Harrison, 1991, p. 312). In both democratic and non-democratic periods, the Punjab had to be appeased. Significantly, this period also saw the non-democratic cooption of Baluchi leaders, and the 'solving' of the Baluchi problem through increasing development funds for the province. This cooption did not extend to Sindhi elites, however, and it is no coincidence that the Movement for the Restoration of Democracy (MRD) had its base in the province, and that the violent agitation in 1983 started there.

The suspicious and still unexplained death of Zia in an air accident (along with the American Ambassador) in 1988 provided the occasion for the election of Benazir Bhutto. Between November 1988 and October 1999, four national elections were held. Benazir Bhutto of the PPP became Prime Minister in 1988 and 1993, and Nawaz Sharif of the Islami Jamhoori Ittehad (IJI) alliance and then the Pakistan Muslim League (PML), in 1990 and 1997. Both were centralizers, and, despite their parties hailing from different provinces, both were dependent on the votes of the Punjab. All four elections were held after the dismissal of the former government by the President, using the Eighth Amendment to the Constitution, introduced by Zia. Between 1988 and 1997, the electorate of Pakistan thus had the opportunity to vote a government into office, but not to remove it, an essential part of a 'real' democracy.[14]

## RECENT DEVELOPMENTS IN PAKISTAN'S FEDERATION

General Musharraf came to power in a bloodless coup in October 1999. Nawaz Sharif had been elected Prime Minister in 1997 with a large majority, but had appointed his own men to prominent positions, including the President and the Chief Justice (who was forced out by Sharif) and the previous army chief (who was also forced out by Sharif). Being a Mohajir head of a Punjabi-dominated army, Musharraf was appointed as a 'safe bet' who would not be able to challenge Sharif (parallels can be made with Zulfikhar Ali Bhutto's mistaken appointment of Zia-ul Huq). The Kargil intervention of 1999 had exposed Pakistan to international criticism, and Sharif backed down under US pressure. Tension between Musharraf and Sharif grew. Rumours of a military coup were rife. Sharif sacked Musharraf when the latter was on a plane returning from Sri Lanka, famously refusing permission for the General's plane to land at Karachi airport despite extremely limited fuel supplies. But this action rebounded when forces loyal to Musharraf arrested Sharif (Rizvi, 2000, p. 211).

After his assumption of power, Musharraf identified several 'aims and objectives' for Pakistan. One of these concerned the need for better centre–province relations, and the need was identified to '[s]trengthen federation, remove inter provincial disharmony and restore national cohesion' (Musharraf, 1999). Little has effectively changed and several arenas of conflict, partially based along ethnic lines, have occurred since he assumed office. As noted, the federation is centrist, and this also applies in the financial field. The centre retains the main sources of revenue collection and allocates a share of the federal divisible pool to the provinces (currently

40 per cent of this pool). Resources are allocated between provinces on the basis of population, benefiting the most populous province, Punjab. This reinforces existing tensions relating to Punjabi domination of the army and the bureaucracy. Because the provinces are almost totally dependent on the centre for their revenues, the share of the pool that each province receives is vitally important. Baluchistan, as a large undeveloped province with a small population, has demanded that the pool be divided according to land mass as well as backwardness. Sindh has demanded that a certain amount be allocated according to revenue generation (as this is an area in which the province performs well), while NWFP, similarly to Baluchistan, demands allocation according to backwardness.

The formula currently under discussion proposes that 90 per cent will be allocated according to population, with only 2 per cent split between the criteria of backwardness, revenue generation and inverse population density (Kiani, 2006). The tensions between the Punjab and the rest of the provinces are compounded by the fact that the majority of the resources produced in NWFP (hydroelectric electricity) and Baluchistan (gas) are allocated to the Punjab. Punjab claims that, as it is the most developed and populous province, it can rightfully claim the largest share. This reasoning is resented by the other provinces. Most federations possess redistributive mechanisms to ensure a degree of equity in the interests of national unity. Punjab has been unwilling to make these sacrifices, which poses a severe test to national unity in Pakistan.

One of the issues discussed above has been the relationship between federalism and democracy and whether federalism has been used to strengthen authoritarian structures. The devolution plan articulated by General Musharraf in 2001 cannot be separated from this debate as it is intimately tied to centre–province relations in Pakistan. Bringing government closer to the people is one of the justifications for federal forms of government, and devolution of powers to a lower level of government enhances this. The plan was introduced by General Musharraf in 2001, and *party-less* local government elections were held in 2002 and again in 2005. The plan bears many similarities to Ayub Khan's 'basic democracies'. The aim of the devolution proposals was to 'empower people at the grassroot level . . . [through] an elaborate structure of councils and committees' (Khan, 2004, p. 7). Many developmental powers were devolved to the local governments, significantly bypassing the provincial governments. Several politicians in Pakistan have argued that an increase in local government powers would be a positive development *if* powers were simultaneously devolved to the provincial governments. This has not been the case and the devolution therefore only serves to encroach on the powers of a potential layer of opposition to the centre.

Opinion has been radically divided on the issue. International Crisis Group has condemned the reforms for 'strengthen[ing] military rule' (International Crisis Group, 2004, p. i), but international donors have argued that '[i]nstalling this array of new structures and accountability arrangements is an achievement that can hardly be overstated' (ADB, DFID, World Bank, 2005, p. 1). In such a centralized federation, with a history of centre–province conflict, however, removing the powers of the provinces without compensation can only lead to more tensions. In addition, as was the case with the introduction of the 'basic democracies' by Ayub Khan, in the absence of land reforms, devolution of powers does not empower the people, but, rather, the landowning rural elite of Pakistan.

A final development that makes a mockery of Musharraf's claim to '[s]trengthen federation . . . and restore national cohesion' is the situation that has been developing in Baluchistan since early 2005. As noted earlier, the province was embroiled in a major conflict with the centre in the 1970s but had been relatively quiescent since Zia-ul Huq came to power. This does not mean that old grievances relating to the distribution of resources and the lack of development in Baluchistan had gone away. Proximate causes of the renewed conflict were related to the development of Gwadar Port in the province (this is controversial because Punjabi labourers have been drafted into the province to work on the project, which is perceived to benefit Punjab's economic development rather than Baluchistan's),[15] the 'alleged' rape of a female doctor at the Sui gas facility, as well as the results of the 2002 provincial elections that brought the religious alliance, the MMA, into a coalition government in the province. This has alienated the traditional Baluchi leadership, ensuring that issues over which the Baluchi elite had previously been quiescent raised their heads again, the issue of Sui gas notable among them. Recommendations were made by two commissions set up by the centre in order to increase development in the province and to distribute the share of resources in a more equitable fashion. However, these recommendations have not been implemented and, at the end of 2005, the conflict took a violent turn. An attack on Musharraf during a visit to the province in December 2005 precipitated a military operation in response. A military 'solution' to the conflict had been on the table for months, and could have occurred even if the attack on Musharraf had not been launched. This operation has hardened attitudes against the centre in the province, particularly as previous military operations in the province suggest that it will be perceived as a force of Punjabi occupation. In August 2006, Nawab Bugti was killed by government forces, but levels of violence have continued at their previous levels. Although the Baluchi leaders remain divided, and the majority of their demands relate to changes *within* the existing state structure, the centre risks provoking more serious conflict through ignoring the demands of Baluchi politicians for more equitable distribution of resources and the removal of cantonments from the province (Akbar, 2006).

## CONCLUSION

Pakistan has not been democratic for much of its existence (1958–70, 1977–88 and 1999–2002), But it has been a federation, and a federation that has experimented with different structures. The federation has experienced extreme conflict between members of different communities. Some of these conflicts have been related to the lack of democracy, such as the Awami League being denied the right to convene the National Assembly in 1970 and form the government, and the MRD, primarily in Sindh, in the mid-1980s. Others have been related to the lack of ethnic cooption: the Baluchistan conflict today and the Bengalis in the 1950s and 1960s. This cooption need not have taken place within elected institutions to have managed ethnic relations more equitably. Indeed, one of the problems of Pakistan's federation has been that its structure has introduced destabilizing demographics into an electoral race. Thus, before 1971, the majority of the population were in one unit, East Bengal/Pakistan, and, since 1971, they have been in one unit, Punjab. Democracy has been no panacea to ethnic accommodation in Pakistan, especially because quotas for the bureaucracy are determined on the basis of provincial populations and the federal spending patterns and subsidies for the provinces have, since 1971, when Punjab possessed the majority of the population, been determined on the basis of population. The last review of this formula did not radically change the outcome.

The fact remains that, even in times of democracy, too many undemocratic forces prevail. The federal system does not help to ameliorate this. There is no particular reason why it should do so because, as noted above, federal forms of government may lead to the permanent exclusion of particular groups from government. Although the prevailing wisdom is that federal forms of government are good for a democracy, as federations take many different forms, it is difficult to sustain this proposition. Lane and Ersson only find a relationship between federalism and democracy where the existence of federalism is measured by the amount of political decentralization that exists within the constitutional structure (Lane and Ersson, 2005, pp. 175–6). Even then the 'impact is not straightforward'. In addition, not all federations are decentralized; the example of India is a case in point. Unitary states may be more decentralized than some federations, and indeed, some are. Although the overwhelming numbers of federations in the world today are democratic, federal states do not have to be democratic. There is nothing intrinsic about federalism that requires democracy.

The particular form of the Pakistani federation, where one province possesses the majority of seats in the lower chamber, and also dominates the undemocratic institutions of state, creates an instability that persists during democratic periods (Adeney, 2004, pp. 161–75). Hale has noted that ethnonational federations where the dominant group is contained within one unit have a high rate of dissolution (Hale, 2004, pp. 172–6). Pakistan is not in danger of splitting up, but this does not mean that tensions do not exist. The size of the Punjab, reflected in its electoral dominance, means that national political parties have to win in the Punjab if they wish to form a national government. Political parties that articulate regionalist agendas either are consigned to a small number of seats in their respective provinces (the ANP in NWFP, and the Pashtun and Baluchi regionalist political parties in Baluchistan) or cannot gain the support of the Punjab for their regionalist agendas as these agendas normally have an anti-Punjabi hue.

Although such parties allege that the military establishment conspires against them, in reality their support has tended to be low in all elections, and the small numbers of seats available to them ensures their impact is limited. Few Punjabi regionalist parties exist, but this is not surprising: the Punjabis, although not homogeneous (Samad, 1995b, pp. 23–42) are the *staatsvolk* of the federation. Sindhis are the major anomalous group: the second largest ethnic group, in a province beset with strife between Sindhis, Mohajirs, Pashtuns and Punjabis, does not possess a successful Sindhi *regionalist* party. The PPP are a Sindhi political party, but, in aiming for national power, they need the support of the Punjab. They therefore tone down their demands, but at times have been able to outflank Sindhi regionalist political parties, through selective measures such as the introduction of Sindhi as a provincial language. Therefore democracy would not solve the problems of federalism in Pakistan, as Punjabis, although not a monolith, are dominant in a democratic system.

Many of the tensions in the federation of Pakistan are therefore related to the fact that one province has the majority of the population. This tension would exist independently of whether or not Punjabis dominated the army and the bureaucracy because it is related to issues of representation and resource allocation. Resources can be reallocated and representation solutions can be devised, but to combat the large size of the Punjab would require more radical solutions that are most unlikely. As noted above, Punjabis are not a monolith, but they are perceived to be so. The division of the Punjab into three or more provinces would enable more creative solutions with regard to resource allocation and representation, and reduce the perception of the domination which also poisons relations between provinces. This is easier said than done. Military regimes have spoken of the need to divide the provinces, but they have done so as a means to undermine further the provinces' strength. This means that this is a problematic solution to propose, also because the areas that most academics propose creating, the Siraiki and Potwa provinces of north and south Punjab, have very weak movements agitating for their creation.[16] Whether it is even possible to subdivide the 'heartland' of Pakistan at this stage in its history is also an important consideration: if it is not possible, then other solutions should be concentrated upon. But it is instructive to consider comparative examples as federations with a small number of units have tended to fail or to experience severe conflict (Adeney, 2007, pp. 171–4).

This chapter has identified that there were elements of federal design that exacerbated conflict in the past and that there are federal reforms that could be made that would make a difference. Whether these reforms are likely is another story, but, without them, democratic federalism will remain as problematic as non-democratic federalism in accommodating the smaller communities in Pakistan.

## NOTES

1.  Most federations have a bicameral legislature to represent the territories that comprise it, but not all do so (currently, Micronesia, St Kitts and Nevis, and Venezuela are unicameral).
2.  The language policy is discussed in more detail below.
3.  Muslim leaders in the United Provinces had founded the Muslim League (see Robinson, 1993).
4.  The census of 1998 was contested, and its figures disputed. It had been delayed for political reasons as the changed demographics were expected to lead to increased ethnic tensions in Baluchistan and Karachi, and potentially provide calls for a redistribution of resources if the Punjab was revealed to have lost population. After the results were released, the population total recorded was below UN estimates, and the relative proportions of the provinces had changed suspiciously little since the 1981 census, despite all the demographic changes Pakistan had experienced during that period. For more details, see Anita Weiss, 'Much ado about counting: the conflict over holding a census in Pakistan', *Asian Survey*, **39**(4), 1999, p. 691.
5.  Mohajir literally translates from Urdu as 'refugee'. Many refugees entered Pakistan from India after the partition, but most of them crossed the borders between the divided Punjab and Bengal and were absorbed within these provinces.
6.  See Roy (1993, pp. 102–32) for an excellent summary of revisionist (who claim that partition was not the intended consequence of Jinnah's campaign) and orthodox (who claim Jinnah demanded and received partition) theories of partition.
7.  More languages were recognized for the 1981 census than were for the 1951 census. One of these was Siraiki, a language spoken predominantly in the south of Punjab province, but also the north of Sindh. The status of Siraiki is contested, with many Punjabis claiming it is only a dialect of Punjabi.
8.  A discussion of the politics of Sindh is beyond the scope of this chapter. An excellent discussion can be found in Kennedy (1991, pp. 938–55).

9. The PPP's 1970 election manifesto had promised that Sindhi would become the provincial language. The provincial wing of the PPP made good on this promise, in the process alienating the Mohajir community who saw their privileges as under threat. The conflict was exacerbated because the PPP proposed to replace Urdu rather than have a dual language policy. After violent conflict in which 55 people died and many thousands were injured, a compromise was imposed on the centre which effectively maintained the two-language formula in the province.
10. Bengalis were also viewed with suspicion because they were seen as being too close to the 'fifth column' of Hindu Bengalis, who comprised 22 per cent of East Bengal's population.
11. It should be noted that Pakistan pre-emptively attacked India after it became clear that an invasion force was being prepared.
12. It must be stressed that this provision was also retained in the Indian constitution and has been used 116 times since independence. (See Adeney, 2007, pp. 185–9.) In the 1970s, Indira Gandhi, another populist leader, used it extensively.
13. In the 1970s all these leaders sought to centralize and personalize power.
14. After his election in 1997, Nawaz Sharif used his large parliamentary majority to remove the Eighth Amendment from the Constitution, one of the reasons for Musharraf formally taking over Pakistan with the military in 1999.
15. In addition, the cantonments set up to house the workers from outside Baluchistan have a much higher standard of living than the nearby villages.
16. Personal conversation with Professor Mohammad Waseem, LUMS, Lahore.

# REFERENCES

ADB, DFID, World Bank (2005), 'Devolution in Pakistan: an assessment and recommendations for action', Islamabad: ADB, DFID, World Bank.

Adeney, K. (2002), 'Constitutional centring: nation formation and consociational federalism in India and Pakistan', *Commonwealth and Comparative Politics*, **40**(3), 8–33.

Adeney, K. (2004), 'Between federalism and separatism: India and Pakistan', in Ulrich Schneckener and Stefan Wolff (eds), *Managing and Settling Ethnic Conflicts: Comparative Perspectives from Africa, Asia, and Europe*, London: Hurst, pp. 161–75.

Adeney, K. (2007), *Federalism and Ethnic Conflict Regulation in India and Pakistan*, New York: Palgrave.

Akbar, M.S. (2006), 'Centralised federalism vs provincial autonomy', *The Friday Times*, November, 17–23.

Alavi, H. (1990), 'Authoritarianism and legitimation of state power in Pakistan', in Subrata K. Mitra (ed.), *The Post-colonial State in Asia: Dialectics of Politics and culture*, New York and London: Harvester Wheatsheaf, pp. 19–72.

Amin, T. (1988), *Ethno-national Movements of Pakistan: Domestic and International Factors*, Islamabad: IPS.

Ballard, R. (1991), 'The Kashmir crisis: a view from Mirpur', *Economic and Political Weekly*, **2**(9), 513–17.

BBC (2006), *New Kashmir government sworn in*, (http://news.bbc.co.uk/1/hi/world/south_asia/5211686.stm), 24 July.

Bogra, M.A. (1953), *Presented to the Constituent Assembly on Wednesday, October 7*, Karachi: Ferozzons.

Bose, S. (1997), *The Challenge in Kashmir: Democracy, Self-Determination and a Just Peace*, New Delhi: Sage Publications.

Ellis, P. and Z. Khan (1999), 'Partition and Kashmir: implications for the region and the diaspora', in Ian Talbot and Gurharpal Singh (eds), *Religion and Partition: Bengal, Punjab and the Partition of the Subcontinent*, Oxford: Oxford University Press, pp. 269–97.

European Union (2002), *European Union's Election Observation Mission to Pakistan 2002*, (http://ec.europa.eu/comm/external_relations/human_rights/eu_election_ass_observ/pak/prestat.htm), last accessed 8 July 2005.

Hale, H. (2004), 'Divided we stand: institutional sources of ethnofederal state survival and collapse', *World Politics*, **56**, 165–93.

Harrison, S. (1991), 'Ethnic conflict in Pakistan: the Baluch, Pashtuns and Sindhis', in Joseph Montville (ed.), *Conflict and Peacemaking in Multiethnic Societies*, New York: Lexington Books, pp. 301–25.

He, B. (2007), 'Democratization and federalization in Asia', in Baogang He, Brian Galligan and Takashi Inoguchi (eds), *Federalism in Asia*, Cheltenham, UK and Northampton, MA, USA: Edward Elgar Publishing, pp.1–32.

Hewitt, V. (1996), 'Ethnic construction, provincial identity and nationalism in Pakistan: the case of Baluchistan', in Subrata Mitra and Alison Lewis (eds), *Subnational Movements in South Asia*, Colorado: Westview Press, pp. 42–67.

Huntington, S. (1991), *The Third Wave: Democratization in the Late Twentieth Century*, Norman, OK: University of Oklahoma Press.

International Crisis Group (2004), 'Devolution in Pakistan: reform or regression?', *Asia Report*, **77**, Islamabad/Brussels.

Jalal, A. (1995), *Democracy and Authoritarianism in South Asia*, Cambridge: Cambridge University Press.

Kennedy, C. (1991), 'The politics of ethnicity in Sindh', *Asian Survey*, **31**(10), 938–55.

Khan, A. (1967), *Friends not Masters: A Political Autobiography*, Oxford: Oxford University Press.

Khan, S.R. (2004), *Pakistan Under Musharraf (1999–2002)*, Lahore, Karachi, Islamabad: Vanguard.

Kiani, K. (2006), 'NFC: provinces not satisfied', *Dawn*, 2 January.

Kymlicka, W. (2005), 'Liberal multiculturalism: western models, global trends and Asian debates', in Will Kymlicka and Baogang He (eds), *Multiculturalism in Asia*, New York: Oxford University Press, pp. 22–55.

Lane, J. and S. Ersson (2005), 'The riddle of federalism: does federalism impact on democracy?', *Democratization*, **12**(2), 163–82.

Lijphart, A. (1977), *Democracy in Plural Societies: A Comparative Exploration*, New Haven: Yale University Press.

Marwah, O. (1979), 'India's military intervention in East Pakistan, 1971–1972', *Modern Asian Studies*, **13**(4), 549–80.

McGarry, J. and B. O'Leary (1993), 'Introduction: the macro-political regulation of ethnic conflict', in John McGarry and Brendan O'Leary (eds), *The Politics of Ethnic Conflict Regulation: Case Studies of Protracted Ethnic Conflicts*, London and New York: Routledge, pp. 1–40.

McGarry, J. and B. O'Leary (2005), 'Federation as a method of ethnic conflict regulation', in Sid Noel (ed.), *From Power-Sharing to Democracy: Post Conflict Institutions in Ethnically Divided Societies*, Montreal: McGill Queens University Press, pp. 263–96.

Musharraf, P. (1999), *Address to the Nation by Chief Executive Islamic Republic of Pakistan General Pervez Musharraf, 17 October*, (http://www.presidentofpakistan.gov.pk), last accessed 22 May 2006.

Nordlinger, E. (1972), *Conflict Regulation in Divided Societies*, Cambridge, Mass.: Harvard University Press.

Pakistan, Government of (1951), *Census of Pakistan, 1951, Volume 1: Reports and Tables*, Karachi: Government of Pakistan.

Pakistan, Government of (1956), *The Constitution of the Islamic Republic of Pakistan*, Karachi: Ferozzsons.

Parekh, B. (1992), 'The cultural particularity of liberal democracy', *Political Studies*, Special Issue, 160–75.

Pirzada, S.S. (ed.) (1969), 'Resolution II of the fifteenth session of the Muslim League 1924', *Foundations of Pakistan: All India Muslim League Documents 1906–1924 Vol. 1*, Dacca: National Publishing House Ltd.

Population Census Organization, Government of Pakistan (1998), *Area, Population, Density and Urban/Rural Proportion by Administrative Units*, (http://www.statpak.gov.pk/depts/pso/statistics/area_pop/area_pop.html), last accessed 4 April 2005.

Rizvi, H.A. (2000), 'Pakistan in 1999: back to square one', *Asian Survey*, **40**(1), 208–18.

Robinson, F. (1993), *Separatism among Indian Muslims: The Politics of the United Provinces' Muslims 1860–1923*, Delhi: Oxford University Press.

Roy, A. (1993), 'The high politics of India's partition. The revisionist perspective', in Mushirul Hasan (ed.), *India's Partition: Process, Strategy and Mobilisation*, Delhi: Oxford University Press, pp. 102–32.

Samad, Y. (1995a), A *Nation in Turmoil: Nationalism and Ethnicity in Pakistan 1937–1958*, New Delhi: Sage Publications.

Samad, Y. (1995b), 'Pakistan or Punjabistan: crisis of national identity', *Indian Journal of Political Science*, **2**(1), 23–42.

Sen, A. (1999), 'Democracy as a universal value', *Journal of Democracy*, **10**(3), 3–17.

Stepan, A. (1999), 'Federalism and democracy: beyond the US model', *Journal of Democracy*, **10**(4), 19–34.

Talbot, I. (2005), *Pakistan: A Modern History: Expanded and Updated Edition*, London: Hurst.

Weiss, A. (1999), 'Much ado about counting: the conflict over holding a census in Pakistan', *Asian Survey*, **39**(4), 679–93.

Wheare, K. (1963), *Federal Government*, London: Oxford University Press.

# 6. Semi-democracy and minimalist federalism in Malaysia

## William Case

By delineating tiers of power and authority between central and state-level governments, federalism is often credited with promoting democracy. It endows, yet limits, central governments, therein accommodating diversity and far-flung localities in ways that are consultative and pragmatic. At the same time, it stimulates competitiveness and popular participation, helping to encourage innovation and policy responsiveness on multiple levels. And where its terms are rooted firmly in constitutionalism, it deepens rule of law, therein raising the value of citizenship (Watts, 1999, p. 14).

In Malaysia, however, federalism has done less to promote democracy than to reinforce semi-democratic politics, a shifting amalgam of authoritarian controls and democratic space by which the central government has efficiently – and interminably – extended its tenure. Accordingly, the main aims of this chapter are, first, to demonstrate that Malaysia's federalist arrangements possess greater substance than is usually acknowledged, but, secondly, despite this substance, to show that the central government, in sharing power with state-level governments, only strengthens its political grip. It shows too that, by organizing federalism along territorial, rather than multinational, lines, the government disorganizes the social minorities that sometimes grate under its rule. And, by adjusting even its territorial federalism to minimalist levels, the government prevents regionalist sentiments from cohering in secessionist movements.

This chapter begins by briefly rehearsing the strategies by which Malaysia's central government has perpetuated its semi-democracy. Next, in addressing its main task of showing how these politics can be reinforced by federalism, analysis turns to recounting the early introduction of federalist arrangements in Malaysia, the functional need for which is not readily apparent. It then charts the distinctive ways in which federalism is articulated in Malaysia today. To be sure, the central government has infringed deeply upon the powers possessed by state-level governments, thereby correlating with the authoritarian controls that are constitutive of semi-democracy. But it has also permitted some autonomous forms of revenue

124

raising and policy making at the state level, squaring with the regime's democratic procedures. Power is thus partially withheld, but also genuinely shared, producing complex strategies by which semi-democracy is reinforced through what is conceptualized in this chapter as minimalist federalism. Within this discussion, the territorial and adjustable dimensions of minimalist federalism are also addressed, features that enable the government to dampen minority and regionalist sentiments.

## SEMI-DEMOCRACY IN MALAYSIA

However self-interested and imperial its design, a framework of administrative structures and democratic procedures was bequeathed to Malaysia through British colonial experience. Central to this framework was a workable and reasonably impartial state bureaucracy and elections that were regularly and competitively waged (Weiner, 1987).

After independence, however, the government steadily truncated, though never fully dismantled, these structures and procedures. In brief, amid economic imbalances in a rapidly urbanizing setting, rivalries sharpened between the country's 'indigenous' Malays and 'migrant' Chinese, precipitating fearsome ethnic rioting in 1969 that is locally coded as the May 13 incident (Von Vorys, 1975). The government responded by greatly expanding the state bureaucracy, then gearing it to reverse discrimination through which to 'uplift' the Malays. Thus, through a series of programmes that were collectively labelled the 'New Economic Policy', quotas favouring Malay followings were imposed upon university placement, public sector hiring, business licences and equity ownership. In its swollenness and new arbitrariness, then, much of the bureaucracy's workability and impartiality were lost. But however partisan bureaucracy became, some programmatic benefits still seeped across ethnic lines to rival social forces. As one example, the state-funded educational system has maintained support for Chinese-language instruction at the primary level, unique among Southeast Asian countries with Chinese minorities.

Next, the government insulated its power over the bureaucracy by curbing the competitiveness of elections. It did this in several ways. First, it advantaged its main party vehicle, the ethnically delimited United Malays National Organisation (UMNO), by filling party coffers with public resources, especially state contracts. At the same time, it weakened opposition parties by drawing many of them into the fold of its ruling coalition. Thus, while husbanding its longstanding, but subordinate, non-Malay partners – the Malaysian Chinese Association (MCA) and the Malaysian Indian Congress (MIC) – the government absorbed upwards of ten more parties into its coalition. This formation was christened the 'Barisan Nasional' (National Front), and UMNO's paramountcy was heightened within it. Finally, the few parties that remained in opposition were muffled by new limits on civil liberties, most signally made manifest in media licensing requirements and preventive detention laws. They were hindered too by new manipulations of electoral procedures, including highly partisan re-districting and an uneven enforcement of campaign laws.

Despite the ways in which elections were skewed, however, two major opposition parties – the Parti Islam Se-Malaysia (Islamic Party of Malaysia, PAS), characterized today by intense religiosity, and the Democratic Action Party (DAP), made up largely of ethnic Chinese – have persisted on either flank of the UMNO-centred Barisan. Moreover, they have each retained an organizational autonomy and capacity for popular mobilization that is rare for parties in opposition in Southeast Asia. PAS and the DAP have been able, then, to exploit such competitiveness as remains to win a toehold in parliament, there to stimulate public debate and keep the government at least mildly accountable.

In analysing the semi-democracy that has thus taken shape, alloying authoritarian controls with democratic space, there are many dimensions of political life that might be explored. From the perspective of this chapter, however, what most bears underscoring is a partisan bureaucracy and skewed elections, their obliqueness crucial to the government's extending its tenure. More specifically, through its bureaucracy, the government delivers programmatic benefits, usually boiling down to base patronage. Among its favoured constituencies of UMNO elites and Malay followings, then, the government earns instrumentalist support. It takes care, however, to secrete some benefits to rival social forces of Islamists and Chinese, softening these groups' alienation. Similarly, by curbing the competitiveness of elections, the government systematically advantages its Barisan coalition, but, by ceding some democratic space to PAS and the DAP, it attracts some legitimating cover.

In sum, Malaysia's government uses its partisan bureaucracy to win instrumentalist support among favoured followings. It uses elections to gain some legitimacy among forces that are less favoured. Thus, these latter forces, never wholly denied state benefits or democratic space, hold enough stake in the order not to resort to anti-system behaviours which, while doubtless repressible, would significantly raise the cost of ruling. Semi-democracy, then, much better than hard authoritarianism with its inefficient coerciveness; and fuller democracy, with its uncertainties over outcomes, has enabled Malaysia's government to perpetuate its incumbency. This chapter's task now is to investigate the ways in which this semi-democracy has been more finely articulated through minimalist federalism.

# MALAYSIA'S MINIMALIST FEDERALISM

While analysts have given Malaysia's semi-democracy much attention, they have largely ignored the regime's federalist arrangements. Failing to match the government's more sophisticated use of a partisan bureaucracy and skewed elections, federalism is typically dismissed as fake or inconsequential. This chapter tries to demonstrate, then, that semi-democracy can be more finely articulated by federalism, helping calibrate patronage and democratic space in order to earn additional increments of support and legitimacy.

To be sure, the functional resonance of federalism in Malaysia does not register quickly on standard indicators. Given the country's small population and modest number of constituent units (a mere 13 states), federalism promises fewer administrative efficiencies and policy experimentation than the duplication of programmes and battles over turf. Moreover, with the country's social communities increasingly interspersed, rather than territorially segmented, federalism does little to protect the cultural identities and autonomy of minorities. On the contrary, as we will see, federalist arrangements were first introduced at the behest of leaders of the ethnic Malay majority in order to preserve their indigenous claims to 'sovereignty'. Federalism was thus organized in territorial, rather than multi-national ways.

Further, as a small and open economy, Malaysia might seem to benefit more readily from cooperating regionally with neighbouring countries than from fragmenting power across states which, in the unevenness of their wealth, might react to rivalries that take root by imposing barriers against commerce and movement. Hence, the international pressures and broader globalized dynamics in which Malaysia is embedded seem to militate against federalism. More generally, one notes that, apart from Russia, there are no countries in East Asia that are organized along federalist lines, thus providing Malaysia with only the weakest of demonstration effects.

Thus, in seeking to account for the origins and persistence of federalism in Malaysia, one begins with the vagaries of the historical record. The British extended their reach across maritime Southeast Asia by fits and starts, first carving out a crown colony, known as the Straits Settlements, in disparate entrepôts along the Strait of Malacca. Next, they gained sway over those parts of the peninsula's hinterland that were rich in mineral or agricultural resources (or, in the case of Pahang, that appeared to possess such natural wealth). Here, the British imposed what they delicately framed as indirect rule, nominally respecting the authority of indigenous potentates (collectively labelled the Malay Rulers) at least over Islam and Malay culture. Meanwhile, the large numbers of ethnic Chinese and Indians that were recruited in these territories to work tin mines and plantations were viewed as sojourners, thus entitling them to few protections.

Four of these territories were then linked together in a protectorate labelled the Federated Malay States (FMS). Further afield, those parts of the peninsula that had been under Thai suzerainty, yet possessed so few resources that they were deemed unworthy of close administration (or that, in the case of Johor, simply declined to join the FMS), were more loosely associated as the Unfederated Malay States (UMS). The Straits Settlements, the FMS and the UMS came collectively to be labelled British Malaya. Across the South China Sea, a dynasty was established by a British adventurer in Sarawak; a chartered British company took charge of Sabah; and a Resident was thrust up alongside the sultan of Brunei, enterprises that came to be called British Borneo.

After the Second World War, the British sought to reorganize administration on the peninsula under the Malayan Union Scheme, effectively imposing a unitary system. The British were partly motivated by concerns over rationalization, but they were moved also by the Rulers having done little to oppose Japanese occupation, while ethnic Chinese, though mobilized under Communist banners, mounted some daring resistance. Hence, under the Union, the sovereignty of the Rulers and the birthright of their Malay followings were to be abolished, with equal citizenship to be granted to Chinese and Indians. State-level authority would thus have diminished. However, resentments among the Malays grew so fierce, finding expression in the formation of UMNO, that the British backed down, agreeing instead to the Federation of Malaya in 1948 (Allen, 1967). Accordingly, states regained much of their standing and, with federalism thus organized along territorial lines, it did less to safeguard minorities than to institutionalize their inequalities.

These arrangements were extended further when, six years after Malaya's independence in 1957, the British proposed also to inject their remaining territories of Singapore, Sarawak, Sabah and Brunei into the new nation, heralding the Federation of Malaysia. Brunei remained aloof, however, while Singapore departed in 1965. Malaysia thus settled into a federation of 13 states – 11 in Peninsular Malaysia, two in East Malaysia – each of which possesses a head of state and governing framework that parallels the monarch (yang di-pertuan agong), the parliament and cabinet at the national level. A Ruler or appointed governor thus serves as the head of each state, while a 'menteri besar' or chief minister leads an executive council (exco) in the state assembly.

Nonetheless, just as bureaucratic neutrality and electoral competitiveness were diminished over time, so too was federalism, never robust, pared back to more modest dimensions. At first sight, this might seem unexpected, with the complex pressures emanating from the two-step process by which federation took place appearing to create countervailing forces for both limited and more substantive power sharing. More specifically, we have seen that, after the Second World War, federalist arrangements grew first from the devolution of unitary rule to state-level governments on the peninsula, then in a second step, in 1963, from the aggregation of the separate territories of Sarawak and Sabah. Historical pressures were thus unleashed respectively for both scant and extensive power sharing across tiers.

More specifically, one might find in this two-step process the basis for parallel, though distinct, sets of federalist arrangements, with states on the peninsula gaining fewer prerogatives than their counterparts on Borneo. And, indeed, as part of the 'merger' agreement, Sarawak and Sabah were awarded a package of guarantees labelled the '20 points', giving their respective governments control over immigration, while softening requirements for Islamization and the introduction of Malay as the national language (Means, 1976, p. 376). But, in making these concessions, the central government feared that the Borneo states, despite their own complex social pluralism, would nurse a sense of regional distinctiveness that might cohere over time in secessionist movements. Thus the assurances contained in the 20 points were either left unfulfilled or scaled back over time. Save the nominal controls over immigration that state-level governments can still wield, levelled largely today at social activists and environmentalists from elsewhere in the country, Sarawak and Sabah have retained no greater powers than their counterparts on the peninsula. Notwithstanding the two-step process, then, by which federalism was introduced, the terms of power sharing have nearly gained consistency across Pensinsular and East Malaysia, descending uniformly, even if at different rates, into minimalist federalism. Accordingly, federalism has been delineated not only territorially along lines that disorganize social minorities, but also in ways that are retractable, allowing the means by which quickly to suppress secessionism.

Even so, while the capacity of state-level governments to operate independently from the centre has been limited, it remains substantive. Most importantly, while the central government delivers the bulk of funding, state-level governments retain some autonomy in raising revenue and making policies. Thus, where state-level governments are aligned with the central government, they appear nearly to operate as franchises, serving the centre, but usually in ways that meet mutual needs. In particular, state-level governments dispense patronage along lines that resonate locally, hence generating an instrumentalist support that refracts back to bolster that which the central government has accumulated more directly.

In turn, state-level governments are permitted to consume some of their patronage resources locally. To be sure, these governments sometimes take too much, hence alienating constituent followings and threatening, rather than augmenting, the central government's support. One example involves the UMNO-led state government in Terengganu during the 1990s which, after squandering the royalties bequeathed to the state for the exploitation of natural gas deposits offshore, was heavily defeated by PAS in a general election at the end of the decade. Sometimes, too, state-level governments have clashed with the central government, frequently over the appropriate tier upon which state contracts or licensing approvals should be granted. In these circumstances, the central government may impose its greater power, even purging the state's 'menteri besar'. But, more in the spirit of minimal-ist federalism, the central government usually reaches a compromise with its state-level counterpart, however asymmetric.

On the other hand, where state-level governments are aligned with the opposition at the national level, their latitude is more tightly constrained by the central government. Budgetary grants may be reduced or delayed, while policies may be left unimplemented by civil servants who are federally appointed. Nonetheless, what stands out is the extent to which these parties remain able to win state assembly elections, form state-level governments and, notwithstanding the hurdles that they face, raise some revenues and initiate new policy directions. In permitting this, of course, the central government gains little in terms of support from the distributions of patronage that result. Instead, it derives some legitimating cover from the limited democratic space that it has ceded. Competitiveness, then, is dis-played not only by opposition parties gaining some seats in parliament, but also by their capturing a few state assemblies outright. The rightfulness of the central government's return to power at the national level, then, is reaffirmed by the opposition's state-level victories, signalling that voters can make choices and turnover can take place.

Of course, where parties in opposition at the national level control state-level governments, they may, in avidly pursuing new policies, be reinter-preted by the central government as less a legitimating aid than a gathering irritant. This is especially the case where these parties had earlier been part of the Barisan coalition, then 'defected' to the opposition, generating a sense of profound betrayal. James Chin (1997) records that PAS, forming the state-level government in Kelantan during the 1970s, abandoned the Barisan that it had so recently joined. The central government responded by instigating unrest in the state, creating the pretext by which to impose emergency rule, order new elections, then usher UMNO candidates into office. Further, in Sabah, the United Sabah Party (Parti Bersatu Sabah, PBS), made up principally of ethnic communities labelled officially today as 'Kadazan-Dusun', turned from Barisan to the opposition in the midst of campaigning for elections in 1990. The central government, vexed by this 'treachery' and the desires for greater autonomy, perhaps even secession, that were implied, machinated ceaselessly afterwards, persuading enough state assemblymen to switch back to the Barisan that PBS's thin majority was lost. Thus, after being cast into opposition at the state level too, PBS pleaded for re-entry to the Barisan fold.

In Malaysia, therefore, federalism is not only territorial, rather than multinational, thereby disorganizing social minorities; it is also retractable, with the central government sometimes trampling federalism's provisions to dislodge state-level governments, especially in East Malaysia where threats of secessionism have sometimes loomed. It is this retractability, then, that prompts most analysts to dismiss the significance of federalism in Malaysia. While acknowledging that the terms by which power is shared are uneven, however, this chapter contends federalism is minimalist, rather than vacuous. In these conditions, the prerogatives of state-level governments, whether formed by parties aligned with the central government or in opposition, remain at least lightly insulated. Indeed, it is only by according some substance to federalist arrangements that the central government can enjoy their supportive and legitimating benefits, correlating more broadly with semi-democratic politics.

## TERMS OF POWER SHARING

Where parties that make up the central government's Barisan coalition have also operated state-level governments, Browne et al. (2004, p. 6) assert that 'the federal factor has been relatively unimportant, with state governments generally acquiescing to their political masters in Kuala Lumpur'. And, where leaders of these state governments have resisted, the central government has, according to Jomo and Wee (2002, p. 44), brought them to heel, purging menteri besar and chief ministers who have grown 'independently minded'. What is more, where parties in opposition at the national level have formed state-level governments, the central government has squeezed them, reducing budgetary grants, hampering policy implementation and sometimes seizing power directly. This retractability has been more rigorously applied by the government in Sarawak and Sabah.

Of course, even as Malaysia's two-step federalism was instituted, the terms of power sharing were modestly parsed. Modelled initially on the Government of India Act (1935), which was based in turn on the British North America Act (1867), federalism in Malaysia was characterized from the start 'by a high degree of centralisation' (Watts, 1999, p. 28). In brief, powers were delineated across three tiers: those enjoyed exclusively by the central government, those held at the state level, and those to be exercised concurrently. Further, as is standard in federalist arrangements, the central government first asserted its authority over foreign policy, defence, monetary policy and constitutional amendments. But it then claimed much more, cutting deeply across areas typically shared with, or reserved for, state-level governments. It thus took control over most forms of revenue raising, imposing a monopoly on direct taxation (that is, income and corporate tax, capital gains taxes and petroleum tax), while assuming the lion's share too of indirect taxation, namely, import and export duties, excise and sales tax, and lotteries (Jomo and Wee, 2002, p. 9). It gained control also over many policy areas, including internal security, justice, education, health and welfare.

But, just as bureaucratic neutrality and electoral competitiveness were diminished over time by the central government, so too were the terms of federalist power sharing made even leaner. While, under the original Federation of Malaya agreement of 1948, residual powers were left to the states, they were reallocated under the Federation of Malaysia in 1963 to the central government. Imbalances in revenue flows grew steeper too. Jomo and Wee (2002, p. 29) observe that, between 1985 and 1999, the central government's revenue increased from four times the consolidated state-level government revenues to seven times.

In part, the central government enhanced its revenue by tapping sources that had initially been reserved for the states. Most importantly, through the National Petroleum Act of 1974, it took control over the returns on petroleum and gas sales from the oil-producing states of Terengganu, Sarawak and Sabah. These states were afterward compensated, though poorly, receiving only a 5 per cent royalty. Moreover, as mentioned above, even these payments were revealed later to be as conditional as they were paltry. When PAS formed a new state-level government in Terengganu after the election of 1999, the central government suddenly withheld the royalty. Then, in seeking to win over mass followings, it issued patronage directly to village-level recipients through a range of ad hoc and discretionary programmes and payments (Jomo and Wee, 2003, pp. 46–7). PAS sought to compensate for this by proposing to levy kharaj, a form of agricultural land tax. But the plan drew such ire from the central government that it was abandoned (Jomo and Wee, 2002, p. 39, fn. 19). Similarly, in Sabah, two years after the PBS government withdrew from the Barisan, the central government imposed a ban on the export of logs. Though this was rightly portrayed as necessary for conservation, the timing of the decree suggested that the central government's deeper motivation was to starve the PBS of revenue (ibid., p. 28).

The central government has been obliged to make up some of the shortfall by issuing various budgetary grants. But in Kelantan and Terengganu, where state-level governments have been formed by PAS, these grants have frequently been reduced or delayed until the end of the fiscal year. Large portions of them have also been converted to loans, deepening the indebtedness of state-level governments. And, in their penury, these governments have surrendered control over some of their agencies and social services, 'leading to further centralisation since the formation of Malaysia' (ibid., pp. 29–30). Thus, unlike in India, where federalism has been invigorated by opposition and regional parties that flourish at the state level, the central government in Malaysia has responded to opposition by perpetuating, indeed tightening, the initial terms of power sharing across tiers (Watts, 1999, p. 28).

What powers might be left, then, to state-level governments in Malaysia, justifying our understanding of federalism there even as minimalist? We have seen that, in terms of revenue, the central government has nearly monopolized taxation, leaving to state-level governments only a small range of indirect taxes and export duties. Even if the central government has thus exponentially increased its revenue take, however, the distributions that result, though asymmetrical, are not at great variance with some other countries on the roster of recognized federations (see Table 6.1).

In addition, after amassing its revenue, the central government distributes large parts of it back to the states through the budgetary grants mentioned above. These grants take various forms, including tax-sharing grants, general grants and specific grants. Further, in determining their

*Table 6.1*    *Federal government revenues before intergovernmental transfers as a percentage of total (federal–state–local) government revenues*

|                | 1986 | 1996 |
|----------------|------|------|
| Malaysia       | 87.2 | 89.9 |
| Spain          | 87.9 | 84.0 |
| Austria        | 71.6 | 72.8 |
| Australia      | 74.4 | 69.1 |
| United States  | 64.7 | 65.8 |
| India          | 68.2 | 64.6 |
| Germany        | 64.5 | 64.5 |
| Canada         | 48.4 | 47.7 |
| Switzerland    | 48.1 | 44.7 |
| European Union | 0.9  | 1.2  |

*Source:*    Ronald L. Watts, 'The spending power in federal systems: a comparative study', Institute of Intergovernmental Relations, Queens University, Kingston, 1999, p. 52.

size, consultations are held in the National Finance Council, a body comprising the prime minister, several federal ministers, and one representative from each of the state-level governments (Jomo and Wee, 2002, p. 28). To be sure, the prime minister retains the upper hand in these dealings, firstly by exercising his prerogative to select the council's membership. Accordingly, Selangor and Johor, two of the country's wealthiest states and both controlled firmly by Barisan, are in proportional terms the largest recipients of grants (ibid., p. 30). By contrast, as noted above, Kelantan and Terengganu, two of the poorest states on the peninsula and episodically controlled by PAS, have found their grants reduced or delayed. Nonetheless, however marred by manipulations, this granting process is enshrined in Article 108 of the Constitution. And such a constitutional guarantee (and the government's regular, if grudging observing of it) helps to ensure that state-level governments, even those operated by parties that at the national level are in opposition, enjoy some autonomy, thereby lending some substance to the country's federalist arrangements.

Similarly, just as the central government has tempered its near monopolization over taxation with budgetary grants, so too has it offset its withholding of petroleum-based revenues by respecting state-based control over land, a prerogative that, like grant funding, is constitutionally protected. Accordingly, state-level governments have been able to raise revenues and make policies by overseeing the usage of lands that they control, especially timber concessions and plantation schemes. They gain revenues, too, through their regulatory powers, enabling them to issue licences and permits. Indeed, through licensing, most state-level governments favour local contractors, especially for state-contracted projects, 'creat[ing] barriers of entry to peninsula-based and foreign contractors' (Ng, 2005, p. 44). To be sure, much local corruption and, in many states, environmental degradation and the dispossession of indigenous people, have resulted. But the independent capacity of state-level governments to pursue even nefarious ends evokes federalism's substance.

Finally, in turning from revenue raising to policy making, one notes that the colonial-era principle by which the Rulers held jurisdiction over religious affairs has been preserved, with each state today operating a large Islamic apparatus (Martinez, 2001). As Islamic sentiments have deepened in Malaysia, especially since the early 1980s, the relevance of control over religion and culture for setting policy directions and mobilizing followings has vastly increased. With the mufti and other top Muslim officials thus appointed by the Rulers, mosques have emerged as important bases from which to pursue their activities, sometimes in opposition to the central government. In turn, the central government has tried to pressure state-level officials and tighten surveillance. But it has been prevented by the constitution from purging these officials outright.

Finally, if the central government has clawed back the residual powers once left to state governments, many concurrent powers remain. In particular, the central government often relies on the state-level apparatus to implement many of its policies and deliver services (Watts, 1999, p. 37). To do this, state-level governments recruit large numbers of civil servants to their bureaucracies. Accordingly, Watts (1999, p. 41) observes that, while federalist arrangements may be 'relatively centralised legislatively, they are much more decentralised administratively'. And, as students of public administration know well, this confers upon state-level governments much de facto autonomy over the directions that policies take.

## PATRONAGE AND DEMOCRATIC SPACE

If federalism can be shown to possess substance in Malaysia, it must bear consequences for politics. Just as the bureaucratic and electoral dimensions of semi-democracy have elevated the central government and its followings, so too have the terms of power sharing associated with minimalist federalism. Put simply, the central government has used federalist arrangements as conduits by which to lengthen the patronage that earns instrumentalist support, as well as extend some democratic space that attracts legitimating cover.

To see this, our investigation turns first to some state-level governments operated by parties that are aligned with the central government, helping to mediate patronage and support. It then examines some state-level governments operated by parties that, at the national level, are in opposition, evoking the competitiveness and democratic space by which the central government's tenure gains some legitimacy.

### Barisan State Governments

Except in Kelantan and occasionally Terengganu, state-level governments aligned with the central government have usually prevailed across Peninsular Malaysia. In Penang, the only state with a Chinese majority, the predominantly Chinese Gerakan Rakyat Malaysia (Malaysian People's Movement, GRM) has been permitted to hold the chief ministership, though only because of this party's deep absorption into Barisan. In East Malaysia, the Parti Pesaka Bumiputra Bersatu (United Traditional Bumiputra Party, PBB), made up principally of indigenous Melanau and Iban, has led a ruling coalition with considerable autonomy. But this is ascribed to its ruling so dutifully on behalf of the central government. In neighbouring Sabah, the central government rules more directly through its new state-level formation, UMNO Sabah, despite its having readmitted PBS to the Barisan in 2002 and the near absence in the state of ethnic Malays.

Thus, across most of Malaysia, the central government has extended its control through the UMNO-centred Barisan. And, in forming state-level governments, these parties have extended the central government's patronage more finely – into the pockets of regional elites and out to mass followings. Through federal budgetary grants and local revenues, state-level governments acquire the bulk of their funding. They then release this funding through various programmes, projects and services. Low-cost housing programmes are especially salient. And, in return for energizing the support that feeds back to the central government, menteri besar, executive councillors and key state assemblymen are permitted to snare much patronage for themselves.

At its most intense, this activity takes place where stands of tropical hardwood are still substantial enough for state-level governments to be able to organize concessions. Menteri besar and relevant exco members thus award licences to favoured timber companies, usually operated by ethnic Chinese. They also grant approvals for many other kinds of land use, especially plantation agriculture. Through complex exchanges, favoured recipients then filter official fees and informal payments to top state-level officials. These officials then invest in political 'war chests' through which to mobilize instrumentalist support more broadly, while sinking their surpluses into personal high living (Mersat, 2005).

Hardly pausing over land use, top state-level officials award infrastructure contracts in similar ways, sometimes to their own companies or those of their family members. As one example, the PBB-led government of Sarawak has developed plans for a new state assembly building in the state capital of Kuching. The contract, valued at RM300 million, was issued without tender in mid-2005 to a joint venture company spearheaded by PPES Works Sdn Bhd, a wholly-owned subsidiary of Cahya Mata Sarawak Bhd (CMS), a prominent firm controlled by the son of the chief minister, Abdul Taib Mahmud. What is more, the project's construction was shortly afterward subcontracted to a listed infrastructure company, Bina Puri Holdings, for less than RM230 million, raising questions over the difference in amounts. Over the years, PPES is reported to have won more than RM2 billion worth of road projects in Sarawak, usually subcontracting them out afterward. Thus a local consultant observed that 'a lot of local companies are . . . benefiting from contracts awarded to the CMS Group, which guarantees itself a reasonable profit while ensuring that its many subcontractors are appropriately rewarded' (quoted in Thien, 2005), making plain the ways in which patronage flows can be extended, instrumentalist support generated and state-level officials enriched.

To be sure, where stakes are high, frictions sometimes set in between the central and state-level governments over the sharing of patronage. An illustration of such strains, as well as the ways in which they may be resolved, can also be found in Sarawak. During Mahathir's prime ministership, construction of the Bakun Dam, the largest of its kind in the world, commenced in the state. The project's initial rationale was to produce hydroelectricity that could be transferred profitably by undersea cable to Peninsular Malaysia and other Southeast Asian markets. The nascence of necessary technologies has prevented this, however, ensuring that the dam's enormous volumes of energy be consumed locally. In thinly populated Sarawak, one of the few industries that would require energy on this scale is aluminium smelting, increasingly 'frowned upon [in many countries] because of potential environmental hazards and the electricity it guzzles' (Shanmugam, 2005, p. 70).

But with Malaysia mostly untroubled by environmental risks, while desperately seeking new energy markets, it has attracted proposals from rival investors seeking to set up smelters and purchase hydroelectricity. Some of these proposals have been launched by major international firms with long experience in aluminium production. Despite the dearth of foreign direct investment that Malaysia attracts today, however, no approvals have yet been offered to these companies by the government. Rather, the central government has appeared strongly to favour a bid mounted by Smelter Asia Sdn Bhd, a Malaysian firm controlled by Syed Mochtar Al-Bukhary, one of the few ethnic Malay business elites who has remained buoyed by state contracts after the economic crisis of the late 1990s. The central government's approval of Syed Mochtar's bid has been held up too, however, with the state-level government of Sarawak, whose approval is needed for land use, appearing to support yet another bid. Specifically, the state's chief minister, Taib, favours a proposal made by a consortium led by CMS Bhd, the company run by his son.

Nonetheless, with the central and state-level governments aligned in this case, a compromise outcome has been presaged. In particular, while the central government keeps foreign investors at arm's length, it will probably award a purchase power agreement to Smelter Asia. But, to placate the state-level government, another hydroelectricity project, the Murum dam, has been proposed, 'cater[ing] for a second aluminium smelter in Sarawak' (Shanmugam, 2005, p. 70) and enabling CMS Bhd to proceed. Despite the mounting risks of overproduction, the frustrations of foreign investors could be mitigated too by bringing some of them into expanded consortia or working as subcontractors. Thus the Bakum dam project evokes the tensions over patronage which, even in states where central and state-level governments are aligned, can sometimes set in across tiers, but also the restraint that the substance of federalism can impose.

## State Governments in Opposition

Through state-level governments with which it is aligned, the central government extends its patronage and deepens its support. However, in states that are controlled by parties that at the national level oppose it, the central government derives few such benefits. Thus, it reduces or delays budgetary grants, then uses the watchdog agencies and media outlets that it controls to scrutinize closely the revenues that are raised autonomously. But, while restricted and checked, funding from the central government is never fully withheld. Rather, minimalist federalism ensures that state-level governments receive enough grants to be able to function. They remain able also to raise some revenues through indirect taxation, concessions and approvals. And their leaders and assemblymen gain regular salaries and sundry allowances. In this way, the alienation of those forces who support these state-level governments can be softened.

On the other hand, the central government has little to gain by ceding so much democratic space to opposition parties that control state-level governments that full competitiveness prevails. Accordingly, the advantages given to Barisan, the limits on civil liberties and the distortions in voting that are practised at the national level are imposed coterminously upon the states. Even so, minimalist federalism ensures that parties in opposition to the central government can, at least, gain formal control over a few state assemblies. And, provided that they have not defected recently from the Barisan, they can persist in office for long periods.

In this way too, forces that support the opposition gain a stake in the order. But, just as importantly, the rightfulness of their inability to widen this stake, or even to retain at some junctures their existing state-level redoubts, finds basis in even such competitiveness as skewed elections permit. We see here clearly, then, the ways in which semi-democratic politics intersect with, and are more finely articulated by, federalist arrangements. And as an integral part of, or at least a useful supplement to, Malaysia's semi-democracy, federalism helps the central government in avoiding the high costs of coercion that are normally associated with clinging perennially to power.

In which states have parties in opposition at the national level been able to form state-level governments? The central government appears most willing to abide these parties coming to power in states distinguished by

Islamic religiosity, rather than in those that bristle with historical grievances and secessionist sentiments. It is thus in the 'Malay heartland', the
northern states of Peninsular Malaysia, rather than in the more distant
states of East Malaysia, that the central government has relied more on
skewed electoral processes than on forceful intervention. It recognizes that,
despite the potency that Islam can gain in the northern states, there is little
secessionist threat. And, with these states populated largely by Malays, it
can mount competing cultural appeals, holding out prospects of its one day
winning state-level elections. Meanwhile, in biding its time, the central
government attracts legitimating cover. In these circumstances, PAS has
been able to form state-level governments in Kelantan from 1955 to 1978
and again after 1991. It was also able to form governments in Terengganu
from 1959 to 1961, and again from 1999 to 2004. Of course, the central government ousted PAS from government in Kelantan in 1978, though, as we
have seen, only after the party had abandoned Barisan the year before.

In East Malaysia, the central government has turned more readily from
skewed elections to forceful intervention, making plain the retractability of
federalism. Here, ethnic identities and historical lineages depart sharply
from those in Pensinsular Malaysia, leaving the UMNO-led Barisan less
able to make competing appeals than in the Malay heartland. Unfiltered
resentments threaten, then, to rise up in the spectre of secessionism. For
these reasons, in 1966, the government plotted to bring down the Sarawak
National Party (SNAP) government after its chief minister, Stephen
Kalong Ningkan, in seeking to exercise guarantees contained in the
20 points, resisted the adoption of Malay language and the recruitment of
civil servants from the peninsula. We have seen too that the central
government scuttled the PBS in Sabah after the party defected from the
Barisan to join a new coalition in opposition. It then fabricated a new
ruling party, UMNO Sabah. Even more fundamentally, the central government has sought periodically to alter the state's social structure, conducting campaigns by which to convert indigenous communities to Islam, while
balancing up those who resist conversion by allowing large-scale in-migra-
tion of Muslims from the southern Philippines and Kalimantan, then
awarding these new arrivals national identity cards and even voting rights.
In these circumstances, Kadazan-Dusun groups that cling to various
denominations of Christianity harbour deep nationalist resentments, but
they find too that their capacity to act politically on their grievances has
been sharply eroded. Thus it is not federalism in East Malaysia, but rather
its retractability which, in combination with profound alterations in social
structure, effectively prevents secessionist movements.

Thus, in those states where governments are formed by parties in opposition at the national level, minimalist federalism retains more substance on

the peninsula than it does in Sarawak and Sabah. To show this, the remainder of this section focuses on the state of Kelantan. Widely characterized
as steeped in religiosity, yet materially impoverished, Kelantan has, except
during the 1980s, been governed by PAS. The central government has
responded with tireless machinating by which to weaken the party, delay-
ing budgetary grants and distorting voting patterns. But with PAS's defection from the Barisan long having passed, and with Malay identities
predominating in Kelantan, the party has been left by the central government to rule in the state.

PAS has probably been more seriously weakened, then, by its own reck-
lessness, in particular its calling for jihad after US retaliation in
Afghanistan over September 11. In this situation, many middle-class Malay
followings, recoiling from newly militant PAS postures, have gravitated
back to the UMNO-centred Barisan. Thus, in the general election held in
March 2004, Barisan was able to make deep inroads into Kelantan (and to
reclaim Terengganu), leaving the state assembly precariously perched with
24 seats for PAS and 21 for Barisan. In early December 2005, after the death
of a PAS state assemblyman, a by-election was held. Though the constituency had traditionally been controlled by PAS, it was this time cap-
tured by UMNO, sharpening margins in the state assembly to 23–22.

With some UMNO leaders opining that PAS's position had grown
'untenable', analysts expected that the central government would persist
until PAS was forced to call a state election, one that it seemed bound to
lose. But the central government then hesitated, indicating clearly that it
finds advantages in leaving parties that oppose it at the national level in
control of a small number of state-level governments.

This chapter has argued that, under minimalist federalism, the central
government can gain some legitimacy simply by ceding some democratic
space. But in cases like Kelantan, where prospects for development are
modest, it may find additional advantages in avoiding the responsibilities
of office. Thus, just as underfunded state-level governments may surrender
to the central government authority over services that they are unable to
deliver, so too may the central government remain content to leave a state-
level government that opposes it in power, spotlighting the latter's policy
failings. Far from regarding states in federalist arrangements as a labora-
tory for policy innovation, then, the central government may eschew such
innovation, instead modulating cunningly the sharing of resources in ways
that keep state-level rivals functioning, but on drip.

The response of Malaysia's deputy prime minister, Najib Abdul Razak,
to the Barisan by-election victory is instructive. Despite UMNO's mounting presence in Kelantan, Najib struck a modest note: 'we hope the win will
be the starting point towards a bigger change, but the change cannot be in

the form of pressures, but the aspiration of the people'. Further, amid media queries over whether the central government should now push the PAS to dissolve Kelantan's state assembly, Najib implied that restraint would better enhance his government's legitimacy: any dissolution of the assembly 'could be perceived as putting pressure on PAS and reflect[ing] as though [Barisan] was power-crazy' (*Malaysiakini*, 7 December 2005).

Finally, an even stronger indicator, perhaps, of the central government's deriving legitimating benefits from the limited democratic space that it cedes can be found in the response of Kelantan's menteri besar, Nik Aziz Nik Mat, to his party's by-election defeat. Though he insisted that the contest had been marred by cheating, prompting PAS to refuse to sign off the by-election results, he conformed to his party's longstanding avoidance of anti-system behaviours. Far from counselling terrorist activities, then, he advised, 'we cannot afford to be hostile toward the federal government and vice-versa . . . I sincerely hope that the relationship can be maintained or improved so that Kelantan can be developed' (*The Star*, 15 December 2005, p. 29). Insofar as these outlooks in opposition can be encouraged through federalist arrangements, they help to strengthen the central government's standing.

## CONCLUSIONS

This chapter has argued that, in Malaysia, federalist arrangements have been minimalist, thereby helping to perpetuate the country's semi-democratic politics. Where the central government is aligned with the parties that control state-level governments, federalism thus aids in mediating distributions of patronage, earning it instrumentalist support. And, where the central government is confronted at the state level by parties that oppose it, federalism cedes some democratic space, generating legitimating cover. Through the partisanship of the state bureaucracy and skewness of elections, Malaysia's government has operated a semi-democracy through which to extend its tenure interminably. Minimalist federalism has helped to anchor this regime type more deeply.

While modulating the patronage and democratic space upon which semi-democracy depends, minimalist federalism bolsters the central government's more fundamental kit of controls. Specifically, with federalism arranged along territorial, rather than multinational, lines, Malaysia's social minorities, in their dispersion, are effectively denied even state-level power through which they might realize more fully their economic and social aspirations. To be sure, the Chinese still form a majority in the state of Penang, enabling them to claim the chief ministership. They can do so, however, only because the party that represents them, the MCA, subsists dutifully as junior partner in the UMNO-centred Barisan. Were the DAP to win a state election in Penang, it is difficult to imagine that the central government would allow it to remain unhindered for long.

It is on this count, then, that minimalist federalism helps to underpin the government in a second way, offering terms that are not only territorially delineated, but readily retractable. The central government has tolerated the PAS's gaining power at the state level in Peninsular Malaysia, even if squeezing funding afterwards. In East Malaysia, however, the central government has not been willing to accept a state-level government formed by a party that opposes it. Here, Malay communities are small and, hence, federalism's territorial delineation may not be enough to prevent ethnic resentments cohering in secessionist movements. In both Sarawak and Sabah, then, the central government has sometimes dispensed with feder-alism's safeguards, resorting to bribery, intimidation and emergency rule, underpinned by social restructuring. Thus it is not so much federalism, but rather the retractability of its minimalist practice, that has in the end kept Malaysia together.

Thus, in Malaysia, minimalist federalism has helped to articulate semi-democracy at the state level, with a partisan bureaucracy extending patron-age, while skewed elections cede some democratic space. This generates a fund of support and legitimacy, enabling the central government to keep its grip. In addition, federalism's territorial delineation disorganizes non-Malay social minorities, thus preventing their resentments from gaining traction. And, where even this is not enough, federalism's retractability, rather than its placatory effects, obviates secessionist movements.

# REFERENCES

Allen, James de V. (1967), 'The Malayan Union', New Haven, Yale University, Monograph Series No. 10.

Browne, Graham. K., Siti Hawa Ali and Wan Manan Wan Muda (2004), 'Policy levers in Malaysia', Centre for Research on Inequality, Human Security and Ethnicity (CRISE), Queen Elizabeth House, Oxford, CRISE Policy Context Paper 4.

Chin, James (1997), 'Politics of federal intervention in Malaysia, with reference to Sarawak, Sabah, and Kelantan', *Journal of Comparative and Commonwealth Politics*, **35**(2) (July).

Jomo, K.S. and Wee Chong Hui (2002), 'The political economy of Malaysian fed-eralism: economic development, public policy and conflict containment', United Nations University, World Institute for Development Economics Research, Discussion Paper No. 2002/113.

Jomo, K.S. and Wee Chong Hui (2003), 'The political economy of petroleum revenue under Malaysian federalism', paper presented to Human Rights and Oil in Southeast Asia and Africa workshop, University of California at Berkeley, 31 January.

*Malaysiakini* (2005), 7 December.

Martinez, Patricia (2001), 'The Islamic state or the state of Islam in Malaysia', *Contemporary Southeast Asia*, **12**(1).

Means, Gordon (1976), *Malaysian Politics*, London: Hodder & Stoughton.

Neilson, Ilan Mersat (2005), 'Politics and Business in Sarawak (1963–2004)', PhD thesis submitted to Department of Political and Social Change, Australian National University, January.

Ng, Kar Yean (2005), 'HSL stands out in land reclamation', *The Edge Malaysia*, 19 December, p. 44.

Shanmugam, M. (2005), 'Aluminium intrigue', *The Edge Malaysia*, 19 December, p. 70.

*The Star* (2005), 'Nik Aziz wants better ties with Federal Govt', 15 December, p. 29.

Thien, Tony (2005), 'Taib family-owned firm to bag RM70m for doing nothing', *Malaysiakini*, 25 August (http://www.malaysiakini.com/news/39518).

Von Vorys, Karl (1975), *Democracy Without Consensus: Communalism and Political Stability in Malaysia*, Princeton: Princeton University Press.

Watts, Ronald, L. (1999), *Comparing Federal Systems*, Montreal and Kingston: McGill-Queen's University Press.

Weiner, Myron (1987), 'Empirical democratic theory', in Myron Weiner and Ergun Ozbudun (eds), *Competitive Elections in Developing Countries*, Durham, NC: Duke University Press, pp. 3–34.

# 7. Indonesia's post-revolutionary aversion to federalism

## Anthony Reid

Indonesia and China are the only very large, multi-ethnic states to have rejected the federal model in favour of a unitary state. This chapter will investigate, for the Indonesian case, the hypothesis that the revolutionary path by which these and other countries arrived at modern nation-statedom is the most important factor in this choice. Comparisons will be drawn with Indonesia's federal neighbour Malaysia to explore the relative strengths and weaknesses of the federal and unitary models, particularly from a democratic perspective. And finally the experiments with regional autonomy and asymmetric statehood in post-Suharto Indonesia will be examined with particular reference to Aceh.

States which achieved their current form through revolution have some advantages over those which evolved in the incremental manner of multiple compromises. They have powerful symbols, a clear identity, a centralized system of government and education, and an ideology that favours complete uniformity in the rights and duties of citizens. France has these advantages in comparison with the United Kingdom, but it also has some disadvantages, particularly from the viewpoint of regions or minorities that feel themselves profoundly different. In Asia too, the portentous comparison of post-revolutionary China with evolutionary, federal and democratic India is central to understanding the effects of modern political ideals on ancient and diverse cultures. The case of Indonesia is perhaps more manageable as a lesson in the strengths and dangers of rejecting federalism for political uniformity.

## COLONIAL HERITAGE AND THE PATH TO INDEPENDENCE

The 1940s and early 1950s were a crucial watershed in the history of Asian states. This mid-century upheaval is usually portrayed in terms of war, revolution, independence or the end of colonialism. Looking back in a world-historical perspective, however, it needs more attention as the mother of all regime changes; as the birth-period of new states that have endured surprisingly effectively over the subsequent half-century. Some of those Asian states – India, Pakistan, Malaysia – were born as federations and have continued to be so. The remainder, including all those that asserted their independence through revolution, embraced a unitary model. In Asia, as elsewhere, revolution has proved to be hostile to federalism in the name of the sovereignty of the people.

Island Southeast Asia in the centuries preceding this watershed appeared most unlikely to be on a path leading towards strong, unitary states of this kind. Its highlands and smaller islands, where most of the pre-1800 population had been concentrated, never developed bureaucratic, law-giving states on a significant scale and were wary of the externally supported states in their midst. Even the highly complex polities of pre-colonial Java and Bali seemed to have 'an alternative conception of what politics was about' (Geertz, 1980, p. 135). Much of the recent historical scholarship has been devoted to seeking to establish what it was 'that looks like a bureaucracy, in early as well as contemporary times, but is not one, according to a Weberian definition?' (Day, 2002, p. 288). Explanations have centred on the spiritual, charismatic nature of power, the system of complementarities between distinct parts of a plural system, and the environmental obstacles to centralized power.[1]

For the colonial powers in this region it seemed clear that they were dealing with political traditions in which power was diffused into a great diversity of hierarchies, kinship networks and sacred centres. The English and Dutch sought to rule through a façade of very diverse rajas, sultans, *adathoofden*, *bupati* and chiefs, even while providing their own bureaucratic 'steel frame' which for the first time around 1900 acquainted Southeast Asians with the effective tools of a modern nation-state. Insofar as they thought of democratizing or decolonizing, feebly in the 1920s and 1930s but almost frenetically after 1945, they thought of complex federal structures as the only viable option. Most of the aristocratic elites who had a share in the colonial system agreed with them (Emerson, 1937; Reid, 1974).

The more radical nationalists of the 1930s and 1940s, however, perceived the underlying reality of centralized colonial power, and dismissed the indigenous inheritance of diversity as an anachronistic and 'feudal' façade, its perpetuation being no more than a colonial trick to divide and rule. Moreover they took seriously what they learned in English and Dutch schools about the history and ideology of the modern nation-states who ruled them, with their ideals of the sovereignty of a free and equal people.

In terms of the massive regime change of the 1940s and 1950s, therefore, the major question would be which of these visions prevailed in the post-colonial successor states. Here we have to distinguish two quite different paths, of which Malaysia and Indonesia might be held to be quintessential types – the evolutionary–pragmatic and the revolutionary. In evolutionary Malaysia the communist-led revolutionaries were defeated and marginalized by an alliance of British Commonwealth forces and the conservative Malay establishment, and the latter fully accepted the symbolic compromises made by the colonial state towards pre-existing political institutions and communities. In Indonesia the revolutionary nationalists were far more strongly placed, and rode a revolution uneasily to power, suppressing their communist extreme wing and thereby gaining the support of the US-led international community against the Dutch. The evolutionary Malaysian path led in the direction anticipated by the British, towards federalism with its constitutional sharing of powers, as well as an electoral democracy. The revolutionary Indonesian one abolished traditional monarchies and autonomies in its march towards a unitary state and the imagined equality of all citizens.

## WERE BRITISH COLONIES MORE LIKELY TO ACHIEVE INDEPENDENCE AS FEDERATIONS?

There have been few examples of British colonies following the revolutionary path to independence since the early cases of the United States and Ireland. The classic Asian cases of anti-imperial revolution in our times – Philippines (the first, 1896), Indonesia (1945–50), Vietnam (1945–54), Laos (1954–75), Cambodia (1954–78), East Timor (1975) – have all been against continental European states which had their own more direct experience of the French revolution, Napoleon and the revolutionary upheavals of 1848 and 1870. Of British decolonizations in Asia, none have generally been classified as 'revolutionary' by the historians, despite the degree of violence accompanying them in India, Burma and Malaya. A revolution *was* attempted by the Malayan Communist Party from 1948 and, if it had succeeded, would probably have produced a unitary state with no serious place for the sultans. But, since that revolution was crushed by military intervention from Britain, Australia and New Zealand, it had no opportunity to affect the shape or ideology of government, even for a brief period, as in the Philippines.

The correlation between federalism and a non-revolutionary, negotiated path to independence seems very clear in Asia, unless the post-revolutionary Soviet Union were to be accepted as a true federation. Without seriously entering this complex issue, I am here following most recent authorities in regarding it as authoritarian and unitary in practice even if federal in many of its formal constitutional arrangements. The centralizing roles of an authoritarian party and a radically egalitarian ideology rendered meaning-less the division of powers which should mark a true federation (Kahn, 2002, ch. 3; Ross, 2003).

The chief examples which obtained their independence in federal form (Malaysia, India, Pakistan and Australia) were all also under former British colonial control. Can we go so far as to say that there was a causal relation between colonial government by the British constitutional monar-chy in the twentieth century, evolutionary paths to independence, and forms of government that entrenched local, traditional autonomies behind a system of federalism? An adequate answer to that question would have to look carefully at the ambivalent case of Burma, treated elsewhere in this book. Considering Malaysia and Indonesia alone, there is much to be said for the hypothesis.

Since Malayan/Malaysian federalism arose in large part as a way to incorporate multiple monarchies within a single polity, we must consider also why monarchies survived in Malaya. One factor was also the colonial one. British of the age of Victoria and subsequently appeared more likely to believe in monarchy as a natural system compatible with modernization than did their Dutch colleagues, even though these also lived formally under the constitutional monarchy established in 1815 at the Congress of Vienna. Both sought to preserve and protect Malay rulers in Malaya and Sumatra respectively, but very differently. As Emerson remarked in the 1930s,

> The sovereignty of these [British Malayan] States has remained intact in the sense that they do not fall within the jurisdiction of the Imperial Parliament, that persons residing within their territories are subject only to the jurisdiction of the State within which they reside . . . Several well-known cases in the British courts have testified to the fact that the sovereigns of the Malay States are immune from suit save at their own pleasure.
>
> In the Netherlands Indies the legal and administrative structure rests on quite a different basis since no protected states recognisable in international law have been left in existence. All the territories form a part of the Dutch colonial domain, and a common citizenship exists throughout. (Emerson, 1937, p. 54).

The sultans on the peninsula, all too weak politically or militarily to offer serious resistance to the British, were placed on exalted pedestals where their sovereignty and royal prerogatives were respected even though they had to follow the advice of the British Resident (as the British monarch had to follow that of the Prime Minister) in all matters except 'Malay religion and culture'. By contrast, the sultans of East Sumatra, very similar in their Malay origins to those of the Peninsula, were frequently refashioned, sub-divided or interfered with in the interests of greater administrative efficiency. Having been reduced largely to expensive figureheads in the first

decades of the twentieth century, they were given new powers in decentralization schemes of the 1930s which were patently motivated by a fear of
Indonesian nationalist sentiment. Some monarchs of Bali and South
Sulawesi were restored after 30 years of direct rule, and there was active
discussion of bringing back the kings of Riau and Aceh, heirs to much
more substantial pre-colonial sultanates.

Yet modern minded Dutch officials, as well as Indonesian nationalists,
regarded the extravagant rulers with dismay or even contempt. Their
present maintenance by the Dutch as semi-foreign bodies in the colonial
empire, irritatingly dividing powers and functions and yet, because of their
special attributes, not fitting properly into the general decentralization
schemes, is to be explained less in terms of a concern for the spiritual and
material ease of their people than in terms of Dutch dread of Indonesian
communism and nationalism (Emerson, 1937, p. 464).

Given the use of indirect rule as a means to curb and control the national
movement, it was hardly surprising that even moderate members of that
movement had little use for the rulers. The early stage of the national revolution of 1945–49 generated a radical 'social revolution', largely inspired
by the Marxist left, which drove all the rulers of Republican-controlled Java
and Sumatra from their thrones (with the notable exception of pro-
Republican Yogyakarta). By contrast, the Malayan sultans survived this
critical period because they 'had been better prepared for a role as constitutional monarchs by the British Resident system; their prestige had not
been sapped by such flamboyant excesses in the 1930s nor by such humili-
ation at the hands of the revolution [in 1945–46]' (Reid, 1979, p. 262).

It was the survival of the rulers, not democracy, which was the crucial
initial ingredient of the unique Malayan (Malaysian) system of federalism,
retaining nine monarchs within a single state. The advocates of more democratic outcomes in the 1940s were mostly on the other, anti-monarchic, side
of the debate. But it can nevertheless be argued that Malaysian federalism
has allowed a training-ground and safety valve for opposition which has
served democracy relatively well. This is the subject of another chapter in
this book.

## INDONESIA'S COMMITMENT TO THE UNITARY STATE

The more radical section of the national movement, comprising the
Marxist left and the nationalists around Sukarno and Hatta, had never had
much interest in federalism. They were intellectually committed to the sovereignty of the people, and believed that independence could only come

through a revolutionary kind of mass action to assert it. The much more numerous Muslim movement was also concerned for the solidarity of the *ummat* (Islamic community), not its division into ethnic units. Support for local autonomy in the 1930s came from ethnonationalist movements such as Pasundan and the South Sulawesi party of Nadjamoedding Daeng Malewa, and from traditional elites and *adat* (customary law) leaders less committed to independence in any form. The Japanese military administration in Java (1942–45) encouraged Sukarno and Hatta as nationalist leaders, and downgraded further the status and autonomy of self-governing rulers, thereby weakening any voice in favour of federalism.

The principal Japanese contribution to the unitary idea, however, was paradoxically by accelerating preparations for independence in Java, while inhibiting any participation in that process from the other islands. Only Java-based delegates attended the principal opportunity to debate the shape of the future independent Indonesia, the Body for the Investigation of Indonesian Independence (Badan Penjelidik Kemerdekaan Indonesia, or BPKI) at the end of May 1945. Although a tenth of its 62 members had been born outside Java, there was no voice at that meeting for the concerns of the ethnic minorities. Not surprisingly, the body voted for a unitary republic. The Java-based nationalist Johannes Latuharhary, an Ambonese Christian, found only one supporter in the 19-man constitutional sub-committee for his plea for a federal state. Only six delegates in the full body favoured a monarchy rather than a Republic (Yamin, 1959, I, p. 259). The revolutionary *ideal* of the unitary state appeared, in the hothouse atmosphere of the late Japanese occupation, untroubled by any practical diversities on the ground, since most of these same delegates believed their future unitary Indonesian state should include Malaya, British Borneo and Portuguese Timor, as well as Netherlands India.

Tokyo subsequently overruled the desire of the local military authorities in Sumatra, Borneo and the East to keep these areas separate from the more rapid independence preparations in Java. On the very day of the Japanese surrender, 14 August 1945, three delegates from Sumatra and five from Borneo and the East arrived in Jakarta for what was intended to be the next step in Japanese-sponsored 'independence' for Indonesia. Suddenly the theatre became reality. After independence was hastily proclaimed in a manner the Japanese could accept on 17 August, the Japanese-sponsored Committee for the Preparation of Indonesian Independence (PPKI) was called upon to authorize the constitution prepared earlier in Java, and lay the basis for a new state in a hurried three-day meeting.

The delegates from outside Java were uniformly concerned about the Java-centred state that was likely to result, but they had little effect on a format that had already been determined without them. The most articulate of them, Dr Mohamad Amir from Medan, pleaded 'that the maximum decentralization be allowed for the islands outside Java, that governments be set up there, and that the people there be given the right to manage their domestic affairs to the widest extent' (Yamin, 1959, I, pp. 410, 419). But, far from allowing natural ethnocultural units their own expression, the PPKI decided to establish only eight large provinces for the whole country – one each for Sumatra, Borneo and Sulawesi. Apart from the three in Java, each of the other five provinces was a mosaic of pluralism, with no dominant ethnicity nor even religion (Reid, 1974, pp. 19–29). But the governors appointed to these provinces had negligible power on the ground. The revolutionary dynamic marched to its own drum in each of the major regions in the period 1945–47, and the Dutch occupation of the most lucrative areas thereafter gave even more responsibility to military units around the Dutch perimeter. The local Republican-appointed officials in Sumatra initially had to accept the self-governing rajas as a political reality, and began pragmatic negotiations about democratizing them. It was the unplanned 'social revolution' that swept these rulers away, killing some and humiliating all. Although there was ambivalence in the Republican leadership about these violent actions, the Republic accepted their consequences as meaning the end of monarchy in Sumatra (Reid, 1979; Ariffin Omar, 1993).

Aceh was the most critical test of the Republic's intentions for regional autonomy. It was a crucial bastion of Republican strength after the elimination during the 'social revolution' of the 102 little 'self-governments' on which the Dutch had relied. Until the victory of the Republic through the transfer of sovereignty at the end of 1949, therefore, the modernist ulama leadership which had led the 'social revolution' was accepted as the local government with complete autonomy. The Dutch aggression in 1947 allowed Yogyakarta to appoint the most influential of these ulama, Daud Beureu'eh, as Military Governor of Aceh. This de facto provincial status was revoked in 1951, however, when the Republic felt strong enough to return to a uniform system of provinces and districts (*kabupaten*). Sumatra had in 1948 been acknowledged to be too big to govern as one province, but the three units it was broken into remained multi-ethnic amalgams, incapable of generating loyalty on an ethnic or historic basis. It was against this amalgamation into a North Sumatra Province that the revolutionary *ulama* (religious scholar) leadership of Aceh revolted in 1953 (Sjamsuddin, 1985; Sulaiman, 1997; Reid, 2006).

The Dutch embrace of a federal model for post-war Indonesia sealed the eventual doom of any such policy for republicans. The Dutch Lieutenant Governor-General, H.J. van Mook, first developed a strategy of surrounding and incorporating Republican Java by erecting large federal states in Sumatra, Borneo and the 'Great East'. These large units had already been established as part of an ineffective decentralization programme in the 1930s. They replicated the large, multi-ethnic provinces of initial Republican design and proved equally impractical on the ground. Sumatra had to be conceded as also de facto Republican territory at the Linggajati Conference in November 1946. Nationalist sentiment and internal jealousies proved too strong even in Dutch-occupied Borneo to allow that state to come into being. Eventually five weak federal states emerged in Borneo: two federations of rajas in the east, one 'special region' in the the west, and two 'neo-lands' still too inchoate to have much sense of identity. Only the Great East was assembled into a single large state, the Negara Indonesia Timur, at a conference in Bali in December 1946. A fragile new edifice of Cabinet, Parliament and civil service for this new state was quickly put together in its capital, Makasar. Internally it rested on an extraordinary mosaic of local bodies. Some, representing pro-Dutch Christian areas like South Maluku (Ambon) and Minahasa, had indirectly elected representative councils; others were little more than confederations of traditional rulers, such as those of Bali and South Sulawesi (Reid, 1974, pp. 106–9; Chauvel, 1990, pp. 233–57).

In a two-week campaign in July–August 1947, Dutch troops occupied the most economically important Republican-held areas, notably including plantation areas of East Sumatra and West Java, and the oil-rich Palembang area of South Sumatra. This made it possible for the Dutch to encourage two important new federal states, an ethnically complex Negara Sumatera Timur in East Sumatra, and a Sundanese-majority state in West Java which turned out to be markedly pro-Republican in orientation (Kahin, 1950; Reid, 1974, pp. 115–19).

The Netherlands eventually transferred sovereignty unconditionally, on 27 December 1949, to a federal republic, the Republik Indonesia Serikat (RIS), known in English as the Republic of the United States of Indonesia (RUSI). United Nations intervention had undercut the military advantage held by the Dutch, and led to an atmosphere of mutual recognition between the Republic, responsible for about half of Java and three-quarters of Sumatra (minus its three major conurbations) and the 15 states of federalist Indonesia erected under Dutch auspices.

The RIS emerged as a negotiated compromise, the kind of evolutionary independence that marked Malaysia eight years later. But in Indonesia this compromise uneasily cloaked the revolutionary mindset of Republican 'victory' over those who had been considered traitors to the revolution. As the Republican Chief of Staff described the military aspect of this compromise, 'BFO [federalist] people who were previously traitors against the 17 August 1945 proclamation now have to be accepted as never having been traitors to the Republic and having similar positions and offices together with the Republicans; KNIL [colonial army] units, auxiliaries, federalists etc., the old enemies of the TNI [Republican army] have to be accepted as part of the new Indonesian National Army' (General Nasution, as translated in Chauvel, 1990, p. 324).

In the event federal Indonesia lasted only eight months. As Herb Feith put it, the fact that the compromises on which the transfer of sovereignty had been based were so quickly torn up 'is barely relevant to a situation where revolutionary political reality was so rapidly outstripping legalities of every kind' (Feith, 1962, p. 71). Beginning with the states in Java, where republican and unitary sentiment was always strongest, federal states dissolved themselves into the Republic under pressure of both long-term republican sympathizers in their midst and those eager to be on the winning side. The strongest federalist figures with some degree of military support, notably Sultan Abdul Hamid II in West Borneo and the Christian Ambonese leader Soumokil in the NIT, became compromised by association with abortive military coups designed to stop the incorporation of KNIL soldiers into a Republican-led national army. Abdul Hamid was arrested and the state he headed collapsed following the Westerling coup in January, 1950. In April, Soumokil fled the NIT capital, where he had been Attorney-General, after the failure of the Captain Andi Azis coup against the landing of Republican troops. With the demise of his initial hope to preserve the autonomy or independence of the Negara Indonesia Timur, he inspired a declaration of independence of the Republic of the South Moluccas (RMS) on 25 April. This put up a strong resistance against the ten Indonesian battalions sent against it in November, and continued a guerrilla resistance in adjacent Ceram until 1962 (Chauvel, 1990, pp. 347–92)

The sense conveyed by the revolutionary winners that continuing support for federalism was a kind of treachery gained ground with each of these incidents. One Medan journalist rode the wave for dissolving the NST state by proclaiming that 'as long as there are in Indonesia elements which defend Van Mook's colonial legacy . . . as long as those elements are not swept out, political tensions will continue to exist like a thorn in a man's flesh'.[2] Unitarism became a part of the victorious nationalist package, and hence something that was not negotiable. As viewed particularly in the key nationalist agencies, including the nationalist and communist parties and the army, people outside Java placing a high value on their ethnic identity 'became tantamount to being pro-Dutch' (Feith, 1962, p. 74).

The most prominent Sumatran in the short-lived federal government, Vice-President Hatta, conceded in 1953 that 'a federal system is in fact suitable for such a far-flung archipelago and might be expected to strengthen the feeling of unity', but any such ideas had to be abandoned in face of the antipathy towards any schemes supported by the Dutch (Hatta, 1953, cited in Feith, 1962, p. 72). The victory of the revolutionary approach to state formation, in other words, equated unitarism with patriotism and federalism with treachery and foreign influence.

Demands for greater regional autonomy were quick to resurface in the 1950s, but they almost never used the label 'federal' because of its negative associations. The regional rebellions of the 1950s, emerging as they did from the revolutionary winners, went to considerable lengths to suppress their ethnonationalism. The armed rebellion of Republican guerrillas in West Java under S.M. Kartosuwirjo declared its cause to be the Islamic State of Indonesia (Negara Islam Indonesia – NII), in 1949. In January 1952, another disgruntled group of Makasar-Bugis guerrillas in South Sulawesi, under Kahar Muzakar, declared for this organization, even though its spirit was anything but national. Finally the most explicitly regional of all the rebellions, that of the revolutionary-period Aceh leadership under Daud Beureu'eh in September 1953, began by declaring itself part of NII. It dressed its demands in theological terms, insisting that violence against the Dutch had only been justified by pursuit of an Islamic state. But its practical grievances were all about the loss of the total autonomy and control of local resources which they had enjoyed in the period 1946–50 (Feith, 1962, pp. 54–5, 212–14; Sulaiman, 2000; Sulaiman, 2006).

It was not long before the Acehnese heritage of separate statehood began to show beneath this cloak. From his position in New York, attached to the Indonesian mission to the UN, Hasan Tiro reacted to the rebellion by developing his desired format for a federal and Islamic Indonesia (Tiro, 1958, pp. 98, 103–4, 150–53). Similar ideas were taken up at the Batee Kureng Congress of groups supporting the rebellion on 23 September 1955. On the same date Daud Beureu'eh declared Aceh to be no longer a 'command' of NII but a federal state (*negara bagian*) with himself as its head of state (*wali negara*).

Following the rebellion and the heavy bloodshed involved in suppressing its passionate followers, the central government realized the fundamental mistake of having tried to amalgamate Aceh into a North Sumatra Province. As part of the negotiations to end the rebellion, provincial status was restored to Aceh on 1 January 1957. Many of the rebels, including the man appointed first Governor, Ali Hasjmy, were satisfied with this and other concessions, and made their peace with Jakarta. Daud Beureu'eh had meanwhile become convinced of the case for federalism, however, and he refused any arrangements that did not include it. Hasan Tiro returned to Aceh during a period of ceasefire and negotiations in 1959, and stiffened resistance to the idea of a mere province. He could then argue that many other rebel groups outside Java, who had joined the PRRI uprising in

1958, were coming around to the idea of a federal state (Sulaiman, 2000, pp. 400–419; Sulaiman, 2006, pp. 132–3).

These rebel movements were however militarily defeated and politically divided by 1960. If anything, their flirtation with federalism confirmed the belief of the nationalist establishment that unitarism was a non-negotiable part of the post-revolutionary state. During the 'Guided Democracy' period, when Sukarno's ideas became dominant and the free expression of dissenting views increasingly restricted, public discussion of federalism was impossible. Only some remaining guerrillas in the outer islands illegally promoted the idea.[3] Those of the rebels who survived into the Suharto era, however, increasingly opted for independence rather than a federal Indonesia.

Despite its hostility to federalism, post-revolutionary Indonesia during its liberal beginnings, when it did not in practice control its regions, offered them impressive-sounding legal autonomies. Laws passed in 1956 and 1957 allowed elected province and Kabupaten (district) assemblies to choose their local executives, as well as providing guaranteed proportions of state revenues for them. Neither law was ever effective. They were overtaken first by Sukarno's brand of revolutionary authoritarianism, and then by General Suharto's long period of bureaucratic authoritarianism (1966–98). Suharto for the first time also had the military control needed to move the country towards an unusually centralized form of government. The law no. 5 of 1974 revoked the autonomy package of the 1950s, and replaced it with a system where governors were effectively chosen by the centre and received their budgets and guidelines from it (Malley, 1999). Another law no. 5, in 1979, removed the ancient autonomies and electoral practices of villages all over Indonesia, replacing village heads and councils with a top-down and uniform bureaucracy across the whole country.

The fall of Suharto in May 1998 therefore released a great deal of pent-up frustration over these centralizing trends. For the first time federalism was openly debated in the press, the distinguished writer, architect and priest ,Y.B. Mangunwijaya, making an effective case that it was the best and fairest means to keep Papua and Aceh in Indonesia.[4] Radical new autonomy laws were passed in 1999, providing elected local officials and a generous sharing of revenues.

## THE ACEH CONCESSION

Attempts to reach agreement on autonomy for Aceh within the Indonesian framework began with the passing of an Aceh Autonomy Law by the Indonesian Parliament in July 1999. This was widely rejected in Aceh as trying to give life to the totally ineffective and discredited 'special region' (*Daerah Istimewa*) deal of 1959. A more consensual drafting effort under the Wahid government led to the NAD Law of July 2001, so called because it renamed the Province Nanggroe Aceh Darussalam (NAD), using the ambiguous Acehnese term *nanggroe* rather than either of the Indonesian terms – traditional *negeri* (town, principality or community) or modern *Negara* (sovereign state). Because it included a generous concession to Aceh of 70 per cent of the oil and gas revenues for eight years, and 50 per cent thereafter, it did gain support among many Acehnese politicians working in the Indonesian structures. It appeared to do little, however, to attract those who had been fighting a guerrilla war for independence since 1976, nor even the much larger element campaigning for self-determination through a referendum (Miller, 2006).

In any case none of this was effectively implemented before military rule was re-established in Aceh by President Megawati on 19 May 2003, making it once again the least autonomous of Indonesia's provinces. Between 45 000 and 60 000 army and policy units were concentrated in Aceh during the ensuing two years, substantially the largest force in Aceh's 130 years of intermittent military occupation.

On 26 December 2004, Aceh was hit by the most destructive tsunami and one of the worst earthquakes of modern times. Fortunately, President Yudhoyono (SBY) was by then better established with a popular mandate than any of his predecessors. He responded effectively to the devastation, allowing the military forces of the US, Australia, Singapore, Malaysia and other countries to move relief supplies in quickly. SBY had already shown a cautious interest in renewing negotiations with the GAM leadership in Sweden. In the aftermath of the massive international relief effort, he authorized ministerial-level negotiations and substantial concessions. Both sides appreciated the need for a new start to reconstruct Aceh in peace. This time it was the Helsinki-based Crisis Management Initiative which brokered the peace deal, agreed in July and implemented immediately upon its signature on 15 August 2005.

In relation to the unitary bias of Indonesian state nationalism since 1945, the peace agreement was a remarkable reversal. It granted to Aceh 'authority within all sectors of public affairs' except defence, foreign affairs, monetary and fiscal matters, justice and freedom of religion. National laws and international agreements 'of special interest to Aceh' would only be agreed after consultation with the Aceh legislature. Aceh would have its own flag, crest and hymn, and a ceremonial head of state called a *wali nanggroe*, the term which GAM had applied to Hasan Tiro. Aceh could raise its own external loans and international investments, administer its ports and airports, and enjoy 70 per cent of the revenues from oil and gas 'and other natural resources' in perpetuity. In return for GAM's acceptance of Aceh's place within Indonesia, its fighters would receive an allocation of land or a pension, and be permitted to play their part in the regional election of officials to be held in April 2006 (though in the end postponed). An exception would be made to the rule that only nationally organized political parties could contest elections in Indonesia, giving GAM the opportunity to create or support an Aceh-specific party for the first time.

There are many reasons to be sceptical about whether this federalism-by-another-name will succeed as a democratic solution to Aceh's problems, yet it is already a remarkable departure from Indonesia's unitarist, post-revolutionary traditions. Though the F-word is carefully avoided, the agreement would inaugurate the kind of 'asymmetrical government' already long practised in the United Kingdom and, to a lesser extent, Canada, Spain and Malaysia. As Michael Keating has argued persuasively, when communities come together with different nationalist expectations and experiences, providing for differential claims on the state can be the strategy most compatible with justice and democracy (Keating, 2001, pp. viii, 102–33). Acehnese have a different memory of state and tradition of nationalism from most Indonesians. Aceh's relationship to Indonesian state nationalism is strong but distinctive. It may be that an anomalous or asymmetric status is the best way to keep Aceh within Indonesia voluntarily. If so, Indonesia will have discovered through a bitter and painful route a formula that Malaysia (not to mention the UK) adopted at the start.

## MALAYSIA'S ASSYMETRIC FEDERALISM

The British domain in the 'Malay World' was always a patchwork of constitutionally very different pieces. Singapore, Melaka and Penang on the Peninsula formed one Crown Colony; Labuan off Borneo another. Four 'protected' Malay monarchies on the Peninsula were federated under a common government in 1896, even though sovereignty was held to continue to reside with their sultans. Johor declined to join this federation despite its very long links to Singapore, and so did four more sultanates transferred from Siamese suzerainty in 1909. These five states remained 'protected' but 'unfederated'. Sarawak, Brunei and North Borneo were also 'protected' by Britain, though the first two were sovereign monarchies under English and Malay kings, respectively, and the third was governed by a chartered company.

Turning this into a country or countries was a challenge, to which federalism was the only evolutionary answer. Only if the revolutionary path taken by the Malayan Communist Party had prevailed could Malaya have emerged as a unitary republic. The British Labour post-war government sought to fold the sovereignty of nine sultans in the Peninsula into a Malayan Union, and to assume sovereignty over Sarawak (from the Brooke rajas) and North Borneo (from the Company). On the Peninsula this was defeated by a Malay popular movement supported by many old Malaya hands in Britain. A Federation of Malaya replaced the Malayan Union in 1948, and became independent in 1957, as explained in another chapter.

The nine sultans remained hereditary monarchs of their respective states in this federation, and with residual rights over religious affairs and land. The premiers had to dance carefully around the foibles of their still powerful sultans. The nine sultans took turns becoming head of state of the whole country for five-year terms as supreme king or *Yang di Pertuan Agong*.

The formation of Malaysia in 1963 brought more diversity into a still more asymmetric federation. Brunei's autocratic Sultan Omar Ali Saifuddin was strong enough to say 'no', but Sarawak and Sabah (North Borneo) were bundled in by a Britain bent on decolonization. Singapore under an elected Lee Kuan Yew government found this an ideal way to finesse the pro-China sentiment of a probable majority of its people. Each of the new states had different constitutional guarantees. Sarawak and Sabah were overrepresented in the federal Parliament, and Singapore underrepresented, since part of the rationale was to use the two Borneo territories to balance the Chinese population of Singapore. In return Singapore enjoyed autonomies in financial and legal arrangements. Sparsely-settled Sarawak and Sabah, fearful of being swamped, obtained control over internal migration into their states. They were also reassured with guarantees that English would remain the official language and that Islam would not be the state religion as it always had been in the sultanates.

Malaysia's peculiar federalism therefore provides one kind of asymmetry, whereby citizens do not all have the same rights. The racial equation provided another. Where post-revolutionary Indonesia asserted the sovereignty and equality of the people, Malaya and Malaysia have constitutionally qualified their citizens by race, obliging the state to give certain unequal rights to Malays or *bumiputra*. Like the federal asymmetry, these features came about through the difficult pragmatic compromises needed to bring groups into the nation, not by revolutionary assertions of principle.

## MALAYSIA AND INDONESIA: COMPARING THE RECORD

Malaysia and Indonesia are both truly new states, unable to draw on the state nationalism of a pre-colonial monarchy which had a claim to continuity with the post-colonial state as Burma, Vietnam, Korea and others did. The post-colonial states would have to be artificial constructs in both cases, within the artificial boundaries Britain, Holland and France had drawn between the Archipelago and the Peninsula, and across the Peninsula and Borneo. The two names 'Malaysia' and 'Indonesia' are alternative scholarly inventions to describe broader identities of the 'Malay world', or the world of Austronesian languages, taken over by politicians who had no satisfactory word for their imagined state.

But the path to that new identity divided them sharply. The revolutionary path gave the name 'Indonesia' a supernatural aura demanding loyalty. The blood of revolutionary martyrs was held to sacralize the flag, the independence declaration, the constitution and the sacred sites and dates of dead heroes. The success of this revolutionary process, completed in 1950 with the destruction of the complex federal architecture of RIS, was almost magical. The steel of the Dutch colonial bureaucracy was inherited by the army, but now married to a new passionately held ideology of the sovereignty of the *Indonesian* people.

Malaysia, on the other hand, inherited a great variety of older political forms of monarchy and of authority within separated communities, only gradually establishing the higher authority of Kuala Lumpur among them. Sultans continued to have outrageous prerogatives and immunities from the law; political parties were based on what they considered immutable 'race' rather than on programmes or ideologies.

On the positive side of the revolutionary path, one might list many valuable coherences in which Indonesia rejoices, which Malaysia lacks to its cost:

1.  An unquestioned national language.
2.  A strong sense of identity as Indonesians, despite extraordinarily diverse histories.
3.  Acceptance of the 'one man one vote' idea, with no special privileges in constitutional theory. Indonesian sultans have been trying to make some sort of comeback recently on a platform of *adat*, but it feels like a lost cause, as it would be in France or Russia.
4.  Acceptance of the irrelevance of race, not mentioned in census data (until 2000), and thus the possibility of Chinese, Dayaks and Papuans being simply accepted as Indonesians.

On the negative side of the balance, the revolutionary assertion of these principles brought some clear political disadvantages.

1.  The way heroic myths of revolutionary struggle take the place of history, denying all Indonesia's peoples, but especially the more

marginal, their roots and their identity. By contrast Malaysia's Dayaks, Kadazans, Chinese and Kelantanese know their distinct histories, even if the federal government does little to support that knowledge.

2. The huge gap between revolutionary expectations and Indonesia's diverse realities virtually required that the state fill the gap with force and the threat of force. People were expected to act as though Indonesia was united around these unifying ideals, and legitimate differences were often therefore equated with treason and suppressed by force. Even in times of democracy (1949–57 and since 1998) it has been difficult for Indonesia to legitimate these differences, though progress is being made.

3. The unitary system, interpreted as meaning that there needed to be uniform administrative, educational and judicial systems throughout the country, drove particularists in Aceh, Papua and East Timor, and Islamists everywhere, into a cycle of rebellion and suppression. By contrast, Malaysia has become, through a succession of unsatisfactory but workable compromises, a striking example of what Keating (2001) calls 'plurinational democracy' and 'asymmetric government'.

4. Basing the rights of endangered minorities such as Chinese and Christians on the myth of nationalist equality rather than legality and the right of redress has in practice not served them well. A pattern developed of affluent minorities having to buy protection and justice rather than relying on constitutional and legal means. In the process the rule of law was further eroded.

The toll of political violence is one factor that can be measured, and Indonesia comes out on the wrong side of that equation. Both countries got off to a bad start in the violent aftermath of the Japanese occupation, but the British reoccupation of Malaya and the Borneo territories gave rise to far fewer casualties in both the short and long term than the failed attempt by the Dutch to do the same in Indonesia.

The tally of deaths in Malaysia would have to include the following:

1. 1945: a hundred or more killed in Malay–Chinese clashes immediately after the Japanese surrender.

2. 1948–56: thousands of casualties of the Malayan emergency, which pitted (predominately Chinese) guerrillas of the MCP against British, Australian and (predominately Malay) Malayan troops

3. 1963–67: some hundreds of casualties, chiefly in Sarawak, of the violent resistance to the formation of Malaysia, sustained first by Indonesia with the infiltration of military 'volunteers', then by pro-communist Chinese in Sarawak and Indonesian Borneo.

4.  1969: around a hundred mostly Chinese casualties at the hands of Malay mobs, in the 13 May violence following the modest advances of left-wing (predominately Chinese) parties in the 1969 elections.

As against this, the Indonesian toll is unfortunately very heavy.[5]

*1945*: Thousands of Chinese, Eurasian and Ambonese victims of the *bersiap* time in the early revolution.

*Nov. 1945*: tens of thousands killed in the 'Battle of Surabaya' against British troops, after General Mallaby is killed trying to make peace.

*1945–46*: thousands of victims of the 'social revolutions' in Aceh, East Sumatra, West Sumatra, Pekalongan area, Solo.

*1946*: hundreds of victims of '3 July affair'; hundreds of Republican sympathizers killed by Lt Westerling in Sth Sulawesi.

*1947*: Dutch aggression kills hundreds of Indonesian defenders; hundreds of Chinese, aristocrats and others killed in 'scorched-earth' actions by Republicans in East Sumatra and elsewhere.

*1948*: Republican military units clash in Central Java, Tapanuli.

*1948*: thousands killed in violent suppression of PKI in so-called 'Madiun rebellion'.

*1948–49*: second Dutch aggression followed by guerrilla activity, with low-level constant violence.

*1949–50*: violence against Federal states in West Borneo, Bali, South Sulawesi.

*1950–51*: Republik Maluku Selatan rebellion put down forcefully.

*1948–63*: DI rebellion led by Kartosuwirjo in West Java, Kahar Muzakkar in South Sulawesi.

*1953–57*: Aceh rebellion. Thousands killed in its violent suppression.

*1958–59*: PRRI rebellion in West Sumatra, Tapanuli, South and North Sulawesi put down forcefully.

*1964–65*: PKI-supported *aksi sepihak* [unilateral actions] against landowners in rural Central and East Java. Often violent land seizures.

*1965–66*: up to a million killed in the aftermath of 1 October 1965 coup attempt, which was used to justify the violent destruction of PKI Indonesia-wide.

*1975–* Invasion of East Timor and subsequent fierce repression of resistance, causing tens of thousands of violent deaths. Technique developed in 1980s of arming pro-Indonesian militias to do much of the killing.

*1976–77*: low-level guerrilla violence recommences in Aceh.

*1982–85*: thousands of 'mysterious killings' (*petrus*) of suspected gangsters by military-backed clandestine units.

*1984*: Tg Priuk affair, at least 27 Muslim victims of military repression (victims say hundreds).

*1989*: Lampung affair, perhaps 200 Muslim students killed by Brimob.

*1959–60, 1963, 1965–67, 1973, 1980, 1982, 1994, 1996*: sporadic violence against Chinese – usually few deaths but much physical damage and much harm to economy.

*1989–91*: about 2000 victims of military crack-down on Aceh rebellion. East Timor technique of arming militias in image of revolutionary pemudas (young activists).

*1996–97, 1999*: thousands killed in Dayak violence against immigrant Madurese in West Kalimantan.

*1998*: over 100 killed in anti-Chinese and other violence accompanying Suharto's fall.

*1999–2002*: about 5000 victims of Muslim–Christian violence in Ambon, spreading also to Poso in Sulawesi.

*1999–2005*: thousands killed in renewal of conflict in Aceh, notably in military crack-down of May 2003–August 2005 (Reid, 2006, chs 11–15).

It is possible to argue that federalism had something to do with Malaysia's better record here, while the unitary dream did have to be imposed by violence. Revolution itself is, however, a larger factor in the contrast. Once legality was breached by violence in the name of the 'people', only a highly disciplined and usually undemocratic force could stop it running out of control. In the Indonesian case this was the army, though in frequent contestation with the communist party before 1965. As Freek Columbijn (Columbijn, 2002, pp. 54–5) has pointed out, state violence was often legitimated by the imagery of the violent foundation of the state in 1945–49, with militia gangs using sharpened bamboo stakes and growing their hair long in evocation of the violent revolutionary youth gangs.

In terms of economic performance, Malaysia has also fared much better than Indonesia since 1945. According to Angus Maddison's figures, in 1913 Indonesia's GNP per capita ($904) was a little more than Malaysia's ($899) though less than Singapore's ($1279). Both countries boomed up to 1929, and staggered thereafter from the blows of the depression and the war. Malaysia, however, left Indonesia progressively further behind in the independent era. By 1965, Indonesia's per capita income ($990) was well below the levels of 1940, scarcely higher than it had been in 1913, and little more than a third of Malaysia's (without Singapore) (Booth, 1998, pp. 53–67; Maddison, 2001, pp. 215, 304).

If there is any link here with federalism it can only be the indirect one of a more stable, open and democratic environment. The post-revolutionary violence and instability of Indonesia had a terrible effect on its economy. Not surprisingly, the other Asian states which made a revolutionary transition to independence, Vietnam, Laos, Cambodia and (more ambivalently) Burma, were the only ones whose economy fared even worse than Indonesia's in this mid-century crisis period.

In conclusion, Indonesia's post-revolutionary drive towards uniformity increased the likelihood of violent outcomes to some regional, ethnic and even ideological tensions. An evolutionary federal path such as Malaysia's would have facilitated a less violent negotiation of the place of Aceh and East Timor, and perhaps also of Ambon, Papua and parts of Sulawesi and Sumatra, within Indonesia. While the possibility could not be ruled out that federal states would move towards secession, the examples of Sarawak and Sabah in Malaysia, and of many disgruntled states in the northeast, northwest and south of the Indian federation, suggest that federations do have effective means to prevent this outcome.

While greater democracy in Indonesia would have provided more space for federal ideas and campaigns, the reverse is less clear, that federalism would have encouraged democracy. One might say rather that some degree of democracy is a precondition for effective federalism, in that the legitimacy and leverage of constituent states can have no other basis than elected governments. Because post-revolutionary Indonesia provided a difficult climate for democracy to flourish, it was also an infertile field for federalism. Developments since 1998, however, should be watched closely for the interplay of democratic procedures and less symmetric political structures.

## NOTES

1. See, among others, Geertz (1980); Reid (1998); Ricklefs (1992); Andaya (1993); Drakard (1999).
2. Mohamad Said, chairman of an 'All East Sumatra People's Congress', lobbying to dissolve the NST, in his opening speech of 27 April 1950, as translated in Feith and Castles (1970, p. 318).
3. In addition to note 23 in Hasan Tiro's book, see the Kahar Muzakar pamphlet of 1960, 'Konsepsi Negara Demokrasi Indonesia', partly translated in Feith and Castles (1970, pp. 330–35).
4. See Mangunwijaya (1998); Simorangkir (2000). A taste of this debate, Mangunwijaya for federalism and General Sudradjat against, is translated in Bourchier and Hadiz (2003, pp. 269–72).
5. An extensive literature has grown around Indonesian political violence in the democratic climate since 1998, though curiously ignored in the earlier authoritarian one. See Anderson (2001), Columbijn and Lindblad (2002), Wessel and Wimhofer (2001), Coppel (2004).

# REFERENCES

Andaya, Leonard (1993), *The World of Maluku: Eastern Indonesia in the Early Modern Period*, Honolulu: University of Hawaii Press.

Anderson, Benedict (ed.) (2001), *Violence and the State in Suharto's Indonesia*, Ithaca, NY: Cornell University Centre for SE Asian Studies.

Ariffin, Omar (1993), *Bangsa Melayu: Aspects of Democracy and Community among the Malays*, Kuala Lumpur: Oxford University Press.

Booth, Anne (1998), *The Indonesian Economy in the Nineteenth and Twentieth Centuries: A History of Missed Opportunities*, Basingstoke: Macmillan.

Bourchier, David and Vedi Hadiz (eds) (2003), *Indonesian Politics and Society: A Reader*, London: Routledge/Curzon.

Chauvel, Richard (1990), *Nationalists, Soldiers and Separatists: The Ambonese Islands from Colonialism to Revolt*, Leiden: KITLV Press.

Columbijn, Freek (2002), 'Explaining the violent solution in Indonesia', *The Brown Journal of World Affairs*, IX(I), (Spring).

Columbijn, Freek and J. Thomas Lindblad (eds) (2002), *Roots of Violence in Indonesia: Contemporary Violence in Historical Perspective*, Leiden: KITLV Press.

Coppel, Charles (ed.) (2004), *Violent Conflicts in Indonesia: Analysis, Representation, Resolution*, Richmond: Curzon.

Day, Tony (2002), *Fluid Iron: State Formation in Southeast Asia*, Honolulu: University of Hawaii Press.

Drakard, Jane (1999), *A Kingdom of Words. Language and Power in Sumatra*, Shah Alam, Malaysia: Oxford University Press.

Emerson, Rupert (1937), *Malaysia: A Study in Direct and Indirect Rule*, New York: Macmillan.

Feith, Herbert (1962), *The Decline of Constitutional Democracy in Indonesia*, Ithaca: Cornell University Press.

Feith, Herbert and Lance Castles (eds) (1970), *Indonesian Political Thinking 1945–1965*, Ithaca: Cornell University Press.

Geertz, Clifford (1980), *Negara: The Theatre State in Nineteenth-Century Bali*, Princeton, NJ: Princeton University Press.

Kahin, George McT. (1950), *Nationalism and Revolution in Indonesia*, Ithaca: Cornell University Press.

Kahn, Jeffrey (2002), *Federalism, Democratisation and the Rule of Law in Russia*, New York: Oxford University Press.

Keating, Michael (2001), *Plurinational Democracy: Stateless Nations in a Post-Sovereignty Era*, Oxford: Oxford University Press.

Maddison, Angus (2001), *The World Economy: A Millennial Perspective*, Paris: Development Centre of OECD.

Malley, Michael (1999), 'Regions: centralization and resistance', in Donald K. Emmerson (ed.), *Indonesia Beyond Suharto*, New York: The Asia Society, pp. 71–105.

Mangunwijaya, Y.B. (1998), *Menuju Republik Indonesia Serikat*, Jakarta: Gramedia.

Miller, Michelle (2006), 'What's special about special autonomy in Aceh?', in A. Reid (ed.), *Verandah of Violence*, pp. 292–314.

Reid, Anthony (1974), *The Indonesian National Revolution*, Melbourne: Longman.

Reid, Anthony (1979), *The Blood of the People: Revolution and the End of Traditional Rule in Northern Sumatra*, Kuala Lumpur: Oxford University Press.

Reid, Anthony (1998), 'Political "tradition" in Indonesia: the one and the many', *Asian Studies Review*, **22**(1), 23–38.

Reid, Anthony (2006), *Verandah of Violence: The Background to the Aceh Problem*, Singapore: Singapore University Press.

Ricklefs, M.C. (1992), 'Unity and disunity in Javanese political and religious thought of the eighteenth century', in V.J.H. Houben et al. (eds), *Looking in Odd Mirrors: The Java Sea*, Leiden University: Department of Southeast Asias Studies, pp. 60–75.

Ross, Cameron (2003), *Federalism and Democratisation in Post-Communist Russia*, Manchester: Manchester University Press.

Simorangkir, B. (ed.) (2000), *Otonomi atau Federalisme: Dampaknya terhadap Pembangunan*, Jakarta: Sinar Harapan.

Sjamsuddin, Nazaruddin (1985), *The Republican Revolt: A Study of the Acehnese Rebellion*, Singapore: Institute of Southeast Asian Studies.

Sulaiman, M. Isa (1997), *Sejarah Aceh: Sebuah Gugatan Terhadap Tradisi*, Jakarta: Pustaka Sinar Harapan.

Sulaiman, M. Isa (2000), *Aceh Merdeka: Ideologi, Kepemimpinan dan Gerakan*, Jakarta: Pustaka al Kausar.

Sulaiman M. Isa (2006), 'From autonomy to periphery: a critical evaluation of the Acehnese Nationalist movement', in Anthony Reid (ed.), *Verandah of Violence*, Singapore: Singapore University Press, pp. 121–48.

Tiro, Hasan Muhammad (n.d. [1958]), *Demokrasi Untuk Indonesia*, Atjeh: no publisher given.

Wessel, Ingrid and Georgia Wimhofer (eds) (2001), *Violence in Indonesia*, Hamburg: Abera.

Yamin, Muhammad (ed.) (1959), *Naskah persiapan Undang-Undang Dasar 1945*, 3 vols, Jakarta: Jajasan Prapantja.

# 8. Federalism versus autonomy in the Philippines[1]

## R.J. May

The Philippines is a unitary state, but one with a high degree of decentralization and a history of experimentation with autonomy arrangements, particularly as a means of addressing the separatist demands of Philippine Muslims in the south. It has also been (apart from a relatively brief interlude under President Ferdinand Marcos) one of the most democratic countries in Southeast Asia. Following the demise of the Marcos regime in the People Power revolution of 1986, the Philippines returned to democracy, and in the aftermath of the regime change there was a significant devolution of political power under a new Local Government Code and attempts were made to accommodate the specific demands of Philippine Muslims in the south and minority cultural communities in the north by regional autonomy arrangements, respectively, in Mindanao and the Cordilleras. Federalism was not on the agenda in 1986–87, however in recent years there seems to have been a widespread belief that federalism offers a means of dealing with continuing problems of regional dissidence and promoting popular participation in government. In 2005, in her State of the Nation address, President Macapagal-Arroyo announced her intention to initiate a constitutional review and endorsed the federal option.

This chapter looks briefly at the history of separatism, autonomy and decentralization in the Philippines, traces the federalist idea in the Philippines, reviews the current debate, with passing reference to the relationship between federalism and democracy, and suggests that the case for a federal system in the Philippines has yet to be established.

# DECENTRALIZATION AND AUTONOMY IN THE PHILIPPINES: AN OVERVIEW

## The Colonial Experience

When the Spanish colonizers arrived in the Philippines in the sixteenth century, Spain's civil and religious authorities created an hierarchical administrative structure based on indigenous *barangays* (communities of around 30–100 families, headed by a *datu*), municipalities and provinces.

In parts of the Philippine islands, particularly in Mindanao and the Sulu Archipelago, the Spanish encountered well-organized Muslim communities within established sultanates. Products of their European history, the Spaniards promptly termed these people 'Moros' and launched a series of military campaigns against them. In Minadanao and Sulu, however, they met strong resistance from the Moros, and were never able to integrate these islands into the Spanish colonial regime. In other areas, also, indigenous people resisted Spanish rule, either militarily or by withdrawing into the hinterland. Such groups were referred to by the Spanish as *'infieles'* or *'tribus independientes'*, and later were identified as 'tribal minorities' or 'cultural communities'.

When, in 1898, the United States took over the Philippines, following the Spanish–American War, they essentially maintained the administrative structure (and the religiously defined ethnic hierarchy) established by Spain. In 1901, a Bureau of Non-Christian Tribes (subsequently renamed Ethnological Survey of the Philippines) was created, to gather information on the non-Christian people of the Philippines (including the Moros) with a view to 'determining the most practicable means for bringing about their advancement in civilization and material prosperity' (quoted in Gowing, 1977, p. 67). The following year a bill passed by the US Congress 'recognized the distinction between the Moros, Pagans and Christian Filipinos and the consequent necessity for providing different forms of government for the different people' (ibid., p. 72).

Under the Americans, a more intensive military campaign against the Moros put an end to hopes of Moro sovereignty. Initially, administration of the Moro homelands in Mindanao and Sulu was placed in the hands of the US Army, though in 1903 an assistant chief of the Bureau of Non-Christian Tribes (a Syrian-born American) was appointed as Agent for Moro Affairs. The same year, a special Moro Province was created, under the supervision of the civil governor of the Philippine Islands and the Philippine Commission (the administrative arm of the colonial regime) but until 1913 headed and predominantly staffed by army officers. The Moro Province comprised five districts (Sulu, Cotabato, Davao, Lanao and

Zamboanga). It had a legislative Council, with limited powers, was subject to national laws except in civil or criminal actions involving only Moros and Pagans, and was expected to be fiscally self-reliant.

In 1913, the Moro Province was replaced by a Department of Mindanao and Sulu, and control passed from the military to civilian authorities headed by a governor. The districts were renamed provinces and the two non-Moro Mindanao provinces of Bukidnon and Agusan were added. The Department was, however, seen as a transitional arrangement, with the seven provinces to assume the same status as provinces elsewhere in the country. It was abolished in 1920.

Elsewhere, a number of 'special provinces' was created, under the secretary of the interior, for the governance of other non-Christian tribes. In the Cordilleras of northern Luzon, where tribal groups, commonly referred to collectively as 'the Igorots', had most strongly resisted Spanish intrusions, the American administration in 1908 established a Mountain Province and the administration of the region was reorganized so that, in the words of a contemporary observer, 'the wild tribes were safely removed from the field of insular [that is, national] politics' (Dean Bartlett, cited in Fry, 1983, p. 52).

Around this time there was some agitation for the administration of non-Christian tribes to be handed over to Filipino provincial and municipal officials. The American secretary of the interior, Dean Worcester, argued, however, that despite their 'common racial origin', the gap between the Filipino, the Igorot and the Moro was very great, and that to hand over control of the non-Christian tribes to Filipinos 'would speedily result in disaster' (*Report of the Philippine Commission, 1909–1911*, cited in Lopez, 1976, p. 113. See also Hayden, 1927–28).[2] Nevertheless, from 1914, responsibility for non-Christian tribes, though nominally in the hands of the secretary of the interior, was exercised increasingly by provincial and municipal authorities.

Dissatisfaction with these arrangements resulted three years later in the reconstitution of the Bureau of Non-Christian Tribes. The Bureau was given responsibility for both tribal areas and, until its demise in 1920, the Department of Mindanao and Sulu (which, as well as the Moros, contained many tribal people, now known as *Lumad*). Between 1917 and 1935, the Bureau of Non-Christian Tribes retained nominal control over the non-Christian groups, though responsibility progressively shifted to the Philippine Legislature. Following the establishment of the Philippine Commonwealth in 1935, the Bureau of Non-Christian Tribes was abolished. The administration of non-Christian tribes passed to the Department of the Interior, though the special circumstances in the south were recognized in the creation of a Commission for Mindanao and Sulu. The same year a group of datus from Lanao met in what is now Marawi City and petitioned the US not to include Mindanao and Sulu in an independent Philippines.

The historical arrangements briefly outlined here reflected the perception of the colonial administration that some degree of regionally based autonomy was needed to safeguard the interests of the Muslim and tribal people of the Philippines. After 1935, the special arrangements lapsed in the drive for national integration. Four decades later, however, regional autonomy arrangements were revived.

### Muslim and Cordillera Autonomy

In the late 1960s, an Islamic resurgence in the south, coupled with growing tensions associated with massive inmigration to Mindanao from the northern, Christian, provinces and encroachment on traditional Muslim and tribal lands, produced an outbreak of armed conflict in which the Philippine government, supported by various Christian militias and private armies, confronted Muslim insurgents under the banner of the Moro National Liberation Front (MNLF). The principal demand of the MNLF was for an independent Bangsa Moro in the 25 provinces of Mindanao, Sulu and Palawan, though under pressure from the Organization of Islamic Conference (OIC) the demand for independence was eventually scaled down to one of autonomy in the 13 provinces of traditional Muslim dominance. A major problem was that, by the end of the 1960s, as a result of immigration, Muslims were a majority in only five of the 13 provinces.

Following a negotiated ceasefire in 1976, the Philippine government of President Marcos and the MNLF signed an agreement, in Tripoli, which provided for autonomy in the 13 provinces. Disagreements over implementation of the Tripoli Agreement (particularly the Marcos government's insistence that the proposed autonomy be subject to a plebiscite in the provinces covered by the agreement), however, led to the MNLF's withdrawal from the peace negotiations. The plebiscite process nevertheless went ahead, without the participation of the MNLF and its supporters, and two autonomous regional governments were set up in administrative regions IX (Western Mindanao) and XII (Central Mindanao), though they lacked popular support and adequate resources.

The Marcos presidency also saw the growing politicization of tribal Filipinos/cultural communities, particularly in the Cordilleras where an armed insurgency emerged, primarily to resist encroachments on ancestral land (see, for example, Buendia, 1991).

Following the 'People Power Revolution' of 1986 a new constitution made special provision to create areas of autonomy in Muslim Mindanao and Sulu (the Autonomous Region of Muslim Mindanao, ARMM) and northern Luzon (the Cordillera Autonomous Region, CAR), and assigned to them a range of legislative powers.[3] Self-exiled MNLF leader Nur Misuari returned to the Philippines in 1986 to take part in talks with President Aquino, but the two failed to reach an agreement on the content of the proposed Muslim autonomy.

The 1987 constitution provided that Congress legislate an organic act for each region, with the assistance of a regional consultative commission created for this purpose. At least in the case of the ARMM, the implementation of the constitutional provision was a deeply flawed process (see Lalanto and Madale, 1989), but by 1989 an organic act had been drafted and put to a plebiscite in the 13 provinces and nine cities of central and western Mindanao and Sulu listed in the Tripoli Agreement, on the basis that only those provinces and cities voting to do so would become part of the ARMM. The MNLF (which by then had split into three factions) boycotted the poll, and in the event only four provinces (Lanao del Sur, Maguindanao, Sulu and Tawi-Tawi) and no cities voted to join the autonomous region. As with the regional governments established earlier under the Marcos government, the ARMM thus lacked popular legitimacy and, with limited authority and funding, proved largely ineffective. In the Cordilleras, an Interim Cordillera Regional Administration was established in 1986, but there too the consultative process proved acrimonious. An organic law was eventually drafted and submitted to plebiscite in 1990, but of the five provinces and one city in the region only one province (Ifugao) voted for the autonomous region.

In 1992, following the election of President Fidel Ramos, negotiations with the MNLF were reopened, with the Organization of Islamic Conference (OIC) playing a facilitative role. These initiatives culminated in 1996 in the signing of a Peace Agreement between the Philippine government and the MNLF. The agreement, which was subtitled 'The Final Agreement on the Implementation of the 1976 Tripoli Agreement', provided for the creation of a Special Zone of Peace and Development (SZOPAD) covering the area defined in the Tripoli Agreement, and a Southern Philippines Council for Peace and Development (SPCPD) with authority to 'control and/or supervise . . . appropriate agencies of the government that are engaged in peace and development activities in the area [of the SZOPAD]'. Provision was also made for a Consultative Assembly, headed by the chair of the SPCPD and dominated by members of the MNLF, for a *Darul Iftah* (religious advisory council) appointed by the SPCPD chair, and for the integration of 7500 former MNLF (Bangsa Moro Army) fighters into the Armed Forces of the Philippines and the Philippine National Police.

Potential jurisdictional problems between the ARMM and the SPCPD were avoided when Misuari, having returned from the Middle East, was appointed chair of the SPCPD and subsequently elected governor of the ARMM. A crucial provision of the 1996 Peace Agreement, however, was that which required a referendum, to be held within two years of the establishment of the SPCPD, seeking approval to extend the ARMM to cover the area of the SZOPAD.

The 1996 Agreement was greeted by many as a major step towards a final settlement of the conflict. But those familiar with the history of the Moro struggle could foresee a number of looming problems. For one, the agreement was specifically with the MNLF. Although the MNLF was the faction of the Moro movement recognized by the OIC (which therefore locked the Philippines government into negotiations with the MNLF), by the mid-1990s the other major faction, the Moro Islamic Liberation Front (MILF), was almost certainly the more powerful group. The MILF was not a party to the 1996 agreement and had vowed to continue the armed struggle. In December 1997, the chairman of the MILF, the late Hashim Salamat, revived the demand for an independent Islamic state. Secondly, there was considerable popular opposition to the 1996 Agreement among Christian communities within the SZOPAD, who were apprehensive about being incorporated into a region of Muslim autonomy, and among members of Congress. As a result of this, the executive order (EO 371) intended to give effect to the Peace Agreement was a substantially watered down version of the agreement signed with Misuari, which was a source of frustration to the Moro leadership. Thirdly, there was no reason to believe that the mandated referendum (which was put off until August 2001) would yield a result any different from that of previous referenda on Muslim autonomy. Added to this, the SPCPD/ARMM leadership complained that it did not receive adequate funding to fulfil its goals, and expected foreign capital inflows did not materialize. In March 1999, Misuari warned that, if conditions did not improve, former MNLF fighters would return to the hills. Moreover, the MNLF leadership of the SPCPD was accused of inefficiency, mismanagement and nepotism, and Misuari's personal leadership came under attack.

In 2001, the required referendum was finally conducted and, predictably, only five of the now 15 provinces and one of the 14 cities voted for an expanded ARMM. Shortly after this, Misuari returned to armed insurgency, and is currently serving a prison sentence. The ARMM continues to function, but with limited popular support (see Bacani, 2005), while the MILF (with whom the Philippine government is currently negotiating) operates as a virtual autonomous region within the autonomous region.

In 1997, the year after the Moro peace agreement, the Philippine Congress legislated to create the Cordillera Autonomous Region and another plebiscite was held. The plebiscite again failed to approve the CAR, which continues to operate as one of the country's 17 administrative regions.

The long saga of attempts to use autonomy arrangements as a means of dealing with ethnic cleavages and ethnoregional separatism in the Philippines thus provides little ground for optimism. In the case of Muslim Mindanao, the disjuncture between the Moro claim to the area described within the Tripoli Agreement (an area already scaled down under pressure from the OIC) and the demographic reality that Philippine Muslims are now outnumbered in all but five provinces and one city creates a continuing obstacle to a lasting settlement.[4] The problems of the ARMM have been exacerbated both by lack of commitment on the part of the national government to provide the resources necessary to support regional autonomy and by the failure of the ARMM to use wisely what resources it has had. It is against this background that, from around the late 1990s, the idea of federalism began to gain support in the Philippines.

### Administrative Decentralization, People Power and the Local Government Code[5]

As noted above, the Spanish colonial regime established an administrative structure based on the *barangay*, with municipalities and provinces between the barangays and the central government. This structure was broadly maintained by the US, though with the special arrangements described above for the Moros and other non-Christian tribes, and the broad features of this system were inherited by the independent republic in 1946.

After independence, a measure of decentralization was enacted through the Local Autonomy Act, the Decentralisation Act and other legislation, but the local government units (LGUs: the barangays, municipalities and provinces) were supervised through the Office of the President and governance remained strongly centralized. At the municipal and provincial level, however, politics was frequently dominated by prominent local families. During the Marcos presidency (1966–86) there were further moves to decentralize: the 'martial law constitution' of 1973 'guaranteed and promoted' the autonomy of LGUs; a system of 'barangay democracy' was introduced by presidential decree; and a Local Government Code was enacted in 1983. But in practice, even though the Philippine state remained fairly weak, political power was centralized, with patronage networks used to ensure the compliance of local officials. Also, in 1972 (the year in which Marcos declared martial law) the Marcos government created a structure of 11 regions, as a basis for economic planning and general administration.

Following the People Power Revolution and the restoration of democratic government, a new Local Government Code was enacted in 1991 which provided for a substantial decentralization of responsibility for the delivery of basic services in health, education, social welfare, agriculture, public works, and environment and natural resources, with a corresponding increase in the allocation of funds to LGUs. Reflecting the new government's commitment to 'people empowerment', the 1991 Code also provided for enhanced participation in local governance by NGOs and POs (people's organizations) and the private sector generally. Amendments to the Code in 1995 strengthened the decentralization of the system.

In the words of the Local Government Code, 1991, 'the barangay serves as the primary planning and implementing unit of government policies, plans, programs, projects and activities in the community, and as a forum where the collective views of the people may be expressed, crystallised and considered, and where disputes may be amicably settled'. Each barangay has a legislative body (*sangguniang barangay*) comprising the chief executive (*punong barangay*), seven elected members and the chair of the local youth organization. The Code also provides for a barangay assembly, composed of all residents of the barangay aged over 14 years, which is required to meet at least twice a year to consider reports of the sangguniang and discuss problems affecting the barangay; it may initiate legislation. Formal provision is made for local dispute settlement. At present there are about 45 000 barangays.

Above the barangays are municipalities, whose function is stated to be 'primarily as a general purpose government for the co-ordination and delivery of basic, regular and direct services and effective governance of the inhabitants within its territorial jurisdiction'. Each municipality is headed by a mayor and a vice mayor, and has its own legislature (*sangguniang bayan*) comprising elected members from the municipality's barangays, the presidents of the municipal league of barangays and youth federation, and three sectoral representatives. The vice-mayor presides over the sangguniang while the mayor exercises 'general supervision and control over all programs, projects, services, and activities of the municipal government'. Although formally responsible to the sangguniang bayan, the mayor has always been a powerful local figure in Philippines politics, and the Local Government Code gives the municipality, and its chief executive, extensive powers. Currently there are 1543 municipalities.

Cities in the Philippines are divided into two categories: 'highly urbanized cities' and 'component cities'. Both are described, like municipalities, as serving 'as a general purpose government'. Each city is headed by an elected mayor and vice-mayor. The latter presides over a *sangguniang panlungsod*, whose composition mirrors that of other local assemblies. The mayor, as chief executive, has powers parallel to those of other chief executives of LGUs. There are 65 highly urbanized cities, which are independent of provincial authority and exercise equivalent functions and responsibilities. Component cities (of which there are many) come under the supervision of the provinces and are similar in structure and function to municipalities.

Provinces are at the top of the LGU structure. There are 79 of them. Each is headed by an elected governor and vice-governor and has a legislature (*sangguniang panlalawigan*) composed of elected members from the provinces, municipalities and component cities, the presidents of the provincial barangay federation and the provincial youth federation, and three sectoral representatives. The vice-governor presides over the sangguniang, while the governor appoints all officials and employees whose salaries derive from provincial funds. The provincial governor is a person of significant power and authority in the Philippines, and an important link between the national government and the municipalities. Even at the provincial level, higher offices are frequently dominated by powerful local dynasties, notwithstanding post-1986 legislation designed to reduce the political power of local elite families.

Authority to exercise 'general supervision' over LGUs resides with the president, but is delegated through the Department of Interior and Local Government. All LGUs have exclusive powers to raise revenue from specified taxes, fees and charges, and may raise loans, accept overseas development assistance, and participate in certain joint-venture business operations. The majority of LGU funding (currently around 60 per cent), however, comes from unconditional block grants from the national government.

It should also be noted that, since 1972, the administrative regions established by Marcos – named Region I to Region XI (to which was added Region XII in 1975) – have acquired some degree of local identity, and seem to be referred to increasingly by locality (for example, 'Region I (Ilocos)', 'Region II (Cagayan Valley)', and so on). Moreover, recent additions (there are now 17 regions) have been given titles (mostly acronyms from the constituent provinces) which identify them with the locality: ARMM, CAR, National Capital Region (NCR), Caraga (Region XIII), CALABARZON and MIMAROPA (Regions IV-A and IV-B, formerly the single region of Southern Tagalog) and SOCCSKSARGEN (the provinces remaining in Region XII (Central Mindanao) following the creation of the ARMM in 1990). In what little discussion there has been about what might constitute the component units of a federal system, the regions seem to have provided the major point of reference.

The Local Government Code of 1991 was a product of the People Power movement of 1986, though it drew on structures established under the authoritarian regime of President Marcos. The Code promised a great deal in terms of participation, transparency, accountability, fiscal redistribution and checks on corruption. After a good deal of initial enthusiasm, however, critics of the decentralization arrangements were quick to emerge. It was noted that provisions for representation of civil society organizations had not always been implemented, that local development councils and other bodies were often ineffective, and that local youth councils were frequently dominated by the children of the political elite (see, for example, Turner, 1999). Critics on the left argued that the Code had simply delivered greater power to local dynasties and 'warlords'. Nevertheless, assessments of the decentralization initiatives of 1991 and 1995 have generally been positive and, in announcing her support for federalism in 2005, President Macapagal-Arroyo specifically referred to the success of decentralization in the Philippines. That said, there is no clear evidence in the Philippines experience either that democracy provides a receptive environment for federalism (except that the Philippines brand of democracy has facilitated debate on the subject and left open the possibility of future progress towards an asymmetric federalism) or that decentralization has fostered greater democratization.

## THE IDEA OF FEDERALISM IN THE PHILIPPINES

While the Philippines has never had a federal system, the federal idea is not entirely new. During the Philippines Revolution against Spain, the first Philippines Republic established at Biak-na-Bato by revolutionary leader General Emilio Aguinaldo had a federal constitution. The republic lasted only six weeks, its leaders going into exile in Hong Kong, but when Aguinaldo returned the following year to proclaim Philippines independence the Biak-na-Bato federal constitution was revived. The 'Malolos Constitution' approved by the Revolutionary Congress in 1899, however, was not federal, though Aguinaldo recognized the separate status of the Moros and proposed that the new government be empowered to negotiate with the Moros 'for the purposes of establishing national solidarity upon the basis of a real federation with absolute respect for their beliefs and traditions' (quoted in Canoy, 1987, pp. 69–70). The Moros declined negotiation, and in the event the revolution ended when the United States took control of the Philippines. The same year, a group of Filipinos submitted a draft constitution for a Federal Republic of the Philippines, with 11 states, but the US, despite its own experience of federal government, did not pursue the federal idea. Several 'little republics' set up during the revolution quickly faded away, though the 'Negros Republic' survived until 1901, anticipating statehood within a federal Philippines republic.

Some 70 years later, delegates to a constitutional convention set up by the Marcos government voiced some support for a federal system; delegate

Antonio de las Alas, for example, argued for a Swiss-style confederation of 20 autonomous states, and Salvador Araneta proposed (under what he called the 'Bayanikasan Constitution') a federal republic comprising five states, to be introduced in ten to 20 years.[6] But in 1972, Marcos declared martial law and the constitutional convention lapsed.

Following the People Power Revolution, in 1986 a Mindanao People's Democratic Movement (later renamed Mindanao Independence Movement) emerged, with the declared intention of establishing a Federal Republic of Mindanao, with 'proportionate cultural representation' of Christians, Muslims and Highlanders (tribal groups/cultural communities/*lumad*). The movement was led by Mindanao politician and former Marcos oppositionist Reuben Canoy,[7] who in 1986 was involved in an abortive attempt to set up an independent state of Mindanao (see May, 1992, pp. 137–8).

When a new constitution was drafted in 1986–87, federalism was not on the agenda, though in the late 1980s and early 1990s there was some discussion of 'federalization', notably in the advocacy of the political group, Unlad Bayan, led by businessman Enrique Zobel, and in a scholarly article by Rizal Buendia (1989). Proposals for a federal system emerged again in the late 1990s. The case for federalism was argued (if at all) largely in terms of resolving the continuing problems of separatism in Muslim Mindanao.

Probably the most prominent advocate of federalism was Senator John Osmeña, a member of the clan which has dominated politics in the Visayan province of Cebu for most of the past century.[8] Another advocate was Aquilino Pimentel, like Canoy a Mindanao politician and former Marcos oppositionist, who became minister for local government in the Aquino government and was principal author of the Local Government Code of 1991, before becoming president of the Senate. In 2000, Senators Pimentel, Osmeña and Francisco Tatad proposed a bill to establish federal government and the chair of the Senate Committee on Constitutional Amendments, Senator Miriam Defensor-Santiago, promised to call for a constitutional convention to consider the proposal, but the initiative lapsed.

About this time also, political scientist and former University of the Philippines president, Jose V. Abueva published a seminal article which supported a shift to a Federal Republic of the Philippines with a parliamentary government, and presented a draft constitution for such a republic (Abueva, 2001; also see Abueva, 2000, 2005). Abueva's proposal was presented to a Mindanao Stakeholders Forum in Cagayan de Oro City in 2001. In Mindanao two civil society organizations, Lihuk Pideral and Kusog Mindanaw, emerged to push for a federal system; these gave birth to the national Citizens' Movement for a Federal Philippines (CMFP), which was launched in Manila in February 2003. Over the next few years the idea of federal government gained ground. The German government, the Konrad Adenauer Stiftung, and the Canadian government sponsored workshops to discuss federalism, and a range of NGOs supported the idea.

Most prominent in the advocacy of federalism has been the CMFP, convened by former Congressman Rey Magno Teves, who is also secretary-general of Kusog Mindanaw. CMFP has a national steering committee, assisted by a 'Resource and Advisory Pool of prominent citizens' headed by Dr Abueva, and international linkages. Abueva is now founding president of the Kalayaan College in Marakina (Metro Manila), which hosts a Federalism Research Project. CMFP has a website (http://www.cmfp.ph/), which includes a 'primer on federalism', a number of pro-federalism articles, and a 'CMFP Draft Constitution for a Federal Republic of the Philippines with a Parliamentary Government' (based on Abueva's 2001 draft, but revised to 14 February 2005), edited by Abueva.

Towards the end of the presidency of Fidel Ramos, who succeeded 'People Power' president Corazon Aquino in 1992, there were proposals for a review (popularly referred to as 'charter change' or 'cha-cha') of the 1987 constitution. In 1997, a Peoples Initiative for Reform and Amendment gathered the constitutionally required number of signatures (12 per cent of registered voters) to petition for constitutional amendment, but the petition was dismissed by the Supreme Court. Although Ramos had generally been considered a good and effective president, the suggestion of a charter change generated considerable angst, with a range of groups accusing Ramos of seeking to extend his term in office (under the 1987 constitution a president may serve only a single six-year term), and some even suggesting that he was on the verge of re-imposing martial law.[9] A consultative commission was created in 1999 by Ramos's successor, Joseph Estrada, primarily to look at issues of national patrimony and economic reform, but little progress was made before Estrada's term in office ended prematurely with the threat of impeachment. Proposals for charter change were revived by incoming president Gloria Macapagal-Arroyo in 2003. 'Federalism,' she suggested, 'will empower regional governments . . . bringing governance and public service closer to the people . . . reducing corruption and making government more responsive and accountable to the people.'[10] In the presidential election the following year she promised if elected to shift to a federal constitution as part of a wider constitutional reform. Macapagal-Arroyo was supported by House of Representatives Speaker Jose de Venecia, who in 2005 told an international conference on federalism that 'Federalism is the best antidote to secession and separatism [in the Philippines]'; he described federalism as 'the wave of the future', and recommended it for Iraq and Myanmar.[11] In 2004, Constantino Jaraula, chair of the House Committee on Constitutional Amendments, introduced a concurrent resolution calling for constitutional change, specifically includ-ing a shift from a presidential and unitary system to a parliamentary and federal system. There followed a period of contention between members of the house, who favoured convening Congress as a constituent assembly, and senators, who mostly demanded a constitutional convention.

Eventually, in her state of the nation address in July 2005, President Macapagal-Arroyo suggested that it was 'time to start the great debate on charter change'. The president went on to say: 'The economic progress and social stability of the provinces, along with the increasing self-reliance and efficiency of political developments and public services there, make a com-pelling case for federalism. Perhaps it's time to take the power from the centre to the countryside that feeds it.'

In August 2005, President Macapagal-Arroyo appointed a Consultative Commission (ConCom) to conduct consultations and studies and propose constitutional amendments and revisions, 'principally the proposals to shift from the presidential–unitary system to a parliamentary–federal system of government'.[12] The 54-person commission, chaired by Professor Abueva, reported in December 2005 (see below).

There appeared to be a good deal of support for the proposed parlia-mentary–federal charter change; nevertheless, as happened with former president Ramos, there was also some strong opposition. President Macapagal- Arroyo had been accused by her critics of 'cheating' in the 2004 presidential election (which she won by a fairly narrow margin) and there have been allegations of corruption against her husband. In the cynical climate of Philippine politics, her opponents accused Macapagal-Arroyo of using charter change as a political diversion and, having failed in an impeachment bid, called on her to step down. Perennial rumours of an immi-nent military coup surfaced again in the latter part of 2005.

## THE DEBATE

### Why Federalism?

An annotated CMFP draft constitution, edited by the CMFP's advisory committee chairman, Abueva, lists six advantages of federalism:

> First, a Federal republic will build a just and enduring framework for peace through unity in our ethnic, religious and cultural diversity, especially in relation to Bangsa Moro or Muslim Filipinos. Responsive Federalism will accommodate their legitimate interests, end the war in Mindanao, and discourage secessionism.
> Second, Federalism will empower our citizens by enabling them to raise their standard of living and enhance their political awareness, participation and

efficacy in elections and the making of important government decisions. Governance will be improved and corruption will be reduced. . . .

Third, Federalism will improve governance by empowering and challenging State and local leaders and entrepreneurs around the country. . . . the people will be more willing to pay taxes that will finance government programs and services for their direct benefit.

Fourth, Federalism will hasten the country's development. . . . There will be inter-State and regional competition in attracting domestic and foreign investments and industries, professionals and skilled workers, good teachers and scholars, artists, and tourists. A renaissance of regional languages and cultures will enrich the national language and culture. The Federal Government will help support the less endowed and developed regions, and the poor and the needy across the land. . . .

Fifth, Federalism, together with parliamentary government, will improve governance by promoting the development of program-oriented political parties that are responsible and accountable to the people for their conduct and performance in and out of power.

Sixth, Federalism will broaden and deepen democracy and make its institutions deliver on the constitutional promise of human rights, a better life for all, a just and humane society, and responsible and accountable political leadership and governance. (*CMFP Draft Constitution*, February 2005, pp. 4–5)

'A Primer on Constitutional Reform/FAQ [frequently asked questions]' by the Institute of Popular Democracy, headed by academic activist Joel Rocamora, asks, 'Why a federal system of government in the Philippines?' and 'What are the advantages of Federal System of Government?' It answers:

The present unitary and centralized form of government of the Philippines is a remnant of its colonial past. It continues to be used as a tool for domination and control. . . .
. . . the federal system will foster closer dialogue and interaction between the people and regional leaders because the locus of power is physically closer to the people . . .

and it provides a list of advantages similar that of the CMFP.

The specific expectation that federalism would help solve the Mindanao conflict has been a recurring theme in the discussion. It is an argument that has been made by Pimentel and by Teves, and also by prominent Muslim lawyer and former Congressman Datu Michael Mastura, who described federalism as 'the antidote to secession' (quoted in Santuario, 2001). More importantly, it is a view that was endorsed as early as 1997 by MNLF leader Misuari and also by the late MILF leader Salamat,[13] and more recently by the Ulama League of the Philippines,[14] the chair of the Islamic Directorate of the Philippines (Macapanton Abbas), the Mindanao Bishops-Ulama Conference, the attorney-general of the ARMM (Jose Lorena), and the newly-formed Muslim Movement for Federal Philippines chaired by Farouk Sampao. Lorena, for example, has argued that, under the present autonomy arrangements, the ARMM is treated as a local government under the supervision of the national government, whereas in a federal system it would have sovereignty within its own sphere of responsibilities. The argument has been questioned, however, by Mindanao-based lawyer and academic Benedicto Bacani (see Bacani, 2003, 2004). Bacani compares the powers of the ARMM under the present organic law and those under the proposed (CMFP) draft constitution, and concludes that 'there are features in the Organic Law that provide for a higher level of self-determination than in the proposed federal system'; perhaps, he suggests, the failure of the present autonomy lies not in autonomy as a framework but in its operationalization (2004, p. 133; also see Diaz-Manalo, 2006).

With respect to claims that federalism would empower citizens and 'broaden and deepen democracy', there has been a good deal of rhetoric but little explanation of how the introduction of a federal structure would change patterns of behaviour that have dominated Philippine politics for decades.

**What Form Might Federalism Take?**

As revised to 14 February 2005, the 'CMFP Draft Constitution for a Federal Republic of the Philippines with a Parliamentary Government' envisaged a Federal Republic of the Philippines (*Ang Republica Federal ng Pilipinas*) with a federal or national government (*Gobyerno Federal*) and ten states (*Estados*): Bangsamoro (ARMM); Central and Southern Mindanao (Regions XI, XII); Northern and Western Mindanao (Regions IX and X and Caraga); Eastern Visayas (Region VII); Western Visayas-Palawan (Region IV and part of Region VI); Bicol (Region V and part of Region IV); Southern Luzon (most of Region IV); Metro Manila; Central Luzon (Region III), and Northern Luzon and Cordillera (Region I and CAR). (A later, June 2005, paper by Abueva refers to 11 states, with Northern Luzon and CAR becoming separate states.) It was proposed to establish a federal capital, New Manila, within the Clark Special Economic Zone, north of Manila (fortuitously, in the home province – Pampanga – of President Macapagal-Arroyo).

The draft constitution proposed a distribution of powers and functions, with 33 subjects listed for exclusive federal jurisdiction, 28 subjects listed for primary state jurisdiction, and another 23 areas for concurrent jurisdiction. The CMFP draft constitution proposed a bicameral federal parliament, with a House of the People (*Balay Sambayanan*), elected mostly from parliamentary districts but in part (60 out of up to 350 members) also on proportional representation from a party list vote, and a *Balay Estados* or Senate, to represent the states and protect their rights and interests. The senators were to be elected by the unicameral state assemblies (*batasang estados*) – two to three per state – 'mostly from among their members'.

The draft constitution made provision for the shift from a presidential to a parliamentary system at both levels of government. The chief executives of the states were to have the title of 'governor'.

In a paper prepared by Abueva it was suggested that 'A transition period is needed to enable the Federal Government and the various states to prepare for, and adjust to, the redistribution of powers, functions and tax bases between the Federal Government (National Government) and the several States (Regional Governments) and their local governments' and that 'The actual formation of the individual States shall depend upon their relative political, economic, fiscal, and administrative capabilities to govern themselves as autonomous regional governments and territories.' It was proposed that the 'more developed and ready' become fully operative in the first five years following ratification of the revised constitution, and the 'less developed' in the next five years. However, the Bangsamoro and Cordillera states (which are amongst the least developed) should be enabled to become operative in the first five years.

The CMFP proposed the holding of a plebiscite in 2007 (when national elections were scheduled) to ratify the proposed revision of the 1987 constitution.

## THE REPORT OF THE CONSULTATIVE COMMISSION

The Consultative Commission commenced work in September 2005, setting up three committees, on national patrimony and economic reforms, form of government, and structure of the republic, and a sub-committee on transitory provisions, and holding several regional consultations. It reported on schedule in mid-December 2005 (as this chapter was being written).

The Commission recommended a unicameral national parliament, with the majority of members voted from district constituencies but 30 per cent of members elected on a party list basis. A prime minister is to be elected by all MPs, and will appoint a cabinet, at least 75 per cent of whom are to be MPs. A presidential head of state is to be elected by MPs.

On the proposed shift to a federal system, however, divisions emerged within the Commission. It was apparent from the outset that several members of the Commission had doubts about the federal idea, though in

November Abueva reported that a 'clear majority' of people consulted strongly or very strongly favoured a shift to a federal system after a ten-year transition (Zamboanga providing a notable exception).[15] These differences became more apparent in the days preceding the submission of the report. On 9 December it was reported that one commissioner, Camaguin Provincial Governor Pedro Romualdo, had said that 'The federal structure is a beautiful mechanism for fragmenting the country.' Romualdo argued that resources were lacking and without adequate resources states could not be effective as independent entities; he cited the ARMM as 'a classic case of failure' and called instead for a strengthening of LGUs. Other commissioners suggested that, if each state could draft its own legislation, it would be difficult to harmonize laws nationally – even that autonomous states could 'seek from outside countries implicated in terrorism activities funding assistance for development'. In the event, it was reported that the commissioners had unanimously agreed 'to junk the mandatory switch to federalism' as proposed by Abueva and instead approved 'a gradual constituent-initiated transition to federalism'.[16]

In fact, the Commission's report makes scant reference to federalism, though provision is made for its eventual realization. In a section on 'Autonomous Territories' (Article XII B), the proposed revision of the 1987 constitution says:

> SEC. 12. An autonomous territory may be created in any part of the country upon a petition addressed to Parliament by a majority of contiguous, compact and adjacent provinces, highly urbanized and component cities, and cities and municipalities in metropolitan areas through a resolution of their respective legislative bodies.
>
> In exceptional cases, a province may be established as an autonomous territory based on area, population, necessity, geographical distance, environmental, economic and fiscal viability and other special attributes.
>
> SEC. 13. Within one year from the filing of the bill based upon the petitions and initiatives, Parliament shall pass an organic act which shall define the basic structure of government for the autonomous territory, consisting of a unicameral territorial assembly whose members shall be elective and representative of the constituent political units. The organic acts shall provide for courts consistent with the provisions of their constitution and national laws.
>
> The creation of the autonomous territories shall be effective when ratified by a majority of the votes cast by their proposed constituent units in a plebiscite called for the purpose.

The autonomous territory assemblies will have legislative power in the following areas (SEC. 16):

1.  Administrative organization, planning, budget and management;
2.  Creation of sources of revenues and finance;

3.   Agriculture and fisheries;
4.   Natural resources, energy, environment, indigenous appropriate tech-
     nologies and inventions;
5.   Trade, industry and tourism;
6.   Labour and employment;
7.   Public works, transportation, except railways, shipping and aviation;
8.   Health and social welfare;
9.   Education and the development of language, culture and the arts as
     part of the cultural heritage;
10.  Ancestral domain and natural resources;
11.  Housing, land use and development;
12.  Urban and rural planning and development; and
13.  Such other matters as may be authorized by law for the promotion of
     the general welfare of the people of the autonomous territory.

In the event of inconsistency between national and autonomous terri-
tory/local government laws, the former will prevail. No mention is made of
concurrent powers.

Under 'Transitory Provisions' (Article XX, SEC. 15, 16), the proposed
revision of the constitution stipulates that, within one year, and after at
least 60 per cent of provinces, highly urbanized cities and component
cities have petitioned through their regional assemblies for the creation of
autonomous territories, parliament will enact the basic law for the
establishment of a Federal Republic of the Philippines, in which the
autonomous territories will become federal states. To this end, a constitutional preparatory commission will be appointed by the prime minister
to study and determine all constitutional, legal, financial, organizational,
administrative, and other requirements necessary or appropriate for a
smooth and orderly transition to the Federal Republic. Special provision is
made (SEC. 14) for the ARMM to 'exercise the powers and . . . be entitled
to benefits given to autonomous territories'.

There is nothing in the proposed revision of the constitution to suggest
how many autonomous territories there should be, or how they should be
constituted, and critical issues such as intergovernmental financial arrangements are left for future discussion.[17]

Controversially, the national election scheduled for 2007 is now to be
held in 2010. In the meantime, members of House and the Senate will
become members of an interim parliament, which will elect an interim
prime minister, and the president will appoint a cabinet from among the
MPs. Amendment or revision of the 1987 constitution may be proposed
by a 75 per cent vote of all members of Congress or a constitutional
convention; ratification requires a majority of votes cast in a plebiscite.

(At the time of writing, the issue of 'charter change' was still under debate.)

## WILL FEDERALISM WORK?

Considering the apparent groundswell of support for a federal system in the Philippines (at least prior to December 2005), it may seem churlish to question the idea. Nevertheless, for anyone familiar with the history of federal experiments in the latter half of the twentieth century, it is difficult to avoid the impression that the advantages claimed for federal over unitary systems read more like statements of faith than reasoned arguments. This is the more so given the long history of unsuccessful autonomy arrangements in the Philippines, and the already high degree of decentralization (at least on paper) prescribed by the amended Local Government Code.

If autonomy arrangements specifically directed to the demands of Philippine Muslims, and arising from negotiations intended to secure a peaceful settlement to the armed conflict, have fallen short of expectations and failed to produce a lasting settlement, what chance is there that the establishment of ten or so states in a federal republic will, incidentally, solve the 'Moro problem'?[18] Most of the prospective benefits claimed – the ability to use shari'ah law (with safeguards for non-Muslim minorities), the boosting of local cultures, greater popular participation in politics, the possibility of pursuing appropriate development paths, and the promise of fiscal redistribution – are available under existing political arrangements. And if the CAR has twice rejected autonomy, why should federalism be any more attractive?

Further, if the elaborate processes of the Local Government Code have not succeeded in further democratizing Philippine society (though some would argue that they have) why should the creation of yet another level of government between Manila and the provinces, cities, municipalities and barangays do so?

Although Abueva and Rocamora have made some attempt to rationalize their list of advantages for federalism, the case has not been strongly argued. Social engineering, through a shift from unitary to federal government, will not necessarily change entrenched patterns of political behaviour; indeed (as with the decentralization of 1990) the transfer of powers and functions to states may well strengthen the position of local elite families. Some cynics argue that this has been one source of the demand for federalism.

Moreover, some of the bigger, and more intractable, questions about a federal form of government have yet to be addressed. The question of how many states and how they are constituted is unlikely to be resolved easily (though the CMFP proposals for ten or 11 states provide a good starting point). And, as in federal and federal-type systems everywhere, the question of intergovernmental fiscal relations will be vexed (as it is already under the Local Government Code). The CMFP claims that, 'The Federal Government will help support the less endowed and developed regions, and the poor and the needy across the land', but to date there is little historical basis for such optimism.[19]

A particular aspect of the Philippine discussion of federalism is that there seems to be little recognition amongst those pressing for a federal system that any workable arrangement almost certainly must recognize the particular demands of Muslim Mindanao, based on historic claims, a sense of separate ethnic identity and relative deprivation – that is, any viable federal arrangement must be asymmetric. In a presentation to an ARMM Legislators' Seminar in Tagaytay in June 2006, Congressman Jaraula, who chairs the House Committee on Constitutional Amendments, spoke of the need to 'expand and strengthen' the powers of the ARMM to bring it *up* to the status of a full federal state. More realistically, Santos (2005, p. 37), argues that federalism in the Philippines 'has to be asymmetrical or with special concessions, particularly when it comes to the Bangsamoro and Cordillera states where there are considerations of compensatory social justice'.

The push for federalism, largely as a response to ethnic or regional tensions, is enjoying something of a renaissance, from the Solomon Islands to Iraq, though there is little evidence that those espousing it have looked at the literature on failed federalism in the second half on the twentieth century (see, for example, Springer, 1962; Franck, 1968; Hazlewood, 1967; May, 1970). Evidence for a posited correlation between democracy and federalism is also thin. Both propositions have enjoyed some support in the Philippines, though there now seems to be growing doubt amongst Philippine Muslims as to whether federalism offers a solution to the 'Moro problem', and there is no real consensus that federalism will promote democracy. Whether or not the Philippines will become a federal republic remains to be seen. Certainly the proposals that there be a transitional period to develop support for the idea, and that the achievement of statehood be geared to individual states' capabilities (though likely to prove contentious) are to be commended. In the meantime, if the issues do not get lost in the personalistic politics that has characterized the Philippines for some decades, there should be some interesting debates.

## NOTES

1.   I am grateful to Rizal Buendia for his comments on an earlier draft of this chapter, and to Benny Bacani, Abhoud Syed Lingga, Robbie Macalde and Steven Rood for helping

me access recent documentation. Some of the ideas in this chapter were presented to an ARMM Legislators' Seminar in Tagaytay City and a Workshop for Senior Staff of Government and Researchers, sponsored by the Konrad Adenauer Stiftung in June 2006.

2. I am grateful to Ishak Mastura for reminding me of Hayden's early paper.
3. The eight areas listed covered administrative organization, sources of revenues, ancestral domain and natural resources, personal, family and property relations, urban and rural planning, economic, social and tourism development, educational policies, preservation and development of cultural heritage and 'such other matters as may be authorized by law for the promotion of the general welfare of the people of the region'. Responsibility for the preservation of peace and order within the regions was also given to the local police agencies.
4. According to an MILF source there are 625 barangays outside the ARMM with a Muslim majority.
5. This section draws on previously published material in May (2002). For a more detailed account see Turner (1999), de Guzman et al. (1988), Sosmeña (1991), Rood (1998) and Tapales et al. (1998).
6. For an account of the Bayanikasan Constitution, see Lina Araneta-Santiago on *inq7.net* posted 28 July 2005 (http://news.inq7.net/viewpoints/index.php?index=1&story_id=45090). Also see Araneta (1962).
7. Canoy's case for Mindanao's independence, together with a copy of the proposed constitution, are set out in Canoy (1987).
8. Other members of the Osmeña clan also supported federalism, notably former Cebu governor and presidential candidate Emilio 'Lito' Osmeña, who founded the regional political party PROMDI and at one stage called for an independent Republic of Cebu.
9. General Ramos had been head of the Philippine Constabulary under President Marcos but, facing arrest, had switched sides to the Marcos opposition in 1986, helping to precipitate the revolt on EDSA.
10. http://www.newsflash.org/2004/02/be/be002800.htm.
11. See de Venecia (2005), summarized at http://www.congress.gov.ph/press/details.php?pressid=611.
12. 'Executive Order No. 453 Creating a Consultative Commission to Propose the Revision of the 1987 Constitution in Consultation with Various Sectors of Society', 19 August 2005. EO 453 was amended by EO 453-A in October to increase the maximum membership from 50 to 55.
13. According to *IslamOnline.net*, Misuari has become ambivalent on the subject, and MILF spokesman Eid Kabalu does not support federalism. (See http://islamonline.net/English/News/2005-08/28/article02.shtml).
14. See, for example, *Philippine Daily Inquirer*, 3 November 2004, p. A19.
15. See www.news.ops.gov.ph/archives2005/nov09.htm. Zamboanga – a predominantly Christian area in a region of traditional Muslim influence – had been strongly opposed to the terms of the agreement negotiated with Misuari in 1996.
16. The quotations here are taken from the Consultative Commission's website, which provided a daily news coverage of the Commission's work (see http://www.concom.ph/news/).
17. Some of these issues are discussed in Diaz-Manalo (2006).
18. Bacani (2004, p. 134) similarly asks: 'If the Bangsamoro state is established with the other states in a Federal Philippines, will not the unique reason for its existence as fought for by the Moros for many years be lost in the broad sweep of a national federal set-up? If autonomy cannot be made to work in one region – the ARMM – how can the federal system bring development to eleven or more states? In these times of scarcity and need, when not enough budget support can be given the ARMM, will the Bangsamoro state further lag behind as resources are siphoned off to more developed regions?'
19. Indeed the president of the Cebu Chamber of Commerce was reported (*Sun Star*, 16 July 2005) as saying that 'We [the Visayas] will not carry the load of the underdeveloped provinces.'

# REFERENCES

Abueva, Jose V. (2000), 'Transforming our unitary system to a federal system: a pragmatic, developmental approach' (downloaded from CMFP website) (http://www.cmfp.ph/).

Abueva, Jose V. (2001), 'Towards a Federal Republic of the Philippines', *IBP* [Integrated Bar of the Philippines] *Law Journal*, **27**(2),1–30.

Abueva, Jose V. (2005), 'Some advantages of federalism and parliamentary government for the Philippines' (downloaded from CMFP website) (http://www.cmfp.ph/).

Araneta, Salvador (1962), 'Our constitutional heritage', *Philippines Law Journal*, **37**(3), 439–44.

Bacani, Benedicto R. (2003), 'Federalism vs. autonomy: roadmaps to peace', *ARMM Roundtable Series* no.6, Cotabato City, Notre Dame University.

Bacani, Benedicto R. (2004), 'Beyond paper autonomy. The challenge in Southern Philippines', Cotabato City, Center for Autonomy and Governance, Notre Dame University College of Law.

Bacani, Benedicto R. (2005), 'MNLF loses the ARMM: a setback for peace?', *Autonomy and Peace Review*, **1**(1), 25–33.

Buendia, Rizal G. (1989), 'The prospects for federalism in the Philippines: a challenge to political decentralization of the unitary state', *Philippine Journal of Public Administration*, **33**(2), 121–41.

Buendia, Rizal G. (1991), 'The Cordillera autonomy and quest for nation-building: prospects in the Philippines', *Philippine Journal of Public Administration*, **35**(4).

Canoy, Reuben R. (1987), *The Quest for Mindanao Independence*, Cagayan de Oro: Mindanao Post Publishing Company.

De Guzman, Raul P., Mila M. Reforma and Elana M. Panganiban (1988), 'Local government', in de Guzman and Reforma (eds), *Government and Politics in the Philippines*, Singapore: Oxford University Press, pp. 207–40.

De Venecia, Jose (2005), 'Federalism as the wave of the global future', statement of Hon. Jose de Venecia, Jr, Speaker of the House of Representatives, Republic of the Philippines. Third International Conference on Federalism at the European Parliament, Brussels, 3 March 2005, unpublished paper.

Diaz-Manalo, Pamela (2006), 'Shifting to a federal government. Some issues to consider', *Occasional Paper No.4*, Quezon City: Congressional Planning and Budget Department, House of Representatives [Congress of the Philippines].

Franck, T.M. (ed.) (1968), *Why Federations Fail. An Inquiry into the Requisites of Successful Federalism*, New York: New York University Press.

Fry, Howard T. (1983), *A History of the Mountain Province*, Quezon City: New Day Publishers.

Gowing, Peter G. (1977), 'Mandate in Moroland. The American government of Muslim Filipinos 1899–1920', Quezon City: Philippine Center for Advanced Studies, University of the Philippines System.

Hayden, Ralston (1927–28), 'What next for the Moro?', *Foreign Affairs*, **6**, 633–44.

Hazlewood, A. (ed.) (1967), *African Integration and Disintegration. Case Studies in Economic and Political Union*, London: Oxford University Press.

Lalanto, M.S. and N.T. Madale (1989), *Autonomy for Muslim Mindanao: the RCC Untold Story*, Marawi City: B-lal Publishers.

Lopez, Violeta B. (1976), *The Mangyans of Mindoro: An Ethnology*, Quezon City: University of the Philippines Press.

May, R.J. (1970), 'Decision making and stability in federal systems', *Canadian Journal of Political Science*, **3**(1), 73–87.
May, R.J. (1992), 'The wild west in the south: a recent political history of Mindanao', in Mark Turner, R.J. May and Lulu Respall Turner (eds), *Mindanao: Land of Unfulfilled Promise*, Quezon City: New Day Publishers, pp. 125–46.
May, R.J. (2002), 'Governance and social safety nets in the Philippines', in OECD (ed.), *Towards Asia's Sustainable Development. The Role of Social Protection*, Paris: Organisation for Economic Co-operation and Development, pp. 91–113.
Rood, Steven (1998), 'Decentralization, democracy and development', in David G. Timberman (ed.), *The Philippines. New Directions in Domestic Policy and Foreign Relations*, Singapore: Institute of Southeast Asian Studies, pp. 111–35.
Santos, Soliman (2005), 'Charter change and the peace process: some key propositions', *Autonomy and Peace Review*, **1**(1), 35–41.
Santuario, Edmundo (2001), 'Federalism: antidote to separatism?' and 'A crisis needing a surgical solution', *Bulatlat*, **10, 11** (20–26 April and 27 April–3 May) [available at http://www.bulatlat.com/archive/].
Sosmeña, Gaudioso C. (1991), 'Decentralization and Empowerment, Manila', Local Government Development Foundation.
Springer, H.W. (1962), 'Reflections on the failure of the first West Indian Federation', Harvard University Center for International Affairs, Occasional Papers in International Affairs, 4.
Tapales, Proserpina Domingo, Jocelyn C. Cuaresma and Wilhelmina L. Cabo (1998), 'Local government in the Philippines: a book of readings', Quezon City, Center for Local and Regional Governance and National College of Public Administration and Governance, University of the Philippines.
Turner, Mark (1999), 'Philippines: from centralism to localism', in M. Turner (ed.), *Central–Local Relations in Asia Pacific. Convergence or Divergence?*, Houndmills, UK: Macmillan Press, pp. 97–122.

# 9. Ethnicity and federal prospect in Myanmar

**Alan Smith**

The boundaries of the Union of Myanmar* are those established by British colonial conquest. They enclose a central plains area which constitutes the ethnic majority Burman heartland which is surrounded on the west, north and east by a horse-shoe of rugged mountains that are home to the non-Burman ethnic nationalities. The seven major non-Burman ethnic groups, nationalities, or national races as they are usually referred to in Myanmar – the Rakhine (Arakanese), Chin, Kachin, Shan, Karenni, Karen and Mon – are each identified with states of the Union within which they constitute the majority. Such a framework of course oversimplifies the reality of a multiplicity of ethnic sub-groups (the military regime emphasizes this ethnic fragmentation, often referring to 135 ethnic groups), as well as the historical factors that distinguish the ethnopolitical perspectives of each of the seven main ethnic groups and some of their sub-groups. Nonetheless, the basic conception of Myanmar as a country with an ethnic Burman heartland and seven ethnic minority states is ubiquitous in public debates and there is a high level of consensus concerning the need for political recognition on a territorial basis of these seven major ethnic groups in addition to the mainly Burman lowland centre. What is more often contested is the division of the heartland area into seven administrative divisions or regions and the appropriate status for some of the ethnic sub-groups within the ethnic states and of course the whole question of the appropriate constitutional structure for the 'union'.

The most important current 'development' in Myanmar's political situation is undoubtedly the military's design for transition from its present total political control to something else, a new constitutional system, through its carefully managed National Convention (NC). This is not a regime transformation of the 'transition to democracy' kind, because it is not being undertaken to achieve a withdrawal of the military from power (return to the barracks), but which will nevertheless change the shape of the political system. This military-managed regime transformation must be seen for what it is, a process through which a military, long and much experienced in holding state power, either directly or indirectly, is seeking to entrench elements of a political system that serve its interests and perpetuate its values but within a framework other than the present total control, with which it is apparently 'uncomfortable'. Through the NC the military is asking a group of mainly hand-picked representatives to endorse its proposals regarding (a) the degree of control it will continue to hold over the various elements of the state and state policy, (b) the space to be allowed other political actors (at the centre) and (c) the division of power between the centre and the units of the Union, especially the ethnic states.

There are many opponents of the military's National Convention and its 'road map to disciplined democracy', including the National League for Democracy (NLD) and its political allies excluded from or boycotting the process, and much of the international community, on the basis of their undemocratic repudiation of the 1990 elections, the unrepresentative composition of the NC and its lack of democratic process. Exile opposition groups are also highly vocal opponents insisting in addition that the only legitimate outcome is a democratic *and* federal union and rejecting what they see as the military's perpetuation of an only quasi-federal structure and its dictatorial approach to the division of powers between the centre and the states. The argument for a truly federal structure relates to the ethnic dissatisfaction (expressed often as armed rebellion) with the structure of the Union of Burma since its formation at independence from Britain in 1948 and alleged discrimination towards ethnic communities and disempowerment of ethnic states.

The outcome of the National Convention in terms of continuing military domination of the new state structure is not going to please many people. It does not have to. The plan, however, is for it to be passed by a referendum, for which the regime is clearly already mobilizing. (This has happened before: the 1974 one-party constitution introduced by General Ne Win was passed by referendum with almost unanimous approval.) The process might be likened to that of a monarch initiating and managing a new constitutional framework for a, still overwhelmingly powerful, monarchy.

The shape of the outcome is already substantially clear concerning the structure of the organs of state and clearly neither democracy nor federalism is 'on the radar'. But since the NC process is not yet completed it is still not clear what political space will be left for political actors other than the military itself. There remain many unknowns even concerning the shape of the new structure at the centre. Undoubtedly the military will continue to control the government. But will the new structure allow for even a slightly more open society in which political views other than those of the military can be legally manifest? Will the new parliament have freedom to debate?

What degree of control will the government have over political parties, civil society and the media? What degree of control will the military and government have over the economy? How hegemonic will be the role of the government's party/mass organization (the United Solidarity and Development Association or USDA)?

In terms of the distribution of power between the 'players' at the centre, the model being prepared looks as though it may be about as democratic as Suharto's Indonesia with a government-supported 'state' party and tolerated but severely managed others. This still leaves unanswered vital questions about the likely space for the development of the 'other' parties and civil society, which currently can perhaps be regarded as 'crippled' and 'emergent', respectively. In terms of the NC, the question of the distribution of power between centre and periphery, especially the ethnic states, is by now sufficiently clear. States will have powers which in most democratic countries would be delegated to 'local government'. For the first time, however, it is envisaged that there will be legislatures at the state level. What remains problematic, however, is more the local reflection of the unanswered question about the structure at the centre; that is, what place will there be in ethnic states for players other than the military? Despite the limitations of powers to be delegated to the states, and despite the clear determination of the military to continue to dominate state structures, will there at least be room at the state level for local, that is, ethnic community political and civil society organizations to begin to emerge into public life? If so, there may be much to be gained in terms of 'political learning' about structures and policies relating to mutual ethnic accommodation, essential if the 'ethnic issue' is to be defused as a key obstacle to the ultimate emergence of a more democratic system. This is a theme to which I will return, after first discussing, in more detail, both the National Convention and opposition responses to it.

## THE NATIONAL CONVENTION

This has been a very long drawn-out process, starting in July 1990, when Maj. Gen. Khin Nyunt, First Secretary of the State Law and Order Restoration Council (SLORC), announced the determination of the military not to transfer power to the election-winning NLD in the absence of a constitution. Referring to the 1947 and 1974 constitutions, he suggested 'because of changing times and conditions, that neither constitution is now suitable or usable'. Instead, he proposed, 'We should draft a new constitution. It is essential to draft such a constitution. For a strong government to emerge, we should proceed systematically according to law . . . As for our SLORC, we will not regard it as something of no concern to us' (quoted in Weller, 1993, pp. 188–94.)

The first concrete step towards what was to become the National Convention did not emerge until after the replacement of SLORC Chairman, Gen. Saw Maung, by Gen. Tan Shwe in April 1992. On 10 July 1992 the composition of the National Convention was announced. The 702 members had been hand-picked by the SLORC and included only 99 elected representatives from the 1990 elections. Hence the NLD had been sidelined.

Whether the military leaders at the outset had a clearly mapped path for the NC (which had a long unexplained adjournment in the middle, 1996–2004) or a clear vision of the outcome is unknown. The National Convention formally opened in January 1993, charged with drawing up not a constitution, but a set of principles on which the future constitution would be based. When the NC opened in January 1993, some of the delegates were alarmed to find that six basic principles had already been laid down by the SLORC, including 'participation of the military in the leading role in national politics'. At its April 1993 session, the NC adopted a set of chapter headings for the future constitution:

1.  State fundamental principles,
2.  State structure,
3.  Head of State,
4.  Legislature,
5.  Executive,
6.  Judiciary,
7.  Tatmadaw,
8.  Citizens and their fundamental rights and duties,
9.  Election,
10. Political parties,
11. Emergency provisions,
12. Amendment of the constitution,
13. State flag, seal, anthem and capital,
14. Transitory provisions,
15. General provisions.

By the end of its third, highly orchestrated, session (September 1993) the National Convention had 'adopted' 104 principles proposed by the SLORC, which essentially established the constitutional framework. Subsequent sessions of the NC worked on producing what are called 'detailed basic principles', chapter by chapter: April 1994, chapters 1–3; April 1995, details concerning autonomous zones (part of chapter 2); March 1996, chapters 4–6.

Aung San Suu Kyi was released from house arrest in July 1995. The NC session scheduled to open on 22 October 1995 was postponed until 28 November and shortly afterwards the NLD demanded that the proceedings of the National Convention be liberalized. When this was rejected by the SLORC, the NLD began a boycott of the proceedings, leading in turn to the expulsion of the NLD by the SLORC. The NLD in protest stated its intention to develop its own version of a new constitution. On 31 March 1996, the National Convention was adjourned and the infamous Law 5/96 promulgated. This law outlaws constitution-drafting activity outside the framework of the National Convention and, in addition, outlaws more or less any action which can be regarded as negative towards the National Convention and its work.[1]

In 1997, following the admission of Myanmar to ASEAN, the military junta was reconstructed and re-emerged as the State Peace and Development Council (SPDC). No further moves towards a new constitution emerged until 2003. Meanwhile Aung San Suu Kyi had been re-arrested in September 2000. Shortly afterwards it became known that Special UN Envoy Razali Ismail was engaged in developing a dialogue between the SPDC and Aung San Suu Kyi and this led to her being again freed in May 2002. Aung San Suu Kyi was re-arrested at the end of May 2003 following an orchestrated attack on her NLD motorcade in the north of the country at Depayin. The incident outraged international opinion and there were demands from every quarter that Aung San Suu Kyi and other detainees be released and that there should be tangible steps towards democratic reform. Shortly afterwards the SPDC announced another regime reconstruction, with Sec. 1 Khin Nyunt named Prime Minister, followed quickly by his August 2003 announcement of a 'roadmap' to 'disciplined democracy', the first step of which would be the reconvening of the National Convention in early 2004.

This presented all political 'actors' inside the country who had access to the military regime with a dilemma: whether to welcome and join this new process as potentially favourable to the cause of democratization and the rights of ethnic minorities, or whether to deride and boycott it as yet another of the military's succession of political charades. The international community was faced with the same dilemma, whether to welcome it or dismiss it.

Overall, faced with assurances by the regime that the release of Aung San Suu Kyi was imminent, and that the procedures of the renewed National Convention would satisfy the NLD, there was cautious agreement between Western and regional countries to welcome the National Convention and to propose what liberalizations would make it acceptable. Finally, however, the regime again demonstrated the shallowness of its assurances when the National Convention was reconvened on 15 May with no procedural reform, with Aung San Suu Kyi still under house arrest, and the NLD still sidelined.

This heightened the dilemma faced by various ethnic organizations invited by Khin Nyunt to join the National Convention. In the end some ethnic actors, especially the United Nationalities Alliance (of ethnic political parties) showed their solidarity with the NLD by declaring a boycott of the proceedings. In fact they had not been invited. Other ethnic actors, who were invited, especially a group of ethnic organizations that had signed ceasefires with the regime (largely through the initiative of Khin Nyunt as chief of Military Intelligence), including notably the Kachin Independence Organisation (KIO) and New Mon State Party (NMSP), decided to participate, though in each case the decision was internally contentious.

Perhaps because of the long adjournment, perhaps because of the (slightly) augmented range of participants, the ensuing 2004–2006 sessions of the NC produced further details concerning the already discussed chapters, namely the distribution of powers between the organs of the state. Two months after the opening of the 2004 session, having heard proposals concerning the principles that should apply to defining the powers of the central government and the states, on 9 July, the National Convention was again adjourned. It was rumoured during the 2004 session that the National Convention Convening Committee was disturbed by sweeping demands put forward by the ceasefire groups concerning 'federal style' division of powers and had urged them to reconsider. Ultimately the proposals they had put forward were not included in those presented to the plenary session. This heightened the clamour within the ceasefire groups to withdraw their participation. When the NC reconvened for a short session in early 2005, they were still present, but when the session opened again in early December 2005, one of the main ethnic ceasefire groups, the New Mon State Party, was represented only by an observer delegation. The December 2005 session was focused initially on relations between the two houses of parliament and the workings of regional and state legislatures. The NC had now reached a very interesting juncture, however, with the Convening Work Committee having to prepare detailed basic principles to place in front of the NC for the chapters 'Tatmadaw' (the military) and 'Citizens and their fundamental rights & duties'. Perhaps this accounts for rather short sessions and rather long adjournments. Importantly, the NC having adjourned in early 2006 and not scheduled to reconvene until October, no detailed basic principles had yet been tabled concerning the chapters on 'Political Parties' and 'Elections'.

What this means is that, at the time of writing (mid-2006), while the outline of the proposed state structure is already clear, the outline with regard to the future political party system (the basic principles of 1994 refer to 'a multi-party system') is not. The country will be divided into seven (ethnic) States and seven Regions (of Burma proper) as was the case under the 1974 constitution (which refers to 'States' and 'Divisions'). The political system will be a presidential one, and there will be two houses of parliament, a lower 'house of the people' and an upper 'house of the seven regions and seven states'. The powerful president will be chosen by an electoral college made up of three groups of representatives in the parliament: elected representatives of each house and military appointees of the two houses. One-quarter of the members of the two houses of parliament will be military appointees. The President will appoint cabinet ministers who cannot also be members of parliament. Any ministers associated with political parties will have to become non-active in their party. Civil servants also must cease their civil service duties. Ministers from the military, however, will not have to give up their military identity. Chiefs of Regions and States will be nominated by the President and approved by the region or state legislature. Military appointees will make up one-third of the members of the regional and state legislatures.

A 1995 session of the NC dealt with the establishment of autonomous zones for ethnic minority communities within established regions and states, basically sub-states, a move which won the support of a number of 'small minorities' who saw themselves as dominated by the 'big minorities' constituting majorities in the various states. The Basic Principles refer twice to 'a genuine multiparty system' and once to the need for a law for systematic formation of political parties. Hence the open question, is the system likely to be similar to the 'Indonesia under Suharto' model (which provided for a dominant 'state party' but with the old major Nationalist and Islamic political parties allowed to play a (circumscribed and closely watched) role in the system? (The previously powerful Communist Party had, of course, been wiped out and outlawed.) A variation on that could be referred to perhaps as the 'Pakistan under Musharaf' model, in which parties can play a role, but the old major parties are proscribed. While the Basic Principles refer to a 'genuine multi-party system', the establishment and mobilization of a state mass organization (proto-state party) is well advanced, as is the crippling of the NLD. Given the familiarity of the state elite with the one-party system of the 1974–88 period, there are good reasons for wondering about the political space to be allowed by the NC for 'other political parties'.

## OPPOSITION RESPONSES AND FEDERALISM

### The Mainstream Opposition: The NLD

Prior to the May 1990 election, the NLD held a number of meetings to start drafting a new constitution that would facilitate transition to democracy following the elections. A draft was submitted to the NLD's Central Executive Committee on 25 April 1990, with further discussion and redrafting in June and July. The process identified a series of amendments to be made to the 1947 constitution that would then serve as a 1990 transitional constitution.

The 1947 constitution provided for a British-style parliamentary system under a powerful Prime Minister and a symbolic President. The regional distribution of power was unusual. It built on to the regional administrative division of the main component of what had been British Burma, a quasi-federal 'union' system that provided for ethnic states with some autonomy. It provided for state 'councils' to be constituted from the representatives from each state in the Union Parliament and the Minister in the Union Government responsible for each state became simultaneously the chief of that state. It was not a classic federal system in that the government of Burma, the major segment of the system, was simultaneously the government of the 'Union'. It was a Burma-plus-satellites system rather than a classic federal system. Controversially, it included a secession clause that allowed the states access to a secession process after ten years from independence.

The NLD's main departure in 1990 from the 1947 constitution was to annul the various sections dealing with the ethnic nationalities, proposing instead that 'with authority derived from the People's Assembly, and as contained in the League's election statement as regards the ability for national races to resolve matters on their own and to held (*sic*) equal rights, call a National Convention and undertake to thoroughly coordinate comprehensive legislation by mutual agreement' (NLD CEC, 1990).

In other words, the existing provisions for minorities, presumably including the provisions for the states and including Article 10 of the 1947 constitution dealing with secession, were to be abolished, but new guarantees would be negotiated 'by mutual agreement' on the basis of the free participation of the ethnic nationalities themselves. Since that time, the NLD has maintained this formula – that is, that dealing with the ethnic issue needs to be postponed until the ethnic groups themselves are able to be fully involved.

**The Exile Opposition: The NDF, DAB, NCGUB and NCUB**

The 1988 'people power' uprising marked a watershed in the civil war, for the bloody crackdown on pro-democracy forces led many to flee to the border areas to join armed insurgent forces. These forces had been grouped together since 1976 in an alliance known as the National Democratic Front (NDF) which was committed to achieving a genuinely federal Burma. This coalescence at the border of the non-Burman nationalities and the mainly ethnic Burman democracy movement exiles was symbolically important. The political basis of the new Democratic Alliance of Burma (DAB), the alliance forged at the end of 1988 between armed ethnic groups and pro-democracy groups, reflected the willingness of the newly-arrived exile democracy groups to support the ethnic minority vision of a future demo-cratic *and federal* Burma. In 1989, the DAB set in motion a process of con-stitution drafting aimed specifically at defining the nature of the 'genuine federalism' demanded by the insurgent ethnic nationalities.

After SLORC overturned the 1990 elections and declared martial law, a new wave of arrests followed, including elected members of the victorious parties, and in December 1990 a group of 12 elected members fled to the rebel-controlled Thai border area to form a government in exile, the National Coalition Government of the Union of Burma (NCGUB). In 1992, the DAB's federal constitution-drafting exercise was given new impetus when, at a conference with a strong international expert presence, the NCGUB declared support in principle for federalism and agreed to join the DAB constitution-drafting process. This common commitment to a federal future was celebrated in the signing of the 'Manerplaw Agreement' and the formation of a new peak alliance known as the National Council of the Union of Burma (NCUB).[2] In May 1995, the DAB constitution-drafting committee was extended to become an NCUB committee. In ad-dition, the Burma Lawyers Council, formed by a group of exiles in 1994, has played a highly proactive role in support. (For the outcome of the process, see NCUB 1997 and 1998.)

Among leaders in exile, a great deal of learning has occurred through par-ticipation in NGO-supported meetings, capacity-building training and ex-posure trips associated with the DAB–NCUB federal constitution-drafting process.[3] More recently, there have been efforts to foster state constitution-drafting processes also, envisaged as leading to a new approach to a federal constitution to be negotiated by representatives of the states (see Williams and Sakhong, 2005). Ethnic leaders in exile have therefore had many oppor-tunities to develop their views and voice their main concerns about a new con-stitution for Burma. Their views are usually stated in terms of how a federal constitution would need to be formulated to satisfy them. Sometimes this is stated in terms of 'genuine federalism' (as distinct from what they see as phony federalism like that of the 1947 Union of Burma). The result is that, amongst exile groups, it has become a kind of accepted orthodoxy that there is only a very narrow range of constitutional options that could satisfy ethnic requirements.

Any popular discussion of the constitutional issue in ethnic circles always produces emotional debate about a number of key issues, including the secession issue. There is a similarly emotional reluctance by ethnic leaders to allow the term 'minorities' to be applied to them or to enter much into discussion of 'minority rights', insisting instead on the language of 'nation' or 'ethnic nationality', or in some cases 'indigenous people', in order to be able to claim what they see as the wider rights of self-determination of 'peoples'. This is understandable but unfortunate as the evolving UN human rights provisions aimed at preventing discrimination and enhancing the situation of ethnic, religious and linguistic minorities can provide a basis for achieving many of the same substantive goals as the 'self determination of peoples'. In many cases, representatives of the non-Burman ethnic nationalities proudly reject the application of the term 'minority' to their community, seeing this as reducing their status to that of immigrant minorities in Burma such as the Chinese and Indians.

The DAB/NCUB draft constitution is essentially a constitution of the classic parliamentary and federal type, envisaging a federal union comprising 'National States and Nationalities States' and with provision for 'National Autonomous Regions' and 'Special National Territories'. It provides for self-determination for the states 'in accordance with this constitution' – a phrasing that is intentionally vague (Constitution Drafting Committee of the NCUB 1998). Those responsible for drafting this constitution have learned from their NGO supporters and academic friends to treat the 'right of secession' as of dubious value and the draft contains no reference to secession. Whenever the draft is subjected to popular scrutiny in opposition/exile circles, however, there is invariably heated argument about the desirability and wisdom of such an omission.

# REGIME TRANSFORMATION

## The Need for Moderation and Working with Softliners

These then are the three main groups of actors: the military regime, the mainstream opposition within Myanmar, and the exile opposition that unites outlawed pro-democracy forces with ethnic insurgents. The first pays lip-service to the idea of an inclusive process of constitution drafting that includes ethnic minorities, but legitimizes its rule on the ground that strong central government is needed to prevent national disintegration; the second is strong on democratic forms and process but avoids taking a clear stand on minority demands for federalism and self-determination, on the grounds that such decisions can only be made in consultation with minorities themselves after conditions of freedom and democracy have been established; and the third is ideologically committed to classic federalism and the principle of self-determination of peoples as well as to democratic forms.

Finding a way of reconciling these views would be difficult under the most auspicious conditions. But conditions today in Myanmar are not auspicious. Far from encouraging or enabling a free exchange of ideas and public deliberation, so as to find common ground amongst these contending actors, the military government has firmly prohibited it, leading to a situation of intellectual isolation for itself, the opposition and the public.

If, as has been suggested by Sundhaussen (1984, pp. 548ff), there are a number of sets of circumstances which will bring about the predisposition of a military regime to transform itself or withdraw from power, essentially they all add up to the same thing: the costs and benefits of continuing to monopolize power against the potential costs and benefits of sharing or handing over power. When the time comes to transform the regime, there are a limited number of paths, greater and lesser degrees of withdrawal, which the military can follow. Which one is chosen will depend on factors both internal and external to the military, and will reflect both the disposition of the military and the availability of opportunity, that is, the military's confidence that its key personal and corporate interests will be protected.

Reviewing a major collection of comparative studies of transitions to democracy edited by Guilermo O'Donnell and Phillippe Schmitter (1986), Nancy Bermeo (1990) wrote a thought-provoking lesson to members of counter-elites. According to Bermeo, O'Donnell and Schmitter were influential observers of the military takeovers and loss of democracy which occurred in South America in the early 1960s. Basically, as Bermeo sees it, O'Donnell and Schmitter blamed the collapse of democracy on 'social and economic structures', causes which, according to Bermeo, sometimes seemed to make the collapse of democracy seem unavoidable, whereas other authors had been more inclined to lay the blame on individual leaders: the failure of leadership and elites.

Bermeo noted that, having studied the reversal, since 1973, of the series of military takeovers, O'Donnell and Schmitter had very substantially changed their ideas. When they examined the cases of transition to democracy from dictatorship, they argued that it is the behaviours of key individuals and elites which determine whether or not an opening to democracy occurs, and whether or not there is a successful transition to democracy.

If the fate of political systems can be determined by wise individual action, we need to know what is 'wise individual action'. This is the question addressed by O'Donnell and Schmitter. And their conclusion is simple: 'play it safe', specifically present moderate images, and demands, opt for gradualism and cooperation with the dictatorship's softliners. In other words, take seriously the need to safeguard the interests of the military, if you are trying to bring about the military's relinquishment of power; that is, provide them with the opportunity to withdraw.

What do we see when we apply this 'moderation and softliners' perspective to Myanmar? I will first attempt to identify what gains might have been made in terms of the constitutional outcome of the NC process, through 'moderation' and the cultivation of softliners. I will then consider the ethnic issue and the federalism demand as a potentially promising example of an opening to 'moderation' and discuss the question of how softliners are to be identified in the military.

## THE NLD AND THE MILITARY: NO MODERATION AND NO SOFTLINERS

It is ironic that Khin Nyunt, who headed the much reviled Military Intelligence (MI), became identified with a 'soft-line'. I would like to put this in context. Within the military regime it was always the Khin Nyunt faction which was responsible for dealing with the opposition, including Aung San Suu Kyi, dealing with the issue of ceasefire talks with ethnic insurgency movements, dealing with the constitutional process and dealing with the international community and international agencies. That is because that responsibility was given to Military Intelligence. I have argued elsewhere (Smith, 2000) that it was also Khin Nyunt who spearheaded the drive for membership of Myanmar in ASEAN (and that Sen. Gen. Than Shwe supported this). In many ways, then, within the military, it was the MI group around Khin Nyunt that constituted the 'outward face' of the government and the regime. It would be too simplistic and misleading to represent the Khin Nyint 'factional outlook' as 'softline', though there were others within the regime who were clearly more 'hardline'. How can we think more practically about these lines?

Perhaps it may be more useful simply to think of more and less outward-oriented groups. There was a group that was more in favour of opening up the country, escaping from the past self-imposed isolationism; and there were those who were much more willing to contemplate an extension of Myanmar's self-imposed isolation, less inclined to open up the country, less inclined to talk with those outside the military, namely, the opposition and Aung San Suu Kyi, to negotiate with rebels and to conciliate the outside world. This less outward-oriented group may also have been simply relieved to be able to take a back seat and allow the Khin Nyunt-headed 'face' of the regime to do the unpleasant job of dealing with outsiders.

In dealing with the Khin Nyunt group, however, ethnic insurgent groups were able to negotiate about ceasefires; the ICRC were able to negotiate access to political prisoners and to conflict areas; starting in late 2000, UN Special Envoy Razali was able to bring about encouraging beginnings of dialogue between Khin Nyunt and Aung San Suu Kyi, and from time to time the international community was able to engage the regime with regard to the need to 'change' its outlook.

Indeed, over a number of years, a series of changes of regime outlook emerged over some specific issues. It started with the ICRC's painstaking negotiation for access to political prisoners. 'After ten years, the Red Cross withdrew in 1995 because it could not get access to prisons and the field. Two years later, [Yangon] said they would like to talk to us' (*Asiaweek*, 2000). This was followed, under pressure from the ILO, by the government's retreat from denial over the internationally unacceptable practice of using forced labour,[4] and it was evident in the government's initial denial but later acknowledgment of the danger of an HIV epidemic. Can these experiences of position-change encounters be repeated and extended?

Were these changes brought about because from the start Khin Nyunt and his group were softliners? Or was it simply that, being positioned as the regime's 'front to the outside world' and, tasked with dealing with these issues under pressure from many directions, and pushed into exposure to international norms, they learned to dialogue, to speak the language of international norms and to sell them to the regime as removing threats? Importantly, were there distinct and contending soft and hard line positions regarding the shape of the future constitution being assembled in the NC right from the start? Or, as I suspect, did Khin Nyunt and the rest of the SLORC/SPDC start out with a common 'vision', with a later divergence of views over what concessions could safely be made to outsiders' demands (which may explain Khin Nyunt's fall)? Unfortunately, answers to these questions can only be guessed at. Long-time supporter of Ne Win and briefly President of the country at the height of the 1988 uprising, Dr Maung Maung recollected that at the critical period in 1988 when the old BSPP regime was under siege, culminating in the SLORC's coup, the differences within the elite were not simply over how the old order should be transformed, but also over whether the old order should be transformed (Maung Maung, 1999). Dr Maung Maung reflected on the foolishness of those among the elite who, at the height of the turmoil, refused to acknowledge that there had to be a change. But he clearly felt also that the popular opposition was being equally foolish in not being willing to follow constitutional-looking procedures to implement change. His own view was that the 'correct' path was to amend the then still-in-force 1974 constitution to allow for a multi-party system and put that to a referendum, as against the 'revolutionaries' who were demanding immediate elections in a constitutional vacuum. It is plausible that his view may have been shared by many military leaders, at the time of the SLORC's 18 September 1988 seizure of power, as they saw the ability of the 'government' to achieve Dr Maung Maung's 'correct path' slip away.

The crucial figure in the SLORC at that time, though, was military chief Gen. Saw Maung and it was Gen. Saw Maung who was responsible for declarations by the SLORC that the military would proceed to elections and honour the election result. Was he a softliner? If so, the spokesperson for the hardline retreat from the recognition of the 1990 elections that had been promised by Gen. Saw Maung was Khin Nyunt, as SLORC Secretary 1. Does this make him a hardliner? More likely it was simply his task to 'put the necessary spin' on the decision by the military leadership that it could not afford to have the victorious NLD take responsibility for the new constitution; that is, in its view it had been a mistake to allow the elections to take place without having first resolved the constitutional issue. Indeed, the move towards establishing a National Convention did not begin to emerge until after the replacement of Saw Maung by Gen. Tan Shwe in 1992. Perhaps from a shared hardline position, a difference opened up over time at the top of the SLORC/SPDC concerning the required future shape of the constitution, especially regarding the role to be allowed the NLD and Aung San Suu Kyi, but perhaps it was simply a divergence based on the confidence of the Khin Nyunt group in being able to defuse threats by dialogue.

Outside observers have tended to see a struggle between the NLD and the military over future control of the political system, but perhaps for the military that was never the case. Perhaps the reality was always only a struggle that emerged within the military between those willing to contemplate a place in the system for Aung San Suu Kyi and the NLD and those who were not. On the face of it, a multi-party system had already been conceded, but the 1990 election had shown that a 'soft' multi-party system would produce a result unacceptable to the military; that is, loss of their own effective control or at least a significant 'final arbiter' role. On the other hand, as I have suggested above, after 1988, maybe most of the military leadership did not seriously contemplate resurrecting the old BSPP-style one-party system, or at least not openly. The compromise solution was therefore what we now see emerging, an executive-dominant system, as under the 1974 constitution (which the military could control), but with decorative multi-party legislatures (which could be dominated by a pro-military party supported by military appointees) which would allow for political parties (maybe or maybe not including the NLD or a decimated version of the NLD) without allowing them to take control. For the NLD, to have followed the advice of O'Donnell and Schmitter, 'moderation and seeking out the soft-liners', would at best have won them survival to play a minor role. For the military (harder and softer lines) and the NLD, in other words, the situation was essentially always a zero-sum game: there was no realistic moderate path, and there were no softliners.

That having been said, is there still more to argue with regard to moderate demands and cooperation with softliners? I believe, in the case of Myanmar, this is the crucial point of intersection of arguments about the relationship between democracy and ethnic autonomy. In my initial encounter with the issue, I had no problem in identifying with the NLD's principled position that taking a stand on the ethnic issue needs to be delayed until a democratic situation prevails and the ethnic communities can freely express their views. I also fully supported the efforts of exile opposition groups to explore the ideal form of federal constitution that would satisfy ethnic aspirations.[5] Grappling, however, with Myanmar's constitutional history on the one hand, and strategic questions regarding the best way to achieve a political transition on the other, I found myself at another conference (in Manila in October 1995), arguing that assembling experts on federalism and 'federalism as the appropriate solution for Myanmar's ethnic problem', was likely to lock people into an inflexible view about federalism as the only conceivable solution for Myanmar's ethnic problems. I began to argue that, in the interests of eventual transition to democracy, the whole range of possible forms of accommodation of ethnic demands needed to be explored. It was not a popular argument. I formalized my view in a conference of 'federalists', arguing that federalism, '. . . seen as an end in itself rather than a means to an end, is as much a part of the problem as it may, one day, be a part of the solution' (Smith, 1997).

It was at that time that I began seriously to explore the elements making up the 'ethnic problem' of Myanmar and at the same time elements that might contribute to its solution, rather than seeking 'the ideal package'. I remember being impressed with Yash Ghai's introduction to his collection, *Autonomy and Ethnicity* (Ghai, 2000) as highly appropriate 'to examine what has been tried, what has worked and not worked and continue on from there'.[6]

At about the same time, I also concluded that the orthodox approach to the question of the sequencing of democracy and ethnic autonomy, namely, that democratic processes were needed in order to be able to address the ethnic issue, needed to be stood on its head in the situation of Myanmar. Initially, I raised the same proposition as I have here, based on Nancy Bermeo's observations (Bermeo, 1990) about O'Donnell and Schmitter's conclusions (O'Donnell and Schmitter, 1986) on 'moderation and softliners', while agreeing that it would be presumptuous to offer advice as to how to expedite the transition to democracy in a case such as Myanmar (Khin Maung Win and Alan Smith, 1998). I became increasingly convinced, however, that there was no prospect for a transition to democracy until the ethnic issue had been resolved (defused?) to the military's satisfaction; that is, conservative nationalist military leaders, obsessed with territorial integrity, would not be prepared to leave this issue to party politicians and ethnic leaders. I began to argue, therefore, that, if there was to be an eventual transition to democracy, effective advocacy must focus on resolving the ethnic issue with the military. I became convinced that, if the ethnic issue and the question of federalism could be dealt with pragmatically rather than dogmatically (specifically, with moderation), this issue could be 'defused', and that this was a strategic necessity in order to open the way towards a more definitive democratization. This means there must be more emphasis on the ethnic issue and support for capacity-building training of the kind which explored a range of possible approaches to dealing with ethnic problems rather than the search for a perfect federalism (Smith, 2003). This was not a popular view, either in exile opposition circles or in the international arena.

## THE ETHNIC ISSUE AND FEDERALISM: IN SEARCH OF MODERATE DEMANDS AND SOFTLINERS

### Ethnic Grievances and Devolution

In discussion amongst ethnic community leaders and educated ethnic people, both quietly inside the country and more openly in the border area, besides an overarching emphasis on the need for federalism or 'genuine' federalism, I see two main themes. First, ethnic states and ethnic leaders occupy an inferior position in the union; second, the rights of ethnic people are not respected by the government and the military.

## ETHNIC STATES AND ETHNIC LEADERS

The feeling is widespread among ethnic people that, owing to Burman-dominated government policies and practices, ethnic areas are either undeveloped or exploited compared with the Burman heartland. They see their areas as lacking infrastructure and economic opportunities, or as being developed only in the sense that their natural resources are extracted in such a way that the local people are bypassed in terms of decision making and benefits. Worse, when development does occur in ethnic areas, local people often find themselves forcibly displaced from their land, usually with highly inadequate (or non-existent) compensation. In short, because of a lack of real autonomy, people of the ethnic states see themselves as treated by successive Burman/military-dominated governments with disdain.

The perception of ethnic people of Myanmar (that is, not only in the ethnic states) is that Burmans always assume that it is the right and responsibility of Burmans to provide national leadership. Since non-Burman ethnic leaders see politics in primarily ethnic terms, they assume that Burman leaders should self-consciously lead the Burman ethnic community, and that national leadership is something that should be shared by leaders of the various ethnic communities, including the Burmans as an ethnic community. For Burmans, however, there is no 'Burman' political position and no effort to represent a Burman ethnic community. For Burmans, politics cuts across ethnicity, and political organizations established by Burmans are usually presented as 'all Burma' or 'all-Myanmar' in nature (although their perception of 'all-Burmese' interests is often unconsciously shaped by their ethnic Burman background). Some non-Burmans respond to this positively; in 1990, for example, the NLD attracted non-Burman candidates and voters. Nevertheless it might be said that Burmans are 'all-Burmese nationalists' while non-Burmans tend to be ethnonationalists. Since ethnic leaders see political action through ethnic eyes, they assume that voters generally vote ethnically and fear that Burmans, being the majority, will inescapably dominate an elected parliament and, without special measures, will always hold (central) government power.

The question, then, is what sorts of special measures do they advocate? Drawing on the independence period debate, some ethnic leaders look to the solution adopted in the 1947 constitution to provide for a strong upper house of parliament weighted in favour of the non-Burman nationalities. This solution, however, requires that there be a single 'Burman' state to complete the ethnic political map of Burma as a classic federation of 'equal' ethnic states.[7] They see this mechanism as having been thwarted by the formula adopted in the 1974 constitution, which created seven administrative divisions within the ethnic Burman heartland ('Burma proper'), alongside the seven ethnic states. In their view, this was intended to dilute the weight of the ethnic states but also to reduce their symbolic status to that of the administrative subdivisions within the ethnic Burman heartland.

The decision by certain ceasefire ethnic groups to participate in the May–July 2004 National Convention sitting seems to have been a very courageous attempt to put pro-democratic and pro-federal issues back on the agenda. The decision was taken on the basis of signs that the newly reconvened NC would be more open for debate and more representative.

By the time the session opened, these signs had evaporated. State powers issues nevertheless were put forward forthrightly by the ceasefire groups, reflecting their perception that it was necessary to take a strong position in order to defuse the opposition to their decision to participate, especially from within the harder line sections of their own organizations and communities, within which there is an established view that only a 'federal solution' can be acceptable.

It may be strategic for political actors in Myanmar to be exposed to a wide range of decentralization and autonomy and minority rights models in order to create a greater space for negotiating ethnic autonomy claims than the either/or, unitary/federal dichotomy now prevailing. Similarly it may be useful to expose them to consociational practices that might be adopted as ways of ensuring ethnic participation in national government and as ways of ensuring all a 'fair deal' in terms of the sharing of national costs and benefits (Smith, 2003).

## THE RIGHTS OF ETHNIC PEOPLE

Grievances specific to the treatment of ethnic communities concern discriminatory policies and practices of the state, such as repressive language policy in education and discriminatory recruitment and promotion in government employment and access to economic opportunities. When discussion about the lack of ethnic rights does occur, it reflects the many and diverse situations in which ethnic people and ethnic areas are seen to be treated unfairly by Burmans, a Burman-dominated state and of course the various Burman-dominated instruments of the state, especially the army.

The language issue is of great importance to the insurgent organizations that control or have controlled territory and population. Where their control of territory has been recognized by ceasefire and a territorial demarcation, as in the case of the Wa, Kachin and Mon, and where they have the will and resources to conduct their own schools, the language of schooling is in accordance with their choice: variously, their ethnic language, Burmese, English or Chinese (in the case of the China-border area). In the case of the New Mon State Party which has sought to defend and expand its influence beyond the pockets of territory left in its control after the ceasefire, it has a long history of negotiating agreements with the local authorities (with mixed success) to be able to conduct Mon language and literacy classes both in government schools, in their own Mon 'National' schools and outside of schools. Ethnic minorities growing up in Myanmar have no choice but to learn Burmese and in many cases are not able to use the ethnic mother tongue. This is in many cases deeply resented, not so much with regard to language use per se, since for most groups being able to use the national language is recognized as having certain practical advantages, but because they see this language shift as manipulated by the authorities to count such people officially as no longer ethnic. In other words, it is seen as Burmanization. Reaction against this practice is quite extreme in the KNU-influenced areas of the eastern border area, where there is popular belief that this is a statistical method of genocide and just part of a wider genocide policy. Popular opinion in the KNU-influenced refugee camps is strongly against learning Burmese at all.

The abuse of the rights of civilians in areas of armed conflict in Myanmar, mainly ethnic areas, has been well documented. It appears to be so widespread and systematic that it must reflect an attitude of scornful disdain for the people, for laws, and for international law on the part of the Myanmar army, its commanders and those responsible for its behaviour in the field. In the end, however, abuses by the military in conflict areas concern the rights of civilians in a place and time of insurgency and civil war. The remedy appears to lie, in the long term, in retraining the armed forces to instill respect for the rights of all civilians, perhaps removing responsibility for internal security from the armed forces and, of course, addressing the causes of insurgency in order to bring about peace and reconciliation.

Perhaps more importantly, however, it seems clear that the types of abuse of the rights of civilians identified with conflict areas now extends beyond the conflict areas and, in post-conflict situations, beyond the conflict into the post-conflict period. The disdainful way that the Myanmar Army has arbitrarily displaced ethnic civilian populations as part of its counter-insurgency operations against ethnic insurgents is a habit that now seems to have become the norm in the way the military authorities treat civilian populations who happen to be in the way of their needs or plans. Ashley South (2006, p. 11) in his study of population displacement in Myanmar, refers to 'state–society conflict' as distinct from more recognizable armed conflict.

Everywhere in the country, in the interests of national development, much celebrated in the government's media, the authorities seek to create or expand infrastructure. Undoubtedly this is necessary and frequently, if not always, an advantage to the local population as well as the authorities. Civilian populations are usually called on to provide labour and/or materials, all too often without payment or (in belated response to the ILO's anti-forced labour campaign) with only a façade of payment. However, this approach to development also extends the disdainful displacement of people in conflict areas to displacement of people from land that is required for development. Land for infrastructure, for the endless expansion of military bases and the surrounding land required to make them self-supporting, land for establishing commercial plantations and other economic enterprises – all such land is simply treated as owned by the state and previous occupants' rights ignored. This does not happen only in ethnic areas, but it is of greatest extent and significance in ethnic areas where development projects are fostered by the military as part of its occupation of previous conflict areas and destruction of traditional ethnic communities a way of securing the civilian population.

In short, any long-term resolution of the ethnic conflicts in Myanmar will require not simply the creation of meaningful territorial autonomies, but also reforming the disdainful way the state treats its citizens (and especially its ethnic minority citizens) and the creative exploration of appropriate policies that can satisfy the demands of a complex multiethnic, multilingual and multicultural society. This in turn will require overcoming a long history of denigration, distrust and authoritarian rule, but it also requires access to information, ideas and experiences from other places. Above all it needs what I call 'opportunities for dialogue' based on willingness to explore such issues.

## CULTIVATING SOFTLINERS

I asked, rhetorically, above, whether Khin Nyunt and his group were, from the start, more predisposed to dialogue, and did they win internal battles to take control of the government's response on issues requiring dialogue. Or was it that, being positioned as the regime's 'front to the outside world' and, under pressure from many directions, and pushed into exposure to international norms, they learned to dialogue, and to speak the language of international norms and learned that this defused threats and problems? The fact is that, until the ousting of Khin Nyunt in October 2004, anybody outside the regime wanting to 'talk' with the regime, came to encounter it through the Khin Nyunt group and that group made it their business to be able to talk. Unfortunately, with regard to the NLD, it appears that talk led nowhere, there was no common ground, or none that could be 'sold' to the military leadership group as a whole.

After Khin Nyunt's fall, those who had developed dialogue with him and his supporters in government, sometimes fruitfully, suddenly found they had lost their old interlocutors and were now meeting new ones ill-versed in the issues and practices around which agreements had slowly been built up with the Khin Nyunt group. Effectively, a regime change had occurred, and it now becomes an important question as to whether the result of the purge of Khin Nyunt and his supporters is to be the systematic application of a 'hard line' because the hardliners have triumphed over the soft, or whether time is needed for dialogue-readiness to emerge again among those of the regime now newly placed at its front. The signs so far are mixed. International agencies that early in 2005 feared that they faced a crisis of access to their project sites now report that there is a new emphasis on working within the letter of formal agreements and that new and tougher rules about access have been proposed, and in many cases that access is being restored. Where there was an intransigent face presented to the ILO's demands and even orchestrated death threats to the ILO representative in the country, it appears that a willingness to try cooperation has re-emerged.

How does this reflect on the necessary 'wise individual action' and the current constitutional process? I am hopeful that the ethnic issue provides room for something other than a zero-sum contest, if only pro-federalists are willing to moderate their demands and learn the language of devo-lution, and help the military at the face of the regime to learn it also. This will take time, however, and it requires that all concerned have access to a wide range of ideas and experience from other countries. Regarding the current constitutional process, we still have to wait for the outcome of the NC with regard to how much space will be left for discussion and debate in the society, once the SPDC has distributed power to new institutions of state in the way that it wants. I have stated that I assume that the parties will be essentially excluded from executive power but included in national and state-level legislative 'talking shop(s)', along with the state party and the military representatives. For ethnic communities, while hostile to the prospect of state executives being controlled by the military, they have no prior experience of state-level legislatures.

The most positive way in which to view the current constitutional process therefore is in terms of the prospect of greater opportunities for dialogue and political learning, in what has been a politically and intellectually iso-lated country since the beginning of the era of the militarized state in Burma. There is no clear timetable to complete the constitution but, according to the roadmap that the regime still acknowledges, on its com-pletion there will be a referendum on the constitution, followed by new elec-tions. These elections will establish the representation in legislatures, and in theory they will determine who becomes the President and forms the gov-ernment. I am assuming that the next elections will be managed in such a way that a new 'state party', probably the USDA, will emerge as dominant, in the same way as GOLKAR was guaranteed electoral victory in repeated elections in Suharto's Indonesia. The 'state party', supported by military appointees, will therefore be in a position to determine who becomes President and who forms the government and this pattern will be repeated in the ethnic states.

The Suharto model was at one time much talked about in exile circles as a deplored and rejected model. However, it needs to be understood that the Suharto model provided a level of freedom of expression and organization far beyond what is known in the SPDC's Myanmar. Inside Myanmar, any public discussion of ethnic rights or constitutional issues is subject to the same repressive intolerance of public debate about all political issues that has prevailed since the 1962 military coup. The period of the 1988 uprising and, to a lesser extent, the period of the 1990 election campaign, were short-lived exceptions.

As a result, published or broadcast views about the constitutional future of Myanmar and about ethnic rights mainly emanate from pro-democracy and ethnic exiles and are designed to extol the virtues of democracy, human rights and federalism and to discredit the regime. Such ideas have no public dissemination inside the country (other than through external sources such as Radio Free Asia, Democratic Voice of Burma) and limited private circulation.

Years of self-imposed isolation and continuing bureaucratic obstacles to travel have compounded the effects of political repression. The military is dominated by a xenophobic nationalist elite, obsessed with threats to the territorial integrity of the country posed by ethnic nationalism.[8] Even within the elite very few people have had any opportunities for sustained exposure to the development of ideas and norms in the international community. There is no access to a modern, analytical history or political science course, there are few independent-minded practising lawyers; there is little knowledge, for example, of comparable situations either within the region or in other parts of the world. In such conditions, views about solutions to the 'ethnic problem' tend to reflect the well-worn debates of the period prior to the military takeover or, in private, the parochial or propaganda views about specific moments in the relations between the authorities and the ethnic insurgent organizations.

Between the 1996 adjournment of the National Convention and its reconvening in May 2004, there was a resounding constitutional silence from the regime. Under military rule, the discussion of ethnic issues is particularly sensitive. Because of the ethnic insurgency there is a total ban on contact with illegal ethnic insurgent and opposition exile organizations and anybody voicing ethnic issues is prima facie suspected of contacts with such organizations. While ethnic insurgents who entered into ceasefires can be said to have enjoyed access to the regime, whenever substantive issues were raised, the military ingenuously responded that, since it is a military junta, it is unable to deal with political issues. Of course, ceasefire groups and their communities are subject to the same restriction of public expression as the rest of the country.

Nevertheless, opportunities have arisen during the NC process both for exile groups, busy mobilizing an alternative to the NC, and ceasefire groups attempting to get their aspirations acknowledged within the NC, for learning: learning new ideas, learning from others' experience. The question is, how can this learning process be extended, over time and to groups not yet exposed or willing to be exposed to such learning? One answer is through expanding and strengthening civil-society activity, and the capacity-building education and training that goes with it, encouraging the necessary confidence for exchange of ideas and the culture of dialogue about solving problems.[9]

Under the Suharto model, much political learning was possible, including that by GOLKAR and the military. This did not bring about the transition to democracy when it occurred. But when the transition began, thanks largely to external events, many political and civil society players and, indeed, much of the military, were somewhat prepared. GOLKAR has been able to make the transition to a pro-democratic political party within a competitive multi-party system. That preparation in Myanmar is currently lacking and the political space provided by the 'Indonesian model' of the Suharto era, however disappointing for those who have looked to a rapid transition to democracy, might be an outcome through which civil society and political parties can learn to shape moderate demands and at the same time cultivate regime softliners.

## NOTES

\*   Burma was renamed Myanmar by the SLORC military junta in 1989. I have used the name Myanmar where I am referring to the country specifically in the period from 1989, otherwise to avoid Burma/Myanmar, in the historical context I have used Burma. I have used the word Burmese to refer to the language and the people of the country as a whole, and the word 'Burman' to refer to the ethnic majority population.
1.  The results of these sessions of the National Convention have been compiled as *The Basic Principles and Detailed Basic Principles Laid Down by the National Convention Plenary sessions up to 30 March 1996*. According to the Convening Committee, results of later sessions will also be published.
2.  At its formation, the NCUB included the NDF, DAB, NLD (Liberated Area) and the NCGUB.
3.  The scope of influences can most easily be gauged by examining the pages of the *Legal Issues on Burma Journal*, published by the Burma Lawyers Council (BLC) and the papers published by the Technical Advisory Network of Burma with the support of the Burma Fund.
4.  '[A] formal understanding negotiated between the ILO and the Union of Myanmar for the establishment of a facilitator to assist possible victims of forced labour in Myanmar' (ILO, Press Release 03/21, 14 May 2003). This is not to say that all the necessary steps were then taken to eliminate forced labour.
5.  My first encounter with the issue occurred in 1992, through an international conference which provided exile opposition groups with access to expert constitutional advice.

6.  Yash Ghai (n.d.), with a career of active constitutional advising, made this very clear in a paper he prepared for the Afghanistan constitution-drafting process, putting federalism into a broader range of approaches to 'devolution'.
7.  The 1947 constitution provided for Shan, Kachin, Karenni and Karen States and a Chin Special Division. The resulting Union of Burma was certainly not a classic federal system. For a discussion of the influences shaping the 1947 constitution and views about it, see Smith (2005). The 1974 constitution introduced a Mon State and an Arakan State but effectively gave the states no powers of autonomy.
8.  For a definitive account of the ethnic insurgent challenges to the state in Burma, see Martin Smith (1999). For a brief recent account of the state of the politics of conflict between the military regime and ethnic groups, see ICG (2003).
9.  On the emerging 'civil society' space in Myanmar, see, for example, ICG (2001), South (2004), Heidel (2006) and Lorch (2006).

# REFERENCES

*Asiaweek* (2000), 28 April, **26**(16).

Bermeo, Nancy (1990), 'Rethinking regime change', *Comparative Politics*, **22**(3), 359–77.

Ghai, Yash (ed.) (2000), *Autonomy and Ethnicity: Negotiating Competing Claims in Multi-ethnic States*, Cambridge: Cambridge University Press.

Ghai, Yash (n.d.), 'Decentralisation of state powers in Afghanistan: unitary or federal: a false choice?', an Options Paper for the Afghan Constitutional Commission.

Heidel, Brian (2006), *The Growth of Civil Society in Myanmar*, Bangalore: Books for Change.

ICG (2001), *Myanmar: The Role of Civil Society* (published on ICG website).

ICG (2003), *Myanmar Backgrounder: Ethnic Minority Politics*, Asia Report no. 52 (published on ICG website).

Khin, Maung Win and Alan Smith (1998), 'Burma', in Wolfgang Sachsenroeder and U. Frings (eds), *Political Party Systems and Democratic Development in East and Southeast Asia, Vol 1: Southeast Asia*, Aldershot: Ashgate, pp. 98–156.

Lorch, Jasmin (2006), 'Civil society under authoritarian rule: the case of Myanmar', *Sudostasien Aktuell, 2*.

Maung, Maung (1999), 'The 1988 uprising in Burma', New Haven, monograph 49, Yale Southeast Asia Studies.

National Council of the Union of Burma (1997), '(Future) constitution of the Federal Union of Burma, proposed first draft', Constitution Drafting Committee of the NCUB.

National Council of the Union of Burma (1998), 'Commentary on the (future) constitution of the Federal Union of Burma, proposed first draft', Constitution Drafting Committee of the NCUB.

O'Donnell, Guillermo and Phillippe Schmitter (1986), *Transitions from Authoritarian Rule: Tentative Conclusions about Uncertain Democracies*, Baltimore: Johns Hopkins University Press.

Smith, Alan (1997), 'Ethnic conflict and federalism: the case of Burma', in Guenther Baechler (ed.), *Federalism against Ethnicity*, Zurich: Verlag Ruegger, pp. 231–59.

Smith, Alan (2000), 'The economic and political consequences of the Asian eco-
    nomic crisis: the case of Burma', in Abdul Rahman Embong and J. Rudolph
    (eds), *Southeast Asia into the 21st Century: Crisis and Beyond*, Bangi: Penerbit
    Universiti Kebangsaan Malaysia, pp. 189–206.
Smith, Alan (2003), 'Ethnic problems and constitutional solutions', *Legal Issues on
    Burma Journal*, **15**, August.
Smith, Alan (2005), 'Burma/Myanmar: struggle for democracy and ethnic rights',
    in Will Kymlicka and Baogang He (eds), *Multiculturalism in Asia*, Oxford:
    Oxford University Press, pp. 262–87.
Smith, Martin (1999), *Burma: Ethnic Insurgency and the Politics of Ethnicity* (revd),
    Dhaka: UP/Bangkok: White Lotus/London: Zed Books.
South, Ashley (2004), 'Political transition in Burma: a new model for democratiz-
    ation', *Contemporary Southeast Asia*, August 2004, ISEAS, National University
    of Singapore.
South, Ashley (2006), 'Forced migration in Myanmar: patterns, impacts and
    responses' (report commissioned by the Office of the United Nations Resident
    Coordinator in Myanmar).
Sundhaussen, Ulf (1984), 'Military withdrawal from government responsibility',
    *Armed Forces and Society*, **10**(4), 548ff.
Weller, Marc (ed.) (1993), *Democracy and Politics in Burma*, Manerplaw: NCGUB.
Williams, David C. and Lian H. Sakhong (eds) (2005), *Designing Federalism in
    Burma*, Chiang Mai: UNLD Press.

# 10.  China's de facto federalism

## Yongnian Zheng*

China does not have a federalist system of government – it has no constitutional division of power between levels of government nor has there
been any separation of power within the government. Constitutionally,
the country is a unitary state. Nevertheless, within China's cultural context,
a formal institutional perspective can hardly help us understand the
country's central–local relations properly. A better understanding of China's
central– local relations should begin with a behavioural perspective. Such a
perspective will enable us to see China's de facto federal structure.

Elsewhere, I have described China's central–local relations as 'semi-
federalism' (Zheng, 1994, 1995), and 'de facto federalism' (Zheng, 2000).
I have also tried to explain the sources of China's de facto federalism
(Zheng, 2006). In this chapter, I will first summarize some of my early works
and sketch an overall de facto federal structure in China's central–local relations. I then discuss briefly three sub-structures of the central–local relations, including formal organizations, procedures and norms, and show
how they can interact with each other in influencing the interaction between
the centre and the provinces. The main purpose of this chapter is to identify
three main features which are embedded in China's de facto federal structure, namely, coercion, bargaining and reciprocity, and discuss how these
institutions have regulated the interaction between the centre and the
provinces in China.

## DEFINING FEDERALISM: FORMAL INSTITUTIONAL V. BEHAVIOURAL

In academic circles, federalism is usually defined in two ways. First, it can be
defined from a formal institutional perspective. In this context, federalism is
often regarded as a form of government that differs from unitary forms of
government in terms of the distribution of power between central and sub-
national governments, the separation of powers within the government, and
the division of legislative powers between national and regional representatives. In this sense, a true federation has both a distribution of political power

specified in the Constitution and a direct relationship between political power and the individual citizen. Only a few countries fit an ideal type of federalism. For example, K.C. Wheare (1964) regards the United States, Canada and Switzerland as federal countries but Malaysia and India only as 'quasi-federal'. This is so because states and local governments in the United States, Canada and Switzerland are not totally dependent on their central government for matters that are local in nature, while in Malaysia and India they depend heavily upon their national government despite the fact that these nations possess a federal structure.

If the Chinese state is defined in terms of formal institutions, it cannot be considered federal. The country has constitutionally remained a unitary state whereby all local governments are subordinate to the central government. The principle of territorial distribution of power has not been changed since 1949, when the People's Republic was established. According to China's Constitution, all provincial governments are local state administrative organs; they must accept the unified leadership by the State Council, implement administrative measures, regulations and decisions by the State Council and be responsible and report to the State Council (Pu Xingzu et al., 1995: 223). On the other hand, the State Council can define the specific functions and powers of the local governments, nullify their decisions, impose martial law in the localities, and direct its auditing agencies to conduct inspections of financial discipline. Similarly, while provincial people's congresses have the right to make local laws, the Standing Committee of the National People's Congress can annul this legislation if it conflicts with national laws. There is also no clear demarcation regarding the scope and content of the respective legislative authority between the central and provincial congresses.

Nevertheless, this should not prevent us from classifying China as de facto federalism. Formal institutions alone cannot guarantee the powers of local governments vis-à-vis the national governments. Constitutional federalism guarantees the power of local governments such as in Australia, Canada and the US, where local governments have a considerable amount of legal authority to determine their governmental form as well as legislative power to make and revise their own laws (Nathan and Balmaceda, 1990). In many other countries with constitutional federalism, especially developing countries, local governments do not have such authority. For example, in India and Brazil, constitutions assign extensive powers to the national government, which has the right to veto state legislation and take over the administration of states under emergency conditions. In Brazil, the federal constitution explicitly specifies how the internal political institutions of the states are to be organized. In India, state powers are constrained by the fact that the governors of the states are appointed by the country's president on the recommendation of the Prime Minister (ibid.). This is also true in the former Soviet Union. Even though there was a federal political structure, little autonomy was granted to local officials, and the central government retained virtually all authority over major economic and political decisions.

More importantly, a formal institutional perspective can hardly help us understand China's central–local relations properly simply because of the lack of a sound legal infrastructure in the country. In the developed world, laws, regulations and contacts often mean the end of business. Once made, they are binding and local governments have to follow. But this is hardly the case in China. China is still in a process of building a system of rule of law. For China's local governments, laws, regulations and contracts often mean the beginning of business. Bargaining in different forms between the centre and the provinces is a must in the enforcement of laws, regulations and contracts. Legal fragmentation is an essential part of China's political system. Therefore, a better understanding of China's central–local relations can begin with a behavioural perspective. Such an approach will enable us to see how China has actually developed de facto federalism and how this system is actually functioning.

There is a behavioural tradition in understanding federalism. Since the 1960s, scholars have attempted to look at different political systems from a behavioural perspective. Scholars in the behavioural school found that the de facto power of local government officials is often much greater than their constitutional authority. Local officials can always defend their local interests in the face of the central power through the use of various local resources, such as social identities, a shared local–political culture, distinct economic activities and interests, the statutory powers of local authorities, and the interests of local political party organizations (Schulz, 1979: 18). Studies of local power in Europe, Latin America, Africa and Japan have all suggested the persistence of local power and local initiative in rather centralized political systems.

Even in the former communist countries, essential local autonomy also existed. Daniel Nelson (1980: i) argued that 'the processes of making and implementing public policies in communist systems . . . cannot be understood unless we observe the roles in these processes which are performed by local party and state organs that constitute day-to-day government for the citizenry'. Jan F. Triska (1980: 2) also found that local governments in communist countries were not mere local extensions of superior governments. They should not be perceived as simply convenient arrangements for national governance, mere local tools of national administration.

Scholars of the behavioural school argued that, even though constitutionally well defined, federalism is so broad and inchoate as a governmental arrangement that it defies close specification. M.D. Reagan and J.G. Sanzone (1981) even argue that federalism as an operational concept is almost bankrupt. Diverse approaches to federalism have led to great differences in judging which country belongs to the club of modern federalism. So, when K.C. Wheare (1964) published his study on comparative federalism in 1946, he believed that the club consisted of only four or five countries. Nevertheless, Daniel Elazar (1987) argued that as high a proportion as 70 per cent of the people in the world live in countries with federal state structures and federal arrangements in some ways.

However, all the above controversies have not prevented scholars from defining federalism in specific contexts. I argue here that federalism can be regarded as an instrument to resolve conflicts between governments at different levels through various measures such as interest representation and decentralization. All political systems have to confront the problem of interest representation; that is, the manner in which local interests can best be expressed and how the central government responds to them. Political systems also confront the problem of policy implementation. If the central government wants to impose its own will on society, it must have policy implementors. Whether policy implementors are bureaucracies or governments, the central government needs a mechanism of interest representation internal to itself because organizations, bureaucracies or local governments have their own interests, which may not necessarily be synonymous with central interests. Obviously, most political systems depend upon intermediary levels of government organizations or political bodies to provide contact between citizens and the central government. How these government organizations or political bodies should be organized is another important question.

Federalism is one means of resolving interest conflicts between governments at different levels. But a key question, which involves the structure of the federal system and the division of power and authority among different levels of government, is whether we define federalism as a system of multiple centres of power in which the central and local governments have broad authority to enact policies of their own choice, or whether we define federalism as a system of decentralization in which the central and local governments essentially implement uniform national policies (Kenyon and Kincaid, 1992:4). If we take the first interpretation, federalism could be the outcome of bargaining or a negotiated working agreement between political actors with conflicting goals, as Willian Riker (1964) understood it. As a matter of fact, federalism has been widely regarded as a means of resolving conflict in a fragmented society and of reducing the burden of the central government.

Moreover, there is a dynamic aspect involved in organizations. A behavioural approach is to look at China's central–local relations in a dynamic way. It helps us understand how changes in local socioeconomic environments will generate changes over the relations of the provinces to the centre. China's political system is not a status quo. Various factors such as economic development, changes in the power distribution of different levels of government and changing expectations of different actors within the system ultimately lead to changes in the way the political system is organized. In this sense, the role of local governments in economic development must be taken into account in understanding changes in China's central–local relations.

Following the behavioural tradition, I define China's central–local relations as de facto or behavioural federalism. One caveat must be added here first. The term 'Federal China' is gaining popularity among Chinese dissident scholars (for example, Yan, 1992; Wu, 2003, 2004). These scholars suggest that China should adopt federalism to solve the issues of national integration such as those related to Taiwan, Hong Kong, Tibet and Xinjiang. This chapter does not deal with these issues. Instead, it investigates how China's existing central–local relations are characterized by de facto federalism. In other words, it only looks at the issue in terms of power distribution between the centre and the provinces. Other factors such as ethnicity, Hong Kong identity and Taiwan nationalism are important in moving China towards federalism, but these factors are beyond the scope of this study.

In a behavioural sense, China's de facto federalism can be defined as follows: A relatively institutionalized pattern which involves an explicit or implicit bargain between the centre and the provinces, one element in the bargain being that the provinces receive certain institutionalized or ad hoc benefits in return for guarantees by provincial officials that they will behave in certain ways on behalf of the centre.

More concretely, China's central–local relationship can be defined as de facto federalism because it satisfies the following conditions:

1. A hierarchical political system in which the activities of government are divided between the provinces and the centre in such a way that each kind of government has some activities on which it makes final decisions.
2. Intergovernmental decentralization is institutionalized to such a degree that it is increasingly becoming difficult, if not impossible, for the national government to impose unilaterally its discretion on the provinces and alter the distribution of authority between governments.
3. The provinces have primary responsibility over the economy and, to some extent, politics within their jurisdictions.

Figure 10.1 illustrates China's de facto federalism. China's Constitution does not describe such a division of power between the centre and the

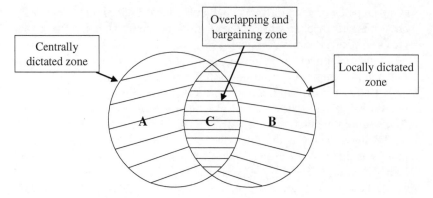

*Figure 10.1    The division of powers between the centre and the provinces*

provinces, but, at a practical and behavioural level, power is divided between the two actors. Some powers such as foreign policy, national defence and birth planning belong exclusively to the central government, and it is very difficult for local governments to have a say on these matters. Some other matters are exclusively dictated by local governments: for example, local public security, road construction and school building. Most economic matters are exclusively handled by local governments. For example, foreign direct investment (FDI) and outflowing investment below a certain limit are decided by local governments. Other powers are shared by the centre and the provinces. There are policies which are made by the centre but implemented by local governments. The central government also has to consult local governments in the formulation of certain policies. Actually, there is no essential difference between China's de facto federalism and other forms of federalism in the world in terms of policy formation and implementation, except that China is not democratic.

## ORGANIZATIONS, PROCEDURES AND NORMS

So, how does the de facto federal structure affect the interaction between the centre and the provinces? In exploring this issue, we can learn a great deal from organizational theories. According to these, organizations consist of three structural aspects (Benson, 1977; Zeitz, 1980; Benz, 1987). First, the political–economic basis of the organizational structure is the power and resource structure formed by the distribution of legally defined authority, financial resources, political support and information among different levels of government. Second, the interaction structure comprises the individual attitudes, action strategies, interests and goals of the actors in the system, which are to be coordinated into collective action. Third, the organizational paradigm, which comprises both the rules of the game and the institutionalized thought structure, is the principles of coordinating and regulating individual actions.

The three levels of the structure normally tend to achieve a state of equilibrium, but they are not totally dependent on one another. Instead, they can vary autonomously, and tensions and contradictions are thus created. All structural variations are determined by the existing power and resource structure, but the system is not deterministic. The political and economic bases can be altered by changes in the organizational paradigm or the processes of resource flow between the organization and its environments. Because the government system depends on resource acquisition from the economic system and needs political support from society, state organizations at different levels affect each other in different ways; shifts in resource flow directly influence the power and resource structure of the political and administrative system.

Changes in the organizational paradigm are also significant for the power and resource structure and the interaction structure. As long as the organizational paradigm is constant, changes in the power and resource structure and the interaction structure will be latent, or the impulse to change will not be effective. According to Benz (1987: 131), 'if the tensions in the inter-organizational political and administrative system rise to a level at which they are evident to all actors and therefore cannot be concealed, they will generate a climate of reform which creates the conditions for a paradigmatic change'. Furthermore, competing ideologies or 'paradigmatic approaches' of governments at different levels can also bring about changes in the organizational paradigm. Thus 'the formulation and implementation of reform conceptions should be regarded as a political process in which the aspirations and interests of different levels of government are at stake as well as maintenance or realization of power position' (ibid.: 136).

These three structural aspects of organizations can help us clarify many issues in China's central–local relations. The de facto federal structure empowered local governments, and power shifted from the centre to the provinces. Intergovernmental decentralization not only meant that the provinces were able to share the economic power that previously was monopolized by the centre but also, more importantly, it implied that the provinces could develop their own independent power bases by increasing their local wealth. Since local governments themselves became economic planners, and local wealth was locally created, the operation of local power, to a great degree, became irrelevant to the centre. Changes in the power structure of central–local relations also had a major impact on the second level of structural aspects, that is, the interaction structure between the centre and the provinces. With increasing power and wealth, local government officials changed their perceptions of interests and their action strategies in their dealings with the centre. They could not only plan local development independent from the centre, but also bargain with the centre to pursue greater power. Furthermore, all these changes went unreflected in the formal institutions of central–local relations. In other words, changes in central–local relations at the operational level did not result in any formal organizational changes. While the behavioural patterns between the centre and the provinces are different from those in the past, the organizational structure of central–local relations remains intact. However, changes in both the structure of power of central–local relations and the interaction between the centre and the provinces could gradually generate new rules and norms of central–local relations in the long run, and eventually lead to a new paradigm. This is the dynamics of China's central–local relations.

To identify institutions which regulate and mediate the interaction between the centre and the provinces, we can go one step further, to look at new institutionalism, which drew much from organizational theories. New institutionalism shows us how collective choices or individual choices are made with the presence of the constraints from these structural factors. Institutionalism aims to explore the impact of both the existing structure and its predecessor, culture, on human behaviour. To see how cultural factors affect behaviour, two important aspects need to be clarified: what are institutions, and how they affect human behaviour. Actors (the centre and the provinces in this study) seek their goals under given institutions which, in turn, provide the context in which actors define their strategies and pursue their interests. In seeking their goals, actors form their own preferences. The formation of their preferences, however, is mediated by institutions. In defining institutions, scholars usually include both formal organizations and informal rules and procedures. But in using 'institution' as an analytical tool, some emphasize formal organizational context, while others emphasize informal rules or cultural context. 'Institutions' is used in this chapter to include not only formal organizations, formal rules, compliance procedures and standard operating practices related to the operation of organizations, but also historically formed informal ones. In other words, this study defines culture as norms, which include organization-generated and historically formed rules.

The next important question is how norms affect behaviour. Traditionally, scholars defined culture as a body of attitudes and beliefs. Many implied that there was a one-to-one correspondence between attitude and behaviour; that is, one set of attitudes leads consistently to one type of behaviour. Clearly, such mechanically deterministic theories were unable to explain disjunctures between practice and thought. A new institutional approach attempts to avoid this trap by defining culture as a body of norms. Culture affects behaviour thanks to its nature of instrumentality. Using Ann Swidler's term, cultural norms affect behaviour by providing actors with a 'tool kit' of habits, skills and styles with which people construct strategies of action. From this point, we can see that the institutions of central–local relations can affect the interaction between the centre and the provinces at least in the following three ways.

First of all, since norms consist of shared decision rules, recipes, standard operating procedures and decision routines, they provide assumptions about the orderliness of the political universe, the nature of causality, principal goals in political life and the trustworthness of other political actors (Elkins and Simeon, 1979: 132). In this sense, norms allow both the centre and the provinces to interpret the game being played, and to figure out what others know, believe and mean. Therefore norms help them predict what reaction will follow if a given strategy is used in their interaction.

Second, norms have direct effect by defining collectively shared standards of appropriate behaviour that validate social identity. This implies that behaviour is shaped not only by goals, alternatives and rules of maximization or satisfaction, as the rationalist model of politics suggested. More importantly, behaviour is shaped by roles and norms that define standards of appropriateness. Since norms are what the centre and the provinces have learned from their interaction in the past, they help the centre and the provinces, not only in what action they should take, but also what action they should not take in their interaction. In other words, norms help the centre and the provinces to reduce, even eliminate, inappropriate behavioural options. In other words, norms and behaviour patterns are not the same, but norms affect behaviour by presenting limited options. In this sense, the interaction between the centre and the provinces is not only motivated by self-interest, but also constrained by their identification with appropriateness. The importance of the instrumentality of norms lies in the fact, as March and Olsen (1989) argued, that obligatory action is different from consequential action.

Third, we can understand the instrumentality of norms in a Gramscian way; that is, norms are the ideational mass product of symbolic manipulation by political actors aimed at creating mass support for their particular choice. This points to two aspects of the interaction between the centre and the provinces. On the one hand, this can imply that the centre (the dominant power actor) can escape from, or rise above, the constraints of norms that it manipulates. On the other hand, political leaders in the centre are also socialized by the norms they produce, and thus over time are constrained by the symbolic or textual myths that they or their predecessors created. In other words, discourses that the centre employs to pursue its interests can be used by the provinces to seek their local interests. As we will see, decentralization is one of such discourses. It is created by the centre to achieve its goals, but is often utilized by the provinces to promote their local interests.

By incorporating norms into the model of central–local relations, we can provide a more effective explanation of central–local relations in the reform era than the ones provided by both the structural approach and the procedural approach, since norms promote and reinforce cooperation between the centre and the provinces.

## COERCION, BARGAINING AND RECIPROCITY: HOW DE FACTO FEDERALISM WORKS

The de facto federal structure affects all the three levels of structural aspects, including the political–economic basis, the interaction structure and the organizational paradigm of China's central–local relations. Many institutions are implicitly and explicitly embedded in such a de facto structure; institutions that affect relations between the state and society, and between the centre and the provinces. This study only deals with these institutions that have governed the interaction between the centre and the provinces. In this regard, three main institutions can be identified, including coercion, bargaining, and reciprocity.

In the China study circles, scholars have emphasized the role of coercion and bargaining in regulating central–local relations. Having recognized the importance of coercion and bargaining, I nevertheless argue that, without a third institution, reciprocity, central–local relations cannot work smoothly. The interaction between the centre and the provinces, be it coercion or bargaining, contains elements of reciprocity. Coercion, bargaining and reciprocity have formed a coherent body of institutions and governed central–local relations throughout the whole reform process. While coercion and bargaining govern aspects of central–local relations, reciprocity regulates the daily businesses of central–local relations. It is worth noting that coercion and bargaining per se contain reciprocity, but generally speaking, when coercion and bargaining end their functions, reciprocity begins. Table 10.1 outlines some main characteristics of these three institutions and how they affect central–local relations. Broadly speaking, these three institutions can be defined as fellows:

- *Coercion* can be defined as a process in which the centre employs coercive means such as the nomenklatura system and massive

*Table 10.1   Institutions governing central–local relations in China*

| Institution | Justification | Motives | Process | Goal |
|---|---|---|---|---|
| Coercion | Necessity of unified leadership and centralization | Central control and coordination | Personnel appointment and campaign, etc | Forced local compliance |
| Bargaining | Mutually advantageous | Self-interest | Negotiations | Conflict resolution |
| Reciprocity | Mutually acceptable | Justification to other, obligation | Self-adjustment, deliberation | Voluntary cooperation |

campaigns to solicit compliance from the provinces. Coercion is unilateral, aiming at guaranteeing central control over the provinces and strengthening the unity of the nation.

- *Bargaining* can be defined as a process in which the two actors (the centre and the provinces) resolve conflicts between them through various forms of bargaining. It is bilateral and both sides utilize their resources to promote their mutual interests or to maximize their respective interests.
- *Reciprocity* can be defined as a process in which the two actors (the centre and the provinces) achieve voluntary cooperation between them through self-adjustment and deliberation. Reciprocity is based on obligation, with each side behaving in a mutually acceptable way or with each side's behaviour justifiable to the other side.

**Coercion**

Coercion as an institution can be formally institution-embedded and informally practice-embedded. Besides these two types of coercion, coercion also can be formally defined. Regarding central–local relations, China's Constitution regulates the country so that it is organized as a unitary state, under which certain aspects of power, such as powers over foreign affairs and national defence, should be and are exclusively monopolized by the central government (Diao et al., 1989). Given that provincial officials are to be punished if they step into these fields, they are not likely to do so unless they are allowed and encouraged by the centre to do so. On the other hand, if they are punished for having done so, they are likely to regard the punishment as a legitimate action by the central government. These different types of formally defined coercion actually point to the formal distribution of authority between the centre and the provinces. Since provincial officials will not step into these fields, these forms of coercion do not function daily. To a great degree, using them to explain central–local relations will not enable us to see how the centre and the provinces have actually interacted with each other. Therefore it is necessary to search for institutions and norms that regulate daily interactions between the two actors. More concretely, we need to examine institution- and practice-embedded norms.

Institution-embedded norms, which play a role of coercion, are formulated in China's economic system and political system as well. China's old planned economic system was highly centralized and, in principle, the central government monopolized all aspects of economic power and left provincial governments no leeway for local autonomy. But the economic reform that Deng Xiaoping initiated in the late 1970s dramatically changed the structure of power centralization. Until Zhu Rongji initiated selective economic recentralization in the mid-1990s, the whole reform era was characterized by excessive decentralization. Many scholars and policy makers believe that excessive decentralization led to a serious crisis of state power and a crisis of national integration. Even though there still existed various economic monitoring systems in which the central government solicited provincial compliance (Huang, 1996: 101–7), decentralization shifted economic power from the centre to provinces, implying that the centre was no longer able to use economic coercive means against the provinces (Lieberthal, 1992). In other words, economically coercive means were no longer available for the central government. So how has the centre been able to control the provinces? Scholars turned to the political side of China's central–local relations and found that, while economic power was drastically decentralized, the political structure remained intact. Indeed, an examination of the political structure of central–local relations is the key to an understanding of how coercion affects provincial behaviour.

In terms of daily interaction between the centre and the provinces, coercion is expressed in both China's structural hierarchy and the nomenklatura system. Constitutionally, China is a unitary state, in which virtually all organizations, whether formally part of the state or not, are assigned particular bureaucratic ranks. The general principle of central–local relations is that provincial governments derive their authority and decision-making rights solely from the central government and their duties at the provincial level are performed on behalf of the central government (Huang, 1996: 28). But one point needs to be emphasized regarding the hierarchical relationship between the centre (for example, the State Council) and the provinces (for example, provincial governments). To say that the relationship between the State Council and provincial governments is one of direct subordination does not mean that all provincial officials have to take orders from the State Council as a whole. According to the system of the bureaucratic rank, central ministries and provincial governments are on the same bureaucratic level. Therefore, though provincial bureaus are lower in bureaucratic rank than their ministerial counterparts in Beijing, provincial bureaus do not necessarily take orders from their ministries. As shown in Table 10.2, provincial bureaus have to answer to two superior units, the central ministry and the provincial government, which are at the same administrative level.[1]

The structural hierarchy means that provincial officials are subordinate to the central government, but subordination per se does not imply coercion. To see how coercion is executed is to see how the system of subordination functions. This requires an investigation of how provincial officials are actually managed. The two most important principles of China's political system are party control of the government and party management of cadres.[2] The two principles are embedded in the nomenklatura system, under which important provincial leaders and cadres are appointed and managed by the central government (see Table 10.3). The nomenklatura system 'consists of lists of leading positions, over which party units exercise the power to make appointments and dismissals; lists of reserves or candidates for these positions; and institutions and processes for making the appropriate personnel changes' (Burns, 1989: ix). The system established was based on the Soviet model. Changes occurred from time to time, but were not drastic.[3] In terms of central–local relations, a significant change was introduced into the system in 1984.

From the mid-1950s and until 1984, the nomenklatura system allowed the Central Committee appointments two ranks 'down' in the system, meaning that the central government had on its nomenklatura list the leaders not only of ministries and provinces, but also of ministerial bureaus

*Table 10.2    Rank equivalents among government organs, China*

| Centre | Province | County |
|---|---|---|
| State Council | | |
| Ministry (*Bu*) | Province (*Sheng*) | |
| General Bureau (*Ju* or *Si*) | Commission | |
| | Provincial department | |
| | (*Ting* or *Ju*) | |
| | Prefecture | |
| Division (*Chu*) | | County |
| Section (*Ke*) | | County department |

*Source:*    Lieberthal and Oksenberg (1988: 143).

*Table 10.3*   *Provincial officials managed by and reported to the Central Committee (1990)*

| Provincial leaders managed centrally | |
| --- | --- |
| *Position* | *Unit* |
| Secretaries, Deputy Secretaries, Standing Committee Members | Party committees of provinces, autonomous regions and centrally administered cities (Beijing, Tianjin and Shanghai) |
| Chairmen, Deputy Chairmen | Party advisory committees (small groups) of provinces, autonomous regions and centrally administered cities |
| Secretaries, Deputy Secretaries | Party discipline inspection commissions of provinces, autonomous regions and centrally administered cities |
| Governors, Deputy Governors | Provincial governments |
| Chairmen, Deputy Chairmen | Autonomous region governments |
| Mayors, Deputy Mayors | Centrally administered city governments |
| Chairmen, Deputy Chairmen | Standing committees of people's congresses of provinces, autonomous regions and centrally administered cities |
| Chairmen, Deputy Chairmen | Chinese People's Political Consultative Conferences of provinces, autonomous regions and centrally administered cities |
| Presidents | Higher-level people's courts of provinces, autonomous regions and centrally administered cities |
| Chief Procurators | People's procuratorates of provinces, autonomous regions and centrally administered cities |
| Provincial cadres reported to the Central Committee | |
| *Position* | *Unit* |
| Secretaries General, Deputy Secretaries General, Department Heads, Deputy Department Heads, Bureau (office) Heads, Deputy Bureau Heads | Party committees of provinces, autonomous regions and centrally administered cities |
| Presidents, Vice Presidents | Party schools of provinces, autonomous regions and centrally administered cities |

*Table 10.3* (continued)

| Provincial cadres reported to the Central Committee | |
|---|---|
| *Position* | *Unit* |
| Editors-in-Chief, Deputy Editors-in-Chief | Newspapers of provincial, autonomous region and centrally administered city party committees |
| Secretaries General, Deputy Secretaries General, Commission Heads, Commission Deputy Heads, Bureau (*ting, ju*) Heads, Bureau Deputy Heads | People's governments of provinces, autonomous regions and centrally administered cities |
| Vice Presidents | Higher People's Courts of provinces, autonomous regions and centrally administered cities |
| Deputy Chief Procurators | People's Procuratorates of provinces, autonomous regions and centrally administered cities |
| Chairmen, Deputy Chairmen | Provincial autonomous region and centrally administered city branches of the ACFTU |
| Secretaries, Deputy Secretaries | Provincial, autonomous region and centrally administered city branches of the Youth League |
| Chairmen, Deputy Chairmen | Provincial, autonomous region and centrally administered city branches of the Women's Federation |
| Presidents (Managers), Vice Presidents (Deputy Managers) | Provincial, autonomous region and centrally administered city branches of the People's Bank of China, various specialized banks and the People's Insurance Corporation of China |
| Secretaries, Deputy Secretaries | Party core groups (committees) of the above banks and insurance company |
| Secretaries, Deputy Secretaries, Standing Committee Members | Party committees of cities under central planning (Shenyang, Dalian, Changchun, Harbin, Xi'an, Chengdu, Chongqing, Qingdao, Nanjing, Ningbo, Xiamen, Wuhan, Guangzhou, Shenzhen) |
| Mayors, Deputy Mayors | People's governments of cities under central planning (see above list) |

*Table 10.3* (continued)

| Provincial cadres reported to the Central Committee | |
| --- | --- |
| Position | Unit |
| Secretaries, Deputy Secretaries | Party committees of prefectures (*di*), cities, districts (*zhou*) and banners |
| Commissioners (*zhuan yuan*), Deputy Commissioners | People's governments of prefectures |
| Mayors, Deputy Mayors | People's governments of cities |
| Heads, Deputy Heads | People's governments of districts |
| Heads, Deputy Heads | People's governments of banners |
| Secretaries, Deputy Secretaries | Party committees of districts directly administered by Beijing, Tianjin and Shanghai |
| Heads, Deputy Heads | People's governments of districts directly administered by Beijing, Tianjin and Shanghai |

*Sources:*   The DOO (1990). The table is adopted from Burns (1994: 479–80, 484–5).

and provincial departments. In 1984, the two-rank down system was changed to a one-rank down system, meaning that the Central Committee only managed directly leaders at the ministerial and provincial level. This change greatly reduced the number of cadres directly managed by the Central Committee. It is important to point out that, by decentralizing nomenklatura authority, the Central Committee aimed to strengthen its power and management efficiency over provincial leaders. The huge numbers of cadres under the two-rank down system had too often resulted in pro forma consideration and de facto approvals of whomever the lower territorial unit nominated (Lieberthal, 1995: 211). The system was thus rather inefficient. By contrast, the one-rank down system enables 'the central authorities to exercise their nomenklatura powers in a more serious fashion' (ibid.).

Scholars have used the nomenklatura system to explain central–local relations, especially why radical decentralization did not lead to the collapse of an already fragmented relationship between the centre and the provinces. Nevertheless, the change from the two-rank down to one-rank down system showed the limitations of the nomenklatura system in explaining the interaction between the centre and the provinces. The change was significant for central–local relations. One point needs to be emphasized specifically; that is, to manage top provincial leaders is not to manage provincial affairs. As emphasized earlier, central–local relations mean not only relations between the central government and provincial governments, but also relations between provincial governments and their territories. Using the nomenklatura system enables us to see only the one level of relations, namely, the central government and provincial governments; nonetheless, it underestimates the second level of relations, that is, the provincial governments and their territories. To explore how China's provinces are governed requires examining this second level of relations. It is in this sense that this study does not regard the provincial government as an agent of the central government, but a level of government within its de facto federal structure.

The change from the two-rank down to one-rank down system has complicated the second level of relations. First of all, the change means that only the very highest officials at each territorial level, that is, the provincial party secretaries and deputy secretaries, the governors and vice-governors, would be appointed and managed by the Central Committee. The new system enabled provincial leaders to gain almost complete control over appointments and dismissals of officials within their territorial jurisdiction. The 1984 change created the possibility that provinces would increasingly become in-grown, since appointments to all but the top-level positions were controlled from within. According to Lieberthal (1995: 211), there was a general increase in the percentage of provincial appointments below the top level in which the appointee's previous position was in that same province. An early study of China's mayors also showed this trend (Li and Bachman, 1989). According to the study, differing from the mayoral recruitment pattern of Mao's time, 70 per cent of Chinese mayors were natives or were born in a neighbouring province in the late 1980s (ibid.: 86).

Second, while the nomenklatura authority over posts previously controlled by the Central Committee was decentralized to provincial party committees, the latter, in turn, decentralized their control over the nomenklatura to prefectural, city and country party committees. Although the new system reduced greatly the number of centrally managed cadres, it did not reduce the total size of the nomenklatura. Rather it changed the distribution of authority over the same number of posts to lower-level party committees. Therefore, while economic decentralization shifted economic power from the centre to the provinces, the new nomenklatura system changed the structural distribution of political power between the two. This shift in turn reinforced the role of provincial governments in governing provincial affairs, be it economic, political or social. In this sense, Lieberthal argued that 'the decentralization of personnel decisions under the reforms has increased the chances of local despotism'

(1995: 212). Put in another way, though the central government still controls top provincial leaders tightly, within the boundary of a given province, the provincial government behaves like an independent actor with total autonomy.

Indeed, by changing the two-rank down system to a one-rank down system, the central government aimed not only at strengthening its control over provincial officials, but also, more importantly, it wanted low level governments to function as a government. According to Burns, who has written the most thorough analyses of China's nomenklatura system,

> By granting more autonomy to local party authorities on personnel matters, the reforms sought to 'spur their initiative' to appoint high-quality local officials and to supervise them efficiently. If local officials had the authority to make more personnel appointments, they would . . . be in a better position to complete their responsibilities. Finally, decentralization of cadre management was necessary to implement new economic reforms, which, among other things, emphasized increased autonomy for enterprises and other local units. (1989: xix)

This major change points to a methodological deficit in using the nomenklatura system to explain central–local relations. To control provincial leaders and to manage provincial affairs are two different matters. Take the transfer system as an example. With the implementation of this system, provincial leaders are frequently transferred from one province to another. Frequent turnover of provincial personnel does not allow consistent provincial policies (that is, policies by provincial leaders). But in reality, provincial policies have been consistent, and provincial affairs have been managed in quite similar ways. This means that the nomenklatura system as a variable is incapable of providing a satisfactory explanation of central–local relations. Therefore we need to go beyond the nomenklatura system to search for a more effective explanation of the way central–local relations have actually worked.

**Bargaining**

Coercion explains why radical economic decentralization did not lead to a collapse of central–local relations. Since the central government has controlled tightly the appointments of provincial leaders, it is hard for the latter to develop independent forces to threaten the centre. The role of coercion in regulating central–local relations depends solely on the position of the central government in China's political hierarchy. As shown in Table 10.1, the aim of coercion is to achieve forced provincial compliance. Therefore coercion hardly explains how provincial leaders make use of local resources to interact with the centre, and how the provinces are actually governed by provincial leaders. The provincial government is not just an agent of the centre, acting on behalf of and subordinating to the latter. It is a government with its own resources and interests. To see how the centre and the provinces have interacted, it is important to explore other variables. In other words, coercion only tells us one side (the centre) of the story of central–local relations; other variables are needed to tell the two sides of the story.

Scholars such as Lieberthal, Oksenberg and Lampton, among others, have developed a new concept, bargaining, to explore how the centre and the provinces have interplayed. The main characteristics are summarized in Table 10.1. The aim of bargaining is to resolve conflicts between the centre and the provinces. The process of bargaining is rather different from co-ercion. Coercion is justified by the necessity of centralization and central control. Provincial leaders do not have any other choice but to be subordi-nated to the centre since the central government can force them to do so through its nomenklatura system. In the process of bargaining, both central and provincial officials are self-interested actors, and the interaction between the two actors is mutually advantageous. Differing from coercion, bargaining refers to a situation in which both the centre and the provinces recognize that negotiations between them can resolve their conflicts while promoting their mutual interests. In this sense, Lampton (1992: 37) argued that bargaining occurs because both central and provincial leaders believe that 'the gains to be made by mutual accommodation exceed those to be made by unilateral action or by forgoing agreement altogether'.

According to Dahl and Lindblom (1976), bargaining commonly means reciprocity among representatives of hierarchies, and it is a form of recip-rocal control among leaders; bargaining occurs because they disagree and expect that further agreement is possible and will be profitable. I should emphasize two main factors in Dahl and Lindblom's definition of bar-gaining. First, bargaining is a form of reciprocal control; second, it aims to resolve conflicts among actors and promote mutual interests.

Bargaining has increasingly become the main dominant form of auth-ority relationship in Chinese politics. In the writings of scholars of the pro-cedural approach, this is so because of structural, procedural and cultural factors:

- Structurally, China's bureaucratic ranking system combines with the functional division of authority among various bureaucracies to produce a situation in which it is often necessary to achieve agree-ment among an array of bodies, where no single body has authority over the others. Moreover, intergovernmental economic decentral-ization has enabled locales and bureaucratic units to accumulate resources to bargain with the central government (Lieberthal, 1992: 8).

● Procedurally, the reform has changed the way of policy formation and implementation, and thus encouraged bargaining to emerge. The leaders reduced the use of coercion against those proposed ideas that are eventually rejected, thus emboldening participants to argue forcefully for their proposals. The stress laid on serious feasibility studies encouraged various units to marshal information to support their own project preferences. The general decline in the use of ideology as an instrument of control increased the 'looseness' of the system, and decentralization in personnel management permitted many bureaucratic units to have their own initiatives (ibid.: 9).

● Culturally, an enduring aspect of the Chinese political milieu is that there has existed a deeply shared value, that is, fairness, among both superiors and subordinates, fairness that requires consultation and just compensation through bargaining among actors (Lampton, 1992: 39).

All these changes made the Chinese bureaucratic system more fragmented and thus increased bargaining among bureaucratic units. As Lieberthal pointed out, 'Fragmentation of authority encouraged a search for consensus among various organs in order to initiate and develop major projects. This consensus, in turn, required extensive and often elaborate deals to be struck through various types of bargaining stratagems' (1992: 9).

Since bargaining as an analytical tool focuses on how actors actually interact, it enables us to see how the central–local relationship functions in the reform era. Bargaining as a paradigm has been widely used to study China's policy-making processes and generated many scholarly works (for example, Lampton, 1987; Lieberthal and Oksenberg, 1988; Lieberthal and Lampton, 1992). Nevertheless, the limitations of this paradigm in explaining central–local relations are also obvious.[4]

First, though scholars have pointed out how structural, procedural and cultural factors have affected bargaining in China, their analytical framework is not well integrated, especially because cultural factors are not an internal part of the paradigm. Overall, bargaining is still structurally determined. Lieberthal argued that 'the structures that link the top and the bottom of the system . . . require negotiations, bargaining, exchange, and consensus building' (1992: 12). This inevitably leaves out cultural factors, which disables the paradigm to see how cultural factors affect central–local relations. Indeed, cultural factors affect and adjust central–local relations in many areas.

Second, and related, since weight is given to structural factors, the focus of bargaining is still on the relations between the central government and provincial governments. Like coercion, bargaining is still not capable of explaining how a given province is governed. Without an examination of how provincial officials govern their territories, it will be difficult to explore the nature of China's central–local relations.

Third, not everything is negotiable in China's central–local relations. There are fields such as national defence and foreign policy that provincial governments will not step in. In using bargaining as an analytical tool, scholars have first to identify 'bargaining areas'. In choosing these, scholars have to focus on the areas in which the centre and the provinces interact. So far, studies on bargaining have all focused on some major policy issues that both the centre and the provinces are involved in. In such policy areas, without negotiations, neither the centre nor the provinces can make or implement a policy. However, the central–local relationship is more than policy making. The centre governs the provinces through making policies, but policies cannot cover all aspects of central–local relations. How the centre and the provinces interact in policy making is not the same as how a given province is governed.

Fourth, and more important, there are also areas that the provinces do not negotiate with the centre. This is so not because the provinces are not eligible to negotiate with the centre as in the cases of national defence and foreign policy making, but because they do not need to. That means that the provincial governments can govern their territories without central intervention. There are 'tacit agreements' (*moqi*) between the centre and the provinces. Provincial officials can exercise their power at will, but will not deviate greatly from what the centre has expected. On the part of the central government, it does not use coercion against the provinces and does not negotiate with the provinces, but it is still capable of soliciting compliance for provincial officials. So the questions become: 'What is a "tacit agreement"? And how does it work to regulate central–local relations?' To answer these questions, are turn to a third institution, 'reciprocity'.

## Reciprocity

A third institution, reciprocity, is needed to explain central–local relations, a paradigm that will incorporate cultural factors into its analytical framework. Central to reciprocal behaviour is obligation. It was formed in a long process of the interaction among actors. It is a process of invisible or tacit interaction among actors, a process regulated not by coercion as in the process of coercion, or explicit negotiations as in the process of bargaining, but by an appropriate standard of behaviour according to which actors adjust their respective behaviour towards each other voluntarily. The questions are: 'How does an institution of reciprocity produce voluntary cooperation between the centre and the provinces, and how does it regulate central–local relations?'

Scholars have searched for ways in which cooperation among egoistic social members can be achieved without coercive intervention from government authorities, how cooperation between governments and people can be achieved without appealing to external forces, and how international co-operation among sovereign states can be achieved without any supra-sovereign authority. Many have found that reciprocity has played a crucial role in facilitating cooperation among egoists. In domestic politics, Robert Axelrod (1984) has advised people and governments to practise and teach reciprocity in order to foster cooperation. Similarly, in international relations, Robert Keohane (1984: 214) strongly argued that reciprocity 'seems to be the most effective strategy for maintaining cooperation among egoists'.

Though reciprocity has been used as an analytical tool in sociology, anthropology and international politics and law for years, its meanings are still vague and scholars often define it in specific contexts. It still remains an ambiguous term. Individual scholars often define terms in accordance with their theoretical purposes.

Reciprocity is used in this study in a sociological sense (for example, Gouldner, 1960; Blau, 1964; Sahlins, 1972). Applying this approach to central–local relations, I argue that reciprocal obligations hold the centre and the provinces together since reciprocity helps the two self-interested actors (the centre and the provinces) to cooperate. Reciprocity can function this way because it is a series of sequential actions which may continue indefinitely, never balancing but continuing to entail mutual concessions within the context of shared commitments and values.

In his classic study of social exchange, Peter Blau (1964) distinguished two types of exchange, economic exchange and social exchange. Social exchange involves somewhat indefinite sequential exchanges within the context of a general pattern of obligation while, in economic exchange, the benefits to be exchanged are precisely specified and no trust is required (Blau, 1964: 8, 93–7). Robert Keohane (1986) applied Blau's concepts to international politics and distinguished two types of reciprocity, specific reciprocity and diffuse reciprocity. According to Keohane, specific reciprocity refers to 'situations in which specified partners exchange items of equivalent value in a strictly delimited sequence'. In diffuse reciprocity, 'the definition of equivalence is less precise, one's partners may be viewed as a group rather than as particular actors, and the sequence of events is less narrowly bounded' (ibid.: 4).

From this distinction, bargaining can be regarded as specific reciprocity or an economic exchange. In the process of bargaining, both the centre and the provinces are motivated by self-interest. Bargaining occurs because both the centre and the provinces believe that it helps resolve conflicts between them and promote their mutual interests. Indeed, in constructing bargaining as an institution regulating Chinese politics, scholars have relied heavily on the rational choice literature and power politics literature (for example, Lieberthal and Oksenberg, 1988). The strength of bargaining in explaining central–local relations is specific policy areas where the centre and the provinces negotiate to increase their own interests. Bargaining is a form of reciprocity since both actors are involved in negotiating over something like 'the price of a house'. Nevertheless, it is game-like or economic bargaining, since here actors behaving 'in a reciprocal fashion respond to cooperation with cooperation and to defection with defection' (Keohane, 1986: 6). This form of game-like bargaining seems to be inefficient in explaining voluntary cooperation between the centre and the provinces. As mentioned earlier, there are areas in which the centre and the provinces do not negotiate with each other.

In this study, 'reciprocity' refers to what Keohane has called 'diffuse reciprocity' and distinguishes it from bargaining, which belongs to what Keohane called 'specific reciprocity'. While the emphasis of bargaining is on self-interest, the type of reciprocity that I emphasize in this study is less based on self-interest, and more on shared concepts of rights and obligations. This implies that the central–local relationship entails obligations of one actor toward another. In a sociological sense, reciprocity can be identified with mutual obligation (Moore, 1978: 506). According to Gouldner (1960: 169–71), there are norms that help impose obligations. For example, people should help those who have helped them, and people should not injure those who have helped them. With the presence of this form of norm, mutual obligation does not require that the actors involved have to be altruistic, since norms consist of standards of behaviour which are widely regarded as legitimate. In this sense, Keohane argued that diffuse reciprocity 'involves conforming to generally accepted standards of behavior' (1986: 4).

While the way reciprocity affects central–local relations will be discussed in the later chapters of case studies, some significant points can be derived from the above basic assumption of reciprocity. First, reciprocity is a conditional action. It usually refers to mutual dependence, mutual influence and mutual exchange of privileges. According to Blau, reciprocity implies 'actions that are contingent on rewarding reactions from others that cease when these expected reactions are not forthcoming' (1964: 6). In the context of central–local relations, reciprocity is also conditional, but whether cooperation can be achieved does not depend on any particular interaction between the centre and the provinces. Rather, it is based on a series of continued interaction between them. In other words, since the interaction between the centre and the provinces is a continuous process, both actors do not necessarily behave in accordance with the principle of 'ill for ill, and good for good', a principle that is prevalent in a condition of anarchy.

Second, since the centre and the provinces have to interact with each other continuously, they are not always motivated by self-interest to bargain with each other. If you become a loser in time *A*, you will not necessarily lose again in time *B*. You may give up something in time *A* in order to gain something in time *B*. You do so because you believe that your altruistic behaviour today will be rewarded in the future.

Furthermore, reciprocity is not equivalence of benefits. In practising reciprocal interaction, neither the centre nor the provinces has identical obligations. It will be misleading to regard the two actors as rationally self-interested. If the centre treats the provinces to a dinner today, it will not necessarily ask the provinces to treat it to a dinner too in the future. For example, in patron–client relationships, the centre and the provinces exchange mutually valued but non-comparable goods and services. But practitioners of obligation-based reciprocity know that they should discharge, in the interest of continuing to receive needed services, their obligations for having received them in the past. This implies that both the centre and the provinces can develop an appropriate standard of behaviour. The formation of such a standard helps voluntary cooperation between them and contributes to the stability of their mutual relations. The one side does to the other side just what is in accordance with the appropriate standard of behaviour. In other words, both sides know what they should do and in what ways.

Third, a further point can be made here. In the context of central–local relations, reciprocity involves not only standards of behaviour but moral codes that supersede self-interest. Reciprocity does not reject the self-interest assumption, but egoists can also undertake obligations. As Keohane pointed out (1984: 57), egoists can also conform to obligations. This is especially true for provincial officials. Under an anarchical condition, no authority exists to enforce moral obligations. But central–local relations are different: the centre and the provinces exist within the same political hierarchy and provincial officials will voluntarily behave in accordance with how they have previously been obligated to perform.

Fourth, and related, the centre and the provinces practise bargaining, but since the centre and the provinces live in the same institutional framework, bargaining, a form of specific reciprocity, tends to turn itself into diffuse reciprocity. Bargaining between the centre and the provinces is not a one-time game, but a series of sequential games. In other words, bargaining is a form of reciprocity. More importantly, it is sequential reciprocity, which promotes long-term cooperation between the centre and the provinces.

## CONCLUSION

I have so far tried to elaborate how different institutions regulate central–local relations in China. The three institutions have played their unique roles in different policy areas and in different historical periods. Since changes in China's central–local relations are mainly driven by local economic development, reciprocity has become an increasingly self-sufficient institution in regulating central–local economic relations. But this does not mean that the other two institutions are irrelevant. Just as coercion-based interactions between the centre and the provinces can generate unwanted consequences, so do reciprocity-based interactions. To solve the problems resulting from reciprocal interactions, coercion and bargaining come in. Moreover, the efficacy and effectiveness of reciprocity in the reform era is also due to the fact that it is affected by the other two institutions, coercion and bargaining. Over the long history of the interaction between the centre and the provinces, all these three institutions were intertwined to effect central–local relations. While coercion and bargaining contain elements of reciprocity, many elements of coercion and bargaining now present themselves in the form of reciprocity.[5]

One particular question which needs to be addressed is why the Chinese government does not want to formalize federalism given the fact that the system has actually functioned in a federal way. For one thing, a de facto structure seems to have functioned well in the reform era. Compared to de facto federalism, the advantages of federalism are obvious. The institutionalization of de facto federalism is favourable for political stability since it reduces the tension between the two actors. Nevertheless, the institutionalization of de facto federalism is also likely to make the system rigid. Given the fact that great diversities among the provinces exist, equal rights among them (implicit in federalism) are not likely. Rich provinces prefer a weak centre while poor provinces prefer a strong one. The recent call for recentralization by poor provinces is not without reason. Without doubt, top leaders fear that federalism will disintegrate a China with great diversities. Also the leadership's priority is to promote economic development rather than to divide power between the centre and the provinces and among the provinces. To do so, it has to adjust continuously its relationship with the provinces as well as mediate between provinces in accordance with changing circumstances. The legitimatization of federalism will render such continuous adjustment less likely. By contrast, de facto federalism has the advantage of flexibility. What the centre needs is creative ambiguity implicit in de facto federalism. In other words, the centre does not need, for the time being, a clear-cut division between the centre and the provinces, but ambiguity between them. As long as the centre maintains its relative power over the provinces, it will be able to adjust central–local relations.

Another major factor is ideology. Ideologically, federalism works counter to the ideology of the CCP. Federalism was linked to chaos during the early twentieth century of warlordism. To many, federalism will result in a divided China, or vice versa. Given the fact that federalism has been discussed in the context of Hong Kong, Taiwan, Tibet, Xinjiang and other territorial issues, the ideological legitimacy of federalism becomes more complicated. Although these territorial factors have pulled China toward federalism, the ideological barrier is not easy to overcome. Indeed, for many within the CCP, federalism is seen as an ideology that divides China. In the West, federalism is a strong ideological foundation for the federal political system, as liberalism supports democracy. As long as federalism cannot be legitimized ideologically, a transition from de facto to de jure federalism is unlikely to take place. While in the long run the establishment of de jure federalism requires great political initiatives or political changes, de facto federalism has actually laid down a sound foundation for such a future development.

## NOTES

*   Portions of this chapter appeared in Zheng Yongnian (2007), *De Facto Federalism in China: Reforms and Dynamics of Central–Local Relations*, Singapore and London: World Scientific Publishing, chs 2 and 8. I am grateful to World Scientific Publishing for permission to use that material here.
1.  For a discussion of the complicated relationship between the provincial government and the ministry, see Huang (1996: 28–32).
2.  For discussions of these two principles, see Lieberthal (1995: ch.6), Huang (1996: ch.4), and Shirk (1993).
3.  For the development of the nomenklatura system, see Burns (1989, 1994).
4.  Indeed, Lampton himself emphasized that 'bargaining is one of several forms of authority relationship in China', and there are other forms of authority relationship such as hierarchy and command, market relations, patron–client ties, pleading, and rent-seeking or corruption, etc (1992: 34). This is certainly true. But my reservations are not about the paradigm leaving out many other forms of authority relations, but over bargaining per se.
5.  For an empirical study of how different institutions govern the interaction between the centre and the provinces in the area of economic development, see Zheng (2007).

## REFERENCES

Axelrod, Robert (1984), *The Evolution of Cooperation*, New York: Basic Books.

Benson, J.K. (1977), 'Organizations: a dialectical view', *Administrative Science Quarterly*, **22**(1), 1–21.

Benz, Arthur (1987), 'Regionalization and decentralization', in Herman Bakvis and William M. Chandler (eds), *Federalism and the Role of the State*, Toronto: University of Toronto Press, pp. 127–46.

Blau, Peter (1964), *Exchange and Power in Social Life*, New York: Wiley.

Burns, John P. (ed.) (1989), *The Chinese Communist Party's Nomenklatura System*, Armonk, NY: M.E. Sharpe, Inc.

Burns, John P. (1984), 'Strengthening central CCP control of leadership selection: the 1990 nomenklatura', *The China Quarterly*, **138**, 458–91.

Dahl, Robert A. and Charles E. Lindblom (1976), *Politics, Economics, and Welfare*, 2nd edn, Chicago: University of Chicago Press.

Diao, Tianding et al. (1989), *Zhongguo difang guojia jigou gaiyao* (An Introduction to Local State Organizations in China), Beijing: Falu chubanshe.

DOO (The Department of Organization of the Central Committee of the CCP) (1990), 'Zhongyang zuzhibu guanyu xiuding "zhonggong zhongyang guanlide ganbu zhiwu mingchengbiao" de tong zhi' ('Notice of the CCP Organization Department on Revision of the "Job Title List for Cadres Managed Centrally by the Chinese Communist Party"'), 10 May 1991 (Zhongzufa (1990) No.2), in The Office of Policy and Regulation of the Personnel Ministry (ed.), *Renshi gongzuo wenjian xuanbian* (Selection of Personnel Work Documents), vol. 13, Beijing: Zhongguo renshi chubanshe, pp. 39–53.

Elazar, Daniel J. (1968), 'Federalism', *International Encyclopedia of the Social Sciences*, vol. 5, New York: Macmillan.

Elazar, Daniel J. (1987), *Exploring Federalism*, Tuscaloosa, AL: The University of Alabama Press.

Elkins, David J. and Richard E.B. Simeon (1979), 'A cause in search of its effect, or what does political culture explain?', *Comparative Politics*, **11**, 127–45.

Gouldner, Alvin W. (1960), 'The norm of reciprocity: a preliminary statement', *American Sociological Review*, **25** (April).

Huang, Yasheng (1996), *Inflation and Investment Controls in China: The Political Economy of Central–Local Relations during the Reform Era*, New York: Cambridge University Press.

Kenyon, Daphen A. and John Kincaid (eds) (1992), *Competition Among States and Local Governments: Efficiency and Equity in American Federalism*, Washington, DC: The Urban Institute Press.

Keohane, Robert O. (1984), *After Hegemony: Cooperation and Discord in the World Political Economy*, Princeton, NJ: Princeton University Press.

Keohane, Robert O. (1986), 'Reciprocity in international relations', *International Organization*, **40**(1) (Winter), 1–27.

Lampton, David M. (ed.) (1987), *Policy Implementation in Post-Mao China*, Berkeley, CA: University of California Press.

Lampton, David M. (1992), 'A plum for a peach: bargaining, interest, and bureaucratic politics in China', in Lieberthal and Lampton (eds), pp. 33–58.

Li, Cheng and David Bachman (1989), 'Localism, elitism, and immobilism: elite formation and social change in post-Mao China', *World Politics*, **XLII**(1) (October), 64–94.

Lieberthal, Kenneth G. (1992), 'Introduction: the "Fragmented authoritarianism" model and its limitations', in Lieberthal and Lamption (eds), pp. 1–30.

Lieberthal, Kenneth G. (1995), *Governing China: From Revolution Through Reform*, New York: W.W. Norton & Company.

Lieberthal, Kenneth G. and David M. Lampton (eds) (1992), *Bureaucracy, Politics, and Decision Making in Post-Mao China*, Berkeley, CA: University of California Press.

Lieberthal, Kenneth G. and Michel Oksenberg (1988), *Policy Making in China: Leaders, Structures, and Processes*, Princeton, NJ: Princeton University Press.

March, James G. and Johan P. Olsen (1989), *Rediscovering Institutions: The Organizational Basis of Politics*, New York: Free Press.

Moore, Barrington, Jr. (1978), *Injustice: The Social Bases of Obedience and Revolt*, White Plains, NY: M.E. Sharpe.

Nathan, Richard P. and Margarita M. Balmaceda (1990), 'Comparing federal systems of government', in B. Bennett (ed.), *Decentralization, Local Governments, and Markets: Towards a Post-Welfare Agenda*, New York: Clarendon Press, pp. 59–77.

Nelson, Daneil N. (ed.) (1980), *Local Politics in Communist Countries*, Lexington: The University Press of Kentucky.

Pu, Xingzu et al. (1995), *Zhonghua renmin gongheguo zhengzhi zhidu* (The Political System of the People's Republic of China), Hong Kong: Sanlian shudian.

Reagan, M.D. and J.G. Sanzone (1981), *The New Federalism*, New York: Oxford University Press.

Riker, William H. (1964), *Federalism: Origin, Operation, Significance*, Boston: Little, Brown & Company.

Sahlins, Marshall (1972), *Stone Age Economics*, Chicago: Aldine-Atherton.

Schulz, Ann (1979), *Local Politics and Nation-States*, Santa Barbara, CA: Clio Books.

Shirk, Susan L. (1993), *The Political Logic of Economic Reform in China*, Berkeley, CA: University of California Press.

Triska, Jan F. (1980), 'Introduction: local communist politics, an overview', in D.N. Nelson, pp. 1–18.

Wheare, K.C. (1964), *Federal Government*, 4th edn, New York: Oxford University Press.

Wu, Jiaxiang (2003), 'Quanqiuhua yu lianbanghua' ('Globalization and Federalization'), *Zhanlue yu guanli* (Strategy and Management), **3**, 95–100.

Wu, Jiaxiang (2004), *Lianbang hua: Zhonghua desan gongheguo zhilu* (Federalization: The Road to the Thrid Republic of China), Hong Kong: The Mirror Press.

Yan, Jiaqi (1992), *Lianbang Zhongguo gouxiang* (The Conception of a Federal China), Hong Kong: Minbao chubanshe.

Zeitz, Gerald (1980), 'Interorganizational dialectics', *Administrative Science Quarterly*, **25**(1), 72–88.

Zheng, Yongnian (1994), 'Fenquan zhanlue yu ban lianbangzhi de yanjin' ('The strategy of decentralization and the evolution of semi-federalism'), in Guoguang Wu (ed.), *Guojia, Shichang yu Shehui: Zhongguo gaige de kaocha yanjiu* (The State, Market and Society: An Investigation into China's Reform), Hong Kong: Oxford University, pp. 72–81.

Zheng, Yongnian (1995), *Institutional Change, Local Developmentalism, and Economic Growth: The Making of Semi-Federalism in Reform China* (Ph. D thesis, Department of Politics, Princeton University.

Zheng, Yongnian (2000), 'Institutionalizing de facto federalism in post-Deng China', in Hung-mao Tien and Yun-han Chu (eds), *China under Jiang Zemin*, Boulder, Colorado: Lynne Rienner Publishers, pp. 215–32.

Zheng, Yongnian (2006), 'Explaining the sources of *de facto* federalism in reform China: intergovernmental decentralization, globalization, and central–local relations', *Japanese Journal of Political Science*, **7**(2), 101–26.

Zheng, Yongnian (2007), *De Facto Federalism in China: Reforms and Dynamics of Central–Local Relations*, Singapore and London: World Scientific.

# 11. Toward federalism in China? The experience of the Hong Kong Special Administrative Region

**Peter T.Y. Cheung**

The People's Republic of China (hereafter the PRC) is a centralized state governed by an authoritarian Communist Party. With the launching of reform and the open door policy by Deng Xiaoping in 1979, however, the country has witnessed unprecedented decentralization of economic policy and extensive local discretion in managing social and economic development. Some scholars have already considered China as a 'quasi-federalist' or a 'behaviourally federalist' system. The incorporation of Hong Kong into the Chinese state under the framework of 'One Country, Two Systems' (hereafter OCTS) further complicates the picture. Although the interpretation of Hong Kong's mini-constitution rests in the hands of Beijing, Hong Kong enjoys a higher degree of autonomy than most local authorities in federalist systems. Some scholars have already argued that a federalist formula is perhaps one of the most feasible platforms for China's unification with Taiwan. Nonetheless, few have examined what the Hong Kong experience means for China and whether it has further strengthened the federalist tendencies in the Chinese political system.

This chapter examines Hong Kong's experience in implementing the OCTS model by reflecting from the perspective of federalism. The chapter is organized into six sections. After this introductory section, section two briefly discusses the literature of federalism. Section three traces the historical context of Hong Kong's transition from a British colony to a special administrative region. Section four introduces the constitutional framework of OCTS and discusses how Hong Kong fares from the federalist perspective. Section five analyses three episodes when the central authorities asserted their authority in handling relations with Hong Kong after 1997. Finally, the chapter concludes the discussion by exploring the prospects of a federalist future for China and Hong Kong's impact on the process.

# FEDERALISM: AN OVERVIEW

Federalism and federalist arrangements can be considered as a practical way of accommodating interests and resolving conflicts in the globalized world. Proponents of federalism believe that it offers an alternative to the modern conception of sovereignty as no state can really dictate all its own affairs. The literature on contemporary federalism is varied and extensive, but seminal works by scholars such as William Riker, Daniel J. Elazar and Ronald Watts are useful in delineating the general features of federalism and federal political systems. For Riker, 'federalism is a political organization in which the activities of government are divided between regional governments and a central government in such a way that each kind of government has some activities on which it makes final decisions' (Riker, 1975, p. 101). The case of the Hong Kong Special Administration Region (hereafter the HKSAR) clearly satisfies his requirement for a federalist arrangement: namely both the central and local governments can act on the people and each has final say over certain sectors.

Other scholars, however, have also suggested various other important conditions for a federal political system. According to Elazar, federal principles are about 'the combination of self-rule and shared rule'. The essence of a federal arrangement is 'one of partnership, established and regulated by a covenant', and such relationships should be 'based on a mutual recognition of the integrity of each partner and the attempt to foster a special unity among them' (Elazar, 1987, p. 5). 'Federal political system,' as an empirical concept, encompasses a wide array of political systems with two or more levels of government which practises shared-rule through common governmental institutions as well as regional self-rule through local or regional governmental units. This broad category includes 'unions, constitutionally decentralized unions, federations, confederations, federacies, associated states, condominiums, leagues, and joint functional authorities' (Watts, 1999, p. 7).

Ronald Watts has generalized six common structural features of federations: (1) at least two levels of government each directly acting on their citizens; (2) formal constitutional distribution of legislative and executive powers and allocation of revenue between different levels of governments to guarantee the autonomy of each respective level; (3) representation of local or regional views in federal policy-making bodies, such as the second chamber of the federal legislature; (4) the provision of a supreme constitution whose amendment could not be done unilaterally because of the requirement of the consent of its constituent bodies (for example through the approval of the regional legislatures); (5) a mechanism to resolve constitutional disputes among the different levels of government, usually in the form of constitutional courts or the provision for referendum; and (6) the existence of intergovernmental processes and institutions in the discharging of shared and overlapping responsibilities (Watts, 1999, p. 7).

Nonetheless, the distribution of power within the units of a federal political system need not be symmetrical. Two forms of asymmetry can be identified. First, the variations in population and economic resources among constituent units will often bring about political asymmetry, which refers to the 'asymmetry in the relative political power and influence' of the constituent units (Watts, 1998, p. 123). Second, constitutional asymmetry refers to 'differences in the status or legislative and executive powers assigned by the constitution to the different regional units' (Watts, 1999, p. 66). Such asymmetry can also be found in the relationship between a smaller state and a larger state (for example a former colonial power) whereby the smaller unit gets the benefits of a union with the larger unit while maintaining autonomy and self-government. This asymmetrical form of federalism is also similar to that of associated states or federacies. According to Watts, federacies refer to 'political arrangements where a large unit is linked to a smaller unit or units, but the smaller unit retains considerable autonomy and has a minimum role in the government of the larger one, and where the relationship can be dissolved only by mutual agreement' (Watts, 1999, p. 8). Hong Kong, however, is constitutionally considered as an 'inalienable part' of China, so it cannot neatly fit the concept of an associate state or federacy.

The OCTS arrangement for Hong Kong is therefore best understood as a unique political compromise. Beijing was willing to offer highly privileged treatment for Hong Kong in order to resolve a difficult historical problem complicated by the huge social and economic gaps and the contrasting political, economic and legal systems and ideologies between Hong Kong and the Mainland. Despite the huge gaps between the two places, Hong Kong has been granted extensive autonomy in different areas, albeit under a restrictive framework that guards the key powers of the central authorities, such as in appointing the top officials of the executive branch and in interpreting the Basic Law.

## THE HISTORICAL CONTEXT OF HONG KONG'S POLITICAL TRANSITION

This section briefly examines the historical context of Hong Kong's transition from a British colony to a special administrative region. Although Hong Kong was a British colony, it enjoyed a great deal of political and economic autonomy in the post-Second World War period. Leo Goostadt, a former policy advisor to the British colonial administration, has offered perhaps the most trenchant analysis of this 'informal devolution' (Goodstadt, 2004, pp. 49–70). When the British Empire began to shrink after 1945 and its ability to tightly control colonial affairs started declining, colonial officials in Hong Kong had devised measures to defend local interests and interests of the business sector in Hong Kong from intervention by London. For instance, in the 1970s, Hong Kong had gained the prerogative to 'fix its own exchange rate, operate its own currency, and manage its own reserve' (ibid., p. 49). Hong Kong's post-1945 economic success demonstrates, among other things, not only the success of market-oriented policy and the industry of its businessmen and people at that particular historical juncture, but also the importance of local autonomy enjoyed by the territory. Despite the stalling of genuine democratic political reform by the colonial administration in Hong Kong, the colony had also enjoyed various types of freedoms and the rule of law, which were indispensable to its social vibrancy and economic prosperity.

The OCTS model was first promulgated by the Chinese leadership as a solution for reunification with Taiwan, but it was adopted to address the Hong Kong issue. In order to entice Taiwan to a future reunion with the Mainland and to avoid jeopardizing the economic dynamism of Hong Kong, which serves Chinese national interests, Beijing had imposed limits on its sovereignty in working out the future blueprint for the territory (Smith, 2001). The Sino-British negotiation over Hong Kong's future was hardly a smooth process, although an agreement was ironed out in 1984. The colony had experienced many more challenges during the run up to 1997. In particular, during the political crisis in China in spring 1989, many people in Hong Kong had staunchly supported the pro-democracy student movement. While the subsequent crackdown in Tiananmen Square shook the confidence of the Hong Kong people in China's promise on OCTS, Beijing also realized that the territory could potentially become a major threat to the Mainland political system, as witnessed by the massive sympathy of the Hong Kong people toward the pro-democracy demonstrators. The political reform proposal initiated by the last Governor, Chris Patten, in 1992, which was seen by critics as something too late and too piecemeal to secure a democratic foundation for Hong Kong, further aroused harsh reactions from Beijing. Among other things, Beijing's insistence on a national security clause (Article 23) in the Basic Law and its reluctance to yield to British demands over the Court of Final Appeal proposals in the 1990s reflects the importance that Beijing assigns to its conventional view on sovereignty.

# THE MODEL OF 'ONE COUNTRY, TWO SYSTEMS': THE CONSTITUTIONAL FRAMEWORK AND ITS PRACTICE SINCE 1997

The OCTS framework practised in the HKSAR offers an interesting context for examining the relevance of federalism for a unitary system like the PRC.[1] Strictly speaking, the OCTS model does not follow the federalist model, because the HKSAR, while being a part of the PRC, adopts a political and legal system radically different from that of the Mainland. The Basic Law – the mini-constitution for Hong Kong – not only provides for a high degree of autonomy not available to other constituent provinces of the PRC, but also sets out the parameters of the relations with the central authorities and guards such a different political community against interventions from other units of the PRC. Hence this highlights the limitation and applicability of the OCTS model because the formula was promulgated in order to help the Mainland recover territories not yet under Chinese sovereign control such as Taiwan, Hong Kong (before 1997) and Macau (before 1999). At least in the case of Hong Kong and Macau, there is a clear duration to which the special treatment applies – only 50 years, which also shows the transient nature of the model. Autonomy is actually secondary in the OCTS framework, which focuses on the preservation of the economic order. This has been indicated by Beijing's rejection of its application to Tibet, as they claimed that the OCTS model applies only to those areas that had a different economic system (Ghai, 1998, pp. 20–22). Further, none of these provisions have immediate impacts on the unitary system of the PRC.

As Yash Ghai has aptly pointed out, the OCTS model reflects the 'remarkable sharing' of power and 'diffusing of the internal sovereignty' from the central authorities to Hong Kong (Ghai, 2005, p. 31). While sovereignty lies in the hands of the central authorities, the local government could enjoy extensive powers in economic, financial and social affairs, including certain areas of international affairs. The central authorities have granted Hong Kong four major areas of autonomy: (1) a distinct 'semi-citizenship', (2) political symbols (separate currency, flag, stamps), (3) extensive law-making power in specific issue areas (that is, most policy-making areas apart from national defence and diplomacy), and (4) the supremacy of the local constitution in the examination of the constitutional status and arrangements of the HKSAR. Nonetheless, there are also important differences between Hong Kong and other autonomy areas (Ghai, 1998, pp. 21–2). For instance, the values of Hong Kong and Mainland China are different. While no one would doubt that China is becoming more and more capitalist and entangled in the capitalist world economy, its social and political ideologies, values and institutions are still very different from those of Hong Kong.

The central government has retained a number of key levers to ensure its exercise of both de jure and de facto sovereign control. First, Article One of the Basic Law dispels any possibility of secession or independence as the HKSAR is an 'inalienable part' of the PRC. Second, Article Two of the Basic Law already indicates that the special autonomy is authorized by the National People's Congress (hereafter the NPC) – China's legislature. The Chinese Constitution which enshrines a unitary political system has adopted Article 31 to provide a constitutional foundation for the creation of Special Administrative Regions (hereafter the SARs).[2] Should China decide to change the provision for the SARs, it can do so at its own will, without having to secure the consent of the HKSAR. Moreover, Article 31 does not specifically guarantee the provision of any form of autonomy, be they substantive or institutional (Ghai, 2005, p. 32). The NPC has the constitutional power to decide on the specific systems to be implemented in the SAR. The HKSAR government has no power to stop or alter the decisions of the central authorities, should it amend, or even repeal, such a provision in the national constitution.

Second, the Basic Law does not prevent the unitary system of the PRC from extending its reach to the highly autonomous HKSAR, if it so wishes. Two powers are particularly noteworthy. The central government maintains effective control over the executive of the HKSAR government because it has the constitutional power to appoint the Chief Executive (hereafter the CE) and the principal officials. The Basic Law also provides for a weak legislature, which basically means that executive power is not as effectively checked as in other democratic political systems. Theoretically speaking, the central government could deliver its preferred policy orientation through its agent in the HKSAR – the CE and his team – although this would have to be done discreetly and covertly. Otherwise, the perception of the erosion of Hong Kong's autonomy could have disastrous consequences. Another key power is the undisputed authority of the Standing Committee of the NPC (hereafter the SCNPC) to interpret the Basic Law. In the post-1997 era, these key features of the unitary state enshrined in the Basic Law have proved to be critical in shaping the relations between Hong Kong and the Mainland.

Third, Hong Kong's high degree of autonomy and its enjoyment of executive, legislative and independent judicial powers are only confined to those provisions set out in the Basic Law. Other autonomous systems can exercise their powers once they are given, often only subject to general principles such as a bill of rights. Whereas the HKSAR has more powers than other autonomous regions or a federal unit, the exercise of these powers are more circumscribed as they would be subject to scrutiny or monitoring. Hence Ghai has concluded that the OCTS is more about the preservation of the existing Hong Kong's pre-1997 systems rather than the protection of autonomy for its own sake (Ghai, 1998, pp. 21–2).

Fourth, the issue of residual powers is not clearly dealt with in the Basic Law (Duchacek, 1986, pp. 118, 141–2). Mainland legal scholars affiliated with the central authorities claimed that the residual powers not stipulated in the Basic Law belong to the central authorities, as this is a common practice in unitary states. The transfer of the residual powers to the local government is a federalist feature, but China is a unitary, not a federalist, state (Wu, 1988). They also maintained that the powers granted to the HKSAR were already broad enough.

Fifth, the central authorities retain the exclusive control over national security and diplomatic affairs. The People's Liberation Army (hereafter the PLA) has established a garrison in the HKSAR as a reminder of Chinese sovereignty. Although the HKSAR police are responsible for its public security, the PLA would only be asked to help with the maintenance of public order and disaster relief when the HKSAR government asks the central government for such assistance. The Office of the Commissioner of the Ministry of Foreign Affairs is stationed in Hong Kong to take care of issues relating to foreign affairs.

Last but not least, in the area of national security, there is a constitutional obligation for the HKSAR government to legislate on national security to prohibit such acts as 'treason, secession, sedition, subversion' against the central government and the 'theft of state secrets' and the establishment of ties between political groups in Hong Kong and other foreign political organizations and their conduct of political activities in Hong Kong. Legislation over this controversial article, which was added to the Basic Law in the aftermath of the 1989 political crisis in China, proves to be a bone of contention in the relations between Hong Kong and Beijing.

The Basic Law, however, is an unusual and pragmatic instrument for a unitary state like the PRC. One of the main features of the OCTS is the 'separation' of the HKSAR from the Mainland body politic. Many provisions in the Basic Law are means to ensure such separateness. For instance, Article 22 maintains that no offices or local authorities of the Mainland may interfere in the affairs of the HKSAR which it administers under the Basic Law. Mainland residents who want to enter the HKSAR must seek approval. Further, in order to ensure the high degree of autonomy, national laws, except those listed in Annex III of the Basic Law, would not be applied to the HKSAR. Nonetheless, the SCNPC can add to or delete from the list of laws to be applied to Hong Kong, after consulting the Committee for the Basic Law of the HKSAR (hereafter the Committee for the Basic Law).

In sum, the insurance underlying Hong Kong's high degree of autonomy is its 'separation' from China's socialist political system. Through the

OCTS framework, Hong Kong is endowed with different economic, social, political and legal systems within the sovereign body of a unitary Chinese state. Hence tensions and contradictions are likely to emerge in defining the boundaries of Hong Kong's high degree of autonomy.

## HONG KONG UNDER 'ONE COUNTRY, TWO SYSTEMS': AN EXPLORATION FROM A FEDERALIST PERSPECTIVE

The OCTS model has not made the PRC a federal state, because it is after all a constitutionally unitary state. Among the most important features of federalist principles is that each level of government derives its authority from the constitution, rather than from the authority of another level of government (Watts, 1999, p. 7). As suggested by Elazar, a federation is a 'polity compounded of strong constituent entities and a strong general government, each possessing powers delegated to it by the people and empowered to deal directly with the citizenry in the exercise of those powers' (Elazar, 1987, p. 7; Watts, 1998, pp. 117–37). Further, what is even more fundamental to federalism is the embodiment of democracy, without which federalist principles will make little sense.

Nonetheless, the constitutional framework set out in the Basic Law exhibited certain federalist characteristics. For instance, there is a clearer delineation of power between the central authorities and the HKSAR (chapter two of the Basic Law). Like other federalist systems, the central government would be responsible mainly for foreign affairs and defence. The OCTS framework in fact grants the HKSAR a much wider range of powers beyond those enjoyed by local governments in a federation. Local authorities in a federation usually do not enjoy, among other things, the powers for final adjudication, a separate monetary system and currency, and a separate customs and immigration mechanism. Nor are they immune to taxation and regulation by the central authority. Unlike other units of a federal country, Hong Kong enjoys extensive powers in external economic relations, and such international links have actually increased since its reunion with the PRC.

The design of the OCTS model is fundamentally different from other federalist models. First, the PRC is a unitary system, and the autonomy enjoyed by the HKSAR under OCTS is the result of the authorization or delegation by the central government. Strictly speaking, the central government could unilaterally change such a framework. Such a scenario may happen if the central government thinks that preserving Hong Kong's special status no longer serves its core interests or that the OCTS has already served its historic purpose of national unification.

Second, the PRC is not a democracy and is unlikely to become one in the near future. The autonomy granted to Hong Kong is not a recognition of the need to respect the special demands of a minority grouping. Nonetheless, as aptly pointed out by Ghai, the key purposes of the OCTS model are on 'the separation and preservation of the two economic, social, political and legal systems through the legal entrenchment of Hong Kong's systems', rather than the preservation of Hong Kong's autonomy per se (Ghai, 1998, p. 32). The primary goal of the OCTS framework is to ensure the continuation of Hong Kong's prosperity and stability following its reunion with China in 1997, which is in the interest of the central government in promoting national unification and economic development, rather than to answer the calls for democracy or autonomy from the populace of Hong Kong. In fact, the democratic prospects for Hong Kong remain precarious when Beijing rules out the possibility of introducing universal suffrage for the executive and the legislature in 2007 and 2008.

Third, the OCTS model allows the HKSAR the power for final adjudication by the local courts, which is unlikely in other federal systems (Duchacek, 1986, pp. 118, 150–51). Although there are two systems of courts in some federal systems, they belong to the same legal system. Nonetheless, an organ of the central authorities, namely the SCNPC, rather than an independent judicial body, enjoys the power in interpreting the Basic Law. If the courts of the HKSAR need to interpret the Basic Law in adjudicating cases involving affairs concerning the central government, or concerning the relations between the HKSAR and the central government, and if such interpretation will affect their final judgements, they shall seek an interpretation from the SCNPC through the Court of Final Appeal (hereafter the CFA), before making their final judgements which are not appealable. The SCNPC only needs to consult its Committee for the Basic Law of the HKSAR before giving such an interpretation.[3] The Mainland relies on the principle of legislative intent in its interpretation and hence many legal experts in Hong Kong would regard this as amounting to an authorization to make new laws.

Fourth, the HKSAR government has limited authority over the amendments of the Basic Law. Aside from the SCNPC, the executive arm of the central government – that is, the State Council – has the power to initiate an amendment. Although the HKSAR could also introduce an amendment, it would require a two-thirds majority from its NPC delegates and the Hong Kong legislators as well as the consent of the CE of the HKSAR. A certain safeguard against the intervention from the central authorities is somehow guaranteed, however, as the Basic Law explicitly states that amendments to the Basic Law shall not contravene the basic policies of the central authorities towards Hong Kong. Further, the SCNPC has no power to amend the laws passed by the HKSAR legislature. But if the SCNPC considers that any law enacted by Hong Kong's legislature is not consistent with the Basic Law regarding matters within the responsibility of the central government or regarding the relations between the central government and the HKSAR, it can return the law, which shall immediately be annulled (Article 17 of the Basic Law).

Fifth, one basic feature of federation is that there are 'two orders of government, each acting directly on their citizens' (Watts, 1999, p. 7). In the Hong Kong case, only the HKSAR government has direct jurisdictions over the local citizens. Unlike other federations, the OCTS framework allows two different legal systems to operate in a single entity (Article 19 of the Basic Law). Indeed, the Chinese constitution does not have direct bearing over the HKSAR because it is the local constitution and the local laws that constitute the law of the land.

Sixth, although chapter two of the Basic Law has set out the division of powers between the central government and the HKSAR, there is still room for interpretations regarding what falls under this category and other grey areas of the Basic Law. Nonetheless, the central authorities have rejected calls for the clarification of such issues, hence allowing it to enjoy much greater flexibility in interpreting the Basic Law, if controversies arise in future (Ghai, 1998). Duchacek pointed out that a loophole in the division of power concerns the emergency provisions which may enlarge the power of the central authorities (Duchacek, 1986, pp. 127–8). According to Article 18 of the Basic Law, the central authorities can declare a state of emergency and apply relevant national laws to Hong Kong in case of war, or 'by reason of turmoil within the Hong Kong Special Administrative Region which endangers national unity or security and is beyond the control of the government of the emergency'.

Seventh, unlike the case in a federal system, there is no provision for territorial representation in a second chamber in China's legislature. Formally, Hong Kong and Macau are each allocated 36 seats in the NPC and hence enjoy considerable representation disproportionate to their population. But these deputies are often seen as agents of the central government, rather than staunch advocates of Hong Kong's interest in the Mainland political system. The central government alone decides on the method of selection of the Hong Kong deputies for both the NPC and the Chinese People's Political Consultative Conference (hereafter the CPPCC). There is some ambiguity concerning the exact role of the Hong Kong delegates in these two bodies. Since they are not directly elected, most Hong Kong people are unlikely to see them as representatives of Hong Kong.[4] These Hong Kong NPC deputies can be involved in the discussions of amendment of the national constitution and national legislation, but they cannot interfere in Hong Kong's local affairs. These deputies are also responsible for submitting amendment proposals of the Basic Law to the NPC for consideration and they are automatically included in the Election Committee choosing the

CE. Nonetheless, the importance of these delegates may increase in the future. The NPC and CPPCC delegates are becoming even more heavily represented in the governmental process in Hong Kong in the last few years, albeit not necessarily as a corporate body. Many prominent members of the political and governmental elites in Hong Kong are either NPC and CPPCC members, including some of the former and existing bureau secretaries, the President of the legislature, head of the Central Policy Unit and members of the top advisory body, the Executive Council. A growing number of NPC and CPPCC delegates have already been appointed to the advisory bodies of the HKSAR government (Cheung and Wong, 2004, pp. 885–8).

Eighth, unlike most other federal units, Hong Kong has a very special status and identity in the international arena, including participation in international organizations and the conclusion of international agreements. As argued aptly by James McCall Smith, the arrangements of the Basic Law included self-imposed and 'limited violations of China's international legal and Westphalian sovereignty' (Smith, 2001, p. 127). The HKSAR government enjoys full member status (separate from the membership of the PRC) in 24 intergovernmental organizations limited to states, 32 intergovernmental organizations not limited to states (including the World Trade Organization, World Customs Organization, World Meteorological Organization and the Bank of International Settlements), and 161 non-intergovernmental organizations.[5] The HKSAR has also ratified 228 multilateral treaties between sovereign states.[6] In fact, not only could the HKSAR government participate in these conferences independently, but it can also take a stand different from that of the Mainland (Xiao, 1993). Further, the central government has authorized the establishment of offices/regional office/sub-offices of international organizations restricted to sovereign states in Hong Kong, although these offices are usually located in the capital of a sovereign nation.[7] On the other hand, Hong Kong can enter into bilateral agreements with foreign nations, as 'Hong Kong, China, in the areas of economic affairs, trade, financial and monetary affairs, shipping, communications, tourism, culture and sports'.[8] Since the establishment of the HKSAR, seven types of bilateral agreements have been reached between Hong Kong and foreign countries.[9] These privileges provide ample evidence to show that Hong Kong has much greater powers in external arenas than the local authorities in a federal political system.

## HONG KONG'S PRECARIOUS AUTONOMY SINCE 1997

Despite the promise of a high degree of autonomy, the tensions between the high degree of autonomy promised in the OCTS model and the prerogatives of the unitary Chinese state are evident even after just eight years of implementation. The following analysis suggests that the framework underpinning Hong Kong's autonomy is far from fully consolidated. No better example in the contention between the central government and the HKSAR could be shown than the occasion when their constitutional relations were at stake.

Three interpretations of the Basic Law have so far been rendered by the SCNPC since 1997. Critics considered these interpretations 'entirely politically motivated', and suggest that the procedures of interpretations shall be 'judicialized' after public consultations (Ghai, 2005, p. 43). In the Mainland, judicial decisions were often influenced by the non-judicial agents of the central authorities, and legislative interpretations may supplement or even amend the original law. Some scholars argued that the CFA in Hong Kong has already developed a system of jurisprudence for the interpretation of the Basic Law, and the common law approach of 'statutory interpretations' has been strictly observed (Lin, 2001). Rather than adhering to the 'subjective theory' of 'original legislative intent' analysis, which focused on the 'subjective intent of lawmakers when they draft a law', the common law tradition of 'objective intent' maintains that 'once a law has been made, it is separate from the will of the lawmakers and acquires an objective existence'. This view is adopted in the common law system in Hong Kong. As a result, the OCTS principles provide significant safeguards for the protection of the common law system practised in the HKSAR (Lin, 2001). While such a perspective on judicial interpretation applies smoothly to most cases sent to the CFA, however, a constitutional crisis could erupt if the interpretation by the CFA concerns aspects of Mainland–Hong Kong relations. A brief analysis of the three interpretations of the Basic Law by the SCNPC serves to illustrate the limits of Hong Kong's autonomy under OCTS and its precarious links with the central government that insisted on unitarist principles. In each of these cases, the central government has reasserted its authority in dealing with Hong Kong and in so doing has demonstrated that its authority as the central government should not be challenged.

The first interpretation concerns the right of abode of the children of Hong Kong residents who were born outside the territory. The provisions in the Basic Law about the rights of this group were not entirely clear. A CFA decision on 29 January 1999 ruled that the requirement of the Certificate for Entitlement for right of abode seekers has violated Article 24(2)(3) of the Basic Law. According to the CFA ruling, Hong Kong courts 'have the jurisdiction to review the legislative acts of the NPC and the SCNPC, on whether such acts were inconsistent with the Basic Law and to declare such acts as invalid if they are determined to be so inconsistent'.

It also granted rights to the Courts of Hong Kong to 'determine whether an act of the National People's Congress or its Standing Committee is inconsistent with the Basic Law', and authorized the CFA to decide whether a case shall be referred to the SCNPC for interpretation under the provision of Article 158 of the Basic Law.[10]

Soon afterwards, four Mainland scholars, who were also former members of the Basic Law Drafting Committee, argued in early February 1999 that the legal authority of the SCNPC should be supreme, and the ruling of the CFA was turning Hong Kong into an 'independent political entity'. One scholar warned that 'no organisation or department can challenge or deny NPC legislation and decisions' (*South China Morning Post*, 8 February 1999, p. 1). The Head of the State Council's Information Office warned that the ruling was against the Basic Law and should be changed (ibid., 9 February 1999, p. 1). In response to such strong reactions from the central government, the HKSAR Government asked the CFA for a 'clarification'. The CFA thus clarified that 'the Hong Kong court's power to interpret the Basic Law is derived from the NPC Standing Committee under Article 158 of the Basic Law; any interpretation made by the Standing Committee under Article 158 would be binding on the Hong Kong courts', and the judgement of 29 January 1999 did not question 'the authority of the NPC and its Standing Committee to do any act which is in accordance with the provisions of the Basic law and the procedure therein'.[11] The clarification was accepted by the central government, at least momentarily.

Nonetheless, on 28 April 1999, the HKSAR government warned that, as a result of the CFA's ruling, an estimated 1.67 million people from the Mainland would be entitled to the right of abode in Hong Kong (*South China Morning Post*, 29 April 1999, p. 1). Hence, a majority of the Hong Kong delegates of the NPC urged the CFA to 'correct its own ruling' (ibid., 4 May 1999, p. 2). In early May 1999, Qiao Xiaoyang, Deputy Director of the Legislative Affairs Commission of the NPC and a member of the Committee for the Basic Law, claimed that the options of both the amendment or the interpretation of the Basic Law as a means to stall the possible influx of the right of abode seekers should not be ruled out (ibid., 6 May 1999, p. 6). In response to this perceived threat, the CE requested the SCNPC to interpret the relevant provisions of the Basic Law in May 1999, by stressing that the interpretation was the 'quickest and most effective option' to resolve the issue (*Hong Kong Commercial Daily*, 19 May 1999, p. A1). Qiao emphasized that the CFA should have consulted the SCNPC on the ruling on the rights of abode issue, and the CFA's ruling had violated the 'true legislative intent' of Article 158 of the Basic Law (*South China Morning Post*, 23 June 1999, p. 1). After discussions with the Committee for the Basic Law, the SCNPC rendered the first interpretation of the relevant provisions of Articles 22 and 24(2)(3) of the Basic Law in June 1999. The interpretation reasserted the authority of the central government on the entry of people from other parts of China to the HKSAR and reversed the CFA's judgement. For the Mainland-born children of Hong Kong residents to qualify for the right of abode in the HKSAR, at least one of the parents must be a permanent resident of the HKSAR at the moment when the child is born. These children are also requested to obtain the Certificate for Entitlement issued by the HKSAR Government and the One-way Permit issued by the Mainland public security authorities before they are allowed to take up residency in Hong Kong (*Ta Kung Pao*, 15 June 1999, p. A11; Chan, Fu and Ghai 2000, pp. 478–80). In the aftermath of this constitutional crisis, Qiao stated that the concept of 'one country' should be strengthened (*South China Morning Post*, 28 June 1999, p. 1).

The second interpretation of the Basic Law concerns the future election method of the CE and the Legislative Council (hereafter LegCo) of the HKSAR. The central government's initiative on the political development of Hong Kong was an attempt to dampen the calls for universal suffrage for the election of the CE and the LegCo from the pro-democracy camp in Hong Kong. In September 2002, the HKSAR government initiated the legislative process for the national security law in accordance with Article 23 of the Basic Law.[12] There were deep divisions in public opinion and strong opposition against the legislation and the legislative process.[13] The HKSAR government planned to table the Draft Bill in the LegCo for the third reading on 9 July 2003. As a result, at least 500 000 people took to the streets on 1 July 2003, protesting against the government. The protest and the ensuing political crisis compelled the HKSAR government to withdraw the Bill on 7 July 2003. Following the protest, the pro-democracy groups stepped up their efforts to call for universal suffrage. The pro-democracy parties successfully highlighted their demands in their campaign for the District Council elections in November 2003, and quite a number of the candidates of pro-democracy parties managed to win over candidates of the pro-Beijing or pro-government candidates (Cheng, 2004).

In view of the political challenges confronting Hong Kong, the central government began to steer the debate on its political development. In December 2003, President Hu Jintao highlighted his concern over the political development in Hong Kong (*Ta Kung Pao*, 4 December 2003, p. A2). Immediately following the remarks, four Mainland scholars articulated five principles on the constitutional development of Hong Kong: that the principle of 'one country' must be upheld and 'must not be compromised' in the implementation of 'one country, two systems'; that the development of the political system has to be 'conductive to maintaining the mutual relationship' between central government and the Hong Kong SAR; that social stability and economic prosperity should not be compromised by political reforms because 'the political system is not just a matter of institutional establishment and electoral mechanisms'; that the interests and democratic participation of all social strata in Hong Kong should be considered; and that considering the changes in the method of the selection of the chief executive and the formation of the Legislative Council as 'purely an internal affair' of Hong Kong was a misunderstanding.[14] In February 2004, through the official media, the central government released 20 commentaries and argued that the 'patriots' shall be 'the main body' that governed Hong Kong (Press Release of the Xinhua News Agency, 10 February 2004). The Deputy Director of the Hong Kong and Macao Affairs Office suggested that the constitutional development in Hong Kong had to follow the principles of 'balanced participation and making gradual and orderly progress' (*South China Morning Post*, 9 April 2004, p. 3).

The central government's concern was about the interpretation of Annexes I and II of the Basic Law regarding the method of selection for the CE and LegCo after 2007, as the provisions were full of ambiguity. Annex I of the Basic Law stipulated that, 'If there is a need to amend the method for selecting the Chief Executives for the terms subsequent to the year 2007, such amendments must be made with the endorsement of a two-thirds majority of all the members of the Legislative Council and the consent of the Chief Executive, and they shall be reported to the Standing Committee of the National People's Congress for approval.' Annex II stipulated that, 'With regard to the method for forming the Legislative Council of the Hong Kong Special Administrative Region and its procedures for voting on bills and motions after 2007, if there is a need to amend the provisions of this Annex, such amendments must be made with the endorsement of a two-thirds majority of all the members of the Council and the consent of the Chief Executive, and they shall be reported to the Standing Committee of the National People's Congress for the record.' These provisions are quite ambiguous. Who could decide 'if there is a need'? Would such provisions allow changes to be made for the CE election and the LegCo election in 2007 and 2008 elections, respectively? Which party could initiate the process for amendments of the method of selection? Should the power to initiate the process reside solely in the HKSAR, or the central government?

In January 2004, Xiao Weiyuan, a Mainland member of the Committee for the Basic Law, promptly suggested that the central government has the power to initiate the constitutional review (*Hong Kong Economic Times*, 19 January 2004, p. A4). Pro-democracy forces and legal experts in Hong Kong believed that the Hong Kong side shall be the 'designer' of its constitutional development and the 'initiator' of the process for constitutional review. They also stressed that the discussion on 'patriotism' was irrelevant (ibid., 20 January 2004, p. A19). Sheng Huaren, Vice Chairman of the SCNPC, however, reiterated that as ' "one country" prevails in the OCTS principle, major constitutional decisions could not be simply decided by the HKSAR Government; the central government had the authority of decision-making on the electoral reforms from the beginning till end' (*Sing Tao Daily*, 12 March 2004, p. A18; *South China Morning Post*, 13 March 2004, p. 1).

In a sudden and unprecedented move, the central government decided to take the initiative to proceed to the interpretation of Annexes I and II of the Basic Law in late March 2004 (*Wen Wei Po*, 27 March 2004, p. A1). The then Chief Secretary Donald Tsang echoed that the issue of constitutional development was the responsibility of the central government, and that consensus among all three sides of the HKSAR Government, LegCo and the central government must be reached to start the process.[15] Qiao Xiaoyang later sought the opinions of the Hong Kong delegates of the NPC and the Committee for the Basic Law, but he stressed that the SCNPC has the right as well as the responsibility to interpret laws.[16] The interpretation clearly stipulated that any amendments of the method of selection of the CE and LegCo must seek the prior approval of the SCNPC.[17] In a lengthy statement, Qiao emphasized that the HKSAR is 'a local administrative region under the central people's government's direct jurisdiction. Its autonomous power is authorized by the central government, and the authority of making decisions rests with the central government'.[18] He also re-emphasized that China is not a federal state: 'Our country implements a unitary system, not a federal system. Local regions of a unitary state have no inherent power, and local power is granted by the central authorities.'[19]

Since the interpretation stated that the method of election could be amended for the next immediate elections scheduled to be held in 2007 and 2008, respectively, the pro-democracy groups soon called for universal suffrage in 2007 and 2008. The central government has responded swiftly. Qiao Xiaoyang met the members of the NPC and members of the Committee of the Basic Law to discuss a report from the CE which stressed that the method of election must follow the principle of 'gradual and orderly progress' (*Hong Kong Economic Times*, 17 April 2004, p. A4). The SCNPC thus made the decision in its ruling that the method for the selection of the CE in 2007 and the legislature in 2008 'shall not be by the means of universal suffrage'.[20] Qiao also stated six reasons for the objection of a 'premature implementation of universal suffrage' in the HKSAR.[21]

The third interpretation emerged from a debate over whether the new CE of the HKSAR shall serve the remaining term of the CE, or whether he/she shall serve a new five-year term, after the resignation of Tung Chee-hwa on 10 March 2005. While the legal community in Hong Kong held the view that the new CE shall have a full term of five years in accordance with Articles 46 and 53 of the Basic Law, Mainland scholars affiliated with the central government argued that the CE shall only serve the remaining term of the outgoing CE. The then Secretary for Justice Elise Leung stated that, after consulting Mainland legal scholars, the original legislative intent of the Basic Law must be taken into account because the term 'new Chief Executive', rather than 'new term of a Chief Executive', was selected as the final wording for the text in Article 53 of BL (Press Release of the HKSAR Government, 12 March 2005). Facing the challenge of a judicial review, the Acting Chief Executive, Donald Tsang, submitted to the SCNPC a request for an interpretation of the relevant provisions of the Basic Law. The SCNPC made the shortest interpretation since 1997, by simply stipulating that, should an incumbent CE fail to complete a full five-year term, the successor could only serve the remaining term of his/her predecessor (*Hong Kong Commercial Daily*, 28 April 2005, p. A1). This led to wide speculation that this 'interpretation' served the political interests of the central government. Some scholars also questioned the role of the Committee for the Basic Law in expressing their opinions on this interpretation (Chen, 2005). In short, the increasing role played by the central government reveals not only its willingness to use its power to steer the political development in Hong Kong, but also the limited scope for Hong Kong over political matters under OCTS.

## CONCLUSIONS: HONG KONG AND THE PROSPECTS OF FEDERALISM IN CHINA

An optimistic assessment would suggest that, although Hong Kong cannot evolve into a genuine democracy soon, the working division of power between the central authorities and the HKSAR, Hong Kong's continuing enjoyment of various kinds of freedoms and its high degree of autonomy can offer important lessons for China's future political reform. Of course, China's political reform may not necessarily follow the path of a federal democracy, but the existence of this kind of quasi-federalist arrangement suggests the possibility of multiple institutional trajectories for the Chinese nation in the longer run.

However, the experience of Hong Kong in implementing the OCTS framework, as shown in the above analysis, does not foreshadow a federalist future for China, at least in the short and medium term. The following issues merit special attention. First, Hong Kong's autonomy under OCTS lacks sufficient institutional guarantees. While the creation of SARs is provided for in Article 31 of the Chinese Constitution, the central government has the prerogative to change such a provision. Second, a number of conditions that were in Hong Kong's favour will no longer be sustained in the future. In the 1980s, the economic gap between Hong Kong and the Mainland was enormous. Even today, on a per capita basis, Hong Kong is still much richer than the Mainland, but its relative importance to the Mainland economy will decline as China further opens up its economy and society. In fact, even Guangdong province's GDP has already surpassed that of Hong Kong in 2004 and if it can sustain its growth rate of 9 per cent per annum for another five to ten years, Hong Kong will fall further behind in aggregate terms. The OCTS framework is arguably more inclined to preserve Hong Kong's economic system than its autonomy, and, should Hong Kong's economic uniqueness be undercut, the very foundation underlying its 'high degree of autonomy' will be subject to change. The growing social and economic integration between Hong Kong and especially south China may pose further challenges to the HKSAR's preservation of its distinct social and economic identity, which may in the longer run spill over to the political sphere as well.

Third, when the OCTS model was proposed, Deng Xiaoping had Taiwan in mind, although he promised even more generous treatment for the island, such as preserving its armed forces and allowing its leaders to become national leaders. Nonetheless, with the growth of pro-independence sentiments in Taiwan and the disillusionment with Hong Kong's OCTS model among the Taiwanese, the OCTS formula is hardly attractive to Taiwan in the near future. Should the Taiwan question be resolved in one way or another before 2047, whether peacefully or not, there would be even less incentive for Beijing to offer Hong Kong another long period of special treatment unless such an arrangement helps to promote the core interests of the PRC. These concerns suggest the possible erosion of the foundations underlying Hong Kong's high degree of autonomy.

Notwithstanding the many proposals from both Mainland and overseas scholars, several conditions which are not conducive to the introduction of federalism in China have to be addressed if some form of federalism can be considered a realistic scenario. First, the Chinese Communist Party, which still holds supreme power, is a hierarchically organized Leninist party. Unless there are fundamental political changes which compel the Party to change its internal organizing principles and territorial organization, the Party itself is unlikely to support the introduction of federalist reforms in the state apparatus, unless it is also ready to go for a federalist route. Second, the fear of chaos with the introduction of federalist reforms and the splitting up of China into competing regions governed by regional strongmen may also be a strong deterrent to any federal political arrangements.

Further, many analyses or advocacies are probably too optimistic about the prospect of a federalist future for China. Genuine federation can only be realistically built upon pluralist, democratic political beliefs that protect the interests of minorities, be they territorial or community-based. Such political toleration and democratic values have not yet taken root in China. Hong Kong's experience with OCTS for eight years has already revealed the many tensions between the quest for democracy and autonomy by local authorities and the insistence on central authority by Beijing. Hong Kong's experience could well be relevant for a federalist China, but the reassertion of central authority in dealing with the HKSAR since 1997 only serves to reveal the deep concern of the Chinese Communist leadership about the centrifugal tendencies of a community of seven million, barely 0.5 per cent of China's total population.

Nonetheless, the OCTS framework for Hong Kong does carry several important elements found in federalist political systems, such as the separation of power between the central and local governments, the autonomy of the local government over taxation, and other special treatments such as allowing English to be used as an official language by the executive authorities, legislature and judiciary. The HKSAR government also enjoys a wide range of economic policy powers which buttress its capacity to govern effectively as a separate and rather independent polity. Further, while Hong Kong people are not ethnically distinct from other Chinese, they do possess a separate identity and a radically different set of social, economic and political values that set them apart from their compatriots in the Mainland. This local identity is further reinforced by the political symbols and privileges they enjoyed, including its issuance of HKSAR passports and the travel privileges that they carry and the co-existence and de facto accommodation of multiple citizenships for Hong Kong residents.

Hence the preferential treatment of Hong Kong under the OCTS may even be interpreted as an incipient stage in the development of asymmetrical federalism. Watts considers both Hong Kong and Macau SAR as examples of decentralized unions with some federal features (Watts, 1999, p. 12). Given the rapid and uneven growth in China's regions and the imperative of national unification, the trajectory of some form of asymmetrical federalism (or federacy) cannot be completely ruled out in the longer run. Actually, the asymmetries between Hong Kong and the coastal regions of China would be very much narrowed by 2047, if the social and economic development of these areas is not seriously disrupted in the coming decades. To what extent the administrative, legal and political systems of the two areas will remain vastly different remains to be seen. In future, the central authorities in Beijing will still have the final say over the political future of the HKSAR, but its actions on the territory will be influenced not only by its own internal political dynamics and the impact of international forces, but also by the way Hong Kong manages its future relations with the central authorities. Different trajectories may still emerge as Hong Kong moves toward the end of the initial term of 50 years.

In short, Hong Kong's post-1997 experience aptly reveals the tensions in China's policy toward the territory. Beijing has largely kept its promise not to intervene in Hong Kong's internal affairs since 1997. However, the mass rally against the national security legislation on 1 July 2003 is a good reminder of the lingering tension between Beijing and Hong Kong. The reorientation of central policy toward Hong Kong since 1 July 2003 shows an increasingly assertive central government in managing Hong Kong affairs. Beijing has fully utilized its power to interpret the Basic Law in order to cope with the tensions in the relations between Hong Kong and the Mainland and the city's demand for more democracy. The lack of an arbitrator in conflict resolution reflects the unitarist tendencies of the Chinese political system. If indeed a genuine federalist framework would be an attractive scenario for managing central–local relations in China today, why did Beijing not adopt federalist instruments in handling the difficulties in its relations with the HKSAR, such as allowing genuine representative democracy to develop and resorting to a judicial solution to resolve the constitutional confrontations over interpretations of the Basic Law? If Beijing is willing to fulfil its promise of a more democratic political system for Hong Kong and sustain its highly autonomous status into the longer future, the federalist elements of the OCTS framework could facilitate the evolution of a federalist China. In other words, the continuation of the OCTS framework for Hong Kong will continue to provide evidence of the beauty of respecting diversity through sharing sovereignty and powers between central and local authorities in a highly centralized political system like the PRC. For such a scenario to work, however, Hong Kong's practice of the OCTS also has to show that its high degree of autonomy will not seriously compromise Beijing's core interests, such as national development and political stability.

# ACKNOWLEDGEMENT

I would like to acknowledge the support from a small project grant of the University of Hong Kong and the assistance provided by Mr Kelvin Sit. I would also like to thank, for their valuable comments, Professor He Baogang and other participants in the 'International Workshop on Democratization and Asian Federalism' held on 9–10 February 2006.

# NOTES

1. Prof. Yash Ghai, for instance, believes that it is more useful to examine the experience of Hong Kong as an example of autonomy systems.
2. Article 31 of the Basic Law states that 'The state may establish special administrative regions when necessary. The system to be instituted in special administrative regions shall be prescribed by laws enacted by the National People's Congress in the light of the specific conditions.'
3. The Committee is under the NPC Standing Committee and currently chaired by Qiao Xiaoyang. Half of its 12 members are from the Mainland and the other half from Hong Kong.
4. Nonetheless, because of their access to the Mainland authorities, Hong Kong citizens would often seek their assistance if they encounter practical problems in the Mainland.
5. The information comes from the following sources: for 'Intergovernmental organisations limited to states', http://www.cab.gov.hk/en/issues/external1.htm; 'Intergovernmental organisations not limited to states', http://www.cab.gov.hk/en/issues/external2.htm; 'List of Non-intergovernmental Organizations', http://www.cab.gov.hk/images/iorg_ngo.xls; 'List of Treaties in Force and Applicable to the Hong Kong Special Administrative Region', http://www.legislation.gov.hk/interlaw.htm.
6. The information comes from the following sources: 'List of Treaties in Force and Applicable to the Hong Kong Special Administrative Region', http://www.legislation. gov.hk/interlaw.htm. Out of those, 76 treaties were not ratified by the Mainland, one of them is partially ratified.
7. The information comes from the 'List of Agreements and Arrangements for the Establishing of International Organisations in Hong Kong (Gazette References)', http://www.legislation.gov.hk/table7ti.htm. Such offices include the office of the Commission of the European Union, the Office of the Bank for International Settlement, the International Monetary Fund, the Regional Office for the International Finance Corporation for East Asia and Pacific, and the Private Sector Development Office for East Asia and Pacific for the World Bank.
8. Further, arrangements for reciprocal juridical assistance, including agreements on surrender of fugitive offenders, agreements on transfer of sentenced persons and agreements on mutual legal assistance in criminal matters, air service agreements and overflight agreements visa abolition agreements, could be reached with foreign sovereign nations under the authorization of the central authorities.
9. These include 53 air service agreements, 14 investment promotion and protection agreements, 14 legal assistance agreements, 13 surrender of fugitive offenders agreements, 7 transfer of sentenced persons agreements, 8 double taxation avoidance agreements and 10 visa abolition agreements. Other international agreements have also been reached between the HKSAR and other foreign bodies, such as with the European Union on mutual cooperation in customs assistance, with Israel on information technology and communications, and with the Ukraine on maritime transport. A full list of the bilateral agreements that are applicable to the HKSAR can be found in the following web pages: http://www.cab.gov.hk/en/issues/external4.htm and http://www.legislation.gov. hk/choice.htm#bf. Other lists of arrangements can be found at 'List of Air Services Agreements and Air Services Transit Agreements', http://www.legislation.gov.hk/ table1ti.htm; 'List of Investment Promotion and Protection Agreements (Gazette References)', http://www.legislation.gov.hk/table2ti.htm; 'List of Mutual Legal Assistance Agreements (Legislative References)', http://www.legislation.gov.hk/ table3ti.htm; 'List of Surrender of Fugitive Offenders Agreements (Legislative References)', http://www.legislation.gov.hk/table4ti.htm; 'List of Transfer of Sentenced Persons Agreements (Gazette References)', http://www.legislation.gov.hk/ table5ti.htm; 'List of Double Taxation Avoidance Agreements (Legislative References)', http://www.legislation.gov.hk/table6ti.htm.
10. [1999] 1 HKLRD 337, para. G; 338, para. A; 342, para. H.

11. [1999] 1 HKLRD 577.
12. Article 23 of the Basic Law stipulated that 'the Hong Kong Special Administrative Region shall enact laws on its own to prohibit any act of treason, secession, sedition, subversion against the Central People's Government, or theft of state secrets, to prohibit foreign political organizations or bodies from conducting political activities in the Region, and to prohibit political organizations or bodies of the Region from establishing ties with foreign political organizations or bodies'. See the full text of the Basic Law of the Hong Kong SAR at http://www.info.gov.hk/basic_law/fulltext/index.htm.
13. Some questioned the approach of the legislative process adopted by the government, while the pro-Beijing groups urged the expeditious passage of the legislation as a fulfilment of duties for the state, and reflected an exercise of national sovereignty. See Question 70 in Democratic Alliance for the Betterment of Hong Kong (2002), *Jibenfa Ershisan Tiao lifa 70 wen* (70 Questions on the Legislation of the Article 23 of the Basic Law), Hong Kong, China: Democratic Alliance for the Betterment of Hong Kong.
14. 'PRC Law Experts on Hu Jintao's Remarks on HK Political System Development', Press Release of Xinhua News Agency, English translation by FBIS.
15. See the Press Release of the HKSAR government, 26 March 2004 and 30 March 2004; (http://www.info.gov.hk/gia/general/200403/26/0326320.htm; http://www.info.gov.hk/gia/general/200403/30/0330222.htm).
16. In 2004, Qiao Xiaoyang held the post of Deputy Secretary-General of the SCNPC, as well as Director of the Committee for the Basic Law of the HKSAR. See the Radio Television Hong Kong Report, 6 April 2004, English translation by FBIS.
17. See the full text of the interpretation at http://www.cab.gov.hk/cd/eng/basic/pdf/es22004080554.pdf.
18. See Xinhua News Agency Domestic Press Release, English translation by BBC Monitoring Asia–Pacific, 'China holds press conference on Hong Kong Basic Law interpretation', 6 April 2004.
19. He also denied that residual powers rest with the HKSAR, as he stressed that 'all residual powers' lie with the central authorities, and only the NPC and the central government could grant such additional power when the SAR 'needs that power and does not have that power'. See 'Qiao Xiaoyang Answers Correspondents' Questions at State Council Information Office', in *Ta Kung Pao* website on 7 April 2004 (http://www.takungpao.com/inc/print_me.asp?url=/news/2004-4-7/GW-247353, htm&date=2004-4-7) and (http://www.takungpao.com/inc/print_me.asp?url=/news/2004-4-7/GW-247349,htm&date=2004-4-7), English translation by BBC Monitoring Asia–Pacific.
20. See the full text of the decision at http://www.info.gov.hk/cab/cab-review/eng/basic/pdf/es5200408081.pdf.
21. The reasons for the objection are that it would 'impose negative impact on national sovereignty and overall interests, the constitutional status of the Basic Law has not yet gained a firm foothold', the 'lack of guarantee of a balanced participation of the industrial and commercial sectors, original capitalism cannot be maintained'; the 'implementation of radical political reform is bound to jeopardize the economic situation which is just starting to turn around'; the operation of the political system 'has not fully met the requirements laid down by the Basic Law'; the 'executive–legislative relations are still at a stage of "adaptation"'; the existence of a 'great divergence of public opinion over the implementation of universal suffrage in 2007 and 2008'; the push forward of universal suffrage in a forceful manner is 'bound to aggravate social contradictions'; the 'introduction of radical reform will surely bring forth fierce confrontations, which is an unbearable political cost'. See the English translation, 'NPC Official Expounds Six Reasons Against Universal Suffrage in HK', in *Ta Kung Pao*'s website translated by FBIS, 28 April 2004.

# REFERENCES

Chan, Johannes M.M., H.L. Fu and Yash Ghai (eds) (2000), *Hong Kong's Constitutional Debate Conflict Over Interpretation*, Hong Kong, China: Hong Kong University Press.

Chen, Albert H.Y. (2005), 'The NPCSC's interpretation in Spring 2005', *Hong Kong Law Journal*, **35**(2), 255–64.

Cheng, Joseph Y.S. (2004), 'The 2003 District Council Elections in Hong Kong', *Asian Survey*, **44**(5), 734–54.

Cheung, Anthony B.L. and Paul C.W. Wong (2004), 'Who advised the Hong Kong government?', *Asian Survey*, **44**(6), 874–94.

Democratic Alliance for the Betterment of Hong Kong (2002), *Jibenfa Ershisan Tiao lifa 70 wen* (70 Questions on the Legislation of the Article 23 of the Basic Law), Hong Kong, China: Democratic Alliance for the Betterment of Hong Kong.

Duchacek, Ivo D. (1986), *The Territorial Dimension of Politics Within, Among and Across Nations*, Boulder, US: Westview Press, pp. 110–57.

Elazar, Daniel J. (1987), *Exploring Federalism*, Tuscaloosa, US: The University of Alabama Press.

Ghai, Yash (1998), 'Autonomy with Chinese characteristics: the case of Hong Kong', *Pacifica Review*, **10**(1), 20–22.

Ghai, Yash (2005). 'The imperatives of autonomy: contradictions of the Basic Law', in Johannes Chan and Lison Harris (eds), *Hong Kong's Constitutional Debates*, Hong Kong, China: Hong Kong Law Journal Limited, pp. 29–44.

Goodstadt, Leo (2004), *Uneasy Partners: The Conflict between Public Interest and Private Profit in Hong Kong*, Hong Kong, China: Hong Kong University Press.

*HKSAR Government, Press Release*, 12 March 2005, (from http://www.info.gov.hk/gia/general/200503/12/03120310.htm).

*Hong Kong Commercial Daily*, 19 May 1999, p. A1; 28 April 2005, p.A1.

*Hong Kong Economic Times*, 19 January 2004, p. A4; 20 January 2004, p. A19; 17 April 2004, p. A4.

*Hong Kong Law Reports and Digest (HKLRD)*, 1999.

Lin, Feng (2001), 'The development of jurisprudence of the Court of Final Appeal in Basic Law litigation', *Journal of Chinese and Comparative Law*, **5**(2), 21–44.

Riker, William (1975), 'Federalism', in Fred I. Greenstein and Nelson W. Polsby (eds), *Handbook of Political Science, Vol. 5*, Reading, MA, USA: Addison-Wesley, pp. 93–172.

*Sing Tao Daily*, 12 March 2004, p. A18.

Smith, James McCall (2001), 'One sovereign, two legal systems: China and the problem of commitment in Hong Kong', in Stephen D. Krasner (ed.), *Problematic Sovereignty: Contested Rules and Political Possibilities*, New York, USA: Columbia University Press, pp. 105–40.

*South China Morning Post*, 8 February 1999, p. 1; 9 February 1999, p. 1; 29 April 1999, p. 1; 4 May, 1999, p. 2; 6 May 1999, p. 6; 23 June 1999, p. 1; 28 June 1999, p. 1; 13 March 2004, p. 1; 9 April 2004, p. 3.

*Ta Kung Pao*, 15 June 1999, p. A11; 4 December 2003, p. A2; 7 April 2004 (website); 28 April 2004 (website).

Watts, Ronald L. (1998), 'Federalism, federal political systems, and federations', *Annual Review of Political Sciences*, **1**, 117–37.

Watts, Roland L. (1999), *Comparing Federal Systems*, 2nd edn, Montreal, Canada and Kingston, Canada: McGill-Queen's University Press.

*Wen Wei Po*, 27 March 2004, p. A1.

Wu, Jianfan (1988), 'Several issues concerning the relationship between the central government of the People's Republic of China and the Hong Kong Special Administrative Region', *Journal of Chinese Law*, **2**, 65–82.

Xiao, Weiyun (1993), *Yiguo Liangzi ru Aomen Tebei xinzheng qu zhiban fa* (One Country, Two Systems and the Basic Law of the Macau Special Administrative Region), Beijing, China: Beijing Daxue Chubanshe.

Xinhua News Agency (2004), 'HKSAR and central government officials exchange views on Hong Kong constitutional development', 10 February.

# 12. Federal traditions and quasi-federalism in Japan

**Takashi Inoguchi**[1]

Japan has had a long tradition of quasi-federalism. In the late 16th century when the Period of the Warring States (1467–1573) ended, what prevailed was not the absolutism of the kind that determined the succeeding history of many Western European countries (Anderson, 1970). Absolutism, Japanese style, floundered mid-way when centralizing absolute power into one person, Nobunaga, who was assassinated in 1582. Nobunaga was a warrior who destroyed what he regarded as barriers and impediments to his military unification of the country. He not only defeated many competing warrior rivals but also crushed the Buddhist temples of Hiei mountain and the merchant republic of Sakai. He was about to usurp the power of the Emperor which had kept its nominal symbolic legitimacy and authority to rule Japan since the 7th century. Since then, first aristocrats (8th–11th centuries), then warriors (11th–mid-16th centuries) had ruled the country without diminishing the power of the Emperor. Nobunaga was open to foreign ideas, technologies, trade and religion. Thus, in 1575, Nobunaga used hundreds of guns in the battle of Nagashino in a way unprecedented in military history. Troops armed with guns systematically crushed the cavalry troops of his adversary. A similar military strategy, albeit on a much smaller scale, was used for the first time in Europe near Leipzig in 1725 by Gustavus Adolphus (Parker, 1996). After Nobunaga's assassination military unification was eventually achieved by his self-proclaimed successor, called Hideyoshi. Hideyoshi, a pragmatic ruler of peasant stock, compromised with his former competitors by allowing virtual autonomy in their domains. His military unification subsequently led to his military campaigns into the Asian Continent in 1592–98. His own death in Japan brought all the troops back to Japan.

Ieyasu then overwhelmed Hideyoshi's allies with two successful military campaigns. Ieyasu emerged as the founder of an early modern arrangement allowing autonomy to 300 odd domains while the Tokugawa government nearly monopolized power in defence, foreign commerce and intelligence. By 'early modern', I mean the preliminary period of modernity in Japan which began in the late 16th century and ended in the mid-19th century (Ikegami, 1995). Ieyasu can be called the founder of modern political arrangements far beyond what he envisaged and executed because his arrangements were to become the basic foundation for federal and democratic arrangements from the mid-19th century onward. The period of Tokugawa rule (1603–1867) was not only noteworthy for its long peace, for which it is sometimes called the Pax Tokugawana, but also for its seeding and rooting of federal and democratic traditions in this early modern period.

## PAX TOKUGAWANA AND DEMOCRATIC AND FEDERAL PREPARATIONS

Pax Tokugawana was noteworthy for its long peace. There was neither external war nor any major civil strife for more than two centuries (Hall, 1991; Jansen and Rozman, 1986). Only on two occasions, once in the mid-17th century to suppress a Christian rebellion in the Shimabara peninsula in southern Japan, and the other in the mid-19th century to suppress the Choshu domain for its anti-Tokugawa policy, did the Tokugawa deploy their troops. Shortly after the great battle in 1600 which led to Tokugawa's rise, Ieyasu and his successors carried out three policy lines.

First came building and consolidating the policy line of *sakoku* (closing the country) (Toby, 1984). Ieyasu was apprehensive about possible reprisal from the Continent for Japan's Continental campaigns in the late 16th century. Chinese rulers changed from Ming to Qing meanwhile. The new Qing rulers ruled the largest Chinese empire since ancient times with Manchu, Mongol, Uigurs, Tibetan and Han all joining the ruling establishment. Portuguese and Spaniards were forbidden from entering the country and carrying out commercial transactions and proselytizing Christianity. Their colonizing ambitions were suspected. Only non-official Chinese and Dutch traders were allowed to use a small port, Deshima, at Nagasaki under the direct rule of Tokugawa. The entire Japanese population was forbidden from entering into commercial transactions with foreigners, who were in turn forbidden from entering the country. This policy line set the 300-odd domains and the entire population on the alert against foreign threats: military, economic and religious. Thus the mid-17th century Christian rebels at Shimabara were massacred and, in the mid-19th century, young men like Yoshida Shoin, who wanted to break the policy line in order to visit foreign countries, were executed. Those domains on the periphery of the country, which by virtue of their location had to handle external neighbours, were assigned the specific role of dealing with those neighbours. Matsumae was assigned to handle Ainus on Hokkaido. Tsushima was assigned to handle Koreans. Satsuma was assigned to handle Ryukyuans. Why did the Tokugawa monopolize foreign trade into their own hands? Foreign trade brought with it new military technology and economic surplus, which, when combined, might be used to topple the power of the Tokugawa. The policy line of closing the country forced each of the 300-odd domains to strive to achieve political self-government and economic well-being within its domain. The military dominance of the Tokugawa, when combined with the policy of placing those domains which were hostile or unfriendly to the Tokugawa in the great battle of Sekigahara of 1600 in peripheral places far away from Edo (Tokyo), helped the long peace to be achieved.

The second policy line was to ensure autonomy for each domain as long as its loyalty to the Tokugawa was assured and its 'good governance' proved. To keep loyalty high and visible the Tokugawa made it a rule for the lords of domains to live intermittently at Edo (Tokyo) while the chief counsellor of the domain took care of domains. To foster good governance the Tokugawa set up the scheme of intelligence whereby violations of a certain set of rules, norms and practices (such as peasant uprisings against heavy tax, internal violent strife among leaders) were to be detected and reported to the Tokugawa. In extreme cases of such incidents, which took place very rarely, the Tokugawa interfered in internal matters by imposing such actions as resignation of lords, and reduction of domain size. Also the Tokugawa government assigned infrastructural building tasks to many domains, with corvé labour for infrastructural construction such as bridges and roads outside their own domains. Other than these two con-straints, much was left to each domain. This second policy line resembles quasi-federal arrangements. To illustrate, let us examine what kind of policy was adopted in view of the budget deficits of domains. The Hirosaki domain in the northernmost Honshu islands used the policy of sending warriors-cum-bureaucrats to the countryside to farm land so that the domain purse would not be burdened; the Yonezawa domain in the northwestern Honshu islands adopted the policy of subsidizing lacquer tree planting and production so that lacquer products could make profits; the Tokushima domain in the Eastern Shikoku islands used the policy of developing the dyeing industry and its market in Osaka, just across the Seto island sea. In all this the general advancement of infra-structure such as roads, bridges, ports and customs was largely left in the hands of Tokugawa.

Other than this infrastructural development, however, much was left to each domain. The Hirosaki domain did reduce the domain expenditure substantially by trimming the size of its bureaucracy. The Yonezawa domain did not trim its bureaucracy; it carried out its industrial policy but it failed because the domain ended up by purchasing most of the lacquer products. There were no large markets to which the landlocked Yonezawa domain could have easy access. The Tokushima domain was very success-ful in its industrial policy of dyeing by developing a huge market in Osaka (Ravina, 1999).

Domain economic policy differed very much, reflecting the differences in agronomical development and demographic change (Hanley and Yamamura, 1986). The Nagaoka domain, through which runs the Shinano river, the longest river in Japan, benefited from the agronomical progress in enabling delta areas to harvest rice. Up to the 17th century, lower stream areas were full of floods, tended to spoil rice with worms, and were thus not suitable for rice agriculture. Technology turned vast delta areas into rice paddies, which increased the size of population inhabiting delta areas. In contrast, the Satsuma domain, a southernmost domain, suffered from a land full of volcanic sand. It had to rely on sending warrior–bureaucrats into the countryside to farm land; it conquered the Ryukyu kingdom to the south to exploit Ryukyuan trade with China and Southeast Asia; it imported arms from foreign countries illegally to achieve its 'revere the Emperor; overthrow the Tokugawa' policy in the mid-19th century.

The above examples are meant to illustrate the degree of autonomy given to each domain to run its affairs. Decentralization was accentuated because the country was closed, because the national economy was being forged steadily, greatly affecting each domain in much the same way that global-ization today profoundly affects each country, and because technological progress was basically slow, if not stagnant.

The third policy line of the Pax Tokugawana was 'democratization'. Two structural conditions existed. First, many lords and their bureaucrats were assigned from elsewhere to their domains as a result of the major political reconfigurations taking place intermittently in the late 16th and early 17th centuries. In other words, elites were strangers. Domain governments were a government of strangers vis-à-vis local peasants (Inoguchi, 1997). Second, the basically zero growth economy forced domains to strive for more product and less expenditure. What is called the 'industrious revo-lution' (Hayami, 1992) had to be engineered. Here democratization comes in. Domains must reflect on what peasants regarded as justice. Bureaucrats must tax people within a reasonable range. Bureaucrats must talk to people. Further, given the basically small size of domains' bureaucracy, those upper elements of non-warrior classes, that is, landlords and rich mer-chants, must be co-opted into street-level bureaucracy. In other words, bureaucrats must develop cooperative working relationship with the non-warrior population within the domains. It is not surprising, therefore, to find that there were not a few philosophical writings during that period pointing to fledgling democratic ideas. For instance, Yamaga Gorui argues, 'A ruler's supreme power is derived from the masses under heaven, thus a ruler must not behave in a selfish manner. . . . It is with the people's support that a ruler emerges, and it is the ruler who establishes the state, thus the essence of the state is the people' (Inoguchi, 2005a). Akita Chiranki also argues, 'The ruler is like a boat and his subordinates like water. Water can carry the boat but it can also sink it' (Inoguchi, 2005a).

Democratization comes in also at the level of decision making. As already noted, warriors were transformed into bureaucrats and settled at castle towns. They developed what Ikegami (1995) calls 'honorific collectivism', as distinguished from honorific individualism, the ethos which shaped warriors during the medieval period. In the early modern period bureaucrats honoured the collectivity of a domain and acted accordingly. Decisions were collectively taken in the council of senior bureaucrats. Thus, when a lord acted in great dissonance with their collective decision, their institutionalized response was to lock a lord up in a confined area of a castle to prevent him from participating in politics. Absolutism was not born. Rather proto-democratic practice was observed in each domain (Kasaya, 1989).

Onto these three structural conditions was set the stage for modernization that was to guide the country in more open, more centralizing and yet more democratic directions.

## MODERNIZATION BASED ON AND ACCELERATED BY EARLY MODERN LEGACIES

Japan was the first country in the non-West to pursue modernization at a fairly early stage. It was in 1868 that the stage for modernization was set with three distinctive prongs: dramatically opening the country, assiduously centralizing the state and steadily democratizing politics. First, opening the country was dramatic, ideationally replacing the Chinese-referenced Japanese order with the Western-referenced Japanese order overnight (Inoguchi, 2005b) and commercially accepting the humiliating and debilitating tariff non-autonomy, making the country vulnerable to foreign economic penetration when the country had no products that were sufficiently competitive in the international market. Second, centralization was steadily achieved: replacing the 300-odd semi-autonomous domains with 50-odd prefectures whose governors were appointed by the central government; setting up a meritocratically recruited civil service; setting a compulsory educational system whereby one standard Japanese language was achieved and national identity was established; establishing the Japanese post service whereby national communications were realized; building the Japanese railway system whereby national transportation was realized; building a national police force; constructing conscriptive national armed forces; building local assemblies first and then the Imperial Diet with popular elections, with gradually decreasing qualifications attached to political rights and civil liberties associated with elections.

Third, there developed steadily if somewhat slowly democratizing politics. A parliamentary democracy with a monarchy was used to build a modern nation state. Local assembly elections were already realized in the 1880s; the Imperial Constitution was promulgated in 1889 and the Imperial Diet was opened in 1890. The qualifications attached to political rights and civil duties were gradually reduced. By 1925, universal suffrage for the entire male population more than 20 years old was achieved. In the same year the internal security preservation law was legislated, somewhat in contradiction to the famous Tocquevillesque dictum that universal suffrage and freedom of expression cannot go together. These moves that gradually strengthened centralization took place over three-quarters of a century after 1868.

At the same time, the early modern legacies of decentralized schemes were kept largely intact in different forms. Most critical was the Imperial Constitution, which allowed a high degree of decentralization at the highest level of the government (Akita, 1967; Banno, 2005). At its pinnacle stood the Emperor who was brought to Tokyo from Kyoto where, for centuries, the imperial power survived all the vicissitudes of history as a symbolic nominal actor which gave legitimizing power to whoever controlled Kyoto and the rest. The Emperor was accorded the highest power constitutionally, but under him were the array of actors whose authority derived from their equal and decentralized access to the ear of the Emperor. Thus not only those founding fathers of the Meiji Restoration (a military coup d'état engineered by bands of lower-class warriors largely from two peripheral domains subsequently consolidated by bringing the Emperor to Tokyo and pacifying the rest of the country militarily under the banner of 'rich country, strong army' and 'enlightenment and entrepreneurship') but also the army, the navy, the Privy Council, the House of Peers, the House of Representatives, major political parties, influential business leaders and all the bureaucratic agencies enjoyed their access to the Emperor, if only often indirectly. The Prime Minister was merely a *primus inter pares* whose cabinet could be constitutionally easily toppled by one dissenter from within the cabinet as well as by a strong dissenting voice coming from without the cabinet.

The semi-sovereignty accorded to each bureaucratic agency is another noteworthy aspect of the modern regime. It was as if old domains had been replaced by new bureaucratic agencies. During the early years of the Meiji Restoration all the warriors lost their jobs and many of them had to find employment in the government. Their high level of literacy and supposedly high moral standards recommended them to such jobs. Given the extremely small numbers of founding fathers and their patronage, it often happened that each bureaucratic agency had some geographical biases derived from old domain affiliations. Thus, for instance, the army was dominated by the Choshu domain, the navy dominated by the Satsuma domain, the Accounting examination office dominated by the Nabeshima domain, the Police Agency thronged by the Higo and Aizu domains, at least until about the First World War. Decentralization during the early modern period in terms of domains remained in the form of decentralization at the highest level of central bureaucracy.

Third, the early modern legacy of democratization played an important role in modern Japanese political development. It was very positive. The introduction of local assemblies in the 1880s was not difficult when local notables, shouldering the bulk of tax revenues, wanted to voice their demands to the central government. Built on local assembly experiences, establishing the Imperial Diet in 1890 went smoothly. The development of political parties and newspapers was most remarkable in the 1880s and 1890s. All this led one noted historian to call the Meiji political regime 'the Meiji democracy' (Banno, 2005), a significant political development attesting to the steady progress of a fledgling democracy in terms of political participation (the introduction of limited suffrage in the early 1880s to universal suffrage of the male population by 1925) and contestation (from the development of political parties in anticipation of the introduction of parliaments, local and national, in the 1880s to the full-fledged party competition in the Taisho democracy in the 1910s and 1920s through the deepening of democracy manifested in the advance of a social democratic party, the Social Masses Party, in the 1930s). Banno calls the last the Showa 'democracy'.

The fact that Japanese democracy in a transition resorted to use of force at home and abroad at the height of its democratic participatory advances may vindicate the proposition that a fledgling democracy is not necessarily peaceful (Mansfield and Snyder, 2006). Yet the half a century development of parliamentary democracy from the 1880s to the 1930s was remarkably steady and smooth and seems to attest to the structural strength acquired historically from the early modern quasi-democratic experiences accumulated in many of the domains for more than two centuries of the Tokugawa era.

After briefly characterizing the Pax Tokugawana and its quasi-democratic and quasi-federal arrangements, we now turn to the discussion on the relationship between democratization and federalism as evolved in Japan's early modern period. I argue that somehow the early Tokugawa period brought about the healthy tension between the centre and localities, that is, the Tokugawa government and 300-odd local domains. First, Tokugawa's military dominance was not supreme. There was no absolutism; rather quasi-federalism existed in early modern Japan. Outer domains tended to be large domains and potentially anti-Tokugawan. Tokugawa's ally domains, which tended to be small domains, were assigned to run Japan at the intermittently high level of decision making. Tokugawa's clans occupied the highest position for two and half a centuries. This configuration allowed quite a big space for autonomy for most domains. The Tokugawa government could not afford to be over domineering for fear of sparking anti-Tokugawa subversion.

Second, domains were free to choose policy strategies in terms of economic development. Under the assumption of no dramatic technological innovations, domains increased gross domestic products (1) by increasing arable lands through good flood control and irrigation technologies, especially in delta areas, (2) by giving incentives to peasants through a scheme of more margins being kept in the hands of peasants once harvests were very good, which led peasants to work much harder than before (which is called by Akira Hayami (1992) 'the industrious revolution' in early modern Japan), and (3) by developing national economic markets centring on Osaka and Edo through building sea route and land route infrastructures, linking most parts of the whole of Japan without too high tariffs being imposed at domain borders. In other words, nation-wide commerce was practised and economic integration on a national scale was achieved steadily. Important was the fact that the degree of competitiveness and ingenuity made differences to the health and wealth of each domain. Quasi-federal arrangements in early modern Japan helped the population to grow and the national economic market to develop. Quasi-federal arrangements encouraged diligence and competition.

Third, within each domain many, if not most, domain leaders were strangers to the local peasants. Domain leaders kept their followers as their bureaucratic troops wherever they were assigned, which was not uncommon at a time of great political upheavals. Domain bureaucrats, therefore, had to treat peasants and merchants with care. They developed a consciousness of peasants' well-being as being one of the highest priorities. Here was the basis of quasi-democratic development in many domains. Class distinctions, warriors, peasants, artisans and merchants, were kept more or less strictly separate in early modern Japan. Warriors-cum-bureaucrats, however, had to treat the rest with care. Furthermore, their number tended to be large when labour productivity was not very high. Bureaucrats lived on harvests generated by peasants. Their number tended to increase slowly but steadily as time went by since governing increasingly needed more manpower as the realm of policy expanded. Rich land-owning peasants and merchants were increasingly coopted to the governing corps of domains. Quasi-democratic development in early modern Japan was genuine and endogenous in many ways. Some of the basic conditions for the emergence of fledgling endogenous proto-democratization were there.

Laurence Whitehead (2002) argued that there were only three democracies which developed democracy endogenously: England, Sweden and Switzerland. In other words, so he argues, of all the 120-odd democracies that exist today, only those three did not have democracy imposed on them by outsiders. Salient among basic conditions for endogenous democratic development is, it seems to me at least, the structural need to develop a communitarian spirit in peripheral locales. Let me take up England and Japan for quick comparison in late 16th and early 17th centuries. Elizabeth I and Ieyasu were the key figures. In the late 16th century, England was a peripheral country in Europe. More importantly perhaps, Europe itself was peripheral to the Middle East, where the highest level of science and technology was generated. Japan was very peripheral to the higher civilization entity called China. England was troubled by foreign entanglements with the Vatican, Spain, France, Scotland and so forth. These foreign powers sometimes allied to aristocrats and local notables who represented themselves in a higher collective body called the parliament. Local collective interests were very strong in England largely because outside invaders and occupiers (the Normans) had to coopt local notables by giving away a significant amount of autonomy. The number of Normans was very small. The language they brought to England, French, affected English considerably. But for governing they had to rely on the inhabitants. England had to execute drastic disentanglements because otherwise they would have kept England divisive. Because England was divisive, Elizabeth had to build absolutism.

In Japan, Ieyasu took a similar and different path (Toby, 1984). Disentanglement was chosen by Ieyasu clearly because of the disasters brought about by Hideyoshi's continental campaigns in late 16th century. Ieyasu even went back to the traditional foreign policy line developed when Japan was defeated in Korea by China in the 7th century. That is the one of 'friendship with distance' focusing primarily on commercial transactions and cultural interactions. Thus Japan had no diplomatic relationship with China, for instance, between the late 14th century and mid-19th century. Ieyasu chose disentanglement by closing off the country from outside. Only commercial transactions at the port of Deshima, Nagasaki were allowed. What Ieyasu was apprehensive about had to do with illicit weapons trade conducted by some domains with foreign countries, and with Christian missionary activities, both of which were suspected of being conducive to schisms and cleavages in Japanese society, engineered by traders and missionaries. What Ieyasu did was to close off the country from missionary activities and to conduct monopolistic trade with non-missionary-minded Dutch and Chinese merchants only. After all, Catholic missionaries from Portugal and Spain were allied with Catholic domain rulers in the late 16th century and early 17th century. Similarly some domains, especially in Japan's peripheries, which were located closer to foreign countries were suspected of smuggling weapons from foreign countries. Ieyasu's successors banned Japanese nationals from going abroad.

Unlike Elizabeth I, however, Ieyasu adopted quasi-federal arrangements instead of absolutism (Hall, 1991). This choice differentiated Japan from England. Once the country was sealed off from foreign influence by monopolization, the matter of governing had better be left to each domain, as long as each domain was not defiant towards the Tokugawa government. As summarized before, quasi-democratic development in early modern Japan started off in many domains. To summarize Japan's development, disentanglement took place; quasi-federal arrangements developed quite solidly; quasi-democratic development proceeded in many domains. In contrast, in England, disentanglement took place and in tandem absolutism was consolidated (Starkey, 2003). Localist traditions, in the form of class representation in the parliament, died hard. Religious entanglements were embedded with localist traditions and parliamentary representation, hence the establishment of the Anglican Church, headed by the Queen or the King. Its purpose was threefold: (1) to detach England from the Vatican, (2) to reduce antagonism between Catholics and non-Catholics in England, and (3) to disentangle England from the meddling by the Continent and to 'isolate', as it were, the Continent with the fog over the English Channel.

The contrast between the two countries in the modern period is no less striking. In England, democratic development proceeded first by getting the aristocratic voice better heard by the absolutist monarch. It was a backlash against the strong absolutism set up by Elizabeth and other sovereigns who were frustrated by the decentralized English political system, especially in view of the English vulnerability to the balance of power and religious influences from the Continent. As the Parliament expanded its recruiting base in tandem with the industrial revolution and its associated call for better representation, the relationship with the Continent changed: the Anti-Corn Law, a protectionist law, was repealed and free trade enabled England to benefit from it (McCord, 2005) whereas the Royal Navy kept a pre-eminent position in Europe by its offshore balancing policy until the late 19th century (Burne, 1990). All this deepened English democratic development steadily at home (Moore, 1966). In contrast, Japan resolved to open the country and to centralize the political system from the mid-19th century without experiencing absolutism. Yet the drive toward centralization was constrained enormously.

First, government revenue was limited as its revenue depended primarily on landowners' tax and its tariff revenue was zero because Japan was denied tariff autonomy by Western powers from the mid-19th century until 1911. Japan's competitiveness was extremely low for agricultural and industrial products at that time. Second, the decentralized system changed its manifestation from the Tokugawa–domain relationship to the intragovernmental or interbureaucratic agency relationship. In the early modern period the decentralized feature was very strong geographically, whereas in the modern period the decentralized feature manifested itself at the highest level of the government, that is, in the form of quasi-autonomy accorded to each of the bureaucratic agencies and institutions, which enjoyed access to the Emperor in varying degrees. Centralization took place most saliently in the relationship between the central government and local governments. Governors were appointed by the central government, yet, ironically, most of the expenditure items, like compulsory education, were left to local governments. It was not until 1918 that expenditure on compulsory education was shouldered by the central government. Gaps in the quality of teachers revealed themselves embarrassingly from one prefecture to another.

Poor local governments paid teachers a poor salary. In the postal service the central government depended upon the donations from local notables to build post offices throughout the country as the central government did not have sufficient revenues in the formative years of the Meiji Restoration. This became one of the bases of local notables and local assemblies upon which political parties (which by definition were opposition parties for the half a century since 1868) built their political and electoral strength. The influence of designated postal offices which were built on the donations from private individuals is still being felt even after the devastating blows to the post-related vested interests of the postal privatization law legislated in 2005. The strength retained by the early modern-originating decentralized forces was one of the engines of democratization in modern Japan. After all, the Meiji government consisted mostly of former warriors-cum-bureaucrats striving for a rich country and a strong army during the formative half a century since 1868. Agricultural and industrial interests were only gradually being asserted politically. Their assertion accelerated democratization: political participation in the 1880s and 1890s in the first wave; normalization of political parties from mostly opposition parties to intermittently power-holding political parties in the 1900s through the 1920s; expansion of social democratic parties through universal suffrage (enacted in 1925) in the 1930s.

Much was changed by the Occupation by Allied Powers between 1945 and 1952 (Iokibe, 2005). Decentralization of power was one change. It is not a coincidence that the Occupation accelerated democratization. Decentralization or quasi-federalization goes hand in hand with democratization. Governors were not appointed any more. They are now popularly elected. At least one nationally funded university was established in each prefecture. An autonomous prefectural educational commission was established in each prefecture. But two impetuses accelerated a counterstrike in the direction of centralization. The Cold War forced further centralization as it led to having Self Defence Forces. More importantly, the deepening of the developmental state from the 1950s to the 1970s led to further centralization, with its instruments being target investments and subsidies to potential national champions in each of the industrial sectors. With the advent of global financial integration in the mid-1980s and beyond, however, the developmental state slowly but steadily gave in to the tide of globalization through the 2000s (Inoguchi, 2006a). Here decentralization is a key word. As important is 'government deregulation'. The tide of globalization is also a tide of decentralization and further democratization. I will advance this argument further by examining the postal privatization issue that highlighted the structural features related to globalization, federalization and democratization.

## POSTAL PRIVATIZATION

Postal privatization has been prompted essentially by globalizing market forces (Inoguchi, forthcoming). Japan Post has been carrying out a number of diverse tasks including postal service, postal insurance and postal savings. Postal service has been strong only at home. Only from post offices at home can one use its overseas service. Unless the postal service is enhanced for worldwide services, its growth has its limits. Therefore a privatized postal service company is about to be born. Postal insurance and postal savings are areas where foreign companies have been eagerly awaiting further government deregulation to take place. Both handle a huge amount of money. What the postal savings register is the largest in the world. Much of postal insurance and postal savings has been closely tied to government spending as the government uses them as if they are government revenue. The weakness is that the government may not use such money most efficiently and effectively. Hence the imminent birth of privatized postal insurance and a privatized postal savings company. Privatizing and fragmenting the essentially mammoth state company called Japan Post is the first aim of the privatization law. While privatization will deepen and the autonomy of these companies will be enhanced, the aim of the Japanese government is somehow to retain coordination with the government. One of the important aims of the coordination will be not to have those companies purchased by foreign capital beyond a certain level. So the private companies will be allowed to do business but they will not be allowed to create the kind of situation in which foreign capital dominates. To this end enhanced competitiveness will be encouraged. The relationship between the private companies and the government will be like the relationship between the Tokugawa government and 300-odd domains in the early modern centuries. It may be called 'quasi-federal practice in an era of globalization'. I will use my case to further develop my argument about quasi-federal practices and arrangements which are largely ignored by Western scholars.

The general election on 11 September 2005 ended in a resounding victory for the ruling Liberal Democratic Party (Inoguchi, 2006b). When the controversial postal privatization bill was rejected in the House of Councillors on 8 August 2005, Prime Minister Junichiro Koizumi dissolved the House of Representatives right away, saying that, since the National Diet opposed the government policy of postal privatization, he needed to see whether the entire electorate would support him or not. The key campaign issue was deliberately and calculatingly focused on postal privatization. The issue of deregulation in one government sector was in a sense transformed into an issue of confidence in Prime Minister Koizumi. Having seen the sizeable opposition within the Liberal Democratic Party to the postal privatization bill, the largest opposition party, the Democratic Party of Japan, wanted to take advantage of the issue to thwart the bill. However, Koizumi confronted the opposition party by dissolving the House of Representatives and, further, fielding pro-postal privatization candidates in those districts which anti-postal privatization LDP parliamentarians represented and in the entire proportionate representation districts. Campaign-savvy Koizumi effectively stormed his opponents. Not only were many of the anti-postal privatization LDP parliamentarians expelled from the LDP but also many of them were crushingly defeated, along with the opposition party candidates. Postal privatization was legislated in the National Diet session following the general election in October 2005. What does this newly legislated law mean? It means government deregulation, market liberalization and globalization. It also means devolution of central government. Furthermore, it means the deepening of democracy in a sense. It is little more than a first step toward fully fledged deregulation and liberalization. Still it constitutes one of the major watersheds in terms of how to devolve a much overexpanded government bureaucracy, how to meet the steady tide of market globalization and how to meet the demands of an increasingly critical citizenry.

Japan Post was created in 1871. Nowadays it has three key functions: (1) postal communications, (2) postal savings, and (3) postal insurance. Although the modernizing Meiji government wanted to establish a modern postal system, financing the whole operation was not easy. The barely modernizing government lacked revenue sources other than tax on land from landlords, who bitterly resisted the government's efforts at taxation and who sometimes opposed the government's bureaucratic authoritarianism violently, demanding the opening of local assemblies and a national parliament (Banno, 1972). A compromise was struck. What it did was to allow some local notables to acquire a post office master's title in exchange for the offer of space and the establishment of a post office building. They were allowed to put a number of the benefits from postal business into their own pocket. They were also useful to the government in mobilizing and cementing support in elections once local assemblies and the Imperial Diet were opened in the 1880s and 1890, respectively (Ministry of Post, 1992). Even in the 1970s and 1980s, the Liberal Democratic Party was able to count on this post office directors' network to mobilize local votes remarkably effectively (Hirose, 1993).

Through the Japanese Post the government was able to achieve a number of its goals. First, postal communications improved remarkably throughout the country, which had been separated into 300-odd domains. Second, the government was able to seed the local basis of its power, counting increasingly on local notables. Third, the government was able to siphon money to the government purse through postal savings and postal insurance from each and every part of the country. Japan Post had about 13 000 local offices for most of its 135 years. Postal savings and insurance gave the population easy and ubiquitous access in Japan. The modernizing government which desperately needed revenue sources for its modernization found the scheme most effective. The government used the scheme for its infrastructure building purposes in the form of another budget scheme of the government. Without a solid industrial basis until some time after the First World War and without tariff autonomy until 1911, the government needed such a scheme to meet its state-led developmental ambitions. The government did not want the country's financial resources to be diverted into the private sector and was quite determined on this matter especially because its manufacturing sectors were kept poorly developed by the denial of tariff autonomy imposed in 1858. The negative reaction to this liberal trade period of Japanese economic development in 1858–1911 reinforced the determination of leaders to endogenize Japan's industrial capacity in terms of capital and technology and to protect industrial and financial sectors from foreign competition.

The key scheme of Japan Post since 1871 was to use people's savings as state revenue sources for national infrastructural and industrial development and other priorities. Japan Post is the world's number one bank in terms of the amount of savings held. The government has been able to use a vast amount of those savings for the business of the state, but the scheme has become somewhat dysfunctional on a number of fronts. First, Japan Post's predominance has prevented a huge amount of money from flowing into private financial markets; instead it circulates within the government itself. There has been a strong view articulated that a more efficient use of this vast amount of money should be devised.[2] Second, the government priorities of infrastructural and industrial development, such as hydroelectric dams, ports and new bullet trains, have ceased to be the highest priorities and yet the vested interests of the Ministry of Land and Transport have been privileged to spend a great deal of the money.

Pressure has been mounting against what is called the investing and lending programme, the size of which amounts to about half of the ordinary budget. It served the needs of the developmental state in so many splendid ways, but it is now not quite so useful. Why build a new airport amidst rice paddies, and why build a fishery port when fishermen amount to no more than ten families? Third, the government deficits have accumulated to an astronomical degree for the last 15 years, while the Japanese economy experienced one of its longest periods of stagnation. Most of the tax hike initiatives have been killed off or at least stymied for the last 25 years. The two tax hikes in the 1980s and 1990s resulted in the resignation of prime ministers shortly after tax hike legislation. Popular resistance has been very strong. One obvious target for trimming the government is Japan Post, as it employs the largest number of government personnel after the Self Defense Forces (the police are employed by prefectures).

Going more deeply, the Japanese government sees the need to change its expenditure pattern that has much to do with demographic decline (Matsubara, 2004). In 2005, the population started to decrease. While longevity has been on the rise, the number of senior citizens (those who are 65 years old and older) has been increasing, so that they constitute nearly one-third of the entire population. Senior citizens receive a pension and use Medicare, but do not pay much tax. Younger citizens do not necessarily marry in their twenties. They do not produce their children at a rate which will maintain the same level of population. They calculate that marriage costs a lot, as does having children, which often costs a job as well for younger females, since many still believe that children must be taken care of by their mothers without much government help.

In terms of tax revenue, the visible decrease in the size of the productive population (say, 25–55 years old) vis-à-vis senior (65 and older) and younger citizens (25 and under) means that tax revenues have been stagnant for a long time. The prolonged business stagnation of 1991 to 2006 has resulted in a huge accumulation of government deficits. The steady increase in social policy expenditure for the last 25 years, in tandem with the increase in the number of senior citizens, has become so alarming that trimming it has been carried out step by step, yet trimming itself has caused great distress to senior citizens and has been unpopular to the electorate as a whole.

In terms of social policy implementation, it is important to note that much of it rests on the shoulders of local governments. They handle implementation on behalf of the central government and yet local governments do not enjoy much of their own tax revenue sources and are dependent on the transfer of money from the central government. To make things worse from the perspective of local governments, the central government increasingly adopts the scheme of jointly shouldering expenditures in a number of areas where local governments have to bring in their own resources along with the transfer from the central government, even though local governments do not have much tax revenue of their own. Hence local governments have been increasingly vocal about the need to empower them, demanding the shift of taxation authority from central to local governments. A number of equations must be solved, for example: kinds and locations of taxing authority, size of administrative units (central, subnational, grass roots), size of the transfer to local government from the central government, and kinds and locations of policy, planning, implementations and monitoring.

In terms of the health of local government budgets, local governments have been encouraged to merge among themselves to create larger entities so that administrative and personnel expenditures might be trimmed (a large part of which has to do with the relative number of local assemblymen, bureaucrats and servicemen who carry out social and educational policy tasks). Of the 3232 local governments which existed only a decade ago, mergers have left only 1821 in 2006. Emerging on the horizon in tandem with this fast development is the idea of creating from seven to ten regional administrative units by merging four to eight prefectures in each region, Hokkaido, Touhoku, Great Kantou, Tokyo, Chubu, Kansai, Shikoku and Chugoku, Kyushu and Okinawa. Competition is strong among adjacent prefectures in terms of which prefectural capital city should be granted the status and privilege of a regional capital city. This competition in turn speeds up the merger of local governments (Asahi shimbun, 2005).

Furthermore, in parallel with the administrative regionalization initiatives, a scheme has been introduced to elect Lower House members on the proportional representation list on a regional, not national, basis. While those lower house members elected on a 'one person per district' basis represent some 1500 local governments more directly, those lower house members elected on the proportional representation list basis would represent not only national concerns and priorities but also regional ones. The scheme for the latter representation runs closely in parallel with the idea of designating a regional capital city.[3]

At the level of the central government, the administrative reform carried out since 1995 has produced a scheme of merging bureaucratic agencies into a dozen major ones and setting up nine smaller ones. The major bureaucratic agencies includes Welfare, Health and Labor; Education, Science, Sports and Culture; Internal Communications and Affairs; Land and Transport; Agriculture, Fishery and Forestry; Environment; Treasury; Economics and Industry; Foreign Affairs; Justice; Defence; Police. The smaller agencies include Postal Privatization; Science and Technology; Equal Opportunities; State Security; Okinawa and Northern Territories; Administrative Reform; Financial Service Sector; Economic and Financial Policy and Cabinet Legislation.

The thrust of the administrative reform is (1) slimming of personnel and budget size, (2) clearer separation of bureaucratic routines and policy initiatives on some priorities leading to the much sharper and stronger functional division of labour between bureaucratic agencies and the Prime Minister's office on matters to be strategically envisioned and implemented (Shimizu, 2005). The latter includes postal privatization, scientific innovation and gender equality. Also coming to the forefront in policy discussions are official development assistance (now under the Ministry of Foreign Affairs), intelligence (now under a committee of cabinet members) and defence (the Defence Agency was elevated to a Defence Ministry, as a result of which national security has become one of the responsibilities of the Defence Ministry; for now, the Ministry of Foreign Affairs retains its strong responsibility for national security).

## POSTAL PRIVATIZATION GOES WITH GLOBALIZATION AND DEMOCRATIZATION

The implications of postal privatization for the prospects of Japanese quasi-federal practice are simple. Once Japan Post is privatized, competitive and fragmented situations are created in the market. If the precedents of privatization of mammoth Japanese state companies give any hint at the prospects of postal privatization, the Japan National Railway was, perhaps, a good example. It was split into regionally divided private companies which must work in close coordination for transporting operations with each other and yet compete immensely to get profits. The Japan Telephone and Telegraph was split into regionally and functionally different companies which must work competitively with other private companies but which must coordinate somewhat with sister companies if only because they must remain competitive in terms of technological innovation and service provision. Since quasi-federal practice is being envisioned in other areas as well, such as administrative, electoral and educational institutions, postal privatization is more likely to constitute part of the greater pressure for the quasi-federalization of the Japanese society and politics.

In this section I focus on the two contexts of globalization and democratization in relation to postal privatization. Globalization is defined here as the two-way process of fragmenting the national economies into much smaller subunits and re-integrating some of those subunits with other similarly vibrating subunits in other national economies into the global economy (Rosenau, 2002). The level of technology in communications and transportation has made an astronomical advance in the last quarter of the 20th century, which has been a key driver of what is called globalization. Those areas which have not kept abreast of these advances in terms of technology and sustaining infrastructure and services tend to lag behind and become marginalized, while those which have on the whole kept up with these advances tend to flourish. This process is called fragmentation. Fragmentation takes place in nationally organized territorial states. Re-integration takes place in linking those places that have kept abreast with the tide of the era across nation-states. These are the two faces of the globalization phenomena. Since areas that have kept pace with the tide of globalization are in close contact when they are geographically adjacent, regionalization is bound to take place (Katzenstein, 2005). In efforts at expanding markets, regionalization takes place because open and free trade links spots closely.

Kenichi Ohmae (1996) was the first author to point to the primordial importance of regionalization. *Beyond the Nation-State* discusses how Japan divides itself into a few regions, at the same time connecting with other regions in adjacent countries of East and Southeast Asia. Ohmae saw the emerging trend as early as the early 1990s. Ohmae talks about regionalization at two levels: at the sub-national level and at the sub-global level. He envisaged the tide of globalization as facilitating economic transactions, for example, between Naha and Amoy, between Kitakyushu and Busan, between Kobe and Tianjin, between Niigata and Vladivostok, between Inchon and Qingdao, between Dalian and Shanghai. In other words, the hegemonic role of the territorial sovereign state is envisaged as breaking up. The decline of the role of the sovereign state is accompanied by the functional quasi-integration of sub-national units bringing about the creation of sub-global units, here and there. In tandem with the creation of sub-global units which is sometimes called regionalization, administrative and political units are gradually collated. In other words, a very loose, open and weak form of federalism is being forged at various levels. This is the message from Kenichi Ohmae. He was very prescient in light of the evolution that has been taking place very fast in this part of the world.

Democratization is facilitated by privatization. Postal privatization gives rise to the reduction of the power of the sovereign state to a certain degree. By 'a certain degree' I mean that the power of the sovereign state retreats somewhat and puts itself at the mercy of global market forces, on the one hand (Strange, 1996) while on the other hand the sovereign state tries to compete with global market forces and thereby tries to retain its strength by way of shaping the spirit and design of a company as well as legislating the rules affecting such a company. Postal privatization is a complex process. At the first stage the three key functions of the old Japan Post will be separated into three companies, each dealing with postal communications, postal savings and postal insurance, respectively. In all areas, market forces are bound to increase. The dominance of the sovereign state in Japan was reinforced by the idea of state-led developmentalism (Johnson, 1982; Inoguchi, 2006a), that is, the idea that the government should be a primary designer and player in shaping national economic development on the basis of its own capital, technology, labour, rules and institutions. Yet the heyday of state developmentalism is clearly over. Non-governmental forces have been steadily increasing. Privatization permeates not only business but also politics.[4] With the recession of state developmentalism those bureaucratic agencies that claimed to guide national economic development have visibly lost their authority and power in politics. The days are gone when the Economic Planning Agency, Finance, International Trade and Industry were regarded as the flag carriers of national economic advances and management.

National economic development has become largely a matter of business. The business of the state used to be business. But the business of the state now places its emphasis on designing and monitoring norms and rules pertaining to each policy area in forms that are congruent with the ones internationally agreed and practised (Inoguchi, 2006b). Also the government has to place enormous emphasis on its own transparency and accountability (Transparency International, http://www.transparency.org/). With these and other changes, democratization deepens. Japan is not an exception.

## CONCLUSION

Japan presents a uniquely Asian way of federalization. The contour of Japanese history for the past 500 years enables one to realize that Japan has two traditions, unitary and federal, in its political arrangements. The early modern period pushed forward its federal direction while the modern period intensified the unitary direction. The argument of this chapter is that the still uncertain mix of these traditions that is in the making, in meeting the two major challenges of what might be called the post-modern period, the deepening tide of globalization and the steady accumulation of critical citizens, presents a fascinating picture of federalization, Asian style.

Conclusion one is that the quasi-federal arrangements remained resilient after 1868 despite the Meiji Restoration's strong aspiration to become a unitary centralized state. To the West, Japan has given the overtly simplified picture of a centralized unitary state largely because Westerners have tended to focus their reading on the modern period since 1868 and especially the post-World War period since 1945 (O'Dywer, 2005). Their horizon has not gone back to the early modern period during which many of the key features of the Japanese political system we are accustomed to take for granted were shaped. This is clear from key Western writings on Japanese politics. They take it for granted that Japan, as they understand it, 'started' only in 1868 or in 1945. This is unfortunate. This tendency has reinforced the image of Japan as being a unitary and centralized state embarking on the path of modernization and industrialization. The image of a modernizing authoritarian state was impressed on the minds of many Westerners. As a matter of fact, the Imperial Constitution prescribed a fairly decentralized picture at the highest level. The monarch sat at the top, but very many had access to the ear of the Emperor. First of all, the Prime Minister was a *primus inter pares*. One cabinet minister's dissent could easily topple the government. The Imperial Army and Navy were directly responsible to the Emperor. So was the Privy Council. So were a bundle of senior statesmen.

Second, each of the bureaucratic agencies of the central government were almost sovereign. They enjoyed their own autonomy in much the same way as the 300-odd domains enjoyed their autonomy in the early modern period. There are two gatekeepers to force compromises with their autonomy. One is the Cabinet Legislative Bureau, an agency which checks a legislative bill drafted by a bureaucratic agency in terms of whether there are inconsistencies of the bill with all the existing laws and the Constitution. The other is the Ministry of Treasury, which checks the bill in terms of whether its budgetary implications can be accommodated or not by state finance. Needless to say, other gatekeepers did exist, as described above. In the early period immediately after 1868, it was not uncommon to find that some ministries retained some geographical features. After all, the Meiji Restoration started as a military coup d'état of small bands of warriors-cum-bureaucrats drawn largely from the two peripheralized domains of

Choshu and Satsuma. The former took in the Army, the latter the Navy. Prime Ministers were more or less alternated between them in the early years. The major anti-government armed rebellion originating from the former reduced the power of the latter in subsequent years. This almost explains why Choshu has given birth to many Prime Ministers in modern Japanese politics. Any geographical features attached to bureaucratic agencies, however, were more or less lost by 1945.

Conclusion two is that all the emphasis on authoritarianism reinforced by such drivers as the strong aspiration to achieve a strong army and a rich country cannot hide the undercurrent of quasi-democratic arrangements originating from the early modern period. Shortly after successfully suppressing the major anti-government rebellion in 1876, the government moved ahead to heal the wounds of local notables from their heavy tax burdens and of former warriors-cum-bureaucrats for their having no jobs, by announcing the opening of local assemblies, the establishing of political parties and the promulgation of a Constitution. The government realized painfully but very clearly that, without mobilizing the support and resources from below, the government could not achieve much of what it wanted to achieve. The tradition of decentralized and quasi-democratic arrangements worked well in the government's establishing modern parliamentary democracy under the monarch. It was assiduous and agile also in such tasks as co-opting landowners for taxation, giving bureaucratic positions to local notables in the postal service and giving job opportunities as policemen and soldiers to jobless former warriors-cum-bureaucrats. Democratization went on more or less continuously from 1876, first, with democratic participation (1880s and 1890s), second, with democratic contestation (1900s to 1920s) and democratic consolidation (1930s). The rise of military dictatorship and authoritarian politics in the wartime period did not hide the continuous democratic practice through the 1930s.

Conclusion three is that, in the postmodern period, the relentless tide of globalization and the emergence of increasingly critical citizens pose two major challenges. Japanese political arrangements have to mix the two traditions in a most calculated way, as in the revival of the early modern arrangement of the relationship between the Tokugawa government and 300-odd localities. The prospect for Japan's quasi-federalization is not dim. Rather, it is very strong. One of the manifestations of the Japanese approach of mixing the traditions is examined in the initial phase of the legislation of postal privatization and associated politics. Bureaucracy reduces its power. Politics is given more space. Meeting the challenge of globalization requires astute calculation and agile action. Otherwise, increasingly critical citizens, now bereft of state developmentalism's networks, can act violently against the government, with their instinctive apprehension that the tide of globalization destroys the fruits of their democratic achievements. The summer–autumn of 2005 showed that citizens can be persuaded, even when the medicine is bitter, at least in the short run.

## NOTES

1. For the most helpful comments by the participants of the Melbourne workshop, especially Baogang He and John Uhr, I am most grateful. I am also grateful for the support from the Ministry of Education and Science for the grant I received, project number 17002002 (2005–09) and to the Mitsubishi Foundation for the grant I received.
2. This is best represented by Heizo Takenaka, a Cabinet member of the Koizumi government. It is also succinctly articulated by the United States Government in its annual list of requests to the Japanese Government.
3. The general election on 11 September 2005 was the first general election, the campaigns in which reminded one of this parallelism.
4. How globalization has an impact on democracy has been examined on the basis of the 18-country (nine from Asia and nine from Europe) cross-national survey of 2000. See Inoguchi Takashi (2004). The results are moderately positive, although more empirical examinations are necessary to have stronger results. See also Daron Acemoglu and James A. Robinson (2006).

## REFERENCES

Acemoglu, Daron and James A. Robinson (2006), *Economic Origins of Dictatorship and Democracy*, Cambridge: MIT Press.

Akita, George (1967), *Foundations of Constitutional Government in Modern Japan 1868–1900*, Cambridge: Harvard University Press.

Anderson, Perry (1979), *Lineages of the Absolutist State*, London: Verso.

Asahi, Shimbun (2005), *Heisei daigappei* (Great Merger of local governments during the Heisei), 4 December.

Banno, Junji (1972), *Meiji kempo taisei no seiritsu* (The Establishment of the Meiji Constitutional System), Tokyo: University of Tokyo Press.

Banno, Junji (2005), *Meiji Demokurashi* (Meiji Democracy), Tokyo: Iwanami shoten.

Burne, Kenneth (1970), *The Foreign Policy of Victorian England 1830–1902*, Oxford: Oxford University Press.

Hall, John Whitney (ed.) (1991), *The Cambridge History of Japan, vol.4: Early Modern Japan*, Cambridge: Cambridge University Press.

Hanley, Susan and Kozo Yamamura (1986), *Economic and Demographic Change in Japan 1600–1868*, Princeton: Princeton University Press.

Hayami, Akira (1992), *Kinsei Nobi Chiho no jinko, keizai, shakai* (The Population, Economy, and Society of Nobi in Early Modern Period), Tokyo: Sobunsha.

Hirose, Michisada (1993), *Hojokin to seikento* (Subsidies and the Governing Party), Tokyo: Asahi shimbunsha.

Ikegami, Eiko (1995), *Taming the Samurai*, Cambridge: Harvard University Press.

Inoguchi, Takashi (1997), 'The pragmatic evolution of Japanese democratic politics', in Michele Schmiegelow (ed.), *Democracy in Asia*, New York, St Martin's Press, pp. 217–31.

Inoguchi, Takashi (2004), 'Globalization wa yoi governance o motarasuka (Does Globalization Bring About Good Governance)', *Nempo seijigaku* (Annals of Political Science), pp. 199–227.

Inoguchi, Takashi (2005a), *Japanese Politics: An Introduction*, Melbourne: Trans Pacific Press.

Inoguchi, Takashi (2005b), 'Korea in Japanese visions of regional order', in Charles Armstrong et al. (eds), *Korea at the Center*, New York: M.E. Sharpe.

Inoguchi, Takashi (2006a), 'Has Japan ceased to be a magnet in Asia?', in Ian Marsh (ed.), *Democratization, Regionalism and Governance in East and Southeast Asia*, London: Routledge, pp. 204–22.

Inoguchi, Takashi (2006b), 'Bilateralism at any cost?', in G. John Ikenberry and Takashi Inoguchi (eds), *The Uses of Institutions*, New York: Palgrave, pp. 51–3.

Inoguchi, Takashi (2006c), 'Japanese foreign policy toward Asia in the 1980s', in Gilbert Rozman et al. (eds), *Japanese Strategic Thought*, New York: M.E. Sharpe, pp. 35–55.

Inoguchi, Takashi (forthcoming), 'Japanese politics – towards a new interpretation', in Heita Kawakatsu and Rien Segers, *Towards a New Japan?*, Kyoto: International Research Center for Japanese Studies.

Inoguchi, Takashi et al. (eds) (2005), *Values and Lifestyles in Urban Asia: A Cross-Cultural Analysis and Sourcebook Based on the AsiaBarometer Survey of 2003*, Mexico: Siglo XXI.

Inoguchi, Takashi (2006), *Human Beliefs and Values in Striding Asia – East Asia in Focus: Country Profile, Thematic Analyses and Sourcebook Based on the AsiaBarometer of 2004*, Tokyo: Akashi shoten.

Iokibe, Makoto (2005), *Nichibei senso to sengo nihon* (The Japan–U.S. War and Post War Japan), Tokyo: Kodansha.

Jansen, Marius and Gilbert Rozman (eds) (1986), *Japan in Transition*, Princeton: Princeton University Press.

Johnson, Chalmers (1982), *MITI and the Economic Miracle*, Stanford: Stanford University Press.

Kasaya, Kazuhiko (1989), *Shukun oshikome no kozu* (Lord Locked In), Tokyo: Yoshikawa kobunkan.

Katzenstein, Peter (2005), *A World of Regions*, Ithaca: Cornell University Press.

Mansfield, Edward and Jack Snyder (2006), *Electing to Fight: Why Emerging Democracies Go to War*, Cambridge: MIT Press.

Matsubara, Satoshi (2004), *Jinko gensho jidai no seisaku kagaku* (Policy Science in an Era of Demographic Decline), Tokyo: Iwanami shoten.

McCord, Norman (2005), *The Anti-Corn Law League 1838–1946*, London: Routledge.

Ministry of Post (ed.) (1972), *Yusei hyakunenshi nempo* (A Historical Table of the Hundred Year History of the Postal Policy), Tokyo: Yoshikawa kobunkan.

Ministry of Post (ed.) (1992), *Yubin sogyo 120 nen no rekshi* (A 120 Year History of Postal Service), Tokyo: Gyosei.

Moore, Barrington (1966), *The Social Origins of Democracy and Dictatorship*, Boston: Beacon Press.

O'Dywer, Jane (2005), 'Inoguchi pens a timely guide to Japan's political theater', *The Daily Yomiuri*, 28 August.

Ohmae, Kenichi (1996), *End of the Nation-State: The Rise of Regional Economies*, New York: Touchstone Books.

Parker, Geoffrey (1996), *The Military Revolution: Military Innovation and the Rise of the West, 1500–1800*, Cambridge: Cambridge University Press.

Ravina, Mark (1999), *Land and Lordship in Early Modern Japan*, Stanford: Stanford University Press.

Rosenau, James (2002), *Distant Dynamics: Dynamics beyond Globalization*, New York: Cambridge University Press.

Shimizu, Mahito (2005), *Kantei shudo: Koizumi Junichiro no kakumei* (Prime Minister's Office Leads: Koizumi's Revolution), Tokyo: Nihon keizai shimbun.

Starkey, David (2003), *Elizabeth I*, London: Chatto and Windus.

Strange, Susan (1996), *The Retreat of the State*, Cambridge: Cambridge University Press.

Toby, Ronald (1984), *State and Diplomacy in the Tokugawa Bakufu*, Princeton: Princeton University Press.

Transparency International (2006), http://www.transparency.org/.

Whitehead, Laurence (2002), *Democratization: Theory and Experience*, Oxford: Oxford University Press.

# 13. Federalism and Asia

## Brian Galligan

There has been an international resurgence of interest in federalism, both theoretical and as an institutional means of achieving decentralized government as well as providing for multinational representation within and among nations (Ferejohn and Weingast, 1997; Frey and Eichenberger, 1999; Lazar, Telford and Watts, 2003; Filippov, Ordeshook and Shvetsova, 2004; Imbeau and Petry, 2004; Ortino, Zagar and Mastny, 2005; Orbinger, Leibfried and Castles, 2005; Ahmad and Brosio, 2006). This is most evident in the institutional reconfiguration of Europe which is at the 'epicentre' of a worldwide 'federalizing tendency' (Russell, 2005, p. 13). While the European Union is not strictly a federation, and many Europeans shy away from using the term to describe their increasingly integrated political and economic arrangements, the European sphere of governance is shaping up as a new model of transnational federalism. Federalism remains a defining feature of many national systems of government and is spreading to others. During the last half-century, federalism has continued as a defining, although changing, feature of well-established federations such as the United States, Switzerland, Canada and Australia, and has been re-established in Germany and Austria, countries with long federal traditions, after the Second World War. Some unitary countries have become more federal, most notably Spain, with autonomous regional communities, Belgium, in accommodating its distinct French and Dutch-speaking peoples, and Great Britain with devolution to Scotland, Wales and Northern Ireland. Russia is unusual but has also embraced aspects of federalism in its transition from Communist centralism. But these are all European or Anglo-American countries.

Federalism has not fared so well in the rest of the world; nor has it been embraced with the same enthusiasm as a constitutional foundation for decentralized government or for accommodating multi-ethnic diversity within nations. India is the outstanding exception in Asia with its vibrant federal system, and to some extent Malaysia and Pakistan that both have quasi-federal systems. In Latin America, Argentina, Brazil, Venezuela and Mexico have important federal features, as do South Africa, Nigeria and, now, Ethiopia in Africa. Nevertheless, the question as to why federalism flourishes more in certain countries rather than others is a crucial one.

Aggregate studies of federalism have tended to wash out this uneven pattern of take-up and success among different sorts of countries and between different continents. This is due to their methodology of assessing particular countries on a case-by-case basis against a set of standard federal features and deciding whether each has the necessary institutional attributes to qualify as federal or quasi-federal. Leading comparative scholars like Ron Watts and Daniel Elazar have been concerned with the organizational definition of federalism, and with the individual classification of countries and compiling an overall list of federal ones. A comprehensive overview by Ron Watts lists 24 federal countries with about 40 per cent of the world's population, although the bulk of these live in India (Watts, 1999, pp. 8–10). Watts' list includes quasi-federations or hybrids that, as he specifies, are 'predominantly federations in their constitutions and operation but which have some overriding federal government powers more typical of a unitary system'. Examples are India, Pakistan and Malaysia, because of their overriding central emergency powers, and South Africa, that retains some unitary features. Watts builds on Elazar's earlier 1987 list (1987, pp. 43–4), adding the recently formed federations of Belgium, Spain and South Africa, and the two tiny island federations of St. Kitts and Nevis, and Micronesia, as well as Ethiopia. The collapse of Yugoslavia has reduced Watts' list to 23.

Comparative studies of federalism typically focus upon the established federations where federal institutional features and processes are most prominent: the Anglo-American ones, Australia, Canada and the United States; and the European ones, Germany, Switzerland and, to a lesser extent, Austria. This is to be expected if we are concerned with analysing the distinctive features common to federalism that will likely be more prominent in well established and functioning federations (Galligan, 2006). It is also appropriate if we are assessing how federalism affects policy processes – for example, whether it facilitates policy innovation or restricts the adoption of welfare state policies (see Obinger, Leibfried and Castles, 2005). Having similar functioning federal systems with historical experience of implementing a particular set of policies is necessary for such investigation. It is not the purpose of such studies to tell us why federalism is strong in the federal countries studied, and not in other countries that are not included precisely because they are not federal or have weak or partial federal traditions.

Federalism's current resurgence is in part due to its compatibility with the new world order and the demise of national sovereignty orthodoxy. The world environment has changed from the twentieth century's primary focus on national sovereignty and centralized government to the twenty-first century's concern with cosmopolitanism, interdependency and multiple sphere government. This is especially the case in Europe where national sovereignty has been sacrificed to membership in a transnational association of nation states. If federalism was at risk in the mid-twentieth century world of nation building and sovereign nation states, it is more likely to thrive in the twenty-first century of complex interdependency, multiple citizenship allegiances, interdependent and overlapping jurisdictions and multiple centres of law and policy making. Watts identifies a 'paradigm shift . . . from a world of sovereign nation-states to a world of diminished state sovereignty and increased interstate linkages of a constitutionally federal character' (Watts, 1999, p. ix). Imbeau (2004) claims that federal systems can provide 'working models' of a new world order. How modern globalization affects federal systems is an important consideration for federal scholars (see Lazar, Telford and Watts, 2003), but again the focus is upon established federations, and mainly the well-established Anglo-American and European ones. In the extensive literature on federalism, there has been little systematic focus upon Asian countries.

This chapter puts the discussion of federalism back into a broader historical and comparative perspective, showing that it serves multiple purposes, only one of which is multinational governance. Constitutional federalism allows for decentralization and complexity of government, and works best in liberal democratic political cultures characterized by tolerance and commitment to limited government. To work at all, federalism requires some significant presence of factors that will support a complex system of divided and limited government. Such an account of constitutional federalism draws upon the traditional meaning of federalism in Western political thought and constitutional design. It articulates some of the main attributes or propensities that have been identified in, or claimed by studies of, federalism. From this we can derive a more comprehensive understanding of the complexities of federalism that help our investigation of why federalism has not been so prominent in Asian countries, and where it has and why that has been the case. The chapter ends with some concluding observations on federalism in Asia.

## CONSTITUTIONAL FEDERALISM

Federalism is characterized by two spheres of government, national and state, operating in the one political entity according to defined arrangements for sharing powers so that neither is sovereign over the other. According to William Riker's definition, 'the activities of government are divided between regional governments and a central government in such a way that each kind of government has some activities on which it makes final decisions' (Riker, 1975, p. 101). For Daniel Elazar, 'the constituting elements in a federal arrangement share in the processes of common policy making and administration by right, while the activities of the common government are conducted in such a way as to maintain their respective integrities'. Elazar summed this up in the neat epigram *'self-rule plus shared rule'* (Elazar, 1987, p. 12) – self-rule in regional communities and shared rule at the national level. Implicit in these definitions, and essential to federalism in its traditional form, is a common territorial base that is both a national entity for one level of government and a contiguous number of distinct regional entities for other government purposes.

Whether we take my opening definition of 'two spheres of government, national and state, operating in the one political entity according to defined arrangements for sharing powers so that neither is sovereign over the other' or that of Riker or Elazar, the basic meaning is clear: this is a constitutional system of dual spheres of government with powers divided between them (see also Wheare, 1963; Sawer, 1976; Davis, 1978) for the complex intergovernmental mixing and mingling that federalism entails (Grodzins, 1966). The set of essential federal institutions that writers typically identify are the organizational means for putting such a system into political practice. The three key ones are a written constitution that defines the respective powers of the two spheres of government and is hard to amend, a bicameral legislature with a strong federal chamber representing the constituent states or provinces, and a constitutional court to resolve jurisdictional disputes and keep governments within their constitutional limits. A fourth one, that concerns us less here, is a system of intergovernmental institutions to facilitate collaboration between governments in areas of shared or overlapping jurisdiction (Galligan, 2006). While this set of institutions is widely considered to be the institutional hallmark of a federal system, none of them is exclusively federal. Unitary constitutions like that of Japan, for instance, have bicameralism and deeply entrenched constitutionalism.

Federalism requires more than this set of political institutions because effective institutions do not work as paper prescriptions or in a cultural and historical vacuum. Rather, living constitutions that order political life are embedded in supportive political cultures that sustain them. They embody certain political values that they represent and reinforce in political practice. There is a symbiotic interrelationship between effective institutions and the norms and values of the polity they serve. Even more so, institutional theorists define institutions in the broadest sense as 'stable, valued, recurring patterns of behavior' (Huntington, 1968, p. 12, quoted in

Goodin, 1996, p. 21). In this sense, constitutional federalism is a stable, valued and recurring pattern of complex governance by multiple governments of limited powers. It requires a level of sophistication and moderation on the part of political leaders, and also on the part of individual citizens and groups. To a considerable but varying degree, the norms and values of federal constitutionalism have to be sufficiently internalized in the polity and among its political leaders. 'A well-designed institution', as Robert Goodin points out, is 'one that is both internally consistent and externally in harmony with the rest of the social order in which it is set' (Goodin, 1996, p. 37). This is especially the case for a federal constitution that divides political activity and policy making between different levels of government, and limits the powers of each.

The modern federal paradigm was set by the American founders who added an overlay of national government directly accountable to the people to the old federal form that was essentially a league or confederation of distinct political entities. The old federal form of a league or confederation of member states was a system for sharing certain matters of collective decision making, often for strategic or trade purposes. A more substantial account of an older version of federalism was Johannes Althusius' notion of an association of associations (Carney, 1965). Confederation was the institutional form of the earlier American Articles of Confederation that provided a weak form of national government, unsuited to raising taxes and armies necessary to fight the American War of Independence. The American colonies declared their independence from Britain and united in a strategic alliance to conduct the war and pursue common policies especially in international affairs, but the central institutions were made up of delegates from the member colonies and directly answerable to their home colony. Needless to say, this made for a rather weak central authority that was constrained in its decision making.

In 1787, the American constitutional founders restructured federalism, strengthening central government through making its key offices independent of the member states and directly responsible to the people. The Americans' redesign of traditional federalism to incorporate a national level of unitary government was highly pragmatic, as it retained the established self-governing colonies as quasi-sovereign states while at the same time limiting their powers and adding a new level of national government. The new sphere of national government was far stronger than in the older confederation because it was made directly accountable to the people, who in this federal republic were the sovereign body. It would be better equipped to act with authority and dispatch in areas of vital national interest such as defence, diplomacy and trade. But it was also constrained and its powers curbed by the basic federal structure that entailed the allocation of specified powers, with the balance remaining under independent state juris-diction. The national government was restrained further through the well-known system of checks and balances in having the legislature, executive and judiciary separately constituted, the legislature bicameral with the Senate constituted by representatives of the states, and a powerful court to uphold the constitution that underpinned this elaborate institutional design. The institutional detail and theoretical justification for what was a novel exercise in constitutional federalism received its classic articulation in the *Federalist Papers*. The Americans had created a 'compound' or 'com-posite' system that combined smaller states in a federal arrangement, but reinforced that with features of national unitary government (Diamond, 1961). Alexis de Tocqueville affirmed this American innovation in federal constitutional design: it 'rests in truth upon a wholly novel theory, which may be considered as a great discovery in modern political science' – namely making citizens, rather than states or societies, members of the national union (Tocqueville [1835] 1945, p. 162).

American federalism was not simply a clever constitutional means of uniting existing smaller states into a viable nation; it was also a way of ensur-ing stable democracy over a geographically large area with diverse political economies. From classical Greek times and as recently as in the writings of Rousseau on the eve of American federation, political theorists had main-tained that democracy was possible only in small states that had a large measure of equality in social rank and material goods. Rousseau thought that democracy required 'many things that are difficult to have at the same time': 'First, a very small state, where the people may be readily assembled and where each citizen may easily know all the others. Secondly, a great sim-plicity of manners and morals, to prevent excessive business and thorny dis-cussions. Thirdly, a large measure of equality in social rank and fortune, without which equality in rights and authority will not last long' ([1792] 1968, p. 113). This was vastly different from the large and diverse American republic that representative democracy and federalism allowed. In addition, history seemed to show that, when democracies existed, they tended to be faction-ridden and short-lived. By substituting representative democracy for direct participation of citizens in government decision making and enlarging the area of the state, thereby introducing a greater number and variety of interests and groups, the American founders both stabilized democratic governance and provided an alternative model of strong, but at the same time decentralized, government for large states. The institutional key to this ingenious solution was federalism, and so successful was the American experiment that their innovation became the new federal paradigm.

A key feature of this new federalism was dual citizenship; individual citizens had membership of the new national union and continuing

membership of the older and smaller state unions. This was a major innovation not only in institutional design but also in popular government.
Indeed, the two are inextricably linked with the two spheres of government
being independently based in popular sovereignty (Beer, 1993). Obviously,
such dual citizenship requires special qualities or public virtues on the part
of its individual citizens and civil society groups, most importantly moderation and pluralism. To retain dual allegiance to both nation and regional
state, individuals and groups cannot have a single overriding commitment
to, or identification with, one cause. Single-minded commitment to a
regional ethnic or religious group, on the one hand, or national unity that
would override such regional alliance, or the other, are equally antithetical
to federalism. For example, Lowi (1984) explains how federalism made
socialism unlikely in the United States. Successful federalism requires
robust democracy in which citizens share membership of two political communities and participate politically in both. The corollary requirement of
such dual citizenship is real but moderate attachment to both spheres of
government. Federalism presupposes a sophisticated citizenry with multiple allegiances and a constitutional culture of limited government
(Sharman, 1990). Clearly, it is not for everyone and does not suit some
countries without at least some basic elements of diversity and moderation
in their political histories and cultures.

## MULTINATIONAL FEDERALISM

Will Kymlicka provides an alternative view of federalism in Chapter 2 of
the present volume and in his previous contribution to *Multiculturalism in
Asia* (2005) that he edited with Baogang He. This is summed up in the term
'multinational federalism', which he defines as 'creating a federal or quasi-
federal subunit in which the minority group forms a local majority, and so
can exercise meaningful forms of self-government', and where 'the group's
language is typically recognized as an official state language, at least within
their federal subunit, and perhaps throughout the country as a whole'
(ibid., pp. 23–4). Security concerns that such groups might collaborate with
foreign countries of similar ethnoculture, however, have dampened the
enthusiasm for federalism in many multicultural countries, especially in
Asia. How federalism serves multinational representation is a key question
both for federal theory and also for assessing federalism in Asia. What is
proposed here is an alternative view of how federalism might best serve a
multinational purpose: by *intra-state* interactions between different ethnic
communities rather than *inter-state* representation of the dominant ones.
But first we need to examine the tradition of using sub-national states to

represent ethnic communities that are dominant in their local region but a minority within the larger nation.

Although he does not claim the lineage, Kymlicka's multinational take on federalism has some similarity with an earlier sociological view that federalism was a consequence of ethnically diverse societies. The most notable proponent of this view was William Livingston, who claimed, 'Federalism was a function not of constitutions but of societies' (1956, p. 4). In this functionalist view, institutional form was derived from, and needed to be grounded in, distinctive societal character and perform a related function. Federalism seemed tailor-made for a country made up of ethnically diverse societies, or, in Kymlicka's terms, multiple nations. It would provide an institutional basis for their political organization and representation, while at the same time allowing unity and a national government at the aggregate level. William Riker's earlier reflections on federalism were based on a similar sociological rationale: he questioned why Australia bothered with federalism when it had no ethnically based differences (1964) and argued federalism was trivial without such differences (1970). Riker, however, was to change his mind about federalism, moving from sociological to institutional explanations, and from being a New Dealer critic to an advocate concerned with big government (1975; 1987, pp. xii–xiii). Riker concluded his federal odyssey on a traditional note that vindicated Madison and the American founders: 'Taking together all federations in the world at all times, I believe that federalism has been a significant force for limited government and hence for personal freedom' (1993, p. 513).

The well recognized problem of using federalism to provide an institutional basis for ethnically distinct peoples is well known: it can also facilitate secession. Depending on the circumstances and the kind and relative strength of the ethnic allegiances and divisions, 'federalism can either exacerbate or mitigate ethnic conflict', as Donald Horowitz has pointed out (1985, p. 603). This is true not only for developing and newly democratizing countries, but also for the heartland federations of North America, as Lawrence Anderson points out in a recent study: 'Federalism may actually whet a given region's appetite for secession by creating opportunities for conflict and providing the region with the opportunity and the institutions needed to mobilize support for secession' (Anderson, 2004, p. 96). Secession of the Southern states of the United States and Canada's long-standing national crisis with Quebec separatism are illustrative cases. Studies of failed federations and attempts to deal with regions of ethnic conflict provide further evidence of this dangerous aspect of federalism (Dorff, 1994). Federalism is in trouble where there is too little national sense among the people, and too sharp differences among regionally based ethnic, religious and linguistic groups. The continuing crisis of Canadian federalism is a consequence of both: Canadians never properly constituted themselves as a sovereign people, according to Peter Russell (2004), and there has been a lasting struggle to head off Quebec separatism that has periodically threatened the nation (Smiley, 1980). Yet Canada and the United States are two of the handful of leading federal countries. Not surprisingly, federalism has failed in countries with shorter and more turbulent political histories. Examples abound in post-colonial federations hastily drawn up by retreating European powers (Franck, 1968), or in the recent failure of Yugoslavia where, as Mitja Zagar (2005, p. 123) explains: 'The existing constitutional and political system failed to provide for the necessary cohesion of the multiethnic Yugoslav community.'

Nevertheless, providing an institutional outlet for sub-nationally distinct peoples as in Switzerland, Canada, Belgium and India is one of a number of purposes that federalism serves. In the cases of Canada and, especially, India, federalism also allows a combination of national and decentralized government in geographically large and diverse countries. But despite the periodic crises of Canadian federalism and the newness of Belgian federalism, this is a proven purpose and, where it works, a significant achievement of federalism. We need to explore how federalism serves this second major purpose of providing a system of government suited to multinational countries. In other words, how does multinational federalism fit with constitutional federalism? As suggested above, constitutional federalism works best in pluralist countries with multiple interests. Multinational federalism works best through representing and accommodating multinational communities within the sub-national unit or regional state; that is, through intra-state rather than inter-state multiculturalism.

Kymlicka has summed up why Western countries have embraced multinational federalism and Asian nations, by and large, have not. In a nutshell, Western acceptance of multinational federalism is due to three factors: one, the absence of security threats from an adjacent nation with the same ethnic composition as the bordering sub-national group; two, a deep consensus across ethno-national lines on basic liberal democratic values and human rights; and three, an acceptance all round that the distinct ethnic groups will endure. In contrast, Asian countries that eschew federalism have opposite beliefs on all three points: one, there are apparent security threats from minority ethnic groups; two, it is doubtful that such groups will respect democratic values and human rights; and three, there is the belief that such groups can be made to integrate and blend into the larger nation. National security, deep consensus on liberal democratic values and the relative strength and concentration of ethnically distinct minorities are major factors in explaining why certain multinational countries embrace federalism and others eschew it.

Multinational federalism, however, is not some novel institutional structure but simply the utilization of constitutional federalism for a multinational purpose. Nor is this something new, as the venerable Swiss federation and also Canada attest. If there is greater opportunity now for employing federalism in this way, it is in countries and continental regions where there are no security risks and deep consensus on liberal democratic values and respect for human rights, including the recognition of and tolerance for ethnic differences. The main theatre for new multinational federations is Europe where the European Union has ensured joint security and reduced the sovereign independence of nation states. Moreover, there is a deep consensus on liberal democratic values. As Europe itself takes on the form of a transnational federation, it is not surprising that its multinational member states like Belgium and Spain will see federalism as an attractive domestic constitutional structure. Countries without an overarching transnational association to ensure national security and without a deep consensus on liberal democratic values will not be drawn to federalism in the same way.

Moreover, if there is a deep consensus on liberal democratic values, Kymlicka's multinational federal model – having regional state boundaries coincide with ethnic fault lines and state institutions represent distinctive ethnic communities – is rather a special case, and one fraught with secessionist tendencies even in mature federations like Canada. It would be more appropriate on liberal democratic grounds and more conducive to political stability to have multiculturalism working at the sub-national state level. Ethnically distinct regions are invariably not monocultural but will usually be interspersed with other sub-minority ethnic communities or minority groups of the nationally dominant group. These should have representation and language rights at that sub-national level, just as the dominant ethnic group in the regional state should have representation and language rights in the larger national sphere. Federalism works best where this is the case: it has a salutary moderating influence as well as ensuring greater political representation for all ethnic groups by virtue of providing an additional regional as well as a national sphere of government. This is more in keeping with the traditional theory of federalism and accords with David Brown's preference for regional federalism that promotes intra-state political and civil interactions between diverse ethnic communities at the sub-national state level, set out in Chapter 3. It is also the ideal, and more often than not the case, for Indian federalism that Gurpreet Mahajan describes in Chapter 4.

Finally, in all our discussions we do need to keep in mind that federalism is not a functional necessity for any society but a matter of historical contingency and political choice. Depending on its historical legacy, political culture, strategic location and contemporary politics, a country might or might not choose constitutional federalism. The three factors that Kymlicka articulates for explaining multinational federalism are necessary but not sufficient ones. A multinational country might have all of these and not adopt federalism; just as a large and diverse country that is not multinational might also not adopt federalism to serve the purpose of decentralizing government. Republican France founded in a revolutionary manner according to radical democratic principles is an unlikely candidate for federalism. For centuries prior to Communist Party rule, Russia was a highly centralized state and the antithesis of federalism. Perhaps more surprisingly, Britain retained its unitary system for centuries despite its distinctive Scottish, Irish and Welsh nations, and has only recently gone some way towards partial recognition with devolution. The reasons were strategic and a strong commitment to principles of centralized national government through a sovereign parliament. On the other hand, the United States, Canada and Australia all had well established self-governing colonies with deep traditions of liberal, and increasingly democratic, governance prior to establishing their federal systems. In federating, each was able to establish an appropriate national government while retaining their state and provincial governments. Germany had a long-standing federal tradition that was suspended during the upheavals of national socialism and Nazi militarism, but revived federal constitutionalism as an institutional alternative under Allied, particularly American, supervision. Asian countries have different traditions and politics that help explain why they have or have not adopted federalism that are articulated in detail in the chapters of this book, and briefly reviewed in the last section of this chapter.

## FEDERALISM'S ATTRIBUTES AND PROPENSITIES

As pointed out above, federalism is not simply a system that a country might choose to adopt for a multinational purpose. This is only one of a number of purposes that federalism can serve, and it is not one that can be neatly quarantined from the other attributes and propensities of federalism. These multiple purposes and propensities need to be taken into account for a deeper understanding of federalism and appreciation of why it might or might not suit particular countries at certain times.

From our analysis of constitutional federalism above, and drawing upon recent theorizing and comparative work, we can distill a number of major attributes or propensities of federalism that are crucial considerations in determining whether federalism suits a particular country or not. In discussing these attributes or purposes of federalism, we need to be clear on a couple of points. First, our subject is the full-bodied sense of institutions in harmony with the rest of the social order, or stable, valued and recurring patterns of behaviour, as discussed earlier. We are not concerned with paper blueprints that have little practical salience, but rather with those that embody the society's norms and values and structure its constitutional politics. Second, our focus is upon federalism as an institutional entity, not the particular variations in one or other federal country.

One important purpose of federalism – representing multiple nations within the one country – has already been discussed in the earlier section on multinational federalism. There it was pointed out that, although an important purpose that federalism can serve, this is not an inherent or necessary purpose. Countries that are not multinational, like the United States, Australia and Germany, have federal systems for other reasons. Hence, multinational representation is a contingent purpose of federalism because it depends upon whether a country has multiple nations, and many federations do not. As well, a distinction was made between two kinds of multicultural federalism: intra-state and inter-state. Inter-state multicultural federalism is the type advocated by Kymlicka and entails the minority group forming a local majority and exercising meaningful forms of self-government and having its language recognized as an official state language for that subunit. Intra-state multicultural federalism builds in multiculturalism and political sharing and recognition of diversity at the subunit level.

A more fundamental purpose that federalism serves is that of democratic representation, creating two spheres of government in which the people of a nation participate in government. The sort of democracy that federalism best serves is not any kind, but rather liberal and pluralist democracy instead of egalitarian and majoritarian democracy. The American founding, that also set the paradigm of modern federalism, was based upon representative and republican democracy; that is, indirect democratic rule with the people being ultimately sovereign but conducting the continuing business of politics through elected representatives and appointed officials. Participatory and majoritarian forms of democracy were considered unstable and illiberal, and federalism part of the institutional remedy. The object was to filter and refine popular sentiment, and to break up and prevent mass majority factions or populist movements, for example of debtors and paupers against property institutions and owners. Federal constitutionalism was supposed to solve the problem of the tyranny of the majority, and has generally worked to do so.

This propensity of constitutional federalism can be framed in an alternative way in terms of rights protection. Constitutional federalism is an institutional system for protecting individual rights. This was evident in the American founders' view at the drafting convention, and justified by Madison and his co-authors in *The Federalist Papers*. They explained how a system of dividing and checking powers based upon federalism was fundamentally about protecting individual and property rights. So much so that a bill of rights was not considered necessary in the original constitutional design, and was only added during the ratification debates to satisfy those anti-federalists who still thought that democracy was only possible in smaller states and any centralization of power in a large national government would inevitably lead to tyranny. The old style anti-federalists were proved wrong. Rights protection has remained a key feature of American-style federal systems, and been significant in the Australian case (Galligan, Knopff and Uhr, 1990) and the experience of other Western democracies.

But there is another more communitarian form of democracy that federalism can be seen to foster, at least in part, through preserving regional communities and providing them with the political infrastructure to govern themselves while at the same time being part of the larger national association. Nor do these regional communities need to be ethnically different or multinational; they might be geographical groupings of peoples with more or less the same ethnic characteristics who have established political communities: for example, the Maritime provinces in Canada, or states like Queensland and Tasmania in Australia. Nevertheless, representing regionally distinct communities is most dramatically evident in instances of multinational federalism, and manifest in the Swiss model and more recently in Belgium. Many federations have a mix of regional and ethnic provinces, such as for example, Canada, Spain and India. Federalism does not necessarily presuppose a political culture based upon Lockean individual rights protection; it can also serve regional communities, some of which might be ethnically distinct with group rights to language and religion. There is an important proviso: the ethnic communities must be moderate in their community demands, extending to others what they themselves enjoy, and be committed to the overarching nation. Federalism best serves a multinational purpose when there is multiculturalism and political sharing among ethnically diverse communities within the local state; in other words, intrastate multinational federalism.

Economists have become more interested in federalism in recent decades, producing a vast literature on economic and fiscal federalism (for leading examples, see Brennan and Buchanan, 1980; Grewal, Brennan and Matthews, 1980; Weingast, 1995; Ferejohn and Weingast, 1997; Rodden, 2003; Ahmad and Brosio, 2006). Market preserving is the attribute of federalism that economists champion. The term comes from Weingast (1995) and draws upon traditional constitutional constraints and checks on central government for the purpose of protecting markets. James Buchanan, founder of the public choice school of economics, was a champion of free markets and of federalism as a way of constraining government and protecting individual rights, particularly property rights and private enterprise (Lynch, 2004). According to this view, anti-Leviathan is achieved partly through constitutional and political restrictions on central government, and partly by fiscal constraints upon the states and/or by competition among governments with taxpayers able to vote with their feet. These constraints upon government help ensure the space for market capitalism.

Policy facilitation is the attribute of federalism that flows from having multiple spheres of government to deal with multiple types of policy with different jurisdictional boundaries. Certain types of policy are best handled at the national level; for example, redistribution or defence, and others like education and health provision at the sub-national level (Ahmad, Hewitt and Ruggiero, 1994). Some make theoretical cases for multiple jurisdictions to handle multiple policies (Frey and Eichenberger, 1999), and there are strong practical reasons for decentralizing policy even if that requires fiscal transfers to achieve (Bahl and Linn, 1994). Moreover, there is room for national and state governments establishing additional regional structures for particular policy purposes (Rainnie and Grobbelaar, 2005). Since major policy areas like the environment and aspects of public health have multiple dimensions, including national, state and local, as well as international, they can be best dealt with by multiple governments plus a system of intergovernmental relations. Moreover, a system of multiple governments can favour innovation or the status quo, and either can be progressive or regressive depending on what is in place and what is being proposed. Federalism provides a multiplicity of veto points (Tsebelis, 2002) but also a multiplicity of entry points and sites for experimentation. Federalism provides an institutional and political means for making and delivering certain public policies at a decentralized level, and also for constraining the central government (Souza, 2002).

Federalism can serve all or some or these multiple purposes, and appeal to particular countries and commentators for one or other of these purposes. Whether these factors are mutually reinforcing or not will depend on their dynamic and variable interaction and this can differ between countries and from time to time during the historical development of a particular country. Brazilian federalism, for example, 'has always been a means of accommodating deep-rooted regional disparities' (ibid., p. 1). But as well as serving the purpose of decentralization it is also a means of furthering democratization by bringing government closer to citizens (Stepan, 2000). By attending to the multiple aspects of federalism, we can better appreciate its complexity. If federalism's multiple aspects and propensities are at odds with significant attributes of particular countries, it is unlikely that they will adopt a federal system, and if they do it is unlikely to work well.

## FEDERALISM IN ASIA

Whether federalism is adopted by a country at a particular time, and whether it works or works well, will depend not only on institutional design, foundational values and the propensities of federalism that we have been discussing so far, but also crucially on mediating factors and intervening assumptions and expectations. Kymlicka has pointed out that intervening political institutions, practices and customs are significant for multinational federalism (2005, pp. 41–2). That is the case for federalism more generally because it is only one, albeit an important one, of the structural factors that goes to make up a country's system of government. Political history and established traditions are also important, as is the balance of domestic and international forces at the particular time a country's system of government is formed. Hence, in exploring why a particular country or regional grouping of countries has or has not embraced federalism, we need to go beyond issues of federal theory and institutional design, and also beyond aspects or propensities of federalism that can be distilled from federal theory and the comparative practice of established federations. The fine-grained country and historical analysis of particular country settings, cultures, established public opinion, traditions and so on – indeed pretty much everything that goes to make up the nuanced political situation of a particular country at a particular time – are necessary and make up the bulk of chapters in this book. This section reviews the findings regarding federalism in Asia.

Federalism works best where there is deep consensus on liberal democratic values and established traditions of limited and complex government. For newly democratizing countries and those without traditions of limited and complex government, federalism is unlikely to be an option, and if chosen is unlikely to work well. Federalism is not compatible with revolutionary politics, or with radical or mass democracy, since it requires the division of government powers and a semi-autonomous sub-national sphere of government. Anti-colonial and post-colonial liberation movements are unlikely to turn to federalism in uniting and mobilizing a society that has been dominated by a colonial power, especially if that colonial power has to be repelled by armed struggle rather than negotiated and phased withdrawal. A revolutionary movement that is mobilized to challenge and defeat an external ruling power or displace a domestic ruling class will need unity of purpose and action. Similarly, militaristic governments that are in a constant state of alert to counter foreign threats or pacify their own people or unruly ethnic minorities are unlikely to choose federalism or to respect it if it is already part of the constitutional system. Federalism requires limited government, so if the country requires strong government, either because of its poverty or fragmentation, or because the ruling party is committed to imposing a new social order, federalism is an unsuitable instrument. The limited government that federalism offers presupposes a viable and robust non-government realm of activity for much of production and exchange, in other words a market system. If this is lacking or rudimentary, federalism will struggle.

These propositions are all based upon the defining attributes or consequences of federalism that have been analysed above. They help us explain why fewer Asian countries than Western ones have adopted it as a system of government, why some like India, Pakistan and Malaysia have, and why it does not work well in Pakistan and Malaysia. India and Malaysia have traditions of British colonial rule that incorporated elements of established local rule and achieved self-government mainly by negotiation. This provided a basis for federalism that incorporated elements of sub-national as well as national government. Apart from some common federal aspects, however, these three Asian federations are quite different in ways that are relevant for our study of federalism. So too are the unitary countries that have eschewed federalism, Indonesia, the Philippines and Myanmar, because their non-federal traditions are also instructive in showing why federalism is not adopted by countries that have obvious geographic and multinational regions whose governance federalism might facilitate.

China provides an in-between case of economic decentralization combined with centralized political rule, but with Hong Kong enjoying a high degree of independence in economic, domestic and international affairs as an autonomous state. Finally, Japan is of primary significance because, as Takashi Inoguchi shows in Chapter 12, 'Japan presents a uniquely Asian way of federalization' – a surprising conclusion to those influenced by a simplified Western perception of Japan as a centralized unitary state reconstituted from a militarist to a democratic polity by the Americans after the Second World War. Japan, however, has a much older autonomous political tradition of decentralization and democratization. As Asia's most advanced democracy and economy, and as one of the world's leading postmodern nations, Japan is currently responding to globalization in ways that can help inform our thinking about federalism and the future.

India is the most truly federal of Asian countries, although it has a centrist element in its constitutional design and political traditions. As Gurpreet Mahajan explains in Chapter 4, at the time of independence, 'concerns of national unity and integrity dominated and provided the core reasons for keeping the political arena free of cultural identities', and the states of the federation were formed 'primarily for reasons of administrative continuity and convenience, in addition to political necessity'. However, some state boundaries were subsequently adjusted to enable adjacent linguistic communities to form one political unit, and later on new states were created in the northeast to give territorial and political autonomy to tribal communities. So, while cultural and community identity was an important ordering principle in modifying federal structures and creating new states after India's founding, most states have a shared cultural and community identity. Federalism has provided the space for accommodating such diversity and has enabled greater political participation of ethnic and regional communities. An important part of this has been the development of ethnic and regional political leaders, some of whom have become prominent at the national as well as the state level. Federalism entails dual citizenship, and one indicator of the success of Indian federalism is the high level of dual allegiance in states like Tamil Nadu and the Punjab that also have strong autonomy traditions. India has adjusted its original constitutional or territorial federalism partly to include multinational representation of ethnic communities. The larger pattern, however, is one of providing enlarged but shared political space for multiple communities and identities.

Although grouped as a federal country in usual classifications, Pakistan is quite different from India and has a much weaker federal system. Although heir to the same British colonial experience, Pakistan separated from India and 'had to build its state institutions from scratch' as well as manage two wings separated by 1000 miles of increasingly hostile Indian territory, as Katharine Adeney explains in Chapter 6. After subsequently losing Eastern Pakistan, which became Bangladesh, Pakistan was left with a more manageable domain of four provinces, but with a powerful military and a ruling administrative elite that lacked provincial roots, having moved from India at separation, and operated in a centralist way. Democracy remains weak in Pakistan, with long periods of military rule, and nonmilitary governments have also been highly centralist. While Pakistan remains a federation despite all of this, in Adeney's terms it is definitely an 'illiberal' and 'centralised' one.

Malaysia has a different style of illiberal and centralized federalism. As William Case describes it in Chapter 6, Malaysia has a system of 'semidemocracy' and 'minimalist federalism', both managed and manipulated by a dominant and well entrenched central government. Rather than being 'fake or inconsequential', Malaysian federalism has been used for a mix of political purposes, providing the central government with 'conduits by which to lengthen the patronage that earns instrumentalist support', but as well extending 'some democratic space that attracts legitimating cover'. Malaysian federalism is territorially based and, while serving primarily a national purpose of integrating diverse geographic territories and ethnic communities, it also cedes limited democratic space for their representation.

Some state political autonomy is allowed and even from time to time moderate governments by political parties in opposition to the central ruling party are tolerated. The central government, however, remains dominant. It has infringed deeply on the powers of state governments through whittling down their powers and centralizing taxation revenue, and is quick to intervene in state politics in what Case neatly describes as 'retractable' federalism. So, while federalism has been subverted to serve a dominant centrist government's enduring hold on power, it nevertheless serves partial federal purposes of political decentralization and representation of sub-national regions.

Indonesia, in contrast to Malaysia, had a less amenable Dutch colonial experience and was forged by revolution and armed struggle, leading to a strong nationalist ethos. Indonesia's aversion to federalism is an Asian example of the more general trend that Tony Reid identifies: 'In Asia, as elsewhere, revolution has proved to be hostile to federalism in the name of the sovereignty of the people.' The exception of course was the American revolution, but it was a conservative revolt against imperial British rule and financial imposts – 'No taxation without representation' – justified in terms of pre-revolutionary principles of self-government and individual rights on the part of people already governing themselves in fairly autonomous states. Indonesia's founding was based upon embracing new national norms, fostering uniformity and abolishing or not recognizing historical and cultural differences. That has increased the likelihood of violent outcomes in some regional and ethnic conflicts that federalism might have prevented or moderated, according to Reid's account. Whether the Aceh concession of special status can work in such national circumstances is still to be seen.

Like Indonesia, the Philippines does not have a federal system. While it shares some of the same features of geographic dispersion and ethnic diversity, the Philippines has a different history of colonial rule under the Spanish, until their ousting at the end of the nineteenth century, and subsequently for half a century under United States rule. Although a federal constitution was proposed by revolutionary leaders, it was not implemented when the United States took control in 1898 after the Spanish–American war. Instead, the Americans adapted the administrative structures put in place by the Spanish, crushed the Moro claim to sovereignty, and managed ethnic communities through decentralized administrative means. Federalism has continued to be advocated from time to time by political leaders and commentators, and is currently on the political agenda as a means of dealing with ethnic and regional tensions. Ron May sets out the development and consolidation of the Philippines as a unitary state with an elaborate system of local government in Chapter 8. He is sceptical about federalism's prospects in the Philippines despite its periodic invocation, and dubious that it would further assist democratization.

Federalism works best where there is a deep consensus on liberal democratic values: that is true for constitutional federalism, and perhaps even more so for multicultural federalism. Conversely, where democracy is weak, federalism is unlikely to be embraced or to prosper. Furthermore, both liberal democracy and federalism depend on vigorous intermediate or civic associations and institutions. The market system is an important component of liberal democratic polities, and provides a powerful alternative source of power and resources to that of government. Where intermediate institutions and the market are lacking or weak, the prospects for federalism are unpromising. It is hardly surprising, then, that federalism does not feature in countries with weak democratic traditions and high incidences of military rule and martial law and that are also economically poor. This helps explain the absence of federalism in Indonesia and the Philippines, and its partial presence in Pakistan and Malaysia. It also helps explain Japan's continuing decentralization that has provided a counterbalance to national government and the framework for a vibrant democracy.

Myanmar provides the most extreme case of military despotism and persecution of opposition and ethnic leaders, with such anti-democratic politics precluding federalism that might otherwise provide a framework for multinational representation of its non-Burman ethnic peoples. Alan Smith explains in Chapter 9, however, that the military dictatorship is unsustainable and there is in process a 'military-managed regime transformation' that will likely entrench its interests in a system of less than total military control. The envisaged model is neither democratic nor federal but will likely approximate Suharto's Indonesia with a dominant governing party and other groups severely constrained and managed. While there will be legislatures at the state level, these will function more like local governments. The ruling military elite and the ethnic communities have been diametrically opposed on federalism, with the former legitimizing its rule on the ground that strong central government is necessary to prevent national disintegration, and the latter demanding political autonomy and devolution of power. Smith is hopeful that moderation on both sides might produce 'soft-liners' better able to achieve more acceptable compromises on both constitutional and multinational outcomes.

Decentralization of government in large and varied geographic nations is one of the key purposes federalism serves. Hence we might expect it to be an obvious feature of government in China as well as India. But there are obvious qualifications and national differences that help explain why China has only 'de facto' federalism compared to India's thriving federal system.

In China's case, a revolutionary Communist Party seized power by force of arms and imposed a centralized unitary government dedicated to class warfare and social restructuring. Its politics were based upon dictatorial central rule in the name of the undifferentiated and radically egalitarian masses. Regional and ethnic differences and institutions had no status or legitimacy. The subsequent adoption of a decentralized market system that is fuelling uneven regional growth and making seaboard provinces comparatively rich and independent of the centre has changed the dynamics of Chinese government. So, while China's formal institutions remain unitary and centralist with all provincial governments subordinated to the central government, Yongnian Zheng, in Chapter 10, explains how China has developed de facto federalism and actually functions in a quasi-federal manner (see also Davis, 1999). This is because it satisfies three important federal conditions: one, each level of government has some activities on which it makes final decisions; two, decentralization has developed to such a degree that the national government finds it increasingly difficult, if not impossible, to impose its will on the provinces unilaterally; and three, the provinces have primary responsibility over the economy and certain aspects of politics in their jurisdiction. For instance, provincial governments control foreign direct investment, as well as local public security, and road and school building. There is a large zone of overlapping control where outcomes are determined by bargained agreement rather than central coercion. Indeed, according to Zheng, bargaining has become the dominant form of authority relationships in Chinese politics. This is due to local economic development and the market economy. While top leaders remain suspicious of federalism, and also of democracy, de facto federalism has allowed political flexibility. Thus while de jure federalism remains unlikely without substantial political change to the Communist one-party system, de facto federalism provides the foundation for such change.

Further indication of China's flexibility and pragmatism is the granting of special status to Hong Kong. As Peter Cheung explains in Chapter 11, Hong Kong enjoys a higher degree of autonomy than most state governments in federal systems, in areas of monetary policy and external economic relations as well as social and international affairs, although final authority over its constitution remains with the Chinese central government. Cheung is more sceptical than Zheng about the federal elements of Chinese politics and the likely spillover of economic to political decentralization that others have predicted. Moreover, Hong Kong's post-1997 autonomy experience has contradictory implications for China that depend upon the relative economic strength of Hong Kong and the kind of settlement made with Taiwan. With China's rapid economic growth, the economic gap is narrowing, with the adjacent Guangdong province already surpassing Hong Kong economically. With continuing high economic growth in China and resolution of Taiwan's separation, Hong Kong would become less of a special case. Hence, its future remains uncertain.

In many ways Japan stands out as the exceptional country in Asia: a constitutional democracy with an affluent economy, and a long history of independence and autonomy punctuated by militarism, occupation and reconstitution after the Second World War. As Takashi Inoguchi explains in Chapter 12, Japan had three centuries of quasi-federal state tradition with relatively decentralized administration, from the sixteenth to the nineteenth centuries, which endured through the following century of modern nation-state building. Such quasi-federal arrangements promoted the 'industrious revolution' of more efficient economic practices in the various domains, and enabled the growth of population and a national economic market: in other words, an instance of 'market facilitating federalism' somewhat comparable to that of Britain and the United States (Weingast, 1995). This continued after the opening of Japan's economy to Western trade in the mid-nineteenth century because the Japanese government was denied tariff powers until 1911. The Japanese experience is central to our focus on federalism and democracy in this chapter and book because, as Inoguchi puts it: 'Decentralization or quasi-federalization goes hand in hand with democratization.' This interdependent relationship evolves in conjunction with a third key factor, the development of a national market that becomes increasingly sophisticated through the nineteenth and twentieth centuries, including the accelerated democratization during occupation from 1945 to 1952. Decentralization has been only one element, however, as Japan is a complex nation where centralized government has also been highly significant in uniting and integrating the country early on, and ensuring integrated and rapid economic development through national investment during the postwar decades.

The Japanese case is also significant because it is one of the world's leading post-modern countries with affluent and increasingly critical citizens who are highly attuned to personal choice. This, coupled with globalization, has brought about a recent structural shift in Japanese political economy, from national government marshalling of private savings and state investment to privatization and market provision. The notable test case, over which the 2005 election was successfully fought, was the dismantling of Japanese Post, a peculiarly Japanese agglomeration of centralized government investment funding sourced by decentralized private banking. The Japanese response to globalization is producing a new market-driven decentralization that caters more directly to democratic demands for private affluence and choice, and changing the role of national government, away from state-managed capitalism and the provision of giant infrastructure projects, to regulation and social provision.

For those who assume that federalism is suited to multinational governance, the lack of federalism in Asia compared to Western countries presents a puzzle. Federalism, however, is primarily a constitutional system of government with all the attributes and propensities sketched above: it presupposes liberal democratic values and traditions of limited government; it limits national government by empowering sub-national governments which have independent authority over major areas of politics and policy; it is complicated and requires dual allegiances on the part of citizens; and it works best in market economies. Having federalism serve the purpose of multinational representation is something of a special case, and an unlikely one for countries where the other factors are not present at least in part. Multinational federalism works best where political multiculturalism operates at the intra-state rather than the inter-state level. As countries become more liberal democratic and market-oriented, and provided they are secure from external and internal threats, federalism has greater potential and inter-state federalism more promise.

But opting for a federal system still remains a matter of national preference and choice. While federalism does not have to be adopted at an initial defining national moment – Belgium and Spain are examples of countries subsequently adopting federal arrangements – this sort of 'staying together' federalism remains something of a special case. Institutions need to be embedded in the political culture of a nation and based at least in part on its indigenous traditions. But in addition they need to be flexible as well as resilient, able to anchor stability while accommodating change. Once a constitutional system is imbedded there is an accompanying crystallization of interests and forces that tend to keep it in place. Nor is formal federalism the only way of achieving many of the purposes that federalism serves: for example, quasi-federalism can underpin strong constitutional government and democracy, as has been the case in Japan, or decentralization through administrative means and strong local government, as in the Philippines. Institutions have an important reflexive dimension that allows different institutions to be made to work for similar purposes or vice versa.

Nor do Asian countries have to stick with established federal forms. After all, the American federal model was a bold innovation in institutional design that suited its particular aspirations and purposes at a moment in history, and has been adapted by the United States and other federal countries in significant ways. Asymmetric and special arrangements, as China has with Hong Kong and Indonesia with Aceh, might be appropriate for special regional states to provide a level of autonomy while preserving national unity. Asymmetric models of political association between comparable countries that remain sovereign but adopt some shared federal style arrangements, such as the Australasian association between Australia and New Zealand (Galligan and Mulgan, 1999), are also possible. Such an arrangement might well suit Asian countries in the future: for example, Malaysia and Singapore, or perhaps even China and Taiwan. Nevertheless, the success of such asymmetric arrangements depends on political norms and values similar to those that federalism requires, namely moderation, acceptance of multiple identities, and experience in working complex institutional arrangements. Since that is the case, federalism also remains a live option for many Asian countries into the future.

## REFERENCES

Ahmad, E. and G. Brosio (2006), *Handbook of Fiscal Federalism*, London: Edward Arnold.

Ahmad, Ehtisham, Daniel Hewitt and Edgardo Ruggiero (1994), 'Assigning expenditure responsibilities', in Teresa Ter-Minassian (ed.), *Fiscal Federalism in Theory and Practice*, Washington, DC: International Monetary Fund, pp. 25–48.

Anderson, L.M. (2004), 'Exploring the paradox of autonomy: federalism and secession in North America', *Regional and Federal Studies*, **14**, 89–112.

Bahl, R. and J. Linn (1994), 'Fiscal decentralization and intergovernmental transfers in less developed countries', *Publius: The Journal of Federalism*, **24**, 1–19.

Beer, S.H. (1993), *To Make a Nation: The Rediscovery of American Federalism*, Cambridge, MA: Harvard University Press.

Brennan, G. and J. Buchanan (1980), *The Power to Tax: Analytic Foundations of a Fiscal Constitution*, Cambridge: Cambridge University Press.

Carney, F.S. (ed.) (1965), *The Politics of Johannes Althusius*, London: Eyre and Spottiswoode.

Davis, M.C. (1999), 'The case for Chinese federalism', *Journal of Democracy*, **10**(2), 124–37.

Davis, S.R. (1978), *The Federal Principle: A Journey through Time in Quest of a Meaning*, Berkeley and Los Angeles: University of California Press.

Diamond, M. (1961), 'The federalist's view of federalism', in G.C.S Benson et al. (eds), *Essays in Federalism*, Claremont, CA: Institute for Studies in Federalism, Claremont Men's College, pp. 21–64.

Dorff, R.H. (1994), 'Federalism in Eastern Europe: part of the solution or part of the problem?', *Publius: The Journal of Federalism*, **24**(2), 99–114.

Elazar, D.J. (1987), *Exploring Federalism*, Tuscaloosa: University of Alabama Press.

Federalist Papers (1961 edn), A. Hamilton, J. Madison and J. Jay, *The Federalist Papers*, New York: Mentor, originally published 1787.

Ferejohn, J. and B. Weingast (eds) (1997), *The New Federalism: Can the States be Trusted?*, Stanford: Hoover Institution Press.

Filippov, M., P.C. Ordeshook and O. Shvetsova (2004), *Designing Federalism: A Theory of Self-Sustainable Federal Institutions*, Cambridge: Cambridge University Press.

Franck, T.M. (ed.) (1968), *Why Federations Fail*, New York: New York University Press.

Frey, B. and R. Eichenberger (1999), *The New Democratic Federalism for Europe: Functional, Overlapping and Competing Jurisdictions*, Cheltenham, UK and Northampton, MA, USA: Edward Elgar.

Friedman, T. (2005), *The World is Flat*, New York: Farrar, Straus and Giroux.

Galligan, B. (2006), 'Comparative federalism', in R.A.W. Rhodes, S.A. Binder and B.A. Rockman (eds), *The Oxford Handbook of Political Institutions*, Oxford: Oxford University Press, pp. 261–80.

Galligan, B. and R. Mulgan (1999), 'Asymmetric political association: the Australasian experiment', in R. Agranoff (ed.), *Accommodating Diversity: Asymmetry in Federal States*, Baden-Baden: Nomos Verlagsgesellschaft, pp. 57–72.

Galligan, B., R. Knopff and J. Uhr (1990), 'Australian federalism and the debate over a bill of rights', *Publius: The Journal of Federalism*, **20**(4), 53–67.

Goodin, R.E. (1996), 'Institutions and their design', in R.E. Goodin (ed.), *The Theory of Institutional Design*, Cambridge: Cambridge University Press, pp. 1–53.

Grewal, B.S., G. Brennan and R.L. Mathews (eds) (1980), *The Economics of Federalism*, Canberra: Australian National University Press.

Grodzins, M. (1966), *The American System: A New View of Government in the United States*, ed. D. Elazar, New Brunswick, NJ: Transaction Books.

Horowitz, D.L. (1985), *Ethnic Groups in Conflict*, Berkeley: University of California Press.

Imbeau, L.M. (2004), 'The political economy of public deficits', in Imbeau and Petry, pp. 1–20.

Imbeau, L.M. and F. Petry (eds) (2004), *Politics, Institutions, and Fiscal Policy: Deficits and Surpluses in Federated States*, London: Lexington Books.

Kymlicka, W. (2005), 'Liberal multiculturalisms: western models, global trends and Asian debates', in W. Kymlicka and B. He (eds), *Multiculturalism in Asia*, Oxford: Oxford University Press, pp. 22–55.

Lazar, H., H. Telford and R.L. Watts (eds) (2003), *The Impact of Global and Regional Integration on Federal Systems: A Comparative Analysis*, Montreal: McGill-Queen's University Press.

Livingston, W.S. (1956), *Federalism and Constitutional Change*, Oxford: Clarendon Press.

Lowi, T.J. (1984), 'Why there is no socialism in the United States: a federal analysis', *International Political Science Review*, **5**, 369–80.

Lynch, G.P. (2004), 'Protecting individual rights through a federal system: James Buchanan's view of federalism', *Publius: The Journal of Federalism*, **34**(4), 153–67.

Obinger, H., S. Leibfried and F.C. Castles (eds) (2005), *Federalism and the Welfare State: New World and European Experiences*, Cambridge: Cambridge University Press.

Ortino, S., M. Zagar and V. Mastny (eds) (2005), *The Changing Face of Federalism: Institutional Reconfiguration in Europe from East to West*, Manchester: Manchester University Press.

Rainnie, A. and M. Grobbelaar (eds) (2005), *New Regionalism in Australia*, Abingdon, UK: Ashgate.

Riker, W.H. (1964), *Federalism: Origin, Operation, Significance*, Boston: Little, Brown.

Riker, W.H. (1970), 'The triviality of federalism', *Politics* [now the *Australian Journal of Political Science*], **5**, 239–41.

Riker, W.H. (1975), 'Federalism', in F.I. Greenstein and N.W. Polsby (eds), *Handbook of Political Science, vol. 5: Governmental Institutions and Processes*, Reading, MA: Addison-Wesley.

Riker, W.H. (1987), *The Development of American Federalism*, Boston: Kluwer.

Riker, W.H. (1993), 'Federalism', in R.E. Goodin and P. Pettit (eds), *A Companion to Contemporary Political Philosophy*, Oxford: Basil Blackwell.

Rodden, J. (2003), 'Reviving Leviathan: fiscal federalism and the growth of government', *International Organization*, **57**, 695–729.

Russell, P.H. (2004), *Constitutional Odyssey: Can Canadians Become a Sovereign People?*, 3rd edn, Toronto: University of Toronto Press.

Russell, P.H. (2005), 'The future of Europe in an era of federalism', in Ortino et al., pp. 4–20.

Sawer, G. (1976), *Modern Federalism*, Melbourne: Pitman.

Sharman, C. (1990), 'Parliamentary federations and limited government: constitutional design and redesign in Australia and Canada', *Journal of Theoretical Politics*, **2**, 205–30.

Smiley, D.V. (1980), *Canada in Question: Federalism in the Eighties*, 3rd edn, Toronto: University of Toronto Press.

Souza, C. (2002), 'Brazil: the prospects of centre-constraining federation in a fragmented polity', *Publius*, **32**(2), 23ff.

Stepan, A. (2000), 'Brazil's decentralized federalism: bringing government closer to the citizens?', *Daedalus*, **129**, Spring, 145–69.

Tocqueville, A. de. (1945 edn), *Democracy in America*, New York: Vintage Books; originally published 1835.

Tsebelis, G. (2002), *Veto Players: How Political Institutions Work*, Princeton, NJ: Princeton University Press.

Watts, R.L. (1999), *Comparing Federal Systems*, 2nd edn, Montreal: McGill-Queen's University Press.

Weingast, B. (1995), 'The economic role of political institutions: market-preserving federalism and economic development', *The Journal of Law, Economics & Organization*, **11**(1), 1–31.

Wheare, K.C. (1963), *Federal Government*, 4th edn, Oxford: Oxford University Press; originally published 1946.

Zagar, M. (2005), 'The collapse of the Yugoslav federation and the viability of asymmetrical federalism', in Ortino, Zagar and Mastny, pp. 107–33.

# Index